# Mrs. Rundell's Domestic Cookery: Formed Upon Principles Of Economy, And Adapted To The Use Of Private Families

## Maria Eliza Ketelby Rundell

# MRS. RUNDELL'S

# DOMESTIC COOKERY;

FORMED UPON

## PRINCIPLES OF ECONOMY,

AND ADAPTED TO THE

## USE OF PRIVATE FAMILIES.

With numerous Illustrations.

*REVISED EDITION, WITH ADDITIONS.*

**LONDON:**
ROUTLEDGE, WARNES, AND ROUTLEDGE,
**FARRINGDON STREET.**
NEW YORK: 56, WALKER STREET.
1859.

# ADVERTISEMENT.

As the following directions were intended for the conduct of the families of the Authoress's own daughters, and for the arrangement of their table, so as to unite a good figure with proper economy, she has avoided all excessive luxury, such as essence of ham, and that wasteful expenditure of large quantities of meat for gravy, which so greatly contributes to keep up the price, and is no less injurious to those who eat than to those whose penury obliges them to abstain. Many receipts are given for things, which being in daily use, the mode of preparing them may be supposed too well known to require a place in a Cookery-book; yet how rarely do we meet with fine melted butter, good toast and water, or well-made coffee! She makes no apology for minuteness in some articles, or for leaving others unnoticed, because she does not write for professed cooks. This little work would have been a treasure to herself when she first set out in life, and she therefore hopes it may prove useful to others. In that expectation it is given to the Public; and as she will receive from it no emolument, so she trusts it will escape without censure.

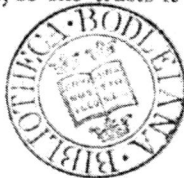

# MISCELLANEOUS OBSERVATIONS

FOR THE USE OF

# THE MISTRESS OF A FAMILY.

———◆———

In every rank, those deserve the greatest praise, who best acquit themselves of the duties which their station requires. Indeed, this line of conduct is not a matter of choice but of necessity, if we would maintain the dignity of our character as rational beings.

In the variety of female acquirements, though domestic occupations stand not so high in esteem as they formerly did, yet, when neglected, they produce much human misery. There was a time when ladies knew nothing *beyond* their own family concerns ; but, in the present day, there are many who know nothing *about* them. Each of these extremes should be avoided : but is there no way to unite in the female character cultivation of talents and habits of usefulness ? Happily there are still great numbers in every situation whose example proves that this is possible. Instances may be found of ladies in the higher walks of life, who condescend to examine the accounts of their house-steward ; and, by overlooking and wisely directing the expenditure of that part of their husband's income, which falls under their own immediate inspection, avoid the inconveniences of embarrassed circumstances. How much more necessary, then, is domestic knowledge in those whose limited fortunes press on their attention considerations of the strictest economy ! There ought to be a material difference in the degree of care which a person of a large and independent estate bestows on money concerns, and that of a person in confined circumstances : yet both may very commendably employ some portion of their time and thoughts on this subject. The custom of the times tends in some measure to abolish the distinctions of rank ; and the education given to young people is nearly the same in all : but though the leisure of the higher may be well devoted to elegant accomplishments, the pursuits of those in a middle line, if less ornamental, would better secure their own happiness and that of others connected with them. We sometimes bring up children in a manner calculated rather to fit them for the station we wish, than that which it is likely they will actually possess : and it is in all cases worth the while of parents to consider whether the expectation or hope of raising their offspring above their own situation be well founded.

A 2

The cultivation of the understanding and disposition, however, is not here alluded to; for a judicious improvement of both, united to firm and early-taught religious principles, would enable the happy possessor of these advantages to act well on all occasions : nor would young ladies find domestic knowledge a burden, or inconsistent with higher attainments, if the rudiments of it were inculcated at a tender age, when activity is so pleasing. If employment be tiresome to a healthy child, the fault must be traced to habits which, from many causes, are not at present favourable to the future conduct of women. It frequently happens, that before impressions of duty are made on the mind, ornamental education commences ; and it ever after takes the lead ; thus, what should be only the embellishment, becomes the main business of life. There is no opportunity of attaining a knowledge of family management at school ; and during vacation, all subjects that might interfere with amusement are avoided.

When a girl, whose family moves in the higher ranks of life, returns to reside at her father's house after completing her education, her introduction to the gay world, and a continued course of pleasures, persuade her at once that she was born to be the ornament of fashionable circles, rather than to *stoop* (as she would conceive it) to undertake the arrangement of a family, though by that means she might in various ways augment the satisfaction and comfort of her parents. On the other hand, persons of an inferior sphere, and especially in the lower order of middling life, are almost always anxious to give their children such advantages of education as themselves did not possess. Whether their indulgence be productive of the happiness so kindly aimed at, must be judged by the effects, which are not very favourable, if what has been taught has not produced humility in herself, and increased gratitude and respect to the authors of her being. Were a young woman brought to relish home society, and the calm delights of agreeable occupation, before she entered into the delusive scenes of pleasure presented by the theatre and other dissipations, it is probable she would soon make a comparison much in favour of the former, especially if restraint did not give to the latter additional relish.

If we carry on our observations to married life, we shall find a love of employment to be the source of unnumbered pleasures. To attend to the nursing, and at *least early* instruction of children, and rear a healthy progeny in the ways of piety and usefulness ; to preside over the family and regulate the income allotted to its maintenance ; to make home the sweet refuge of a husband fatigued by intercourse with a jarring world ; to be his enlightened companion and the chosen friend of his heart ; these, these are woman's duties ! and delightful ones they are, if haply she be married to a man whose soul can duly estimate her worth, and who will bring his share to the common stock of felicity. Of such a woman, one may truly say, "Happy the man who can call her his wife. Blessed are the children who call her mother."

When we thus observe her, exercising her activity and best abilities in appropriate cares and increasing excellence, are we not ready to say, she is the agent for good of that benevolent Being who placed her on earth to fulfil such sacred obligations, not to waste the talents committed to her charge.

When it is thus evident that the highest intellectual attainments may find exercise in the multifarious occupations of the daughter, the wife, the mother, and the mistress of the house, can any one urge that the female mind is contracted by domestic employ? It is, however, a great comfort that the duties of life are within the reach of humbler abilities, and that *she* whose chief aim is to fulfil them, will rarely ever fail to acquit herself well. United with, and perhaps crowning all the virtues of the female character, is that well-directed ductility of mind, which occasionally bends its attention to the smaller objects of life, knowing them to be often scarcely less essential than the greater.

Hence the direction of a *table* is no inconsiderable branch of a lady's concern, as it involves judgment in expenditure, respectability of appearance, and the comfort of her husband and those who partake their hospitality.

The mode of covering the table differs in taste. It is not the multiplicity of things, but the choice, the dressing, and the neat pleasing look of the whole, which gives respectability to her who presides. Too much, or too little dinners are extremes not uncommon : the latter is in appearance and reality the effort of poverty or penuriousness to be *genteel;* and the former, if constantly given, may endanger the circumstances of those who are not affluent.

Generally speaking, dinners are far less sumptuous than formerly, when half a dozen dishes were supplied for what one now costs ; consequently those whose fortunes are not great, and who wish to make a genteel appearance, without extravagance, regulate their table accordingly.

Perhaps there are few incidents in which the respectability of a man is more immediately felt, than the style of dinner to which he accidentally may bring home a visitor. Every one is to live as he can afford, and the meal of the tradesman ought not to emulate the entertainments of the higher classes; but, if two or three dishes are well served, with the usual sauces, the table-linen clean, the small sideboard neatly laid, and all that is necessary be at hand, the expectation of the husband and friend will be gratified, because no irregularity of domestic arrangement will disturb the social intercourse. The same observation holds good on a larger scale. In all situations of life, the entertainment should be no less suited to the station, than to the fortune of the *entertainer* and to the number and rank of those invited.

The manner of carving is now not only a very necessary branch of information, to enable a lady to do the honours of her table, but makes a considerable difference in the consumption of a family ; and though in large parties she is so much assisted as to render this knowledge apparently of less consequence, yet she must at times feel the deficiency ; and should not fail to acquaint herself with an attainment, the advantage of which is evident every day.

Indeed, as fashions are so fleeting, it is more than probable, that before the end of this century, great attention to guests may be again the mode, as it was in the commencement of the last. Some people haggle meat so much, as not to be able to help half-a-dozen persons decently from a large tongue, or a sirloin of beef; and the dish goes away with the appearance of having been gnawed by dogs. If the daughters of the family were to take the head of the table under the direction of their mother, they would fulfil its duties with grace, in the same easy manner as an early practice in other domestic affairs gradually fits them for their own future houses. Habit alone can make good carvers; but some principal directions are hereafter given, with a reference to the annexed plates.

The mistress of a family should always remember that the welfare and good management of the house depend on the eye of the superior; and consequently that nothing is too trifling for her notice, whereby waste may be avoided; and this attention is of more importance now that the price of every necessary of life is so greatly increased.

If a lady has never been accustomed, while single, to think of family management, let her not upon that account fear that she cannot attain it: she may consult others who are more experienced, and acquaint herself with the necessary quantities of the several articles of family expenditure, in proportion to the number it consists of, the proper prices to pay, &c., &c.

A minute account of the annual income, and the times of payment should be taken in writing; likewise an estimate of the supposed amount of each article of expense; and those who are early accustomed to calculations on domestic articles, will acquire so accurate a knowledge of what their establishment requires, as will give them the happy medium between prodigality and parsimony, without acquiring the character of meanness.

Perhaps few branches of female education are so useful, as great readiness at figures. Accounts should be regularly kept, and not the smallest article omitted to be entered; and if balanced every week and month, &c., the income and outgoings will be ascertained with facility, and their proportions to each other be duly observed. Some people fix on stated sums to be appropriated to each different article, and keep the money in separate purses; as house, clothes, pocket, education of children, &c. Whichever way accounts be entered, a certain mode should be adopted, and strictly adhered to. Many women are unfortunately ignorant of the state of their husband's income; and others are only made acquainted with it, when some speculative project, or profitable transaction, leads them to make a false estimate of what can be afforded; and it too often happens that both parties, far from consulting each other, squander money in ways that they would even wish to forget: whereas marriage should be a state of mutual and perfect confidence, and similarity of pursuits, which would secure that happiness it was intended to bestow.

There are so many valuable women who excel as wives, that it is a fair inference there would be few extravagant ones, were they consulted by their husbands on subjects that concern the mutual interest of both parties. Within the knowledge of the writer of these pages, many families have been reduced to poverty by the want of openness in the man on the subject of his affairs; and though on these occasions the women were blamed, it has afterwards appeared, that they never were allowed to inquire, or suffered to reason upon what sometimes seemed to them imprudent.

Many families have owed their prosperity full as much to the propriety of female management, as to the knowledge and activity of the father.

The lady of a general officer observed to her man-cook, that her last weekly bill was higher than usual. Some excuse was offered; —to which she replied :—" Such is the sum I have allotted to housekeeping; should it be exceeded one week, the next must pay for it. The General will have no public day this week." The fault was never repeated.

March's " Family Book-keeper " is a very useful work, and saves much trouble; the various articles of expense being printed, with a column for every day in the year, so that at one view the amount of expenditure on each, and the total sum may be known.

Ready-money should be paid for all such things as come not into weekly bills, and even for them a check is necessary. The best places for purchasing should be attended to. In some articles a discount of five per cent. is allowed for ready-money in London and other large cities, and those who thus pay are usually best served. Under the idea of buying cheap, many go to new shops; but it is safest to deal with people of established credit, who do not dispose of goods by underselling.

To make tradesmen wait for their money injures them greatly, besides that a higher price must be paid, and in long bills, articles never bought are often charged. Perhaps the irregularity and failure of payment may have much evil influence on the price of various articles, and may contribute to the destruction of many families from the highest to the lowest.

Thus regularly conducted, the exact state of money affairs will be known with ease; for it is delay of payment that occasions confusion. A good common-place book should be always at hand, in which to enter such hints of useful knowledge, and other observations, as are given by sensible experienced people. Want of attention to what is advised, or supposing things too minute to be worth hearing, are the causes why so much ignorance prevails on necessary subjects among those who are not backward in frivolous ones.

It is very necessary for a woman to be informed of the prices and goodness of all articles in common use, and of the best times, as well as places, for purchasing them. She should also be acquainted with the comparative prices of provisions, in order that she may be able to substitute those that are most reasonable, when they will answer as well for others of the same kind, but which are more costly. A false notion of economy leads many to purchase as bargains what is not wanted, and sometimes never is used. Were this error avoided, more money would remain for other purposes. It is not unusual among lower dealers to put off a larger quantity of goods, by assurance that they are advancing in price; and many who supply fancy articles are so successful in persuasion, that purchasers not unfrequently go far beyond their original intention even to their future disquiet. Some things are better for keeping, and, being in constant consumption, should be laid in accordingly; such as paper, soap, and candles. Of these more hereafter.

To give unvarying rules cannot be attempted; for people ought to form their conduct on their circumstances, but it is presumed that a judicious arrangement according to them will be found equally advantageous to all. The minutiæ of management must be regulated by every one's fortune and rank; and some ladies, not deficient in either, charge themselves with giving out, once in a month, to a superintending servant, such quantities of household articles, as by observation and calculation they know to be sufficient, reserving for their own key the large stock of things usually laid in for very large families in the country. Should there be several more visitors than usual, they can easily account for increase of consumption, and *vice versâ*. Such a degree of judgment will be respectable even in the eye of domestics, if they are not interested in the ignorance of their employers; and if they are, their services will not compensate for want of honesty.

When young ladies marry, they frequently continue their own maids in the capacity of house-keepers; who, as they may be more attached to their interest than strangers, become very valuable servants. To such, the economical observations in this work will be as useful as the cookery; and it is recommended to be strictly observant of both, which in the course of time will make them familiar in the practice.

It is much to be feared, that for the waste of many of the good things that God has given for our use, not abuse, the mistress and servants of great houses will hereafter be called to a strict account.

Some part of every person's fortune should be devoted to charity; by which "a pious woman will build up her house before God, while she that is foolish (*i.e.* lends nothing to the Lord), pulls it down with her hands." No one can complain of the want of gifts to the poor in this land: but there is a mode of relief which would add greatly to their comfort, and which being prepared from superfluity, and such materials as are often thrown away, the expense would not be felt. In the latter part of this work some hints for preparing the above are given.

By good hours, especially early breakfast, a family is more regular, and much time is saved. If orders be given soon in the morning, there will be more time to execute them; and servants by doing their work with ease, will be more equal to it, and fewer will be necessary.

It is worthy of notice that the general expense will be reduced, and much time saved, if everything be kept in its proper place, applied to its proper use, and mended, when the nature of the accident will allow, as soon as broken.

If the economy of time was duly considered, the useful affairs transacted before amusements were allowed, and a regular plan of employment was daily laid down, a great deal might be done without hurry or fatigue; and it would be a most pleasant retrospect at the end of the year, were it possible to enumerate all the valuable acquirements made, and the good actions performed by an active woman.

If the subject of servants be thought ill-timed in a book upon family arrangement, it must be by those who do not recollect that the regularity and good management of the heads will be insufficient, if not seconded by those who are to execute orders. It behoves every person to be extremely careful whom he takes into his service; to be very minute in investigating the character he receives, and equally cautious and scrupulously just in giving one to others. Were this attended to, many bad people would be incapacitated for doing mischief, by abusing the trust reposed in them. It may be fairly asserted that the robbery or waste, which is but a milder epithet for the unfaithfulness of a servant, will be laid to the charge of that master or mistress who knowing, or having well-founded suspicions of any such faults, is prevailed upon by false pity or entreaty, to slide him into another place. There are, however, some who are unfortunately capricious, and often refuse to give a character because they are displeased that a servant leaves their service: but this is unpardonable, and an absolute robbery, servants having no inheritance, and depending on their fair name for employment. To refuse countenance to the evil, and to encourage the good servant, are actions due to society at large; and such as are honest, frugal and attentive to their duties should be liberally rewarded, which would encourage merit, and inspire servants with zeal to acquit themselves.

It may be but proper to observe that a retributive justice usually marks persons in that station sooner or later even in this world. The extravagant and idle in servitude are ill prepared for the industry and sobriety on which their own future welfare so essentially depends. Their faults, and the attendant punishment, come home when they have children of their own; and sometimes much sooner. They will see their own folly and wickedness perpetuated in their offspring, whom they must not expect to be better than the example and instruction given by themselves.

It was the observation of a very sensible and experienced woman, that she could always read the fate of her servants who married; those who had been faithful and industrious in her service, continued their good habits in their own families, and became respectable members of the community: those who were the contrary, never were successful, and not unfrequently were reduced to the parish.

A proper quantity of household articles should be always ready, and more bought in before the others be consumed, to prevent inconvenience, especially in the country.

A bill of parcels and receipt should be required, even if the money be paid at the time of purchase; and, to avoid mistakes, let the goods be compared with these when first brought home.

Though it is very disagreeable to suspect any one's honesty, and perhaps mistakes have been unintentional, yet it is prudent to weigh meat, sugars, &c., when brought in, and compare with the charge. The butcher should be ordered to send the weight with the meat, and the cook to file these checks, to be examined when the weekly bill shall be delivered.

Much trouble and irregularity are saved when there is company, if servants are required to prepare the table and sideboard in similar order daily.

All things likely to be wanted should be in readiness : sugars of different qualities kept broken, currants washed, picked, and perfectly dry, spices pounded, and kept in very small bottles close corked ; not more than will be used in four or five weeks should be pounded at a time. Much less is necessary than when boiled whole in gravies, &c.

Where luncheons or suppers are served (and in every house some preparation is necessary for accidental visitors) care should be taken to have such things in readiness as are proper for either, and a list of several will be subjoined, a change of which may be agreeable, and if duly managed will be attended with little expense and much convenience.

A ticket should be exchanged by the cook for every loaf of bread, which when returned will show the number to be paid for ; as tallies may be altered, unless one is kept by each party.

Those who are served with brewer's beer, or any other articles not paid for weekly, or on delivery, should keep a book for entering the dates ; which will not only serve to prevent overcharges, but will show the whole year's consumption at one view.

An inventory of furniture, linen, and China, should be kept, and the things examined by it twice a year, or oftener, if there be a change of servants ; into each of whose care the articles used by him or her, should be entrusted, with a list, as is done with plate. Tickets of parchment, with the family name, numbered, and specifying what bed it belongs to, should be sewed on each feather-bed, bolster, pillow, and blanket. Knives, forks, and house-cloths, are often deficient : these accidents might be obviated, if an article at the head of every list required the former should be produced whole or broken, and the marked part of the linen, though all the others should be worn out. The inducement to take care of glass is in some measure removed, by the increased price given for old flint glass.—Those who wish for trifle dishes, butter-stands, &c., at a lower charge than cut glass, may buy them made in moulds, of which there is a great variety that look extremely well, if not placed near the more beautiful articles.

The price of starch depends upon that of flour ; the best will keep good in a dry warm room for some years ; therefore when bread is cheap it may be bought to advantage, and covered close.

SUGARS being an article of considerable expense in all families, the purchase demands particular attention. The cheapest does not go so far as that more refined ; and there is difference even in the degree of sweetness. The white should be chosen that is close, heavy, and shining. The best sort of brown has a bright gravelly look, and it is often to be bought pure as imported. East India sugars are finer for the price, but not so strong, consequently unfit for wines and sweetmeats, but do well for common purposes, if good of their kind. To prepare white sugar, pounded, rolling it with a bottle, and sifting, wastes less than a mortar.

Candles made in cool weather are best ; and when their price, and that of soap, which rise and fall together, is likely to be higher, it will be prudent to lay in the stock of both. This information the chandler can always give; they are better for keeping eight or ten months, and will not injure for two years, if properly placed in the cool; and there are few articles that better deserve care in buying, and allowing a due quantity of, according to the size of the family.

Paper improves by keeping, and if bought by half or whole reams will be much cheaper than if purchased by the quire. It is principally made from rags, of which there is some scarcity, which might be obviated if an order were given to a servant in every family to keep a bag to receive all the waste bits from cuttings out, &c.

Many well-meaning servants are ignorant of the best means of managing, and thereby waste as much as would maintain a small family, besides causing the mistress of the house much chagrin by their irregularity; and many families, from a want of method, have the appearance of chance rather than of regular system. To avoid this, the following hints may be useful as well as economical:—

Every article should be kept in that place best suited to it, as much waste may thereby be avoided, viz.—

Vegetables will keep best on a stone floor if the air be excluded.—Meat in a cold dry place.—Sugar and sweetmeats require a dry place; so does salt.—Candles cold, but not damp.—Dried meats, hams, &c. the same.—Rice and all sorts of seeds for puddings, &c. should be closely covered to preserve from insects.

Bread is so heavy an article of expense that all waste should be guarded against; and having it cut in the room will tend much to prevent it. It should not be cut until a day old. Earthen pans and covers keep it best.

Straw to lay apples on should be quite dry to prevent a musty taste.

Large pears should be tied up by the stalk.

Basil, savoury, or knotted marjoram, or London thyme, to be used when herbs are ordered; but with discretion, as they are very pungent.

The best means to preserve blankets from moths is to fold and lay them under the feather-beds that are in use; and they should be shaken occasionally. When soiled, they should be washed, not scoured.

Soda, by softening the water, saves a great deal of soap. It should be melted in a large jug of water, some of which pour into the tubs and boiler; and when the lather becomes weak, add more. The new improvement on soft soap is, if properly used, a saving of near half in quantity; and though something dearer than the hard, reduces the price of washing considerably.

Many good laundresses advise soaping linen in warm water the night previous to washing, as facilitating the operation with less friction.

Soap should be cut with a wire or twine, in pieces that will make a long square when first brought in, and kept out of the air two or three weeks; for if it dry quick, it will crack, and when wet, break.

Put it on a shelf, leaving a space between, and let it grow hard gradually. Thus, it will save a full third in the consumption.

Some of the lemons and oranges used for juice should be pared first to preserve the peel dry; some should be halved, and when squeezed, the pulp cut out, and the outsides dried for grating. If for boiling in any liquid, the first way is best. When these fruits are cheap, a proper quantity should be bought and prepared as above directed, especially by those who live in the country, where they cannot always be had; and they are perpetually wanted in cookery.

When whites of eggs are used for jelly, or other purposes, contrive to have pudding, custard, &c. to employ the yolks also. Should you not want them for several hours, beat them up with a little water, and put them in a cool place, or they will be hardened and useless. It was a mistake of old, to think that the whites made cakes and puddings heavy; on the contrary, if beaten long and separately, they contribute greatly to give lightness, are an advantage to paste, and make a pretty dish beaten with fruit, to set in cream, &c.

If copper utensils be used in the kitchen, the cook should be charged to be very careful not to let the tin be rubbed off; and to have them fresh done when the least defect appears, and never to put by any soup, gravy, &c. in them, or any metal utensil; stone and earthen vessels should be provided for those purposes, as likewise plenty of common dishes, that the table set may be used to put by cold meat.

Tin vessels, if kept damp, soon rust, which causes holes   Fenders, and tin linings of flower-pots, &c., should be painted every year or two.

Vegetables soon sour and corrode metals, and glazed red ware, by which a strong poison is produced. Some years ago, the death of several gentlemen was occasioned by the cook sending a ragout to table, which she had kept from the preceding day in a copper vessel badly tinned.

Vinegar, by its acidity, does the same, the glazing being of lead or arsenic.

To cool liquors in hot weather, dip a cloth in cold water, and wrap it round the bottle two or three times, then place it in the sun; renew the process once or twice.

The best way of scalding fruits, or boiling vinegar, is in a stone jar on a hot iron hearth; or by putting the vessel into a saucepan of water, called a water-bath.

If chocolate, coffee, jelly, gruel, bark, &c., be suffered to boil over, the strength is lost.

The cook should be encouraged to be careful of coals and cinders; for the latter there is a new contrivance to sift, without dispersing the dust of the ashes, by means of a covered tin bucket.

Small coal wetted makes the strongest fire for the back, but must remain untouched until it cake. Cinders, lightly wet, give a great degree of heat, and are better than coal for furnaces, ironing-stoves, and ovens.

. The cook should be charged to take care of jelly-bags, tapes for the collared things, &c., which if not perfectly scalded, and kept dry, give an unpleasant flavour when next used.

Cold water thrown on cast iron, when hot, will crack it.

In the following, and indeed all other receipts, though the quantities may be as accurately directed as possible, yet much must be left to the discretion of the person who uses them. The different tastes of people require more or less of the flavour of spices, salt, garlic, butter, &c., which can never be ordered by general rules; and if the cook has not a good taste, and attention to that of her employer's, not all the ingredients which nature and art can furnish, will give exquisite flavour to her dishes. The proper articles should be at hand, and she must proportion them until the true zest be obtained, and a variety of flavour be given to the different dishes served at the same time.

Those who require maigre dishes will find abundance in this little work; and where they are not strictly so, by suet or bacon being directed in stuffings, the cook must use butter instead; and where meat gravies (or stock, as they are called), are ordered, those made of fish must be adopted.

---

## DIRECTIONS FOR CARVING.

THE carving-knife for a lady should be light, and of a middling size and fine edge. Strength is less required than address, in the manner of using it: and to facilitate this, the cook shall give orders to the butcher to divide the joints of the bones of all carcase joints of mutton, lamb, and veal (such as neck, breast, and loin), which may then be easily cut into thin slices attached to the adjoining bones. If the whole of the meat belonging to each bone should be too thick, a small slice may be taken off between every two bones.

The more fleshy joints (as fillet of veal, leg or saddle of mutton, and beef) are to be helped in thin slices, neatly cut and smooth; observing to let the knife pass down to the bone in the mutton and beef joints,

The dish should not be too far off the carver; as it gives an awkward appearance, and makes the task more difficult. Attention is to be paid to help every one to a part of such articles as are considered the best.

In helping fish, take care not to break the flakes; which in cod and very fresh salmon are large, and contribute much to the beauty of its appearance. A fish-knife, not being sharp, divides it best on this account. Help a part of the roe, milt, or liver, to each person. The heads of carp, parts of those of cod and salmon, sounds of cod and fins of turbot, are likewise esteemed niceties, and are to be attended to accordingly.

In cutting up any wild-fowl, duck, goose, or turkey, for a large party, if you cut the slices down from pinion to pinion, without making wings, there will be more prime pieces.

**A Cod's Head.**—Fish in general requires very little carving, the fleshy parts being those principally esteemed.  A cod's head and shoulders, when in season, and properly boiled, is a very genteel and handsome dish. When cut, it should be done with a fish-trowel, and the parts, about the back-bone on the shoulders are the most firm and the best.  Take off a piece quite down to the bone, in the direction *a, b, c, d,* putting in the spoon at *a, c,* and with each slice of fish give a piece of the sound, which lies underneath the back-bone and lines it, the meat of which is thin, and a little darker-coloured than the body of the fish itself.  About the head are many delicate parts, and a great deal of the jelly kind.  The jelly part lies about the jawbones, and the firm parts within the head.  Some are fond of the palate, and others the tongue, which likewise may be got by putting a spoon into the mouth.

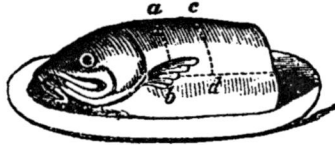

**Aitch-bone of Beef.**—Cut off a slice an inch thick all the length from *a* to *b,* and then help.  The soft fat, which resembles marrow, lies at the back of the bone, below *c :* the firm fat must be cut

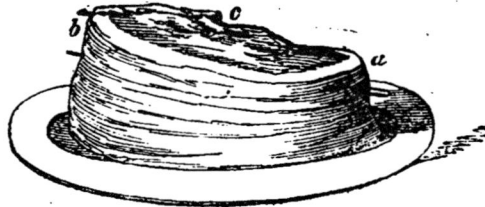

in horizontal slices at the edge of the meat *d.*  It is proper to ask which is preferred, as tastes differ.  The skewer that keeps the meat properly together when boiling is here shown at *a.*  This should be drawn out before it is served up ; or, if it is necessary to leave the skewer in, put a silver one.

**Sirloin of Beef** may be begun either at the end, or by cutting into the middle.  It is usual to inquire whether the outside or inside is preferred.  For the outside, the slice should be cut down to the bones? and the same with every following helping.  Slice the inside likewise, and give with each piece some of the fat.

The inside done as follows eats excellently :—Have ready

some fine shalot vinegar boiling hot; mince the meat large, and a good deal of fat; sprinkle it with salt, and pour the shalot vinegar and the gravy on it. Help with a spoon, as quickly as possible on hot plates.

**Round or Buttock of Beef** is cut in the same way as fillet of veal. It should be kept even all over.

When helping the fat, observe not to hack it, but cut it smooth. A deep slice should be cut off the beef before you begin to help, as directed for the Edge-bone.

**Fillet of Veal.**—In an ox this part is round of beef. Ask whether the brown outside be liked, otherwise help the next slice. The bone is taken out and the meat tied close, before dressing; which makes the fillet very solid. It should be cut thin and very smooth. A stuffing is put into the flap which completely covers it; you must cut deep into this, and help a thin slice, as likewise of fat. From carelessness in not covering the latter with paper, it is sometimes dried up, to the great disappointment of the carver.

**Breast of Veal.**—One part (which is called the brisket) is thickest, and has gristles; put your knife about four inches from the edge of this, and cut through it, which will separate the ribs from the brisket.

**Calf's Head** has a great deal of meat upon it, if properly managed. Cut slices from *a* to *b*, letting the knife go close to the bone. In the fleshy part, at the neck end *c*, there lies the throat sweet-bread, which you should help a slice of from *c* to *d* with the other part. Many like the eye; which you must cut out with the point of your knife, and divide in two. If the jaw-bone be taken off, there will be found some fine lean. Under the head is the palate, which is reckoned a nicety; the lady of the house should be acquainted with all things that are thought so, that she may distribute them among her guests.

**Shoulder of Mutton.**—This is a very good joint, and by many preferred to the leg; it being very full of gravy, if properly roasted, and produces many nice bits. The figure represents it as laid in the dish with its back uppermost. When it is first cut, it should be in the hollow part of it, in the direction of *a, b,* and the knife should be passed deep to the bone.

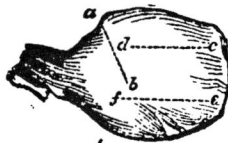

The prime part of the fat lies on the outer edge, and it is to be cut out in thin slices in the direction of *e* to *f*. If many are at table, and the hollow part cut in the line *a, b,* is eaten, some very good

and delicate slices may be cut out on each side the ridge of the
blade-bone, in the direction c, d.  The line between these two dotted
lines, is that in the direction of which the edge or ridge of the blade-
bone lies, and cannot be cut across.

**Leg of Mutton.**—A leg of wether mutton (which is the best
flavoured) may be known by a round lump of fat at the edge of the
broadest part.  The best
part is in the midway. at
b, between the knuckle
and farther end.  Begin
to help here, by cutting
thin deep slices to c.  If
the outside is not fat
enough, help some from
the side of the broad end
in slices from e to f.  This
part is the most juicy;
but many prefer the knuckle, which, in fine mutton, will be very
tender though dry.  There are very fine slices on the back of
the leg; turn it up, and cut the broad end; not in the direction you
did the other side, but longways.  To cut out the cramp-bone, take
hold of the shank with your left hand, and cut down to the thigh-
bone at d; then pass the knife under the cramp-bone on the direction, d, g.

**A Fore Quarter of Lamb.**—Separate the shoulder from the
scoven (which is the breast and ribs), by passing the knife under in
the direction of a, b, c, d; keeping it towards you horizontally, to
prevent cutting the meat
too much off the bones.
If grass-lamb, the shoul-
der being large, put it into
another dish.   Squeeze
the juice of half a lemon
on the other part, and
sprinkle a little salt and
pepper.   Then separate
the gristly part from the
ribs in the line c, c; and help either from that, or from the ribs,
as may be chosen.

**Haunch of Venison.**—Cut down to the bone in the line a, b, c.
in the figure, to let
out the gravy : then
turn the broad end
of the haunch to-
wards you, put in
the knife at b, and
cut as deep as you
can to the end of the
haunch d; then help
in thin slices, observ-
ing to give some fat to each person.  There is more fat (which is a
favourite part) on the left side of c and d than on the other; and

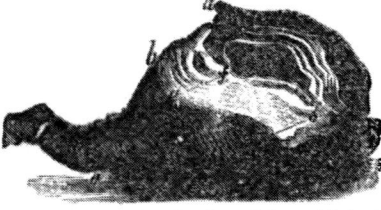

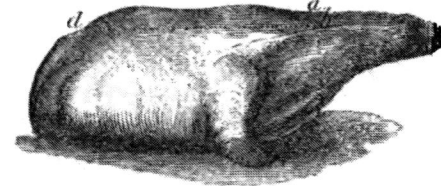

those who help must take care to proportion it, as likewise the gravy, according to the number of the company.

**Haunch of Mutton** is the leg and part of the loin, cut so as to resemble haunch of venison, and is to be helped at table in the same manner.

**Saddle of Mutton.**—Cut long thin slices from the tail to the end, beginning close to the backbone. If a large joint, the slice may be divided. Cut some fat from the sides.

**Ham** may be cut three ways; the common method is, to begin in the middle, by long slices from *a* to *b*, from the centre through the thick fat. This brings to the prime at first; which is likewise accomplished by cutting a small round hole on the top of the ham, as at *c*, and with a sharp knife enlarging that by cutting successive thin circles; this preserves the gravy and keeps the meat moist.

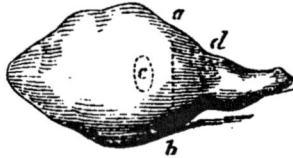

The last and most saving way is, to begin at the hock end, and proceed onwards.

Ham that is used for pies, &c. should be cut from the under side, first taking off a thick slice.

**Sucking Pig.**—The cook usually divides the body before it is sent to table, and garnishes the dish with the jaws and ears.

The first thing is, to separate a shoulder from the carcase on one side, and then the leg according to the direction given by the dotted line *a, b, c.* The ribs are then to be divided into about two helpings; and an ear or jaw presented with them, and plenty of sauce. The joints may either be divided into two each, or pieces may be cut from them.

The ribs are reckoned the finest part; but some people prefer the neck end, between the shoulders.

**Goose.**—Cut off the apron in the circular line *a, b, c ;* and pour into the body a glass of port wine ; and a large tea-spoonful of mustard, first mixed at the sideboard. Turn the neck end of the goose towards you, and cut the whole breast in long slices from one wing to another ; but only remove them as you help each person, unless the company is so large as to require the legs likewise. This way gives more prime bits than by making wings. Take off the leg, by put-

B

ting the fork into the small end of the bone, pressing it to the body, and having passed the knife at $d$, turn the leg back, and if a young bird it will easily separate. To take off the wing, put your fork into the small end of the pinion, and press it close to the body; then put in the knife at $d$, and divide the joint, taking it down in the direction $d$, $e$. Nothing but practice will enable people to hit the joint exactly at the first trial. When the leg and wing of one side are done, go on to the other; but it is not often necessary to cut up the whole goose, unless the company be very large. There are two side bones by the wing, which may be cut off, as likewise the back and lower side-bones; but the best pieces are the breast, and the thighs after being divided from the drumsticks.

Hare.—The best way of cutting it up is, to put the point of the knife under the shoulder at $a$, and so cut all the way down to the rump, on one side of the back-bone, in the line $a$, $b$. Do the same

on the other side, so that the whole hare will be divided into three parts. Cut the back into four, which with the legs is the part most esteemed. The shoulder must be cut off in a circular line, as $c$, $d$, $a$; lay the pieces neatly on the dish as you cut them, and then help the company, giving some pudding and gravy to every person. This way can only be practised when the hare is young; if old, do not divide it down, which will require a strong arm; but put the knife between the leg and back, and give it a little turn inwards at the joint, which you must endeavour to hit, and not to break by force. When both legs are taken off, there is a fine collop on each side the back, then divide the back into as many pieces as you please, and take off the shoulders, which are by many preferred, and are called the sportsman's pieces. When every one is helped, cut off the head, put your knife between the upper and lower jaw, and divide them, which will enable you to lay the upper flat on your plate: then put the point of the knife into the centre, and cut the head into two. The ears and brains may be helped then to those who like them.

Carve Rabbits as directed the latter way for hare; cutting the back into two pieces, which with the legs are the prime.

A Fowl.—A boiled fowl's legs are bent inwards, and tucked into the belly; but before it is served, the skewers are to be removed. Lay the fowl on your plate, and place the joints, as cut off, on the dish. Take the wing off in the direction of $a$ to $b$, only dividing the joint with your knife, and then with your fork lift up the pinion, and draw the wing towards the legs, and the muscles will separate in a more complete form than if cut. Slip the knife between the leg and body, and cut to the bone; then with the fork turn the leg back, and the joint will give way if the bird is not old. When the four quarters are thus removed, take off the merrythought from *a* and the neck-bones; these last by putting in the knife at *c*, and pressing it under the long broad part of the bone in the line *c, b,* then lift it up, and break it off from the part that sticks to the breast. The next thing is, to divide the breast from the carcase, by cutting through the tender ribs close to the breast right down to the tail. Then lay the back upwards, put your knife into the bone half-way from the neck to the rump, and on raising the lower end it will separate readily. Turn the rump from you, and very neatly take off the two sidesmen, and the whole will be done. As each part is taken off, it should be turned neatly on the dish; and care should be taken that what is left goes properly from table. The breast and wings are looked upon as the best parts, but the legs are most juicy in young fowls. After all, more advantage will be gained by observing those who carve well, and a little practice, than by any written directions whatever.

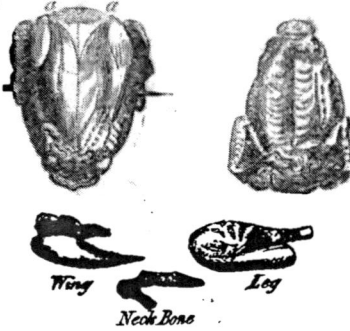

A Pheasant.—The bird in the annexed engraving is as trussed for the spit, with its head under one of its wings. When the skewers are taken out, and the bird served, the following is the way to carve it:—

Fix your fork in the centre of the breast; slice it down in the lines *a, b;* take off the leg on one side in the dotted line *b, d;* then cut off the wing on the same side, in the line *c, d.* Separate the leg and wing on the other side, and then cut off the slices of breast you divided before. Be careful how you take off the wings, for if you should cut too near the neck, as at *g,* you will hit on the neckbone, from which the wing must be separated. Cut off the merrythought in the line *f, g,* by passing the knife under it towards the neck. Cut the other parts as in a fowl. The breast, wings, and merrythought are the most esteemed; but the leg has a higher flavour.

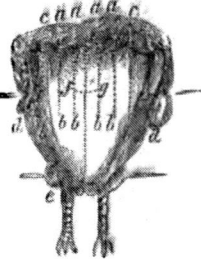

Partridge.—The partridge is here represented as just taken

from the spit; but before it is served up, the skewers must be withdrawn. It is cut up in the same manner as a fowl. The wings must be taken off in the lines *a*, *b*, and the merrythought in the line *c*, *d*. The prime parts of a partridge are the wings, breast, and merrythought. But the bird being small, the two latter are not often divided. The wing is considered as the best, and the tip of it reckoned the most delicate morsel of the whole.

**Pigeons.**—Cut them in half, either from top to bottom or across. The lower part is generally thought the best: but the fairest way is to cut from the neck to *a*, rather than from *c* to *b*, by *a*, which is the most fashionable. The figure represents the back of the pigeon; and the direction of the knife is in the line *c*, *b*, by *a*, if done the last way.

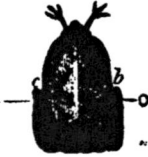

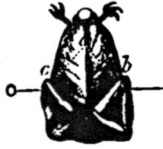

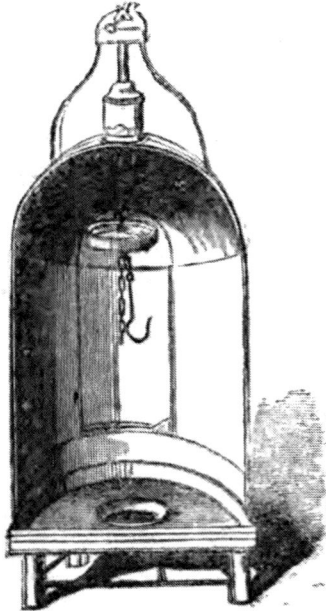

ROASTING APPARATUS.

# DOMESTIC COOKERY.

## FISH.

### To Choose Fish.

**TURBOT**, if good, should be thick, and the belly of a yellowish white; if of a bluish cast or thin, they are bad. They are in season the greatest part of the summer.

**Salmon.**—If new, the flesh is of a fine red (the gills particularly), the scales bright, and the whole fish stiff. When just killed, there is a whiteness between the flakes, which gives great firmness; by keeping, this melts down, and the fish is more rich. The Thames salmon bears the highest price; that caught in the Severn is next in goodness, and even preferred by some. Small heads, and thick in the neck, are best.

**Cod.**—The gills should be very red: the fish should be very thick at the neck, the flesh white and firm, and the eyes fresh. When flabby they are not good. They are in season from the beginning of December till the end of April.

**Skate.**—If good they are very white and thick. If too fresh they eat tough, but must not be kept above two days.

**Herrings.**—If good, their gills are of a fine red and the eyes bright; as is likewise the whole fish, which must be stiff and firm.

**Soles.**—If good they are thick, and the belly is of a cream colour: if this is of a bluish cast and flabby, they are not fresh. They are in the market almost the whole year, but are in the highest perfection about midsummer.

**Whitings.**—The firmness of the body and fins is to be looked to, as in herrings; they are in high season during the first three months of the year, but they may be had a great part of it.

**Mackerel.**—Choose as whitings. Their season is May, June, and July. They are so tender a fish that they carry and keep worse than any other.

**Pike.**—For freshness observe the above marks. The best are taken in rivers: they are a very dry fish, and are much indebted to stuffing and sauce.

**Carp** live some time out of water, and may therefore get wasted; it is best to kill them as soon as caught, to prevent this. The same signs of freshness attend them as other fish.

**Tench.**—They are a fine-flavoured fresh-water fish, and should be killed and dressed as soon as caught. When they are to be bought, examine whether the gills are red and hard to open, the eyes bright, and the body stiff. The tench has a slimy matter about it, the clearness and brightness of which show freshness. The season is July, August and September.

**Perch.**—Take the general rules given to distinguish the freshness of other fish. They are not so delicate as carp and tench.

**Smelts**, if good, have a fine silvery hue, are very firm, and have a refreshing smell like cucumbers newly cut. They are caught in the Thames and some other large rivers.

**Mullets.**—The sea are preferred to the river mullets, and the red to the grey. They should be very firm. Their season is August.

**Gudgeons.**—They are chosen by the same rules as other fish. They are taken in running streams; come in about midsummer, and are to be had for five or six months.

**Eels.**—There is a greater difference in the goodness of eels than of any other fish. The true silver-eel (so-called from the bright colour of the belly) is caught in the Thames. The Dutch eels sold at Billingsgate are very bad; those taken in great floods are generally good, but in ponds they have usually a strong rank flavour. Except the middle of summer, they are always in season.

**Lobsters.**—If they have not been long taken, the claws will have a strong motion when you put your finger on the eyes and press them. The heaviest are the best, and it is preferable to boil them at home. When you buy them ready boiled, try whether their tails are stiff, and pull up with a spring; otherwise that part will be flabby. The cock lobster is known by the narrow back part of his tail, and the two uppermost fins within it are stiff and hard; but those of the hen are soft, and the tail broader. The male, though generally smaller, has the highest flavour, the flesh is firmer, and the colour when boiled is a deeper red.

**Crabs.**—The heaviest are best, and those of a middling size are sweetest. If light they are watery; when in perfection the joints of the legs are stiff and the body has a very agreeable smell. The eyes look dead and loose when stale.

**Prawns and Shrimps.**—When fresh they have a sweet flavour, are firm and stiff, and the colour is bright.—Shrimps are of the prawn kind, and may be judged by the same rules.

**Oysters.**—There are several kinds; the Pyfleet, Colchester, and Milford, are much the best. The native Milton are fine, being white and fat; but others may be made to possess both these qualities in some degree by proper feeding. When alive and strong the shell closes on the knife. They should be eaten as soon as opened, the flavour becoming poor otherwise. The rock oyster is largest, but usually has a coarse flavour if eaten raw.

**Flounders.**—They should be thick, firm, and have their eyes bright. They very soon become flabby and bad. They are both sea and river fish. The Thames produces the best. They are in season from January to March, and from July to September.

**Sprats.**—Choose by the same rules as herrings.

**Observations on Dressing Fish.**—If the fishmonger does not clean it, fish is seldom very nicely done; but those in great towns wash it beyond what is necessary for cleaning, and by perpetual watering diminish the flavour. When quite clean, if to be boiled, some salt and a little vinegar should be put into the water to give firmness, but Cod, Whiting, and Haddock are far better if a little salted, and kept a day; and if not very hot weather, they will be good two days.

Those who know how to purchase fish, may, by taking more at a time than they want for one day, often get it cheap; and such kinds as will pot or pickle, or keep by being sprinkled with salt and hung up, or by being fried will serve for stewing the next day, may then be bought with advantage.

Fresh-water fish has often a muddy smell and taste, to take off which, soak it in strong salt and water after it is nicely cleaned; or if of a size to bear it, scald it in the same; then dry and dress it.

The fish must be put into the water while cold, and set to do very gently, or the outside will break before the inner part is done.

Crimp fish should be put into boiling water; and when it boils up, pour a little cold water in, to check extreme heat, and simmer it a few minutes.

The fish-plate on which it is done may be drawn up to see if it be ready; it will leave the bone when it is. It should then be immediately taken out of the water, or it will soon be woolly. The fish-plate should be set crosswise over the kettle, to keep hot for serving; and a clean cloth to cover the fish to prevent it losing its colour.

Small fish nicely fried, covered with eggs and crumbs, make a dish far more elegant than if served plain. Great attention should be paid to garnishing fish: use plenty of horse-radish, parsley, and lemon.

When well done, and with very good sauce, fish is more attended to than almost any other dish. The liver and roe should be placed on the dish, so that the lady may see them, and help a part to every one.

If fish is to be fried or broiled, it must be wrapt in a nice soft cloth after it is well cleaned and washed. When perfectly dry, wet with an egg if for frying, and sprinkle the finest crumbs of bread over it; if done a second time with the egg and bread, the fish will look much better; then, having a thick-bottomed frying-pan on the fire, with a large quantity of lard or dripping boiling hot, plunge the fish into it, and let it fry middlingly quick, till the colour is a fine brown yellow, and it is judged ready. If it is done enough before it has obtained a proper degree of colour, the cook should draw the pan to the side of the fire; carefully take it up, and either place it on a large sieve turned upwards, and to be kept for that purpose only, or on the under side of a dish to drain; and if wanted very nice, a sheet of cap paper must be put to receive the fish, which should look a beautiful colour, and all the crumbs appear distinct; the fish being free from all grease. The same dripping, with a little fresh, will serve a second time. Butter gives

a bad colour; oil fries of the finest colour for those who will allow
the expense,

Garnish with a fringe of curled raw parsley, or parsley fried,
which must be thus done: When washed and picked, throw it
again into clean water; when the lard or dripping boils, throw the
parsley into it immediately from the water, and instantly it will
be green and crisp, and must be taken up with a slice; this may
be done after the fish is fried.

If fish is to be broiled, it must be seasoned, floured, and put on
a gridiron that is very clean; which, when hot, should be rubbed
with a bit of suet to prevent the fish from sticking. It must be
broiled on a very clear fire, that it may not taste smoky; and not
too near, that it may not be scorched.

**TURBOT.—To Keep Turbot.**—If necessary, turbot will
keep for two or three days, and be in as high perfection as at
first, if lightly rubbed over with salt, and carefully hung in a cold
place.

**To Boil Turbot.**—The turbot-kettle must be of a proper size,
and in the nicest order. Set the fish in cold water sufficient to
cover it completely, throw a handful of salt and a glass of vinegar
into it, and let it gradually boil: be very careful that there fall
no blacks; but skim it well, and preserve the beauty of the
colour.

Serve it garnished with a complete fringe of curled parsley, lemon,
and horse-radish.

The sauce must be the finest lobster, and anchovy butter, and
plain butter, served plentifully in separate tureens.

**SALMON.—To Boil Salmon.**—Clean it carefully, boil it
gently, and take it out of the water as soon as done. Let the
water be warm if the fish be split. If underdone, it is very unwholesome. Serve with shrimp or anchovy sauce.

**To Broil Salmon.**—Cut slices an inch thick, and season with
pepper and salt; lay each slice in half a sheet of white paper well
buttered; twist the ends of the paper, and broil the slices over
a slow fire six or eight minutes. Serve in the paper with anchovy
sauce.

**To Pot Salmon.**—Take a large piece, scale and wipe, but do
not wash it; salt very well, let it lie till the salt is melted and
drained from it, then season with beaten mace, cloves, and whole
pepper: lay in a few bay-leaves, put it close into a pan, cover it
over with butter, and bake it; when well done, drain it from the
gravy, put it into the pots to keep, and when cold cover it with
clarified butter.

In this manner you may do any firm fish.

**To Dry Salmon.**—Cut the fish down, take out the inside and
roe. Rub the whole with common salt after scaling it; let it hang
twenty-four hours to drain. Pound three or four ounces of saltpetre, according to the size of the fish, two ounces of bay salt, and
two ounces of coarse sugar; rub these, when mixed well, into the
salmon, and lay it on a large dish or tray two days, then rub it
well with common salt, and in twenty-four hours more it will be

fit to dry ; wipe it well after draining. Hang it either in a wood chimney, or in a dry place ; keeping it open with two small sticks.

Dried salmon is eaten broiled in paper, and only just warmed through, with egg sauce and mashed potatoes ; or it may be boiled, especially the bit next the head.

**An excellent Dish of Dried Salmon.**—Pull some into flakes ; have ready some eggs boiled hard, and chopped large ; put both into half a pint of thin cream, and two or three ounces of butter rubbed with a tea-spoonful of flour ; skim it and stir till boiling hot ; make a wall of mashed potatoes round the inner edge of a dish, and pour the above into it.

**To Pickle Salmon.**—Boil as before directed, take the fish out, and boil the liquor with bay leaves, peppercorns, and salt ; add vinegar, when cold, and pour it over the fish.

**Another way.**—After scaling and cleaning, split the salmon, and divide into such pieces as you choose, lay it in the kettle to fill the bottom, and as much water as will cover it ; to three quarts put a pint of vinegar, a handful of salt, twelve bay leaves, six blades of mace, and a quarter of an ounce of black pepper. When the salmon is boiled enough, drain it and put it on a clean cloth, then put more salmon into the kettle, and pour the liquor upon it, and so on till all is done. After this, if the pickle be not smartly flavoured with the vinegar and salt, add more, and boil quick three quarters of an hour. When all is cold, pack the fish in something deep, and let there be enough of pickle to plentifully cover. Preserve it from the air. The liquor must be drained from the fish, and occasionally boiled and skimmed.

**Salmon Collared.**—Split such a part of the fish as may be sufficient to make a handsome roll, wash and wipe it, and having mixed salt, white pepper, pounded mace and Jamaica pepper, in quantity to season it very high, rub it inside and out well. Then roll it tight and bandage it, put as much water and one-third vinegar as will cover it, with bay leaves, salt and both sorts of pepper. Cover close, and simmer till done enough. Drain and boil quick the liquor, and put on when cold. Serve with fennel. It is an elegant dish, and extremely good.

**COD.**—Some people boil the cod whole ; but a large head and shoulders contain all the fish that is proper to help, the thinner parts being overdone and tasteless, before the thick are ready. But the whole fish may be purchased at times more reasonably, and the lower half, if sprinkled and hung up, will be in high perfection in one or two days. Or it may be made salter, and served with egg sauce, potatoes, and parsnips.

Cod when small is usually very cheap. If boiled quite fresh it is watery ; but eats excellently if salted and hung up for a day to give it firmness, then stuffed and broiled or boiled.

**Cod's Head and Shoulders** will eat much finer by having a little salt rubbed down the bone, and along the thick part, even if to be eaten the same day.

Tie it up and put it on the fire in cold water which will completely cover it. Throw a handful of salt into it. Great care must be taken to serve it without the smallest speck of black or scum. Garnish with a large quantity of double parsley, lemon, horseradish, and the milt, roe, and liver, and fried smelts if approved. If with smelts, be careful that no water hangs about the fish ; or the beauty of the smelts will be taken off, as well as their flavour. Serve with plenty of oyster or shrimp sauce, and anchovy and butter.

**Crimp Cod.**—Boil, broil, or fry.

**Cod Sounds boiled.**—Soak them in warm water half an hour, then scrape and clean ; and if to be dressed white, boil them in milk and water ; when tender serve them in a napkin, with egg sauce. The salt must not be much soaked out, unless for fricassee.

**Cod Sounds to look like small Chickens.**—A good maigre-day dish. Wash three large sounds nicely, and boil in milk and water, but not too tender ; when cold, put a forcemeat of chopped oysters, crumbs of bread, a bit of butter, nutmeg, pepper, salt, and the yolks of two eggs ; spread it over the sounds, and roll up each in the form of a chicken, skewering it ; then lard them as you would chickens, dust a little flour over, and roast them in a tin oven slowly. When done enough, pour over them a fine oyster sauce. Serve for side or corner dish.

**To Broil Cod Sounds.**—Scald in hot water, rub well with salt, pull off the dirty skin, and put them to simmer till tender ; take them out, flour, and broil. While this is being done, season a little brown gravy with pepper, salt, a tea-spoonful of soy, and a little mustard ; give it a boil with a bit of flour and butter, and pour it over the sounds.

**Cod Sound Ragout.**—Prepare as above ; then stew them in white gravy seasoned, cream, butter, and a little bit of flour added before you serve, gently boiling up. A bit of lemon-peel, nutmeg, and the least pinch of pounded mace should give the flavour.

**Currie of Cod** should be made of sliced cod, that has either been crimped or sprinkled a day, to make it firm. Fry it of a fine brown with onion ; and stew it with a good white gravy, a little currie-powder, a bit of butter and flour, three or four spoonfuls of rich cream, salt, and Cayenne, if the powder be not hot enough.

**To Dress Salt Cod.**—Soak and clean the piece you mean to dress, then lay it all night in water, with a glass of vinegar. Boil it enough, then break it into flakes on the dish ; pour over it parsnips boiled, beaten into a mortar, and then boiled up with cream and a large piece of butter rubbed with a bit of flour. It may be served as above with egg sauce instead of the parsnip, and the root sent up whole, or the fish may be boiled and sent up without flaking, and sauces as above.

**STURGEON.—To Dress Fresh Sturgeon.**—Cut slices, rub egg over them, then sprinkle with crumbs of bread, parsley, pepper, salt ; fold them in paper, and broil gently.

Sauce ; butter, anchovy, and soy.

**To Roast Sturgeon.**—Put it on a lark spit, then tie it on a large spit; baste it constantly with butter; and serve with good gravy, an anchovy, a squeeze of Seville orange or lemon, and a glass of sherry.

**Another way.**—Put a piece of butter rolled in flour into a stew-pan with four cloves, a bunch of sweet herbs, two onions, some pepper and salt, half a pint of water, and a glass of vinegar. Stir it over the fire till hot; then let it become lukewarm, and steep the fish in it an hour or two. Butter a paper well, tie it round, and roast it without letting the spit run through. Serve with sorrel and anchovy sauce.

**An excellent Imitation of Pickled Sturgeon.**—Take a fine large turkey, but not old; pick it very nicely, singe, and make it extremely clean: bone and wash it, and tie it across and across with a bit of mat-string washed clean. Put into a very nice tin saucepan a quart of water, a quart of vinegar, a quart of white (but not sweet) wine, and a very large handful of salt; boil and skim it well, then boil the turkey. When done enough tighten the strings, and lay upon it a dish with a weight of two pounds over it.

Boil the liquor half an hour; and when both are cold, put the turkey into it. This will keep some months, and eats more delicately than sturgeon; vinegar, oil, and sugar are usually eaten with it. If more vinegar or salt should be wanted, add when cold. Send fennel over it to table.

**Thornback and Skate** should be hung one day at least before they are dressed; and may be served either boiled, or fried in crumbs, being first dipped in egg.

**Crimp Skate.**—Boil and send up in a napkin; or fry as above.

**Maids** should likewise be hung one day at least. They may be boiled or fried; or, if of a tolerable size, the middle may be boiled and the fins fried. They should be dipped in egg, and covered with crumbs.

**Boiled Carp.**—Serve in a napkin, and with the sauce which you will find directed for it under the article Stewed Carp.

**Stewed Carp.**—Scald and clean, take care of the roe, &c., lay the fish in a stewpan, with a rich beef gravy, an onion, eight cloves, a dessert spoonful of Jamaica pepper, the same of black, a fourth part of the quantity of gravy or port (cyder may do); simmer close covered: when nearly done add two anchovies chopped fine, a dessert spoonful of made mustard, and some fine walnut ketchup, a bit of butter rolled in flour: shake it, and let the gravy boil a few minutes. Serve with sippets of fried bread, the roe fried, and a good deal of horse-radish and lemon.

**Baked Carp.**—Clean a large carp; put a stuffing as for soles dressed in the Portuguese way. Sew it up; brush it all over with yolk of egg, and put plenty of crumbs; then drop oiled butter to baste them; place the carp in a deep earthen dish, a pint of stock (or, if fast-day, fish-stock), a few sliced onions, some bay-leaves, a faggot of herbs (such as basil, thyme, parsley, and both sor' marjoram), half a pint of port wine, and six anchovies, cover over the pan, and bake it an hour. Let it be done before it is wanted. Pour the liquor from it, and keep the fish hot while you heat up the liquor with a good piece of butter rolled in flour, a tea-spoonful of mustard, a little Cayenne, and a spoonful of soy. Serve the fish on the dish, garnished with lemon, parsley, and horse-radish, and put the gravy into the sauce-tureen.

**Perch and Tench.**—Put them into cold water, boil them carefully, and serve with melted butter and soy. Perch are a most delicate fish. They may be either fried or stewed, but in stewing they do not preserve so good a flavour.

**To Fry Trout and Grayling.**—Scale, gut, and well wash; then dry them, and lay them separately on a board before the fire, after dusting some flour over them. Fry them of a fine colour with fresh dripping; serve with crimped parsley, and plain butter.

Perch and Tench may be done the same way.

**Trout a-la-Genevoise.**—Clean the fish very well; put it into your stewpan, adding half Champagne and half Moselle, or Rhenish, or sherry wine. Season it with pepper, salt, an onion, a few cloves stuck in it, and a small bunch of parsley and thyme; put in it a crust of French bread; set it on a quick fire. When the fish is done, take the bread out, bruise it, and then thicken the sauce; add flour and a little butter, and let it boil up. See that your sauce is of a proper thickness. Lay your fish on the dish, and pour the sauce over it. Serve it with sliced lemon and fried bread.

**MACKEREL.**—Boil, and serve with butter and fennel.

To broil them, split, and sprinkle with herbs, pepper, and salt; or stuff with the same, crumbs, and chopped fennel. Collared, as Eel, page 31.

Potted: clean, season, and bake them in a pan with spice, bay-leaves, and some butter; when cold, lay them in a potting-pot, and cover with butter.

Pickled: boil them, then boil some of the liquor, a few peppers, bay-leaves, and some vinegar; when cold, pour it over them.

**Pickled Mackerel, called Caveach.**—Clean and divide them; then cut each side into three, or, leaving them undivided, cut each fish into five or six pieces. To six large mackerel, take near an ounce of pepper, two nutmegs, a little mace, four cloves, and a handful of salt, all in the finest powder; mix, and making holes in each bit of fish, thrust the seasoning into them, rub each piece with some of it; then fry them brown in oil; let them stand till cold, then put them into a stone-jar, and cover with vinegar; if to keep long, pour oil on the top. Thus done, they may be preserved for months.

**Red Mullet.**—It is called the Sea-Woodcock. Clean, but leave the inside, fold in oiled paper, and gently bake in a small dish. Make a sauce of the liquor that comes from the fish, with a piece of butter, a little flour, a little essence of anchovy, and a glass of sherry. Give it a boil; and serve in a boat, and the fish in the paper cases.

**To Dress Pipers.**—Boil, or bake them with a pudding well seasoned. If baked, put a large cup of rich broth into the dish; and when done, take that, some essence of anchovy, and a squeeze of lemon, and boil them up together for sauce.

**To Bake Pike.**—Scale it, and open as near the throat as you can, then stuff it with the following: grated bread, herbs, anchovies, oysters, suet, salt, pepper, mace, half a pint of cream, four yolks of eggs; mix all over the fire till it thickens, then put it in the fish, and sew it up; butter should be put over it in little bits; bake it. Serve sauce of gravy, butter, and anchovy.

*Note.*—If in helping a pike, the back and belly are slit, and each slice gently drawn downwards, there will be fewer bones given.

**HADDOCK.**—Boil; or broil with stuffing, as under, having salted them a day.

**To Dry Haddock.**—Choose them of two or three pounds weight: take out the gills, eyes, and entrails, and remove the blood from the backbone. Wipe them dry, and put some salt into the bodies and eyes. Lay them on a board for a night; then hang them up in a dry place, and after three or four days, they will be fit to eat; skin and rub them with egg, and strew crumbs over them. Lay them before the fire, and baste with butter until brown enough. Serve with egg-sauce.

**Whitings,** if large, are excellent this way; and it will prove an accommodation in the country where there is no regular supply of fish.

**Stuffing for Pike, Haddock, and Small Cod.**—Take equal parts of fat bacon, beef-suet, and fresh butter, some parsley, thyme, and savoury; a little onion, and a few leaves of scented marjoram shred fine; an anchovy or two; a little salt and nutmeg, and some pepper. Oysters will be an improvement with or without anchovies; add crumbs, and an egg to bind.

**SOLES.**—If boiled, they must be served with great care to look perfectly white, and should be much covered with parsley.

If fried, dip in egg, and cover them with fine crumbs of bread; set on a frying-pan that is just large enough, and put into it a large quantity of fresh lard or dripping, boil it, and immediately slip the fish into it; do them of a fine brown. See to fry, page 28.

Soles that have been fried eat good cold with oil, vinegar, salt, and mustard.

**Stewed Soles.**—Do as Carp, page 27.

**Soles another way.**—Take two or three soles, divide them from the backbone, and take off the head, fins, and tail. Sprinkle the inside with salt, roll them up tight from the tail end upwards, and fasten with small skewers. If large or middling, put half a fish in each roll: small do not answer. Dip them into yolks of eggs, and cover them with crumbs. Do the egg over them again, and then put more crumbs; and fry them a beautiful colour in lard, or for fast-day in clarified butter.

**Soles in the Portuguese way.**—Take one large or two small: if large, cut the fish in two; if small, they need only be split. The bones being taken out, put the fish into a pan with a bit of butter and some lemon juice, give it a fry, then lay the fish on a dish, and spread a forcemeat over each piece, and roll it round, fastening the roll with a few small skewers. Lay the rolls into a small earthen pan, beat an egg and wet them, then strew crumbs over; and put the remainder of the egg, with a little meat-gravy, a spoonful of caper-liquor, an anchovy chopped fine and some parsley chopped, into the bottom of the pan; cover it close, and bake till the fish are done enough in a slow oven. Then place the rolls in the dish for serving, and cover it to keep them hot till the gravy baked is skimmed; if not enough, a little fresh, flavoured as above, must be prepared and added to it.

**Portuguese Stuffing for Soles Baked.**—Pound cold beef, mutton, or veal, a little; then add some fat bacon that has been lightly fried, cut small, and some onions, a little garlic or shalot, some parsley, anchovy, pepper, salt, and nutmeg; pound all fine with a few crumbs, and bind it with two or three yolks of eggs.

The heads of the fish are to be left on one side of the split part, and kept on the outer side of the roll; and when served the heads are to be turned towards each other in the dish.

Garnish with fried or dried parsley.

**An excellent way of Dressing a Large Plaice, especially if there be a Roe.**—Sprinkle with salt, and keep twenty-four hours; then wash and wipe it dry, wet over with egg, and cover with crumbs of bread; make some lard or fine dripping, and two large spoonfuls of vinegar, boiling hot; lay the fish in, and fry it a fine colour, drain it from the fat, and serve with fried parsley round, and anchovy-sauce. You may dip the fish in vinegar, and not put it into the pan.

**To Fry Smelts.**—They should not be washed more than is necessary to clean them. Dry them in a cloth; then lightly flour them, but shake it off. Dip them into plenty of egg, then into bread-crumbs, grated fine, and plunge them into a good pan of *boiling* lard; let them continue gently boiling, and a few minutes will make them a bright yellow-brown. Take care not to take off the light roughness of the crumbs, or their beauty will be lost.

**EELS.—Spitchcock Eels.**—Take one or two large eels, leave the skin on, cut them into pieces of three inches long, open them on the belly side, and clean them nicely: wipe them dry, and then wet them with beaten egg, and strew over on both sides chopped parsley, pepper, salt, a very little sage, and a bit of mace pounded fine and mixed with the seasoning. Rub the gridiron with a bit of suet, and broil the fish of a fine colour. Serve with anchovy and butter for sauce.

**Fried Eels.**—If small, should be curled round and fried, being first dipped into egg and crumbs of bread.

**Boiled Eels.**—The small ones are best: do them in a smal

quantity of water, with a good deal of parsley, which should be served up with them and the liquor.

Serve chopped parsley and butter for sauce.

**Eel Broth, very Nourishing for the Sick.**—Do as above; but stew two hours, and add a onion and pepper-corns : salt to taste.

**Collared Eel.**—Bone a large eel, but do not skin it : mix pepper, salt, mace, allspice, and a clove or two, in the finest powder, and rub over the whole inside; roll it tight, and bind with a coarse tape. Boil in salt and water till done, then add vinegar, and when cold keep the collar in pickle. Serve it either whole or in slices. Chopped sage, parsley, and a little thyme, knotted marjoram, and savoury, mixed with the spices, greatly improve the taste.

**To Stew Lamprey as at Worcester.**—After cleaning the fish carefully, remove the cartilage which runs down the back, and season with a small quantity of cloves, mace, nutmeg, pepper, and all-spice; put it into a small stew-pot, with very strong beef-gravy, port, and an equal quantity of Madeira or sherry.

It must be covered close; stew till tender, then take out the lamprey and keep hot, while you boil up the liquor with two or three anchovies chopped, and some flour and butter; strain the gravy through a sieve, and add lemon-juice and some made mustard. Serve with sippets of bread and horse-radish.

**Eels**, done in the same way, are a good deal like the lamprey. When there is spawn, it must be fried and put round.

*Note.*—Cyder will do in common instead of white wine.

**FLOUNDERS.**—Let them be rubbed with salt inside and out, and lie two hours to give them some firmness. Dip them into egg; cover with crumbs, and fry them.

**Water Souchy.**—Stew two or three flounders, some parsley-leaves and roots, thirty pepper-corns and a quart of water, till the fish are boiled to pieces; pulp them through a sieve. Set over the fire the pulped fish, the liquor that boiled them, some perch, flounders, and some fresh leaves and roots of parsley; simmer all till done enough, then serve in a deep dish. Slices of bread and butter are to be sent to table, to eat with the souchy.

**HERRINGS AND SPRATS.—To Smoke Herrings.**—Clean, and lay them in salt and a little saltpetre one night; then hang them on a stick, through the eyes, in a row. Have ready an old cask, in which put some sawdust, and in the midst of it a heater red-hot; fix the stick over the smoke, and let them remain twenty-four hours.

**Fried Herrings.**—Serve them of a light brown, with onions sliced and fried.

**Broiled Herrings.**—Flour them first, and do of a good colour : plain butter for sauce.

**Potted Herrings** are very good done like Mackerel, see page 28.

**To Dress Red Herings.**—Choose those that are large and

moist, cut them open, and pour some boiling small beer over them
to soak half an hour; drain them dry, and make them just hot
through before the fire, then rub some cold butter over them and
serve. Egg sauce, or buttered eggs and mashed potatoes should
be sent up with them.

**Baked Herrings and Sprats.**—Wash and drain without
wiping them; season with allspice in fine powder, salt, and a few
whole cloves; lay them in a pan with plenty of black pepper, an
onion, and a few bay-leaves. Add half vinegar and half small
beer, enough to cover them. Put paper over the pan, and
bake in a slow oven. If you like, throw saltpetre over them the
night before, to make them look red. Gut, but do not open
them.

**Sprats.**—When cleaned, should be fastened in rows by a
skewer run through the heads, and then broiled and served hot
and hot.

**LOBSTERS AND SHRIMPS.—To Pot Lobsters.**—
Half boil them, pick out the meat, cut it into small bits, season with
mace, white pepper, nutmeg and salt, press close into a pot and
cover with butter, bake half an hour; put the spawn in.. When
cold, take the lobster out, and put it into the pots with a little of
the butter. Beat the other butter in a mortar with some of the
spawn: then mix that coloured butter with as much as will be
sufficient to cover the pots and strain it. Cayenne may be added,
if approved.

**Another way to Pot Lobsters, as at Wood's Hotel.**—
Take out the meat as whole as you can; split the tail and remove
the gut; if the inside be not watery, add that. Season with mace,
nutmeg, white pepper, salt, and a clove or two, in the finest
powder. Lay a little fine butter at the bottom of a pan, and the
lobster smooth over it, with bay-leaves between; cover it with
butter, and bake gently. When done pour the whole on the
bottom of a sieve, and with a fork lay the pieces into potting-pots,
some of each sort, with the seasoning about it. When cold, pour
clarified butter over, but not hot. It will be good next day; or
highly seasoned, and thickly covered with butter, will keep some
time.

Potted lobster may be used cold, or as a fricassee, with a cream-
sauce: it then looks very nicely, and eats excellently, especially if
there is spawn.

**Mackerel, Herrings, and Trout,** are good potted as above.

**Stewed Lobster, a very high Relish.**—Pick the lobster,
put the berries into a dish that has a lamp, and rub them down
with a bit of butter, two spoonfuls of any sort of gravy, one of soy,
or walnut-ketchup, a little salt and Cayenne, and a spoonful of
port; strew the lobster cut into bits with the gravy as above.

**Buttered Lobsters.**—Pick the meat out, cut it, and warm
with a little weak brown gravy, nutmeg, salt, pepper, and butter,
with a little flour. If done white, a little white gravy and cream.

**To Roast Lobsters.**—When you have half boiled the lobster,
take it out of the shell, and, while hot, rub it with butter, and lay

*it* before the fire. Continue basting it with butter till it has a fine froth.

**Currie of Lobsters or Prawns.**—Take them from the shells, and lay into a pan, with a small piece of mace, three or four spoonfuls of veal-gravy, and four of cream: rub smooth one or two tea-spoonfuls of currie-powder, a tea-spoonful of flour, and an ounce of butter: simmer an hour; squeeze half a lemon in, and add salt.

**Prawns and Cray-fish in Jelly, a beautiful Dish.**—Make a savoury fish jelly, and put some into the bottom of a deep small dish; when cold, lay the cray-fish with their backs downwards, and pour more jelly over them. Turn out when cold.

**To Butter Prawns or Shrimps.**—Take them out of the shells, and warm them with a little good gravy, a bit of butter and flour, a scrape of nutmeg, salt, and pepper; simmer a minute or two, and serve with sippets; or with a cream-sauce instead of brown.

**To Pot Shrimps.**—When boiled, take them out of the skins, and season them with salt, white pepper, and a very little mace and cloves. Press them into a pot, set it in the oven ten minutes, and when cold put butter.

**CRABS.—Hot Crab.**—Pick the meat out of a crab, clear the shell from the head, then put the meat with a little nutmeg, salt, pepper, a bit of butter, crumbs of bread, and three spoonfuls of vinegar, into the shell again, and set it before the fire. Dry toast should be served to eat it upon.

**Dressed Crab Cold.**—Empty the shells, and mix the flesh with oil, vinegar, salt, and a little white pepper and Cayenne; then put the mixture into the large shell, and serve. Very little oil is necessary.

**OYSTERS.—To Feed Oysters.**—Put them into water, and wash them with a birch-besom till quite clean; then lay them bottom-downwards in a pan, sprinkle with flour or oatmeal and salt, and cover with water. Do the same every day, and they will fatten. The water should be pretty salt.

**To Stew Oysters.**—Open and separate the liquor from them, then wash them from the grit: strain the liquor, and put with the oysters a bit of mace and lemon-peel, and a few white peppers. Simmer them very gently, and put some cream and a little flour and butter. Serve with sippets.

**Boiled Oysters.**—Eat well. Let the shells be nicely cleaned first, and serve in them, to eat with cold butter.

**To Scallop Oysters.**—Put them with crumbs of bread, pepper, salt, nutmeg, and a bit of butter, into scallop-shells or saucers, and bake before the fire in a Dutch oven.

**Fried Oysters, to garnish Boiled Fish.**—Make a batter of flour, milk, and eggs, season it a very little, dip the oysters into it, and fry them a fine yellow-brown. A little nutmeg should be put into the seasoning, and a few crumbs of bread into the flour.

**Oyster Sauce.**—See SAUCES.

**Oyster Loaves.**—Open them, and save the liquor; wash the

c

in it; then strain it through a sieve, and put a little of it into a tosser with a bit of butter and flour, white pepper, a scrape of nutmeg, and a little cream. Stew them, and cut in dice; put them into rolls sold for the purpose.

**Oyster Patties.**—See PATTIES.

**To Pickle Oysters.**—Wash four dozen of the largest oysters you can get in their own liquor, wipe them dry, strain the liquor off, adding to it a dessert-spoonful of pepper, two blades of mace, a table-spoonful of salt, if the liquor be not very salt, three of white wine, and four of vinegar. Simmer the oysters a few minutes in the liquor, then put them in small jars, and boil the pickle up, skim it, and when cold, pour over the oysters: cover close.

**Another way to Pickle Oysters.**—Open the number you intend to pickle, put them into a saucepan with their own liquor for ten minutes, simmer them very gently; then put them into a jar, one by one, that none of the grit may stick to them, and cover them when cold with the pickle thus made. Boil the liquor with a bit of mace, lemon-peel, and black peppers, and to every hundred put two spoonfuls of the best undistilled vinegar.

They should be kept in small jars, and tied close with bladder, for the air will spoil them.

*Note.*—Directions for making Fish Pies will be found under the head PIES.

---

# MEATS.

## *To Choose Meats.*

**VENISON.**—If the fat be clear, bright, and thick, and the cleft part smooth and close, it is young; but if the cleft is wide and tough, it is old. To judge of its sweetness, run a very sharp narrow knife into the shoulder or haunch, and you will know by the scent. Few people like it when it has much of the *haut-gout.*

**Beef.**—If the flesh of ox-beef is young, it will have a fine smooth open grain, be of a good red, and look tender. The fat should look white rather than yellow, for when that is of a deep colour, the meat is seldom good: beef fed by oil-cakes is in general so, and the flesh is flabby. The grain of cow-beef is closer, and the fat whiter than that of ox-beef, but the lean is not of so bright a red. The grain of bull-beef is closer still, the fat hard and skinny, the lean of a deep red, and a stronger scent. Ox-beef is the reverse. Ox-beef is the richest and largest, but in small families, and to some tastes, heifer-beef is better, if finely fed. In old meat there is a streak of horn in the ribs of beef: the harder this is, the older; and the flesh is not finely flavoured.

**Veal.**—The flesh of a bull-calf is firmest, but not so white. The fillet of the cow-calf is generally preferred for the udder. The whitest is not the most juicy, having been made so by frequent bleeding and having had whiting to lick. Choose the meat of which the kidney is well covered with thick white fat. If the

bloody vein in the shoulder looks blue, or of a bright red, it is ·
newly killed, but any other colour shows it stale. The other part
should be dry and white; if clammy or spotted, the meat is stale
and bad. The kidney turns first in the loin, and the suet will not
then be firm.

**Mutton.**—Choose this by the fineness of its grain, good colour,
and firm white fat. It is not the better for being young; if of a
good breed and well fed, it is better for age, but this only holds
with wether-mutton ; the flesh of the ewe is paler, and the texture
finer. Ram-mutton is very strong-flavoured, the flesh is of a deep
red, and the fat is spongy.

**Lamb.**—Observe the neck of a fore-quarter; if the vein is
bluish, it is fresh ; if it has a green or yellow cast, it is stale. In
the hind-quarter, if there is a faint smell under the kidney, and
the knuckle is limp, the meat is stale. If the eyes are sunk, the
head is not fresh. Grass-lamb comes into season in April or May
and continues till August. House-lamb may be had in great
towns almost all the year, but is in the highest perfection in December and January.

**Pork.**—Pinch the lean, and if young it will break. If the rind
is tough, thick, and cannot easily be impressed by the finger, it is
old. A thin rind is a merit in all pork. When fresh, the flesh
will be smooth and cool ; if clammy, it is tainted. What is called
measly pork is very unwholesome, and may be known by the fat
being full of kernels, which in good pork is never the case. Pork
feed at still-houses does not answer for curing any way, the fat
being spongy. Dairy-fed pork is the best.

**Bacon.**—If the rind is thin, the fat firm and of a red tinge, the
lean tender, of a good colour, and adhering to the bone, you may
conclude it good, and not old. If there are yellow streaks in it, it
is going, if not already rusty.

**Hams.**—Stick a sharp knife under the bone; if it comes out
with a pleasant smell, the ham is good; but if the knife is daubed
and has a bad scent, do not buy it. Hams short in the hock are
best, and long-legged pigs are not to be chosen for any preparation of pork.

**Brawn.**—The horny part of young brawn will feel moderately
tender, and the flavour will be better; the rind of old will be
hard.

**Observations on Purchasing, Keeping, and Dressing
Meat.**—In every sort of provisions, the best of the kind goes
farthest : it cuts out with most advantage, and affords most
nourishment. Round of beef, fillet of veal, and leg of mutton, are
joints that bear a higher price ; but as they have more solid meat,
they deserve the preference. It is worth notice, however, that
those joints which are inferior may be dressed as palatably ; and,
being cheaper, they ought to be bought in turn ; for, when they
are weighed with the prime pieces, it makes the price of these
come lower.

In loins of meat, the long pipe that runs by the bone should be
taken out, as it is apt to taint; as also the kernels of beef. Rumps

and aitchbones of beef are often bruised by the blows the drovers
give the beasts, and the part that has been struck always taints;
therefore do not purchase these joints if bruised.

The shank-bones of mutton should be saved; and, after soaking
and crushing, may be added to give richness to gravies or soups.
They are also particularly nourishing for sick persons.

When sirloins of beef, or loins of veal or mutton, come in, part
of the suet may be cut off for puddings, or to clarify.

Dripping will baste everything as well as butter, except
fowls and game; and for kitchen pies, nothing else should be
used.

The fat off a neck or loin of mutton makes a far lighter pudding
than suet.

Meat and vegetables that the frost has touched, should be
soaked in cold water two or three hours before used, or more if
they are much iced.    Putting them into hot water, or to the fire,
till thawed, makes it impossible for any heat to dress them properly afterwards.

In warm weather, meat should be examined when it comes in;
and if flies have touched it, the part must be cut off, and then well
washed.    In the height of summer, it is a very safe way to let meat
that is to be salted lie an hour in very cold water, rubbing well
any part likely to have been fly-blown; then wipe it quite dry,
and have salt ready, and rub it thoroughly in every part, throwing
a handful over it besides.    Turn it every day, and rub the pickle
in, which will make it ready for the table in three or four days.
If to be very much corned, wrap it in a well-floured cloth, after
rubbing it with salt.    This last method will corn fresh beef fit for
the table the day it comes in, but it must be put into the pot when
the water boils.

If the weather permit, meat eats much better for hanging two
or three days before it is salted.

The water in which meat has been boiled makes an excellent
soup for the poor, by adding to it vegetables, oatmeal, or peas.

Roast beef bones, or shank-bones of ham, make fine peas-soup;
and should be boiled with the peas the day before eaten, that the
fat may be taken off.

In some families great loss is sustained by the spoiling of meat.
The best way to keep what is to be eaten unsalted, is, as before
directed, to examine it well, wipe it every day, and put some pieces
of charcoal over it.    If meat is brought from a distance in warm
weather, the butcher should be ordered to cover it close, and
bring it early in the morning; but even then, if it is kept on the
road while he serves the customers, who live nearest to him,
it will very likely be fly-blown.    This happens often in the
country.

Wash all meat before you dress it: if for boiling, the colour will
be better for soaking; but if for roasting, dry it.

Boiling in a well-floured cloth will make meat white.

Particular care must be taken that the pot is well skimmed the
*moment* it boils, otherwise the foulness will be dispersed over the

meat. The more soups or broth are skimmed, the better and cleaner they will be.

The boiler, &c., should be kept delicately clean.

Put the meat into cold water, but flour it well first. Meat boiled quick will be hard; but care must be taken that in boiling slow it does not stop, or the meat will be underdone.

If the steam is kept in, the water will not lessen much; therefore, when you wish it to boil away take off the cover of the soup-pot.

Vegetables should not be dressed with the meat, except carrots or parsnips with boiled beef.

As to the length of time required for roasting and boiling, the size of the joint must direct; as also the strength of the fire, the nearness of the meat to it, and in boiling, the regular though slow progress it makes; for if the cook, when told to hinder the copper from boiling quick, let it stop from boiling up at all, the usual time will not be sufficient, and the meat will be underdone.

Weigh the meat; and allow for all solid joints a quarter of an hour for every pound, and some minutes (from ten to twenty) over, according as the family like it done.

A ham of twenty pounds will take four hours and a half, and others in proportion.

A tongue, if dry, takes four hours slow boiling, after soaking; a tongue out of pickle, from two hours and a half to three hours, or more if very large; it must be judged by feeling whether it is very tender.

A leg of pork, or of lamb, takes the allowance of twenty minutes, above a quarter of an hour to a pound.

In roasting, beef of ten pounds will take above two hours and a half; twenty pounds will take about three hours and three quarters.

A neck of mutton will take an hour and a half, if kept at a proper distance. A chine of pork two hours.

The meat should be put at a good distance from the fire, and brought gradually nearer when the inner part becomes hot, which will prevent its being scorched while yet raw. Meat should be much basted; and, when nearly done, floured to make it look frothed.

Veal and mutton should have a little paper put over the fat to preserve it. If not fat enough to allow for basting, good dripping answers as well as butter.

The cook should be careful not to run the spit through the best parts; and should observe that it be well cleaned before and at the time of serving, or a black stain appears on the meat. In many joints the spit will pass into the bones, and run along them for some distance, so as not to injure the prime of the meat; and the cook should have leaden skewers to balance it with; for want of which, ignorant servants are often troubled at the time of serving.

In roasting meat it is a very good way to put a little salt and water into the dripping-pan, and baste for a little while with this, before using its own fat or dripping. When dry, dust it with flour, and baste as usual.

Salting meat before it is put to roast draws out the gravy: it should only be sprinkled when almost done.

Time, distance, basting often, and a clear fire of a proper size for what is required, are the first articles of a good cook's attention in roasting.

Old meats do not require so much dressing as young; not that they are sooner done, but they can be eaten with the gravy more in.

A piece of paper should be twisted round the bone at the knuckle of a leg or shoulder of lamb, mutton, or venison, when roasted, before they are served.

When you wish fried things to look as well as possible, do them *twice* over with egg and crumbs. Bread that is not stale enough to grate quite fine, will not look well. The fat you fry in must always be boiling hot the moment the fish, meat, &c., are put in, and kept so till finished; a small quantity never fries well.

**To Keep Meat Hot.**—It is to take it up when done, though the company may not be come; set the dish over a pan of boiling water, put a deep cover over it so as not to touch the meat, and then throw a cloth over that. This way will not dry up the gravy.

**VENISON.**—**To Keep Venison.**—Keep the venison dry, wash it with milk and water very clean, and dry it with clean cloths till not the least damp remains; then dust pounded ginger over every part, which is a very good preventive against the fly. By thus managing and watching, it will hang a fortnight. When to be used, wash it with a little lukewarm water, and dry it. Pepper is likewise good to keep it.

**To Dress Venison.**—A haunch of buck will take three hours and a half or three quarters roasting; doe, only three hours and a quarter. Venison should be rather under than over done.

Spread a sheet of white paper with butter and put it over the fat, first sprinkling it with a little salt; then lay a coarse paste on strong paper and cover the haunch, tie it with fine packthread, and set it at a distance from the fire, which must be a good one. Baste it often; ten minutes before serving take off the paste, draw the meat nearer the fire, and baste it with butter and a good deal of flour to make it froth up well.

Gravy for it should be put into a boat, and not into the dish (unless the venison has none), and made thus:—Cut off the fat from two or three pounds of a loin of old mutton, and set it in steaks on a gridiron for a few minutes, just to brown one side; put them into a saucepan with a quart of water, cover close for an hour, and simmer it gently; then uncover it, and stew till the gravy is reduced to a pint. Season with only salt.

Currant jelly sauce must be served in a boat.

Formerly pap sauce was eaten with venison; which, as some still like it, it may be necessary to direct. Grate white bread and

### VENISON.

1. Haunch.          3. Shoulder.
2. Neck.            4. Breast.

### PORK.

1. Sparerib.        4. Fore Loin.
2. Hand.            5. Hind Loin.
3. Belly or Spring. 6. Leg.

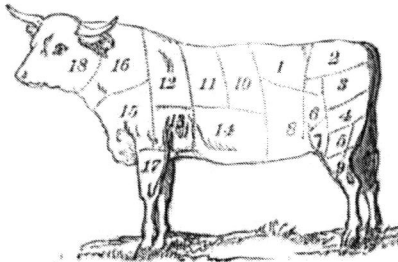

### BEEF.

**Hind Quarter.**

1. Sirloin.
2. Rump.
3. Edge Bone.
4. Buttock.
5. Mouse Buttock.
6. Veiny Piece.
7. Thick Flank.
8. Thin Flank.
9. Leg.
10. Fore Rib; 5 Ribs.

**Fore Quarter.**

11. Middle Rib; 4 Ribs.
12. Chuck; 3 Ribs.
13. Shoulder, or Leg of Mutton Piece.
14. Brisket.
15. Clod.
16. Neck, or Sticking-piece.
17. Shin.
18. Cheek.

### VEAL.

1. Loin, Best End.
2. Loin, Chump End.
3. Fillet.
4. Hind Knuckle.
5. Fore Knuckle
6. Neck, Best End.
7. Neck, Scrag End.
8. Blade Bone.
9. Breast, Best End.
10. Breast, Brisket End.

### MUTTON.

1. Leg.
2. Loin, Best End.
3. Loin, Chump End.
4. Neck, Best End.
5. Neck, Scrag End.
6. Shoulder.
7. Breast. [ Necks.
A Chine is Two
A Saddle is Two
[ Loins.

boil it with port wine, water, and a large stick of cinnamon; and
when quite smooth take out the cinnamon and add sugar.  Claret
may be used for it.

Make the jelly sauce thus.   Beat some currant jelly and a
spoonful or two of port wine, and set it over the fire till melted.
Where jelly runs short, put more wine, and a few lumps of sugar,
to the jelly, and melt as above.  Serve with French beans.

**Haunch, Neck, and Shoulder of Venison.**—Roast with
paste as directed above, and the same sauce.

**To Stew a Shoulder of Venison.**—Let the meat hang till
you think fit to dress it; then take out the bone, beat the meat
with a rolling-pin, lay some slices of mutton fat that have lain a
few hours in a little port wine, sprinkle a little pepper and allspice
over it in fine powder, roll it up tight, and tie it.  Set it in a stew-
pan that will only just hold it, with some mutton or beef gravy not
strong, half a pint of port wine, and some pepper and allspice.
Simmer it close-covered, as slow as you can, for three or four
hours.   When quite tender take off the tape, set the meat in a
dish, strain the gravy over it, and serve with currant jelly sauce.
This is the best way to dress this joint, unless it is very fat,
and then it should be roasted.   The bone should be stewed
with it.

**Breast of Venison.**—Do it as the shoulder, or make it into
a small pasty.

**Hashed Venison** should be warmed with its own gravy, or
some without seasoning, as before; and only warmed through,
not boiled.  If there is no fat left, cut some slices of mutton fat,
set it on the fire with a little port wine and sugar, simmer till
dry, then put to the hash, and it will eat as well as the fat of the
venison.

**For Venison Pasty** look under the head PASTRY; as likewise
an excellent imitation.

**BEEF.—To Keep Beef.**—The butcher should take out the
kernels in the neck-pieces where the shoulder-clod is taken off,
two from each round of beef, and one in the middle, which is
called the pope's eye; the other from the flap: there is also one in
the thick flank, in the middle of the fat.   If these are not taken
out, especially in the summer, salt will be of no use for keeping
the meat sweet.  There is another kernel between the rump and the
aitchbone.

As the butchers seldom attend to this matter, the cook
should take out the kernels; and then rub the salt well into such
beef as is for boiling, and slightly sprinkle that which is for
roasting.

The flesh of cattle that are killed when not perfectly cleared of
food, soon spoils.   They should fast twenty-four hours in winter,
and double that time in summer before being killed.

**To Salt Beef or Pork for eating immediately.**—The
piece should not weigh more than five or six pounds.   Salt it very
thoroughly just before you put it into the pot, take a coarse cloth,
flour it well, put the meat in, and fold it up close.  Put it into a

pot of boiling water, and boil it as long as you would any other salt beef of the same size, and it will be as salt as if done four or five days.

Great attention is requisite in salting meat; and in the country, where large quantities are cured, this is of particular importance. Beef and pork should be well sprinkled, and a few hours afterwards hung to drain, before it is rubbed with salt; which method by cleansing the meat from the blood, serves to keep it from tasting strong. It should be turned every day; and if wanted soon, should be rubbed as often. A salting-tub or lead may be used, and a cover to fit close. Those who use a good deal of salt meat, will find it answer well to boil up the pickle, skim it, and when cold, pour it over meat that has been sprinkled and drained·

**To Salt Beef Red, which is extremely good to eat fresh from the Pickle, or to hang to Dry.**—Choose a piece of beef with as little bone as you can (the flank is most proper), sprinkle it and let it drain a day; then rub it with common salt, saltpetre, and bay salt, but only a small proportion of the saltpetre, and you may add a few grains of cochineal, all in fine powder. Rub the pickle every day into the meat for a week, then only turn it. It will be excellent in eight days. In sixteen drain it from the pickle; and let it be smoked at the oven-mouth when heated with wood, or send it to the bake-house. A few days will smoke it. A little of the coarsest sugar may be added to the salt. It eats well boiled tender with greens or carrots. If to be grated as Dutch, then cut a lean bit, boil it till extremely tender, and while hot put it under a press. When cold fold it in a sheet of paper, and it will keep in a dry place two or three months, ready for serving on bread and butter.

**The Dutch Way to Salt Beef.**—Take a lean piece of beef; rub it well with treacle or brown sugar, and let it be turned often. In three days wipe it, and salt it with common salt and saltpetre beaten fine: rub these well in, and turn it every day for a fortnight. Roll it tight in a coarse cloth, and press it under a large weight; hang it to dry in a wood-smoke, but turn it upside down every day. Boil it in pump water, and press it: it will grate or cut into shivers, like Dutch beef.

**Beef à-la-mode.**—Choose a piece of thick flank of a fine heifer or ox. Cut into long slices some fat bacon, but quite free from yellow; let each bit be near an inch thick: dip them into vinegar, and then into a seasoning ready prepared of salt, black pepper, allspice, and a clove, all in fine powder, with parsley, chives, thyme, savoury, and knotted marjoram, shred as small as possible, and well mixed. With a sharp knife make holes deep enough to let in the larding; then rub the beef over with the seasoning, and bind it up tight with tape. Set it in a well-tinned pot over a fire or rather stove; three or four onions must be fried brown and put to the beef, with two or three carrots, one turnip, a head or two of celery, and a small quantity of water; let it simmer gently ten or twelve hours, or till extremely tender, turning the meat twice.

Put the gravy into a pan, remove the fat, keep the beef covered, then put them together, and add a glass of port wine. Take off the tape, and serve with the vegetables; or you may strain them off, and send them up cut into dice for garnish. Onions roasted, and then stewed with the gravy, are a great improvement. A tea-cupful of vinegar should be stewed with the beef.

**A Fricandeau of Beef.**—Take a nice piece of lean beef, lard it with bacon seasoned with pepper, salt, cloves, mace, and allspice. Put it into a stew-pan with a pint of broth, a glass of white-wine, a bundle of parsley, all sorts of sweet herbs, a clove of garlick, a shalot or two, four cloves, pepper and salt. When the meat is become tender, cover it close; skim the sauce well, and strain it: set it on the fire, and let it boil till it is reduced to a glaze. Glaze the larded side with this, and serve the meat on sorrel-sauce.

**To Stew a Rump of Beef.**—Wash it well and season high with salt, allspice, pepper, Cayenne, three cloves, and a blade of mace, all in fine powder. Bind it up tight, and lay it into a pot that will just hold it. Fry three large onions sliced, and put them to it, with three carrots, two turnips, a shalot, four cloves, a blade of mace, and some celery. Cover the meat with good beef-broth, or weak gravy. Simmer it as gently as possible for several hours, till quite tender. Clear off the fat; add to the gravy half a pint of port wine, a glass of vinegar, and a large spoonful of ketchup; simmer half an hour, and serve in a deep dish. Half a pint of table-beer may be added. The herbs to be used should be burnet, tarragon, parsley, thyme, basil, savoury, marjoram, penny-royal, knotted marjoram, and some chives if you can get them; but observe to proportion the quantities to the pungency of the several sorts; let there be a good handful all together.

Garnish with carrots, turnips, or truffles and morels, or pickles of different colours, cut small, and laid in little heaps separate; chopped parsley, chives, beetroot, &c. If, when done, the gravy is too much to fill the dish, take only a part to season for serving, but the less water the better; and to increase the richness, add a few beef-bones and shanks of mutton in stewing. A spoonful or two of made mustard is a great improvement to the gravy. Rump roasted is excellent, but in the country it is generally sold whole with the aitchbone, or cut across instead of lengthwise, as in London, where one piece is for boiling, and the rump for stewing or roasting. This must be attended to, the whole being too large to dress together.

**Stewed Rump another way.**—Half-roast it; then put it into a large pot with three pints of water, one of small beer, one of port wine, some salt, three or four spoonfuls of vinegar, two of ketchup, a bunch of sweet herbs of various kinds (such as burnet, tarragon, parsley, thyme, basil, pennyroyal, savoury, marjoram, knotted marjoram, and a leaf or two of sage), some onions, cloves, and Cayenne; cover it close, and simmer till quite tender; two or three hours will do it. When done, lay it into a deep dish, set it over hot water, and cover it close. Skim the gravy: put in a few pickled mushrooms, truffles, morels, and oysters if agreeable, but it is good without; thicken the gravy with flour and butter, and heat it with the above, and pour over the beef. Forcemeat-balls of veal, anchovies, bacon, suet, herbs, spice, bread, and eggs, to bind, are a great improvement.

**Beef en Miroton.**—Cut thin slices of cold roast beef and put them into a frying-pan with some butter, and six onions, turn the pan frequently, then mix a little broth, add pepper and salt, and after a few boils, serve up hot. This dish is excellent and econo-mical.

**To Stew Brisket of Beef.**—Put the part with the hard fat into a stew-pot with a small quantity of water; let it boil up, and skim it thoroughly; then add carrots, turnips, onions, celery, and a few pepper-corns. Stew till extremely tender, then take out the flat bones, and remove all the fat from the soup. Serve that and the meat in a tureen, or the soup alone and the meat on a dish, garnished with some vegetables. The following sauce is much admired, served with the beef:—Take half a pint of the soup and mix it with a spoonful of ketchup, a glass of port wine, a tea-spoonful of made mustard, a little flour, a bit of butter, and salt; boil all together a few minutes, then pour it round the meat. Chop capers, walnuts, red cabbage, pickled cucumbers, and chives or parsley, small, and put into separate heaps over it.

**To Press Beef.**—Salt a bit of brisket, the thin part of the flank, or the tops of the ribs, with salt and saltpetre five days, then boil it gently till extremely tender; put it under a great weight, or in a cheese-press, till perfectly cold.

It eats excellently cold, and for sandwiches.

**To make Hunter's Beef.**—To a round of beef that weighs twenty-five pounds, take three ounces of saltpetre, three ounces of the coarsest sugar, an ounce of cloves, a nutmeg, half an ounce of allspice, and three handfuls of common salt, all in the finest powder.

The beef should hang two or three days; then rub the above well into it, and turn and rub it every day for two or three weeks. The bone must be taken out at first. When to be dressed, dip it into cold water, to take off the loose spice, bind it up tight with tape, and put it into a pan with a tea-cupful of water at the bottom, cover the top of the meat with shred suet, and the pan with a brown crust and paper, and bake it five or six hours. When cold, take off the paste and tape.

The gravy is very fine; and a little of it adds greatly to the flavour of any hash, soup, &c.

Both the gravy and the beef will keep some time. The meat should be cut with a very sharp knife, and quite smooth, to pre-vent waste.

**An excellent Mode of Dressing Beef.**—Hang three ribs three or four days: take out the bones from the whole length, sprinkle it with salt, roll the meat tight, and roast it. Nothing can look nicer. The above done with spices, &c., and baked as hunter's beef, is excellent,

**To Collar Beef.**—Choose the thin end of the flank of fine mellow beef, but not too fat; lay it in a dish with salt and saltpetre, turn and rub it every day for a week, and keep it cool. Take out every bone and gristle, remove the skin of the inside part, and cover it thick with the following seasoning cut small: a large handful of parsley, the same of sage, some thyme, marjoram, and pennyroyal, pepper, salt and allspice. Roll the meat up as tight as possible and bind it, then boil it gently for seven or eight hours. A cloth must be put round before the tape. Put the beef under a good weight while hot, without undoing it; the shape will then be oval. Part of a breast of veal rolled in with the beef, looks and eats very well.

**Beef Steaks** should be cut from the rump that has hung a few days. Broil them over a very clear or charcoal fire: put into the dish a little minced shalot, and a table-spoonful of ketchup; and rub a bit of butter on the steak the moment of serving. It should be turned often, that the gravy may not be drawn out on either side.

This dish requires to be eaten hot and fresh-done, and is not in perfection if served with anything else. Pepper and salt should be added when taking it off the fire.

**Beef Steaks and Oyster Sauce.**—Strain off the liquor from the oysters, and throw them into cold water to take off the grit, while you simmer the liquor with a bit of mace and lemon-peel; then put the oysters in, stew them a few minutes, add a little cream if you have it, and some butter rubbed in a bit of flour: let them boil up once, and have rump steaks, well seasoned and broiled, ready for throwing the oyster sauce over the moment you are to serve.

**Staffordshire Beef Steaks.**—Beat them with a rolling-pin, flour and season, then fry with sliced onion of a fine light brown; lay the steaks in a stew-pan, and pour as much boiling water over them as will serve for sauce; stew them very gently half an hour, and add a spoonful of ketchup or walnut-liquor, before you serve.

**Italian Beef Steaks.**—Cut a fine large steak from a rump that has been well hung, or it will do from any tender part: beat it, and season with pepper, salt, and onion; lay it in an iron stew-pan that has a cover to fit quite close, and set it by the side of the fire without water. Take care it does not burn, but it must have a strong heat: in two or three hours it will be quite tender, and then serve with its own gravy.

**Beef Collop.**—Cut thin slices of beef from the rump, or any other tender part, and divide them into pieces three inches long; beat them with the blade of a knife, and flour them. Fry the collops quick in butter two minutes; lay them into a small stew-pan, and cover them with a pint of gravy; add a bit of butter rubbed in flour, pepper, salt, the least bit of shalot shred as fine as possible, half a walnut, four small pickled cucumbers, and a tea-spoonful of capers cut small. Take care that it does not boil, and serve the stew in a very hot covered dish.

**Beef Palates.**—Simmer them for several hours, till they will peel; then cut the palates into slices, or leave them whole, as you choose, and stew them in a rich gravy till as tender as possible. Before you serve, season them with Cayenne, salt, and ketchup. If the gravy was drawn clear, add also some butter and flour.

If to be served white, boil them in milk, and stew them in a fricassee sauce; adding cream, butter, flour, mushroom powder, and a little pounded mace.

**Beef Cakes for a Side Dish of Dressed Meat.**—Pound some beef that is underdone with a little fat bacon or ham; season with pepper, salt, and a little shalot, or garlic; mix them well, and make into small cakes three inches long, and half as wide and thick; fry them a light brown, and serve them in a good thick gravy,

**To Pot Beef.**—Take two pounds of lean beef, rub it with saltpetre, and let it be one night; then salt with common salt, and cover it with water four days in a small pan. Dry it with a cloth, and season with black pepper; lay it in as small a pan as will hold it, cover it with coarse paste, and bake it five hours in a very cool oven. Put no liquor in.

When cold, pick out the strings and fat; beat the meat very fine with a quarter of a pound of fine butter just warm, but not oiled, and as much of the gravy as will make it into a paste; put it into very small pots, and cover them with melted butter.

**Another way.**—Take beef that has been dressed, either boiled or roasted; beat it in a mortar with some pepper, salt, a few cloves, grated nutmeg, and a little fine butter just warm.

This eats as well, but the colour is not so fine. It is a good way for using the remains of a large joint.

**To Dress the Inside of a Cold Sirloin of Beef.**—Cut out all the meat, and a little fat, in pieces as thick as your finger, and two inches long: dredge it with flour, and fry in butter, of a nice brown; drain the butter from the meat, and toss it up in a rich gravy, seasoned with pepper, salt, anchovy, and shalot. Do not let it boil on any account. Before you serve, add two spoonfuls of vinegar. Garnish with crimped parsley.

**Fricassee of Cold Roast Beef.**—Cut the beef into very thin slices, shred a handful of parsley very small, cut an onion into quarters, and put all together into a stew-pan, with a piece of butter and some strong broth: season with salt and pepper, and simmer very gently a quarter of an hour; then mix into it the yolks of two eggs, a glass of port wine, and a spoonful of vinegar; stir it quick, rub the dish with shalot, and turn the fricassee into it.

**To Dress Cold Beef that has not been done enough, called Beef Olives.**—Cut slices half an inch thick, and four inches square: lay on them a forcemeat of crumbs of bread, shalot, a little suet or fat, pepper and salt. Roll them, and fasten with a small skewer; put them into a stew-pan with some gravy made of the beef bones, or the gravy of the meat, and a spoonful or two of water, and stew them till tender. Fresh meat will do.

**To Dress the same, called Sanders.**—Mince beef or mutton small, with onion, pepper, and salt; add a little gravy; put it into scallop-shells or saucers, making them three parts full, and fill them up with potatoes, mashed with a little cream; put a bit of butter on the top, and brown them in an oven or before the fire, or with a salamander.

**To Dress the same, called Cecils.**—Mince any kind of meat, crumbs of bread, a good deal of onion, some anchovies, lemon-peel, salt, nutmeg, chopped parsley, pepper, and a bit of butter warm, and mix these over a fire for a few minutes; when cool enough, make them up into balls the size and shape of a turkey's egg, with an egg; sprinkle them with fine crumbs, and then fry them of a yellow brown, and serve with gravy as before directed for Beef Olives.

**To Mince Beef.**—Shred the underdone part fine, with some of the fat; put it into a small stew-pan, with some onion or shalot (a very little will do), a little water, pepper, and salt; boil it till the onion is quite soft; then put some of the gravy of the meat to it, and the mince. Do not let it boil. Have a small hot dish with sippets of bread ready, and pour the mince into it, but first mix a large spoonful of vinegar with it: if shalot-vinegar is used, there will be no need of the onion nor the raw shalot.

**To Hash Beef.**—Do it the same as in the last receipt, only the meat is to be in slices, and you may add a spoonful of walnut-liquor or ketchup.

Observe, that it is owing to boiling hashes or minces that they get hard. All sorts of stews, or meat dressed a second time, should be only simmered; and this last only hot through.

**Beef a-la-Vingrette.**—Cut a slice of underdone boiled beef three inches thick and a little fat; stew it in half a pint of water, a glass of white wine, a bunch of sweet herbs, an onion, and a bay leaf: season it with three cloves pounded and pepper, till the liquor is nearly wasted away, turning it once. When cold, serve it. Strain off the gravy, and mix it with a little vinegar for sauce.

**Round of Beef** should be carefully salted, and wet with the pickle for eight or ten days. The bone should be cut out first, the beef skewered and tied up to make it quite round. It may be stuffed with parsley, if approved; in which case the holes to admit the parsley must be made with a sharp pointed knife, and the parsley coarsely cut and stuffed in tight. As soon as it boils it should be skimmed, and afterwards kept boiling very gently.

**Rolled Beef that equals Hare.**—Take the inside of a large sirloin, soak it in a glass of port wine and a glass of vinegar mixed, for forty-eight hours; have ready a very fine stuffing, and bind it up tight. Roast it on a hanging spit, and baste it with a glass of port wine, the same quantity of vinegar, and a tea-spoonful of pounded allspice. Larding it improves the look and flavour: serve with a rich gravy in the dish; currant-jelly and melted-butter, in tureens.

**To Roast Tongue and Udder.**—After cleaning the tongue

well, salt it with common salt and saltpetre three days, then boil
it, and likewise a fine young udder with some fat to it, till tolerably tender; then tie the thick part of one to the thin part of the
other, and roast the tongue and udder together.

Serve them with good gravy, and currant-jelly sauce. A few
cloves should be stuck in the udder. This is an excellent dish.

Some people like neat's tongues cured with the root, in which
case they look much larger; but otherwise the root must be cut
off close to the gullet, next to the tongue, but without taking away
the fat under the tongue. The root must be soaked in salt and
water, and extremely well cleaned, before it is dressed; and
the tongue should be laid in salt for a day and a night before
pickled.

**To Pickle Tongues for Boiling.**—Cut off the root, but
leave a little of the kernel and fat. Sprinkle some salt, and let it
drain from the slime till next day: then for each tongue mix a
large spoonful of common salt, the same of coarse sugar, and
about half as much of saltpetre; rub it well in, and do so every
day. In a week add another heaped spoonful of salt. If rubbed
every day, a tongue will be ready in a fortnight; but if only
turned in the pickle daily, it will keep four or five weeks without
being too salt.

When you dry tongues, write the date on a parchment and tie
it on. Smoke them, or dry them plain, if you like best.

When it is to be dressed, boil it till extremely tender; allow
five hours, and if done sooner, it is easily kept hot. The longer
kept after drying, the higher it will be: if hard, it may require
soaking three or four hours.

**Another way.**—Clean as above: for two tongues allow an
ounce of saltpetre, and an ounce of sal-prunella; rub them well.
In two days, after well rubbing, cover them with common salt,
turn them every day for three weeks, then dry them, rub bran
over them, and smoke them. In ten days they will be fit to eat.
Keep in a cool dry place.

**To Stew Tongue.**—Salt a tongue with saltpetre and common
salt for a week, turning it every day. Boil it tender enough to
peel: when done, stew it in a moderately strong gravy; season
with soy, mushroom ketchup, Cayenne, pounded cloves, and salt
if necessary.

Serve with truffles, morels, and mushrooms. In both this receipt and the next, the roots must be taken off the tongues before
salting, but some fat left.

**An excellent way of doing Tongues to eat Cold.**—
Season with common salt and saltpetre, brown sugar, a little bay-
salt, pepper, cloves, mace, and allspice, in fine powder, for a fortnight; then take away the pickle, put the tongue into a small pan,
and lay some butter on it; cover it with brown crust, and bake
slowly till so tender that a straw would go through it.

The thin part of tongues, when hung up to dry, grates like
hung beef, and also makes a fine addition to the flavour of
omelets.

**Beef-heart.**—Wash it carefully; stuff as hare; and serve with rich gravy and currant-jelly sauce.

Hash with the same, and port wine.

**Stewed Ox-cheek Plain.**—Soak and cleanse a fine cheek the day before it is to be eaten; put it into a stew-pot that will cover close, with three quarts of water: simmer it after it has first boiled up and been well skimmed. In two hours put plenty of carrots, leeks, two or three turnips, a bunch of sweet herbs, some whole pepper, and four ounces of allspice. Skim it often; when the meat is tender, take it out; let the soup get cold, take off the cake of fat, and serve the soup separate or with the meat.

It should be of a fine brown; which may be done by burnt sugar; or by frying some onions quite brown with flour, and simmering them with it. This last way improves the flavour of all soups and gravies of the brown kind.

If vegetables are not approved in the soup, they may be taken out, and a small roll be toasted, or bread fried and added. Celery is a great addition, and should always be served. Where it is not to be got, the seed of it gives quite as good a flavour, boiled in and strained off.

**To Dress an Ox-cheek another way.**—Soak half a head three hours, and clean it with plenty of water. Take the meat off the bones, and put it into a pan with a large onion, a bunch of sweet herbs, some bruised allspice, pepper, and salt.

Lay the bones on the top; pour on two or three quarts of water and cover the pan close with brown paper, or a dish that will fit close. Let it stand eight or ten hours in a slow oven; or simmer it by the side of the fire, or on a hot hearth. When done tender, put the meat into a clean pan, and let it get cold. Take the cake of fat off, and warm the head in pieces in the soup. Put what vegetables you choose.

**Marrow-bones.**—Cover the top with floured cloth; boil them and serve with dry toast.

**Tripe** may be served in a tureen, stewed with milk and onion till tender. Melted butter for sauce.

Or fry it in small bits dipped in butter.

Or stew the thin part, cut into bits, in gravy; thicken with flour and butter, and add a little ketchup.

Or fricassee it with white sauce.

**Soused Tripe.**—Boil the tripe, but not quite tender; then put it into salt and water, which must be changed every day till it is all used. When you dress the tripe, dip it into a batter of flour and eggs, and fry it of a good brown.

**Ox-feet or Cow-heels.**—May be dressed in various ways, and are very nutritious in all.

Boil them; and serve in a napkin, with melted butter, mustard, and a large spoonful of vinegar.

Or boil them very tender, and serve them as a brown fricassee; the liquor will do to make jelly sweet or relishing, and likewise give richness to soups or gravies.

Or cut them into four parts, dip them into an egg, and then flour and fry them ; and fry onions (if you like them) to serve round. Sauce as above.

Or bake them as for mock-turtle.

**Bubble and Squeak.**—Boil, chop, and fry with a little butter, pepper, and salt, some cabbage, and lay on it slices of underdone beef, lightly fried.

**VEAL.—To Keep Veal.**—The first part that turns bad of a leg of veal, is where the udder is skewered back. The skewer should be taken out, and both that and the part under it wiped every day, by which means it will keep good three or four days in hot weather. Take care to cut out the pipe that runs along the chine of a loin of veal, to hinder it from tainting. The skirt of a breast of veal is likewise to be taken off; and the inside of the breast wiped and scraped, and sprinkled with a little salt.

**Leg of Veal.**—Let the fillet be cut large or small as best suits the number of your company. Take out the bone, fill the space with a fine stuffing, and let it be skewered quite round ; and send the large side uppermost. When half-roasted, not before, put a paper over the fat; and take care to allow a sufficient time, and put it a good distance from the fire, as the meat is solid : serve with melted butter poured over it.—You may pot some of it.

**Knuckle of Veal.**—As few people are fond of boiled veal, it may be well to leave the knuckle small, and take off some cutlets or collops before it be dressed ; but as the knuckle will keep longer than the fillet, it is best not to cut off the slices till wanted. Break the bones, to make it take less room ; wash it well ; and put it into a saucepan with three onions, a blade of mace or two, and a few pepper-corns : cover it with water, and simmer till quite ready. In the meantime some maccaroni should be boiled with it if approved, or rice, or a little rice-flour, to give it a small degree of thickness ; but do not put too much. Before it is served, add half a pint of milk and cream, and let it come up either with or without the meat.

Or, fry the knuckle with sliced onion and butter to a good brown ; and have ready peas, lettuce, onion, and a cucumber or two, stewed in a small quantity of water an hour : then add these to the veal ; and stew it till the meat is tender enough to eat, but not overdone. Throw in pepper, salt, and a bit of shred meat, and serve all together.

**Shoulder of Veal.**—Cut off the knuckle, for a stew or gravy. Roast the other part with stuffing : you may lard it. Serve with melted butter.

The blade-bone, with a good deal of meat left on, eats extremely well with mushroom or oyster sauce, or mushroom ketchup in butter.

**Neck of Veal.**—Cut off the scrag to boil, and cover it with onion-sauce. It should be boiled in milk and water. Parsley and butter may be served with it, instead of onion sauce.

Or, it may be stewed with whole rice, small onions, and pepper corns, with a very little water.

D

Or, boiled and eaten with bacon and greens.

The best end may be either roasted, broiled as steaks, or made into pies.

**Neck of Veal a-la-braise.**—Lard the best end with bacon rolled in parsley chopped fine, salt, pepper, and nutmeg; put it into a tosser, and cover it with water. Put to it the scrag end, a little lean bacon or ham, an onion, two carrots, two heads of celery, and about a glass of Madeira wine. Stew it quick two hours or till it is tender, but not too much. Strain off the liquor: mix a little flour and butter in a stew-pan till brown, and lay the veal in this, the upper side to the bottom of the pan. Let it be over the fire till it gets coloured: then lay it into the dish, stir some of the liquor in and boil it up, skim it nicely, and squeeze orange and lemon-juice into it.

**Breast of Veal.**—Before roasted, if large, the two ends may be taken off and fried to stew, or the whole may be roasted. Butter should be poured over it.

If any be left, cut the pieces into handsome sizes, put them into a stew-pan, and pour some broth over it, or if you have no broth, a little water will do: add a bunch of herbs, a blade or two of mace, some pepper, and an anchovy; stew till the meat is tender, thicken with butter and flour, and add a little ketchup; or the whole breast may be stewed, after cutting off the two ends.

Serve the sweetbread whole upon it, either stewed or parboiled, and then covered with crumbs, herbs, pepper, and salt, and browned in a Dutch oven.

If you have a few mushrooms, truffles, and morels, stew them with it, and serve.

Boiled breast of veal, smothered with onion sauce, is an excellent dish, if not cold nor too fat.

**To Roll a Breast of Veal.**—Bone it, take off the thick skin and gristle, and beat the meat with a rolling-pin. Season it with herbs chopped very fine, mixed with salt, pepper, and mace. Lay some thick slices of fine ham; or roll into it two or three calves' tongues of a fine red, boiled first an hour or two and skimmed. Bind it up tight in a cloth, and tape it. Set it over the fire to simmer in a small quantity of water till it is quite tender: this will take some hours. Lay it on the dresser, with a board and weight on it till quite cold.

Pigs' or calves' feet, boiled and taken from the bones, may be put in or round it. The different colours laid in layers look well when cut; and you may put in yolks of egg boiled, beet-root, grated ham, and chopped parsley, in different parts.

**Another way.**—When it is cold, take off the tape, and pour over it the liquor; which must be boiled up twice a week, or it will not keep.

**Chump of Veal a-la-daube.**—Cut off the chump end of the loin; take out the aitch-bone; stuff the hollow with good force-meat, tie it up tight, and lay it in a stew-pan with the bone you took out, a little faggot of herbs, an anchovy, two blades of mace, a few white peppers, and a pint of good veal-broth. Cover the veal with slices of fat bacon and lay a sheet of white paper over it. Cover the pan close, simmer it two hours, then take out the bacon, and glaze the veal. Serve it on mushrooms, or with sorrel sauce, or what else you please.

**Veal Rolls of either Cold Meat or Fresh.**—Cut thin slices; and spread on them a fine seasoning of a very few crumbs, a little chopped bacon or scraped ham, and a little suet, parsley, and shalot (or instead of the parsley and shalot, some fresh mushrooms stewed and minced), pepper, salt, and a small piece of pounded mace. This stuffing may either fill up the roll like a sausage, or be rolled with the meat. In either case tie it up very tight, and stew it very slowly in a gravy and a glass of sherry.

Serve it when tender, after skimming it nicely.

**Harrico of Veal.**—Take the best end of a small neck; cut the bones short, but leave it whole: put it into a stew-pan, just cover with brown gravy; and when it is nearly done, have ready a pint of boiled peas, six cucumbers pared and sliced, and two cabbage-lettuces cut into quarters, all stewed in a little good broth; put them to the veal, and let them simmer ten minutes. When the veal is in the dish, pour the sauce and vegetables over it, and lay the lettuce with forcemeat-balls around it.

**A Dunelm of Cold Veal or Fowl.**—Stew a few small mushrooms in their own liquor and a bit of butter, a quarter of an hour; mince them very small, and add them (with their liquor) to mince veal, with also a little pepper and salt, some cream and a bit of butter rubbed in less than half a tea-spoonful of flour. Simmer three or four minutes, and serve on thin sippets of bread.

**Minced Veal.**—Cut cold veal as fine as possible, but do not chop it. Put to it a very little lemon-peel shred, two grates of nutmeg, some salt, and four or five spoonfuls of either a little weak broth, milk, or water; simmer these gently with the meat, but take care not to let it boil, and add a bit of butter rubbed in flour. Put sippets of thin toasted bread, cut into a three-cornered shape round the dish.

**To Pot Veal.**—Cold fillet makes the finest potted veal; or you may do it as follows:—

Season a large slice of the fillet before it is dressed, with some mace, pepper-corns, and two or three cloves; lay it close into a potting-pan that will but just hold it, fill it up with water, and bake it three hours; then pound it quite small in a mortar, and add salt to taste: put a little gravy that was baked to it in pounding, if to be eaten soon; otherwise only a little butter just melted. When done, cover it over with butter.

**To Pot Veal or Chicken with Ham.**—Pound some cold veal or white of chicken, season as directed in the last article, and put layers of it with layers of ham pounded or rather shred; press each down and cover with butter.

**Cutlets Maintenon.**—Cut slices about three quarters of an inch thick, beat them with a rolling-pin, and wet them on both sides with egg: dip them into a seasoning of bread-crumbs, parsley, thyme, knotted marjoram, pepper, salt, and a little nutmeg grated; then put them into papers folded over, and broil them; and have in a boat melted butter with a little mushroom-ketchup.

**Cutlets another way.**—Prepare as above, and fry them; lay them into a dish, and keep them hot; dredge a little flour, and put a bit of butter into the pan; brown it, then pour a little boiling water into it, and boil quick: season with pepper, salt, and ketchup, and pour over them.

**Other ways.**—Prepare as before, and dress the cutlets in a Dutch-oven; pour over them melted butter and mushrooms.

Or, pepper, salt, and broil them, especially neck-steaks. They are excellent with herbs.

**Veal Collops.**—Cut long thin collops; beat them well; and lay on them a bit of thin bacon of the same size, and spread forcemeat on that, seasoned high, and also a little garlic and Cayenne. Roll them up tight, about the size of two fingers, but not more than two or three inches long; put a very small skewer to fasten each firmly; rub egg over; fry them of a fine brown, and pour a rich brown gravy over.

**To Dress Collops Quick.**—Cut them as thin as paper with a very sharp knife, and in small bits. Throw the skin, and any odd bits of the veal, into a little water, with a dust of pepper and salt; set them on the fire while you beat the collops; and dip them into a seasoning of herbs, bread, pepper, salt, and a scrape of nutmeg, but first wet them in egg. Then put some butter into a frying-pan, and give the collops a very quick fry; for as they are so thin, two minutes will do them on both sides: put them into a hot dish before the fire; then strain and thicken the gravy, give it a boil in the frying-pan, and pour it over the collops. A little ketchup is an improvement.

**Another way.**—Fry them in butter, only seasoned with salt and pepper; simmer them in gravy, either white or brown, with bits of bacon served with them.

If white, add lemon-peel and mace, and some cream.

**Scallops of Cold Veal or Chicken.**—Mince the meat extremely small; and set it over the fire with a scrape of nutmeg, a little pepper and salt, and a little cream, for a few minutes: then put it into the scallop-shells, and fill them with crumbs of bread, over which put some bits of butter, and brown them before the fire.

Either veal or chicken looks and eats well prepared in this way, and lightly covered with crumbs of bread fried; or these may be put on in little heaps.

**Fricandeau of Veal.**—Cut a large piece from the fat side of the leg, about nine inches long, and half as thick and broad; beat it with the rolling-pin; take off the skin, and trim off the rough edges. Lard the top and sides; and cover it with fat bacon, and then with white paper. Lay it in the stew-pan with pieces of undressed veal or mutton, four onions, a carrot sliced, a faggot of sweet herbs, four blades of mace, four bay leaves, a pint of good veal or mutton broth, and four or five ounces of lean ham or gammon. Cover the pan close, and let it stew slowly three hours;

then take up the meat, remove all the fat from the gravy, and boil it quick to a glaze. Keep the fricandeau quite hot, and then glaze it; and serve with the remainder of the glaze in the dish, and sorrel sauce in a sauce tureen.

**A Cheaper, but equally good Fricandeau of Veal.—** With a sharp knife cut the lean part of a large neck from the best end, scooping it from the bones the length of your hand, and prepare it the same way as in the last receipt: three or four bones only will be necessary, and they will make the gravy; but if the prime part of the leg is cut off, it spoils the whole.

**Fricandeau another way.—**Take two large round sweetbreads, and prepare them as you would veal; make a rich gravy with truffles, morels, mushrooms, and artichoke-bottoms, and serve it round.

**Veal Olives.—**Cut long thin collops, beat them, lay on them thin slices of fat bacon, and over these a layer of forcemeat seasoned high, with some shred shalot and Cayenne. Roll them tight, about the size of two fingers, but not more than two or three inches long; fasten them round with a small skewer, rub egg over them, and fry of a light brown. Serve with brown gravy, in which boil some mushrooms, pickled or fresh. Garnish with balls fried.

**Veal Cake.—**Boil six or eight eggs hard; cut the yolks in two, and lay some of the pieces in the bottom of the pot; shake in a little chopped parsley, some slices of veal and ham, and then eggs again; shaking in after each some chopped parsley, with pepper and salt, till the pot is full. Then put in water enough to cover it, and lay on it about an ounce of butter; tie it over with a double paper, and bake it about an hour. Then press it close together with a spoon, and let it stand till cold.

It may be put into a small mould: and then it will turn out beautifully for a supper or side dish.

**Veal Sausages.—**Chop equal quantities of lean veal and fat bacon, a handful of sage, a little salt, pepper, and a few anchovies. Beat all in a mortar: and when used roll and fry it, and serve with fried sippets, or on stewed vegetables, or on white collops.

**Scotch Collops.—**Cut veal into thin bits about three inches over, and rather round; beat with a rolling pin, and grate a little nutmeg over them; dip into the yolk of an egg; and fry them in a little butter of a fine brown; pour the butter off, and have ready warm to pour upon them half a pint of gravy, a little bit of butter rubbed into a little flour, a yolk of egg, two large spoonfuls of cream, and a bit of salt. Do not boil the sauce, but stir it till of a fine thickness to serve with the collops.

**To Boil Calf's Head.—**Clean it very nicely, and soak it in water, that it may look very white; take out the tongue to salt, and the brains to make a little dish. Boil the head extremely tender; then strew it over with crumbs and chopped parsley, and brown them; or, if liked better, leave one side plain. Serve bacon and greens to eat with it.

The brains must be boiled; and then mixed with melted butter, scalded sage chopped, pepper, and salt.

If any of the head is left, it may be hashed next day, and a few slices of bacon, just warmed and put round.

- Cold calf's head eats well if grilled.

**To Hash Calf's Head.**—When half-boiled, cut off the meat in slices, half an inch thick, and two or three inches long: brown some butter, flour, and sliced onions, and throw in the slices with some good gravy, truffles, and morels; give it one boil, skim it well, and set it in a moderate heat to simmer till very tender. Season with pepper, salt, and Cayenne, at first; and ten minutes before serving, throw in some shred parsley, and a very small bit of tarragon and knotted marjoram cut as fine as possible; just before you serve, add the squeeze of a lemon. Forcemeat-balls, and bits of bacon rolled round.

**Another way.**—Boil the head till done, and take the meat of the best side neatly off the bone with a sharp knife; lay this into a small dish, wash it over with the yolks of two eggs, and cover it with crumbs, a few herbs nicely shred, a little pepper and salt, and a grate of nutmeg, all mixed together first. Set the dish before the fire, and keep turning it now and then, that all parts of the head may be equally brown. In the meantime slice the remainder of the head and the tongue, but first peel the tongue : put a pint of good gravy into a pan, with an onion, a small bunch of herbs (consisting of parsley, basil, savoury, tarragon, knotted marjoram, and a little thyme), a little salt and Cayenne, a shalot, a glass of sherry, and a little oyster liquor. Boil this for a few minutes, and strain it upon the meat, which should be dredged with some flour. Add some mushrooms, either fresh or pickled, a few truffles and morels, and two spoonfuls of ketchup; then beat up half the brains, and put this to the rest with a bit of butter and flour. Simmer the whole.

Beat the other part of the brains with shred lemon-peel, a little nutmeg and mace, some parsley shred, and an egg. Then fry it in little cakes of a beautiful yellow brown. Dip some oysters into the yolk of an egg, and do the same; and also some relishing force-meat-balls made as for mock turtle. Garnish with these, and small bits of bacon just made hot before the fire.

**Calf's Head Fricasseed.**—Clean and half-boil a head; cut the meat into small bits, and put it into a tosser, with a little gravy made of the bones, some of the water it was boiled in, a bunch of sweet herbs, an onion, and a blade of mace. If you have any young cockrels in the house, use the cockscombs; but first boil them tender and blanch them; or a sweetbread will do as well. Season the gravy with a little pepper, nutmeg, and salt, rub down some flour and butter, and give all a boil together; then take out the herbs and onion, and add a little cup of cream, but do not boil it in. Serve with small bits of bacon rolled round, and balls.

**To Collar a Calf's Head.**—Scald the skin off a fine head, clean it nicely, and take out the brains. Boil it tender enough to remove the bones; then have ready a good quantity of chopped parsley, mace, nutmeg, salt, and white pepper, mixed well; season it high with these; lay the parsley in a thick layer, then a quantity of thick slices of fine ham, or a beautifully-coloured tongue skinned, and then the yolks of six nice yellow eggs stuck here and there about. Roll the head quite close, and tie it up as tight as you can. Boil it, and then lay a weight on it. A cloth must be put under the tape, as for other collars.

**Mock Turtle.**—Bespeak a calf's head with the skin on, cut it in half, and clean it well; then half boil it, take all the meat off in square bits, break the bones of the head, and boil them in some veal and beef broth to add to the richness. Fry some shalot in butter, and dredge in flour enough to thicken the gravy: stir this into the browning, and give it one or two boils; skin it carefully, and then put in the head; put in also a pint of Madeira wine, and simmer it till the meat is quite tender. About ten minutes before you serve, put in some basil, tarragon, chives, parsley, Cayenne, pepper, and salt to your taste; also two spoonfuls of mushroom ketchup, and one of soy. Squeeze the juice of a lemon into the tureen, and pour the soup upon it. Forcemeat balls, and small eggs.

**A Cheaper way.**—Prepare half a calf's head, without the skin, as above: when the meat is cut off, break the bones, and put them into a saucepan with some gravy made of beef and veal bones, and seasoned with fried onions, herbs, mace, and pepper. Have ready two or three ox-palates boiled so tender as to blanch, and cut into small pieces; to which a cow-heel, likewise cut into pieces, is a great improvement. Brown some butter, flour, and onion, and pour the gravy to it; then add the meats as above, and stew. Half a pint of sherry, an anchovy, two spoonfuls of walnut ketchup, the same of mushroom ketchup, and some chopped herbs as before. Balls, &c.

**Another.**—Put into a pan a knuckle of veal, two fine cow-heels, two onions, a few cloves, peppers, berries of allspice, mace, and sweet herbs; cover them with water, then tie a paper over the pan, and set it in an oven for three hours. When cold, take off the fat very nicely; cut the meat and feet into bits an inch and a half square, remove the bones and coarse parts, and then put the rest on to warm, with a large spoonful of walnut and one of mushroom ketchup, half a pint of sherry or Madeira wine, a little mushroom powder, and the jelly of the meat. When hot, if it wants any more seasoning, add some; and serve with hard eggs, forcemeat balls, a squeeze of lemon, and a spoonful of soy.

This is a very easy way, and the dish is excellent.

**Another.**—Stew a pound and a half of scrag of mutton, with from three pints of water to a quart: then set the broth on, with a calf's-foot and a cow-heel, cover the stew-pan tight, and simmer till you can get off the meat from the bones in proper bits. Set it on again with the broth, a quarter of a pint of Madeira wine, or sherry, a large onion, half a tea-spoonful of Cayenne pepper, a bit of lemon-peel, two anchovies, some sweet herbs, eighteen oysters cut into pieces, and then chopped fine, a tea-spoonful of salt, a little nutmeg, and the liquor of the oysters. Cover it tight, and simmer three quarters of an hour. Serve with forcemeat balls, and hard eggs in the tureen.

An excellent and very cheap mock turtle may be made of two or three cow-heels baked with two pounds and a half of gravy beef, herbs, &c., as above with cow-heels and veal.

**Calf's Liver.**—Slice it, season with pepper and salt, and boil nicely : rub a bit of cold butter on it, and serve hot and hot.

**Calf's Liver Roasted.**—Wash and wipe it ; then cut a long hole in it, and stuff it with crumbs of bread, chopped anchovy, herbs, a good deal of fat bacon, onion, salt, pepper, a bit of butter, and an egg : sew the liver up ; then lard it, or wrap it in a veal-cawl, and roast it.

Serve with a good brown gravy, and currant jelly.

**To Dress the Liver and Lights.**—Half-boil an equal quantity of each, then cut them in middling-sized mince, put to it a spoonful or two of the water that boiled it, a bit of butter, flour, salt, and pepper, simmer ten minutes, and serve hot.

**Sweet-breads.**—Half boil them, and stew them in a white gravy ; add cream, flour, butter, nutmeg, salt, and white pepper.

Or do them in brown sauce seasoned.

Or parboil them, and then cover them with crumbs, herbs, and seasoning, and brown them in a Dutch oven. Serve with butter, and mushroom ketchup or gravy.

**Sweet-breads Roasted.**—Parboil two large ones ; when cold, lard them with bacon, and roast them in a Dutch oven. For sauce, plain butter, and mushroom ketchup.

**Sweet-bread Ragout.**—Cut them about the size of a walnut, wash and dry them, and fry them of a fine brown ; pour to them a good gravy, seasoned with salt, pepper, allspice, and either mushrooms, or mushroom ketchup : strain, and thicken with butter and a little flour. You may add truffles, morels, and mushrooms.

**Kidneys.**—Chop veal kidney, and some of the fat ; likewise a little leek or onion, pepper, and salt ; roll it up with an egg into balls, and fry them.

Calf's heart, stuff and roast as a beef's heart, or sliced, make it into a pudding, as directed for steak or kidney pudding.

**PORK, &c.**—Bacon hogs, and porkers are differently cut up.

Hogs are kept to a large size ; the chine (or backbone) is cut down each side, the whole length, and is a prime part either boiled or roasted.

The sides of the hog are made into bacon, and the inside is cut out with very little meat to the bone. On each side there is a large spare-rib ; which is usually divided into two, one sweet-bone and a blade-bone. The bacon is the whole outside ; and contains a fore leg, and a ham ; which last is the hind-leg, but if left with the bacon, is called a gammon. There are also griskins. Hog's lard is the inner fat of the bacon hog.

Pickled pork is made of the flesh of the hog, as well as bacon.

Porkers are not so old as hogs : their flesh is whiter and less rich, but it is not so tender. It is divided into four quarters. The fore-quarter has the spring or fore-leg, the fore-loin or neck, the spare-rib and griskin. The hind has the leg and the loin.

The feet of pork make various good dishes, and should be cut off before the legs are cured. Observe the same of the ears.

The bacon hog is sometimes scalded to take off the hair, and sometimes singed. The porker is always scalded.

**To Roast a Leg of Pork.**—Choose a small leg of fine young pork; cut a slit in the knuckle with a sharp knife: and fill the space with sage and onion chopped, and a little pepper and salt. When half-done, score the skin in slices, but do not cut deeper than the outer rind.

Apple sauce and potatoes should be served to eat with it.

**To Boil a Leg of Pork.**—Salt it eight or ten days: when it is to be dressed, weigh it, let it lie half an hour in cold water to make it white; allow a quarter of an hour for every pound, and half an hour over, from the time it boils up: skim it as soon as it boils, and frequently after. Allow water enough. Save some of it to make peas soup. Some boil it in a very nice cloth, floured; which gives a very delicate look. It should be small and of a fine grain.

Serve peas-pudding and turnips with it.

**Loin and Neck of Pork.**—Roast them. Cut the skin of the loin across, at distances of half an inch, with a sharp pen-knife.

**Shoulders and Breasts of Pork.**—Put them into pickle, or salt the shoulder as a leg: when very nice, they may be roasted,

**Rolled Neck of Pork.**—Bone it; put a forcemeat of chopped sage, a very few crumbs of bread, salt, pepper, and two or three berries of allspice, over the inside; then roll the meat as tight as you can, and roast it slowly, and at a good distance at first.

**Spring, or Forehand of Pork.**—Cut out the bone; sprinkle salt, pepper, and sage dried, over the inside; but first warm a little butter to baste it, and then flour it: roll the pork tight, and tie it; then roast by a hanging jack. About two hours will do it.

**Spare-rib** should be basted with a very little butter and a little flour, and then sprinkled with dried sage crumbled. Apple sauce and potatoes, as for roasted pork.

**Pork Griskin** is usually very hard; the best way to prevent this is, to put it into as much cold water as will cover it, and let it boil up; then instantly take it off, and put it into a Dutch oven; a very few minutes will do it. Remember to rub butter over it, and then flour it, before you put it to the fire.

**Blade-bone of Pork** is taken from the bacon hog: the less meat left on it in moderation, the better. It is to be broiled; and when just done, pepper and salt it. Put to it a piece of butter, and a tea-spoonful of mustard: and serve it covered, quickly. This is a Somersetshire dish.

**To Dress Pork as Lamb.**—Kill a young pig of four or five months old; cut up the fore-quarter for roasting as you do

lamb, and truss the shank close. The other parts will make delicate pickled pork; or steaks, pies, &c.

Pork Steaks.—Cut them from a loin or neck, and of middling thickness; pepper and broil them, turning them often; 
when nearly done, put on salt, rub a bit of butter over, and serve
the moment they are taken off the fire, a few at a time.

To Pickle Pork.—The quantities proportioned to the mid-
dlings of a pretty large hog, the hams and shoulders being cut off.

Mix, and pound fine, four ounces of saltpetre, a pound of
coarse sugar, an ounce of sal-prunel, and a little common salt;
sprinkle the pork with salt, and drain it twenty-four hours: then
rub with the above; pack the pieces tight in a small deep tub,
filling up the spaces with common salt. Place large pebbles on
the pork to prevent it from swimming in the pickle which the salt
will produce. If kept from air, it will continue very fine for two
years.

Sausages.—Chop fat and lean of pork together; season it with
sage, pepper, and salt, and you may add two or three berries of
allspice; half fill hogs' guts that have been soaked and made extremely clean: or the meat may be kept in a very small pan, closely
covered: and so rolled and dusted with a very little flour before
it is fried.  Serve on stewed red cabbage, or mashed potatoes put
in a form, brown with salamander, and garnish with the above,:
they must be pricked with a fork before they are dressed, or they
will burst,

An excellent Sausage to eat Cold.—Season fat and lean
pork, with some salt, saltpetre, black pepper, and allspice, all in
fine powder, and rub into the meat: the sixth day cut it small
and mix with it some shred shalot or garlic, as fine as possible.
Have ready an ox-gut that has been scoured, salted, and soaked
well, and fill it with the above stuffing; tie up the ends, and hang
it to smoke as you would hams, but first wrap it in a fold or two
of old muslin.  It must be high-dried. Some eat it without boiling,
but others like it boiled first.  The skin should be tied in different
places, so as to make each link about eight or nine inches long.

Spadbury's Oxford Sausages.—Chop a pound and a half
of pork, and the same of veal, cleared of skin and sinews; add
three quarters of a pound of beef-suet; mince and mix them;
steep the crumb of a penny loaf in water, and mix it with the
meat, with also a little dried sage, pepper and salt.

To Scald a Sucking Pig.—The moment the pig is killed,
put it into cold water for a few minutes, then rub it over with a
little resin beaten extremely small, and put it into a pail of scalding water half a minute; take it out, lay it on a table, and pull off
the hair as quickly as possible; if any part does not come off, put
it in again.  When quite clean, wash it well with warm water,
and then in two or three cold waters, that no flavour of the resin
may remain.  Take off all the feet at the first joint; make a slit
down the belly, and take out the entrails; put the liver, heart and
lights to the feet.  Wash the pig well in cold water, dry it
thoroughly, and fold it in a wet cloth to keep it from the air.

**To Roast a Sucking Pig.**—If you can get it when just killed, this is of great advantage. Let it be scalded, which the dealers usually do; then put some sage. crumbs of bread, salt, and pepper into the belly, and sew it up. Observe to skewer the legs back, or the under part will not crisp.

Lay it to a brisk fire till thoroughly dry, then have ready some butter in a dry cloth, and rub the pig with it in every part. Dredge as much flour over as will possibly lie, and do not touch it again till ready to serve; then scrape off the flour very carefully with a blunt knife, rub it well with the buttered cloth, and take off the head while at the fire; take out the brains and mix them with the gravy that comes from the pig. Then take it up, and without withdrawing the spit, cut it down the back and belly, lay it into the dish, and chop the sage and bread quickly as fine as you can, and mix them with a large quantity of fine melted butter that has very little flour. Put the sauce into the dish after the pig has been split down the back, and garnished with the ears and the two jaws; take off the upper part of the head down to the snout.

In Devonshire it is served whole, if very small; the head only being cut off to garnish as above.

**Pettitoes.**—Boil them, the liver, and the heart, in a small quantity of water, very gently; then cut the meat fine and simmer it with a little of the water and the feet split, till the feet are quite tender; thicken with a bit of butter, a little flour, a spoonful of cream, and a little salt and pepper; give it a boil up, pour it over a few sippets of bread, and put the feet on the mince.

**To make excellent Meat of a Hog's Head.**—Split the head, and take out the brains, cut off the ears, and sprinkle it with common salt for a day; then drain it: salt it well with salt and saltpetre three days, then lay the salt and head into a small quantity of water for two days. Wash it, and boil till all the bones will come out; remove them, and chop the head as quick as possible; but first skin the tongue and take the skin carefully off the head, to put under and over. Season with pepper, salt and a little mace or allspice-berries. Put the skin into a small pan, press the cut head in, and put the other skin over; press it down. When cold it will turn out, and make a kind of brawn. If too fat, you may put some lean pork, to be prepared the same way. Add salt and vinegar, and boil these with some of the liquor for a pickle to keep it.

**To Roast Porker's Head.**—Choose a fine young head, clean it well and put bread and sage as for pig; sew it up tight, and on a string or hanging-jack roast it as a pig, and serve with the same sauce.

**To Prepare Pig's Cheek for Boiling.**—Cut off the snout, and clean the head; divide it, take out the eyes and the brains; sprinkle the head with salt, and let it drain twenty-four hours. Salt it with common salt and saltpetre: let it lie eight or ten days if it be dressed without stewing with peas, but less if to be dressed with peas; and it must be washed first, and then simmered till all is tender.

**To Collar Pig's Head.**—Scour the head and ears nicely; take off the hair and snout, and take out the eyes and the brain; lay it into water one night; then drain, salt it extremely well with common salt and saltpetre, and let it lie five days. Boil it enough to take out the bones, then lay it on a dresser, turning the thick end of one side of the head towards the thin end of the other to make the roll of equal size; sprinkle it well with salt and white. pepper, and roll it with the ears; and, if you approve, put the pig's feet round the outside when boned, or the thin parts of two cow-heels. Put it in a cloth, bind with a broad tape, and boil till quite tender, then put a good weight upon it, and do not take off the covering till cold.

If you choose it to be more like brawn salt it longer, and let the proportion of saltpetre be greater, and put in also some pieces of lean pork; and then cover it with cow-heel, to look like the horn.

This may be kept either in or out of pickle of salt and water boiled with vinegar, and is a very convenient thing to have in the house. If likely to spoil, slice and fry it, either with or without butter.

**To Dry Hog's Cheeks.**—Cut out the snout, remove the brains, and split the head, taking off the upper bone, to make the chawl a good shape: rub it well with salt; next day take away the brine, and salt it again the following day: cover the head with half an ounce of saltpetre, two ounces of bay salt, a little common salt, and four ounces of coarse sugar. Let the head be often turned; after ten days, smoke it for a week like bacon.

**To Force Hog's Ears.**—Parboil two pair of ears, or take some that have been soused; make a forcemeat of an anchovy, some sage, parsley, a quarter of a pound of suet chopped, bread-crumbs, pepper, and only a little salt. Mix all these with the yolks of two eggs; raise the skin of the upper side of the ears, and stuff them with the above. Fry the ears in fresh butter, of a fine colour; then pour away the fat, and drain them: make ready half a pint of rich gravy, with a glass of fine sherry, three tea-spoonfuls of made mustard, a little bit of flour and butter, a small onion whole, and a little pepper or Cayenne. Put this with the ears into a stew-pan, and cover it close; stew it gently for half an hour, shaking the pan often. When done enough, take out the onion, place the ears carefully in a dish, and pour the sauce over them. If a larger dish is wanted, the meat from two feet may be added to the above.

**Different ways of Dressing Pig's Feet and Ears.**—Clean carefully and soak some hours, and boil them tender; then take them out; boil some vinegar and a little salt with some of the water, and when cold put it over them. When they are to be dressed, dry them, cut the feet in two, and slice the ears; fry, and serve with butter, mustard, and vinegar. They may be either done in batter or only floured.

**Pig's Feet and Ears Fricasseed.**—Put no vinegar into

the pickle, if to be dressed with cream. Cut the feet and ears into neat bits, and boil them in a little milk; then pour that from them, and simmer in a little veal broth, with a bit of onion, mace, and lemon peel. Before you serve add a little cream, flour, butter, and salt.

**Jelly of Pig's Feet and Ears.**—Clean and prepare as in the last article, then boil them in a very small quantity of water till every bone can be taken out; throw in half a handful of chopped sage, the same of parsley, and a seasoning of pepper, salt, and mace, in fine powder; simmer till the herbs are scalded, then pour the whole into a melon-form.

**Pig's Harslet.**—Wash and dry some liver, sweetbreads, and fat and lean bits of pork, beating the latter with a rolling-pin to make it tender; season with pepper, salt, sage, and a little onion shred fine; when mixed, put all into a cawl, and fasten it up tight with a needle and thread. Roast it on a hanging-jack, or by a string.

Or serve in slices with parsley for a fry.

Serve with a sauce of port-wine and water, and mustard, just boiled up and put into the dish.

**Mock Brawn.**—Boil a pair of neat's feet very tender; take the meat off, and have ready the belly-piece of pork salted with common salt and saltpetre for a week. Boil this almost enough; take out the bones, and roll the feet and the pork together. Then roll it very tight with a strong cloth and coarse tape. Boil it till very tender, then hang it up in the cloth till cold; after which keep it in a sousing liquor, as is directed in the next article.

**Souse for Brawn, and for Pig's Feet and Ears.**—Boil a quarter of a peck of wheat-bran, a sprig of bay, and a sprig of rosemary, in two gallons of water, with four ounces of salt in it, for half an hour. Strain it, and let it get cold.

**To make Black Puddings.**—The blood must be stirred with salt till cold. Put a quart of it, or rather more, to a quart of whole grits, to soak one night; and soak the crumb of a quartern loaf in rather more than two quarts of new milk made hot. In the meantime prepare the guts by washing, turning, and scraping with salt and water, and changing the water several times. Chop fine a little winter-savoury and thyme, a good quantity of pennyroyal, pepper, and salt, a few cloves, some allspice, ginger, and nutmeg: mix these with three pounds of beef-suet, and six eggs well beaten and strained; and then beat the bread, grits, &c. all up with the seasoning; when well mixed, have ready some hog's fat cut into large bits; and as you fill the skins, put it in at proper distances. Tie in links, only half filled, and boil in a large kettle, pricking them as they swell, or they will burst. When boiled, lay them between clean cloths till cold, and hang them up in the kitchen. When to be used, scald them a few minutes in water, wipe, and put them into a Dutch oven.

If there are not skins enough, put the stuffing into basons, and boil it covered with floured cloths; and slice and fry it when used.

**Another way.**—Soak all night a quart of bruised grits in as

much boiling-hot milk as will swell them and leave half a pint of
liquid. Chop a good quantity of pennyroyal, some savoury and
thyme; salt, pepper, and allspice, finely powdered. Mix the
above with a quart of the blood, prepared as before directed;
then half fill the skins, after they have been cleaned thoroughly,
and put as much of the leaf (that is, the inward fat) of the pig as
will make it pretty rich. Boil as before directed. A small
quantity of leeks finely shred and well mixed, is a great improvement.

**Another way.**—Boil a quart of half-grits in as much milk as
will swell them to the utmost; then drain them and add a quart
of blood, a pint of rich cream, a pound of suet, some mace, nutmeg, allspice, and four cloves, all in fine powder; two pounds of
the hog's leaf cut into dice, two leeks, a handful of parsley, ten
leaves of sage, a large handful of pennyroyal, and a sprig of thyme
and knotted majoram, all minced fine; eight eggs well beaten,
half a pound of bread-crumbs that have been scalded with a pint
of milk, pepper, and salt. Half fill the skins; which must first be
cleaned with the greatest care, turned several times, and soaked
in several waters, and last in rose-water. Tie the skins in links,
boil and prick them with a clean fork to prevent their bursting.
Cover them with a clean cloth till cold.

**White Hog's Puddings.**—When the skins have been soaked
and cleaned as before directed, rinse and soak them all night in
rose-water, and put into them the following filling: Mix half a
pound of blanched almonds cut into seven or eight bits, with a
pound of grated bread, two pounds of marrow or suet, a pound of
currants, some beaten cinnamon, cloves, mace, and nutmeg, a
quart of cream, the yolks of six and whites of two eggs, a little
orange-flower water, a little fine Lisbon sugar, and some lemon-
peel and citron sliced, and half fill the skins. To know whether
sweet enough, warm a little in a panikin. In boiling, much care
must be taken to prevent the puddings from bursting. Prick them
with a small fork as they rise, and boil them in milk and water.
Lay them in a table-cloth till cold.

**Hog's Lard** should be carefully melted in a jar put into a
kettle of water, and boiled; run it into bladders that have been
extremely well cleaned. The smaller they are the better the lard
keeps; as after the air reaches it, it becomes rank. Put in a sprig
of rosemary when melting.

This being a most useful article for frying fish, it should be prepared with care. Mixed with butter, it makes fine crust.

**To Cure Hams.**—Hang them a day or two; then sprinkle
them with a little salt, and drain them another day; pound an
ounce and a half of saltpetre, the same quantity of bay-salt, half
an ounce of sal-prunel, and a pound of the coarsest sugar. Mix
these well; and rub them into each ham every day for four days,
and turn it. If a small one, turn it every day for three weeks; if
a large one, a week longer; but do not rub after four days.
Before you dry it, drain and cover with bran. Smoke it ten days.

**Another way.**—Choose the leg of a hog that is fat and well fed; hang it as above; if large, put to it a pound of bay salt, four ounces of saltpetre, a pound of the coarsest sugar, and a handful of common salt, all in fine powder, and rub it thoroughly. Lay the rind downwards, and cover the fleshy parts with the salts. Baste it as often as you can with the pickle, the more the better. Keep it four weeks, turning it every day. Drain it, and throw bran over it; then hang it in a chimney where wood is burned, and turn it sometimes for ten days.

**Another way.**—Hang the ham, and sprinkle it with salt as above: then rub it every day with the following in fine powder: half a pound of common salt, the same quantity of bay salt, two ounces of saltpetre, and two ounces of black pepper, mixed with a pound and a half of treacle. Turn it twice a day in the pickle, for three weeks. Lay it into a pail of water for one night, wipe it quite dry, and smoke it two or three weeks.

**Another way that gives it a high flavour.**—When the weather will permit, hang the ham three days; mix an ounce of saltpetre, with a quarter of a pound of bay salt, the same quantity of common salt, and also of coarse sugar, and a quart of strong beer; boil them together, and pour them immediately upon the ham; turn it twice a day in the pickle for three weeks. An ounce of black pepper, and the same quantity of allspice, in fine powder, added to the above, will give still more flavour. Cover it with bran when wiped, and smoke it from three to four weeks, as you approve: the latter will make it harder and give it more of the flavour of Westphalia. Sew hams in hessings (that is, coarse wrappers), if to be smoked where there is a strong fire.

**A method of giving a still higher flavour.**—Sprinkle the ham with salt, after it has hung two or three days; let it drain; make a pickle of a quart of strong beer, half a pound of treacle, an ounce of coriander seeds, two ounces of juniper berries, an ounce of pepper, the same quantity of allspice, an ounce of saltpetre, half an ounce of sal-prunel, a handful of common salt, and a head of shalot, all pounded or cut fine. Boil these all together a few minutes, and pour them over the ham: this quantity is for one of ten pounds. Rub and turn it every day, for a fortnight; then sew it up in a thin linen bag, and smoke it three weeks. Take care to drain it from the pickle, and rub it in bran before drying.

**To make a Pickle** that will keep for years, for hams, tongues, or beef, if boiled and skimmed between each parcel of them. To two gallons of spring water put two pounds of coarse sugar, two pounds of bay and two pounds and a half of common salt, and half a pound of saltpetre, in a deep earthen glazed pan that will hold four gallons, and with a cover that will fit close. Keep the beef or hams as long as they will bear, before you put them into the pickle; and sprinkle them with coarse sugar in a pan, from which they must drain. Rub the hams, &c., well with the pickle, and pack them in close; putting as much as the pan will hold, so that the pickle may cover them. The pickle is not to be boiled at first. A small ham may lie fourteen days, a large one three weeks; a tongue twelve days, and beef in propor-

tion to its size. They will eat well out of the pickle without drying. When they are to be dried, let each piece be drained over
the pan, and when it will drop no longer, take a clean sponge and
dry it thoroughly. Six or eight hours will smoke them, and there
should be only a little sawdust and wet straw burnt to do this;
but if put into a baker's chimney, sew them in coarse cloth, and
hang them a week.

**To Dress Hams.**—If long hung, put the ham into water a
night, and let it lie either in a hole dug in the earth, or on damp
stones sprinkled with water two or three days, to mellow, covering it with a heavy tub to keep vermin from it. Wash well, and
put it into a boiler with plenty of water; let it simmer four, five,
or six hours, according to the size. When done enough, if before
the time of serving, cover it with a clean cloth doubled, and keep
the dish hot over boiling water. Take off the skin, and strew
raspings over the ham. Garnish with carrot. Preserve the skin
as whole as possible to keep over the ham when cold, which will
prevent its drying.

**Excellent Bacon.**—Divide the hog, and take the chine out:
it is common to remove the spare-ribs, but the bacon will be preserved better from being rusty if they are left in. Salt the bacon
six days, then drain it from the first pickle: mix as much salt as
you judge proper with eight ounces of bay salt, three ounces of
saltpetre, and a pound of coarse sugar, to each hog, but first cut
off the hams. Rub the salts well in, and turn it every day for a
month. Drain, and smoke it a few days; or dry without, by
hanging in the kitchen, not near the fire.

**The Manner of Curing Wiltshire Bacon.**—Sprinkle
each flitch with salt, and let the blood drain off for twenty-four
hours: then mix a pound and a half of coarse sugar, the same
quantity of bay salt, not quite so much as half a pound of saltpetre,
and a pound of common salt; and rub this well on the bacon,
turning it every day for a month: then hang it to dry, and afterwards smoke it ten days. This quantity of salts is sufficient for
the whole hog.

**MUTTON.—Observations on Keeping and Dressing
Mutton.**—Take away the pipe that runs along the bone of the
inside of a chine of mutton; and if to be kept a great time, rub
the part close round the tail with salt, after first cutting out
the kernel.

The kernel in the fat on the thick part of the leg should be taken
out by the butcher, for it taints first there. The chine and rib-
bones should be wiped every day; and the bloody part of the
neck be cut off, to preserve it. The brisket changes first in the
breast; and if it is to be kept, it is best to rub it with a little salt,
should the weather be hot.

Every kernel should be taken out of all sorts of meat as soon
as brought in; then wipe dry.

For roasting, it should hang as long as it will keep, the hind-
quarter especially, but not so long as to taint; for, whatever

fashion may authorize, putrid juices ought not to be taken into the stomach.

Mutton for boiling will not look of a good colour if it has hung long.

Great care should be taken to preserve by paper the fat of what is roasted.

**Leg of Mutton.**—If roasted, serve with onion or currant-jelly sauce; if boiled, with caper sauce and vegetables.

**Neck of Mutton** is particularly useful, as so many dishes may be made of it; but it is not advantageous for the family. The bones should be cut short, which the butchers will not do unless particularly desired.

The best end of the neck may be boiled, and served with turnips; or roasted, or dressed in steaks, in pies, or harrico.

The scrags may be stewed in broth; or with a small quantity of water, some small onions, a few peppercorns and a little rice, and served together.

When a neck is to be boiled to look particularly nice, saw down the chine bone, strip the ribs half-way down, and chop off the ends of the bones about four inches. The skin should not be taken off till boiled, and then the fat will look the whiter.

When there is more fat to a neck or loin of mutton than it is agreeable to eat with the lean, it makes an uncommonly good suet pudding, or crust for a meat-pie if cut very fine.

**Shoulder of Mutton Roasted.**—Serve with onion sauce. The blade-bone may be broiled.

**To Dress Haunch of Mutton.**—Keep it as long as it can be preserved sweet by the different modes: let it be washed with warm milk and water, or vinegar, if necessary; but when to be dressed, observe to wash it well, lest the outside should have a bad flavour from keeping. Put a paste of coarse flour on strong paper, and fold the haunch in: set it at a great distance from the fire, and allow proportionable time for the paste; do not take it off till about thirty-five or forty minutes before serving, and then baste it continually. Bring the haunch nearer to the fire before you take off the paste, and froth it up as you would venison.

A gravy must be made of a pound and a half of loin of old mutton, simmered in a pint of water to half, and no seasoning but salt: brown it with a little burnt sugar, and send it up in the dish; but there should be a good deal of gravy in the meat; for though long at the fire, the distance and covering will prevent its roasting out.

Serve with currant-jelly sauce.

**To Roast a Saddle of Mutton.**—Let it be well kept first. Raise the skin, and then skewer it on again; take it off a quarter of an hour before serving, sprinkle it with some salt, baste it, and dredge it well with flour. The rump should be split, and skewered back on each side. The joint may be large or small according to the company; it is the most elegant if the latter. Being broad it requires a high and strong fire.

E

**Fillet of Mutton Braised.**—Take off the chump end of the loin, butter some paper, and put over it, and then a paste as for venison; roast it two hours. Do not let it be the least brown. Have ready some French beans boiled and drained on a sieve; and while the mutton is being glazed, give them one heat-up in gravy, and lay them on the dish with the meat over them.

**Harrico.**—Take off some of the fat, and cut the middle or best end of the neck into rather thin steaks; flour and fry them in their own fat of a fine light brown, but not enough for eating. Then put them into a dish while you fry the carrots, turnips, and onions; the carrots and turnips in dice, the onions sliced: but they must only be warmed, not browned, or you need not fry them. Then lay the steaks at the bottom of the stew-pan, the vegetables over them, and pour as much boiling water as will just cover them; give one boil, skim well, and then set the pan on the side of the fire to simmer gently till tender. In three or four hours skim them; and add pepper, salt, and a spoonful of ketchup.

**To Hash Mutton.**—Cut thin slices of dressed mutton, fat and lean; flour them; have ready a little onion boiled in two or three spoonfuls of water; add to it some gravy and meat seasoned, and make it hot, but not to boil. Serve in a covered dish. Instead of onion, a clove, a spoonful of currant-jelly, and half a glass of port wine, will give an agreeable flavour of venison, if the meat be fine. Pickled cucumber, or walnut, cut small, warm in it for change.

**To Boil Shoulder of Mutton with Oysters.**—Hang it some days, then salt it well for two days, bone it, and sprinkle it with pepper and a bit of mace pounded: lay some oysters over it, and roll the meat up tight and tie it. Stew it in a small quantity of water, with an onion and a few pepper-corns, till quite tender.

Have ready a little good gravy, and some oysters stewed in it; thicken this with flour and butter, and pour over the mutton when the tape is taken off. The stew-pan should be kept close covered.

**Breast of Mutton.**—Cut off the superfluous fat, and roast and serve the meat with stewed cucumbers; or to eat cold, covered with chopped parsley. Or half boil and then grill it before the fire; in which case cover it with crumbs and herbs, and serve with caper sauce. Or, if boned, take off some of the fat, and cover it with bread, herbs, and seasoning; then roll and boil: and serve with chopped walnuts, or capers and butter.

**Loin of Mutton** roasted; if cut lengthways as a saddle, some think it eats better. Or for steaks, pies, or broth.

**To Roll Loin of Mutton.**—Hang the mutton till tender; bone it; and lay a seasoning of pepper, allspice, mace, nutmeg, and a few cloves, all in fine powder, over it. Next day prepare a stuffing as for hare; beat the meat, and cover it with the stuffing; roll it up tight, and tie it. Half-bake it in a slow oven; let it grow cold; take off the fat, and put the gravy into a stew-pan; flour the meat, and put it in likewise; stew it till almost ready: and add a glass of port wine, some ketchup, an anchovy, and a little lemon-pickle, half an hour before serving: serve it in the gravy, and with jelly-sauce. A few fresh mushrooms are a great improvement; but if to eat like hare do not use these, nor the lemon pickle.

**Mutton Ham.**—Choose a fine fresh leg of wether-mutton, of twelve or fourteen pounds weight; let it be cut ham-shape, and hang two days. Then put into a stew-pan half a pound of bay salt, the same of common salt, two ounces of saltpetre, and half a pound of coarse sugar, all in powder; mix and make it quite hot; then rub it well into the ham. Let it be turned in the liquor every day; at the end of four days put two ounces more of common salt; in twelve days take it out, dry it, and hang it up in wood-smoke a week. It is to be used in slices with stewed cabbage, mashed potatoes or eggs.

**Mutton Collops.**—Take a loin of mutton that has been well hung; and cut from the part next the leg, some collops very thin. Take out the sinews. Season the collops with salt, pepper, and mace; and strew over them shred parsley, thyme, and two or three shalots: fry them in butter till half done; add half a pint of gravy, a little juice of lemon, a piece of butter rubbed in flour, and simmer the whole very gently five minutes. They should be served immediately, or they will be hard.

**Mutton Cutlets in the Portuguese Way.**—Cut the chops; and half-fry them with sliced shalot or onion, chopped parsley, and two bay leaves; season with pepper and salt; then lay a forcemeat on a piece of white paper, put the chop on it, and twist the paper up, leaving a hole for the end of the bones to go through. Broil on a gentle fire. Serve with sauce Robart; or, as the seasoning makes the cutlets high, a little gravy.

**Mutton Steaks** should be cut from a loin or neck that has hung; if a neck, the bones should not be long. They should be broiled on a clear fire, seasoned when half done, and often turned: take them up into a very hot dish, rub a bit of butter on each, and serve hot and hot the moment they are done.

**Steaks of Mutton, or Lamb, and Cucumbers.**—Quarter cucumbers, and lay them into a deep dish, sprinkle them with salt and pour vinegar over them. Fry the chops of a fine brown, and put them into a stew-pan; drain the cucumbers, and put over the steaks; add some sliced onions, pepper, and salt; pour hot water or weak broth on them; stew and skim well.

**Mutton Steaks Maintenon.**—Half-fry, strew them while hot with herbs, crumbs, and seasoning; put them in paper immediately, and finish on the gridiron. Be careful the paper does not catch: rub a bit of butter on it first to prevent that.

**Mutton Sausages.**—Take a pound of the rawest part of a leg of mutton that has been either roasted or boiled; chop it extremely small, and season it with pepper, salt, mace, and nutmeg: add to it six ounces of beef-suet, some sweet herbs, two anchovies, and a pint of oysters, all chopped very small; a quarter of a pound of grated bread, some of the anchovy liquour, and the yolks and whites of two eggs well beaten. Put it all, when well mixed, into a little pot; and use it by rolling it into balls or sausage-shape

E 2

and frying. If approved, a little shalot may be added, or garlic, which is a great improvement.

**To Dress Mutton Rumps and Kidneys.**—Stew six rumps in some good mutton-gravy half an hour; then take them up, and let them stand to cool. Clear the gravy from the fat; and put into it four ounces of boiled rice, an onion stuck with cloves, and a blade of mace; boil them till the rice is thick. Wash the rumps with yolks of eggs well beaten; and strew over them crumbs of bread, a little pepper and salt, chopped parsley and thyme, and grated lemon-peel. Fry in butter of a fine brown. While the rumps are stewing, lard the kidneys, and put them to roast in a Dutch oven. When the rumps are fried, the grease must be drained before they are put on the dish, and the pan being cleared likewise from the fat, warm the rice in it. Lay the latter on the dish; the rumps put round on the rice, the narrow ends towards the middle, and the kidneys between. Garnish with hard eggs cut in half, the white being left on; or with different coloured pickles.

**An excellent Hotch Potch.**—Stew peas, lettuce, and onions, in a very little water, with a beef or ham-bone. While these are doing, fry some mutton or lamb steaks seasoned, of a nice brown: three quarters of an hour before dinner, put the steaks into a stew-pan, and the vegetables over them; stew them, and serve all together in a tureen.

**Another.**—Knuckle of veal, and scrag of mutton, stewed with vegetables as above; to both add a bit of butter rolled in flour.

**Mutton Kebobbed.**—Take all the fat out of a loin of mutton, and that on the outside also if too fat, and remove the skin. Joint it at every bone: mix a small nutmeg grated with a little salt and pepper, crumbs, and herbs; dip the steaks into the yolks of three eggs, and sprinkle the above mixture all over them. Then place the steaks together as they were before they were cut asunder, tie them and fasten them on a small spit. Roast them at a quick fire; set a dish under, and baste them with a good piece of butter and the liquor that comes from the meat; but throw some more of the above seasoning over. When done enough, take it up, and lay it in a dish; have half a pint of good gravy ready besides that in the dish; and put into it two spoonfuls of ketchup, and rub down a tea-spoonful of flour with it; give this a boil, and pour it over the mutton, but first skim off the fat well. Mind to keep the meat hot till the gravy is quite ready.

**China Chilo.**—Mince a pint basin of undressed neck of mutton, or leg, and some of the fat; put two onions, a lettuce, a pint of green peas, a tea-spoonful of salt, a tea-spoonful of pepper, four spoonfuls of water, and two or three ounces of clarified butter, into a stew-pan closely covered; simmer two hours, and serve in the middle of a dish of boiled dry rice. If Cayenne is approved, add a little.

**LAMB.**—Leg of Lamb should be boiled in a cloth to look as white as possible. The loin fried in steaks and served round, garnished with dried or fried parsley; spinach to eat with it; or dressed separately, or roasted.

**Fore Quarter of Lamb.**—Roast it either whole, or in separate parts. If left to be cold, chopped parsley should be sprinkled over it. The neck and breast together are called a scoven.

**Breast of Lamb and Cucumbers.**—Cut off the chine-bone from the breast, and set it on to stew with a pint of gravy. When the bones would draw out, put it on the gridiron to grill; and then lay it in a dish on cucumbers nicely stewed.

**Shoulder of Lamb, Forced, with Sorrel Sauce.**—Bone a shoulder of lamb, and fill it up with forcemeat: braise it two hours over a slow stove. Take it up, glaze it; or it may be glazed only, and not braised.

The method for both, see page 75. Serve with sorrel sauce under the lamb.

**Lamb Steaks.**—Fry them of a beautiful brown: when served, throw over them a good quantity of crumbs of bread fried, and crimped parsley; the receipt for doing which of a fine colour will be given under the head of Vegetables.

Mutton or Lamb steaks, seasoned and broiled in buttered papers, either with crumbs and herbs, or without, are a genteel dish, and eat well.

Sauce for them, called Sauce Robart, will be found in the list of Sauces.

**House Lamb Steaks, White.**—Stew them in milk and water till very tender, with a bit of lemon peel, a little salt, some pepper, and mace. Have ready some veal gravy, and put the steaks into it; mix some mushroom powder, a cup of cream, and the least bit of flour; shake the steaks in this liquor, stir it, and let it get quite hot. Just before you take it up, put in a few white mushrooms. This is a good substitute when poultry is very dear.

**House Lamb Steaks, Brown.**—Season them with pepper, salt, nutmeg, grated lemon peel, and chopped parsley; but dip them first into egg; fry them quick. Thicken some good gravy with a bit of flour and butter; and add to it a spoonful of port wine, and some oysters: boil it up, and then put in the steaks warm: let them heat up, and serve. You may add palates, balls, or eggs, if you like.

**Lamb Cutlets with Spinach.**—Cut the steaks from the loin, and fry them: the spinach is to be stewed and put into the dish first, and then the cutlets round it,

**Lamb's Head and Hinge.**—This part is best from a house lamb; but any, if soaked in cold water, will be white. Boil the head separately till very tender. Have ready the liver and lights three parts boiled and cut small; stew them in a little of the water in which they were boiled, season and thicken with flour and butter, and serve the mince round the head.

**Lamb's Fry.**—Serve it fried of a beautiful colour, and with a good deal of dried or fried parsley over it.

**Lamb's Sweetbreads.**—Blanch them, and put them a little while into cold water. Then put them into a stew-pan with a ladleful of broth, some pepper and salt, a small bunch of small onions, and a blade of mace; stir in a bit of butter and flour, and stew half an hour. Have ready two or three eggs well beaten in cream, with a little minced parsley and a few grates of nutmeg. Put in some boiled asparagus-tops to the other things. Do not let it boil after the cream is in, but make it hot, and stir it well all the while. Take great care it does not curdle. Young French beans or peas may be added, first boiled of a beautiful colour.

**Fricasseed Lambstones.**—Skin and wash, then dry and flour them; fry of a beautiful brown in hog's lard. Lay them on a sieve before the fire till you have made the following sauce: Thicken almost half a pint of veal gravy with a bit of flour and butter, and then add to it a slice of lemon, a large spoonful of mushroom ketchup, a tea-spoonful of lemon pickle, a grate of nutmeg, and the yolk of an egg beaten well in two large spoonfuls of thick cream. Put this over the fire, and stir it well till it is hot, and looks white; but do not let it boil, or it will curdle. Then put in it the fry, and shake it about near the fire for a minute or two. Serve in a very hot dish and cover.

**Fricassee of Lambstones and Sweetbreads, another way.**—Have ready some lambstones blanched, parboiled and sliced. Flour two or three sweetbreads, if very thick, cut them in two. Fry altogether, with a few large oysters, of a fine yellow brown. Pour the butter off; and add a pint of good gravy, some asparagus tops about an inch long, a little nutmeg, pepper, and salt, two shalots shred fine, and a glass of white wine. Simmer ten minutes; then put a little of the gravy to the yolks of three eggs well beaten, and by degrees mix the whole. Turn the gravy back into the pan, and stir it till of a fine thickness without boiling. Garnish with lemon.

**A very nice Dish.**—Take the best end of a neck of lamb, cut into steaks, and chop each bone so short as to make the steaks almost round. Egg, then strew with crumbs, herbs, and seasoning; fry them of the finest brown; mash some potatoes with a little butter and cream, and put them into the middle of the dish raised high. Then place the edge of one steak on an other with the small bone upward, all round the potatoes.

Pies of the different meats are directed under the general head of Savoury Pies.

---

# POULTRY, GAME, &c.

## To Choose Poultry, Game, &c.

**A Turkey-cock** if young, it has a smooth, black leg, with a short spur. The eyes full and bright, if fresh, and the feet supple and moist. If stale, the eyes will be sunk, and the feet dry.

**Hen-turkey** is known by the same rules; but if old, her legs will be red and tough.

**Fowls.**—If a cock is young, his spurs will be short: but take care to see that they have not been cut or pared, which is a trick often practised. If fresh, the vent will be close and dark. Pullets are best just before they begin to lay, and yet are full of egg; if old hens, their combs and legs will be rough; if young, they will be smooth. A good capon has a thick belly and large rump, there is a particular fat at his breast, and the comb is very pale. Black-legged fowls are most moist, if for roasting.

**Geese.**—The bill and feet of a young one will be yellow, and there will be but few hairs upon them; if old, they will be red: if fresh, the feet will be pliable; if stale, dry and stiff. Geese are called green till three or four months old. Green geese should be scalded: a stubble-goose should be picked dry.

**Ducks.**—Choose them by the same rules, of having supple feet, and by their being hard and thick on the breast and belly. The feet of a tame duck are thick, and inclining to dusky yellow; a wild one has the feet reddish, and smaller than the tame. They should be picked dry. Ducklings must be scalded.

**Pigeons** should be very fresh; when they look flabby about the vent, and this part is discoloured, they are stale. The feet should be supple; if old, the feet are harsh. The tame ones are larger than the wild, and are thought best by some persons; they should be fat and tender; but many are deceived in their size, because a full crop is as large as the whole body of a small pigeon.

The wood pigeon is large, and the flesh dark-coloured: if properly kept and not over-roasted, the flavour is equal to teal. Serve with a good gravy.

**Plovers.**—Choose those that feel hard at the vent, which shows they are fat. In other respects, choose them by the same marks as other fowl. When stale, the feet are dry. They will keep sweet a long time. There are three sorts:—The grey, green, and bastard plover, or lapwing.

**Hare or Rabbit.**—If the claws are blunt and rugged, the ears dry and tough, and the haunch thick, it is old; but if the claws are smooth and sharp, the ears easily tear, and the cleft in the lip is not much spread, it is young, If fresh and newly killed, the body will be stiff, and in hares the flesh pale. But they keep a good while by proper care: and are best when rather beginning to turn, if the inside is preserved from being musty. To know a real leveret, you should look for a knob or small bone near the foot on its fore leg; if there is none it is a hare.

**Partridges.**—They are in high season in autumn. If young, the bill is of a dark colour, and the legs yellowish; if fresh, the vent will be firm; but this part will look greenish if stale.

**Pheasants.**—The cock-bird is accounted best, except when the hen is with egg. If young, he has short blunt or round spurs; but if old, they are long and sharp.

**Directions for Dressing Poultry and Game.**—All poultry should be very carefully picked, every plug removed, and the hair nicely singed with white paper.

The cook must be careful in drawing poultry of all sorts, not break the gall bag, for no washing will take off the bitter where it has touched.

In dressing wild fowl, be careful to keep a clear brisk fire. Let them be done of a fine yellow brown, but leave the gravy in; the fine flavour is lost if done too much.

Tame fowls require more roasting, and are longer in heating through than others. All sorts should be continually basted; that they may be served with a froth, and appear of a fine colour.

A large fowl will take three-quarters of an hour: a middling one half-an-hour; and a very small one, or a chicken, twenty minutes, The fire must be very quick and clear before any fowls are put down. A capon will take from thirty to thirty-five minutes; a goose an hour; wild ducks a quarter of an hour; pheasants, twenty minutes; a small turkey stuffed, an hour and a quarter; turkey poults, twenty minutes; grouse a quarter of an hour; quails, ten minutes; and partridges, from twenty to twenty-five minutes. A hare will take near an hour, and the hind part requires most heat.

Pigs and geese require a brisk fire, and quick turning. Hares and rabbits must be well attended to: and the extremities brought to the quick part of the fire, to be done equally with the backs.

POULTRY.—To Boil Turkey.—Make a stuffing of bread, herbs, salt, pepper, nutmeg, lemon peel, a few oysters or an anchovy, a bit of butter, some suet, and an egg; put this into the crop, fasten up the skin, and boil the turkey in a floured cloth to make it very white. Have ready a fine oyster sauce made rich with butter, a little cream, and a spoonful of soy, if approved, and pour it over the bird; or liver and lemon sauce. Hen birds are best for boiling, and should be young.

To Roast Turkey.—The sinews of the legs should be drawn, whichever way it is dressed. The head should be twisted under the wing; and in drawing it, take care not to tear the liver, nor let the gall touch it.

Put a stuffing of sausage meat; or if sausages are to be served in the dish, a bread stuffing. As this makes a large addition to the size of the bird, observe that the heat of the fire is constantly to that part; for the breast is often not done enough. A little strip of paper should be put on the bone, to hinder it from scorching while the other parts roast. Baste well and froth it up. Serve with gravy in the dish, and plenty of bread sauce in a sauce tureen. Add a few crumbs, and a beaten egg to the stuffing of sausage meat.

Pulled Turkey.—Divide the meat of the breast by pulling instead of cutting: then warm it in a spoonful or two of white gravy, and a little cream, grated nutmeg, salt, and a little flour and butter; do not boil it. The leg should be seasoned, scored, and broiled, and put into the dish with the above round it. Cold chicken does as well.

To Boil Fowl.—For boiling choose those that are not black-legged. Pick them nicely, singe, wash, and truss them. Flour

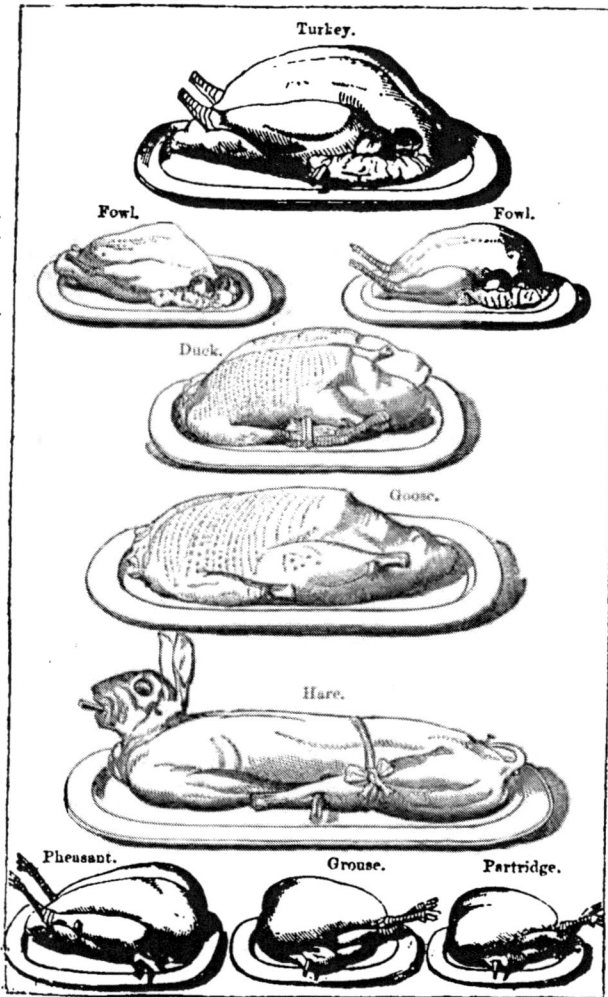

Turkey.

Fowl.                    Fowl.

Duck.

Goose.

Hare.

Pheasant.          Grouse.          Partridge.

them, and put them into boiling water.—See time of dressing,
page 72.

Serve with parsley and butter ; oyster, lemon, liver, or celery
sauce.

If for dinner, ham, tongue, or bacon, is usually served to eat
with them ; as likewise greens.

To Boil Fowl with Rice.—Stew the fowl very slowly in
some clear mutton broth well skimmed ; and seasoned with
onion, mace, pepper, and salt. About half an hour before it
is ready put in a quarter of a pint of rice well washed and
soaked. Simmer till tender ; then strain it from the broth and
put the rice on a sieve before the fire. Keep the fowl hot, lay it
in the middle of a dish, and the rice round it without the broth.
The broth will be very nice to eat as such, but the less liquor
the fowl is done with the better. Gravy, or parsley and butter
for sauce.

Fowls Roasted.—Serve with egg sauce, bread sauce, or garnished with sausages and scalded parsley.

A large barn-door fowl well hung, should be stuffed in the
crop with sausage meat, and served with gravy in the dish, and
with bread sauce.

The head should be turned under the wing, as a turkey.

Fowls Broiled.— Split them down the back ; pepper, salt, and
broil. Serve with mushroom sauce.

Another way.—Cut a large fowl into four quarters, put
them on a bird spit, and tie that on another spit, and half-
roast ; or half-roast the whole fowl, and finish either on the
gridiron, which will make it less dry than if wholly broiled.
The fowl that is not cut before roasted, must be split down the
back after.

Davenport Fowls.—Hang young fowls a night : take the
livers, hearts, and tenderest parts of the gizzards, shred very
small, with half a handful of young clary, an anchovy to each
fowl, an onion, and the yolks of four eggs boiled hard, with
pepper, salt, and mace, to your taste. Stuff the fowls with
this, and sew up the vents and necks quite close, that the
water may not get in. Boil them in salt and water till almost
done : then drain them, and put them into a stew-pan, with
butter enough to brown them. Serve them with fine melted
butter, and a spoonful of ketchup, of either sort, in the dish.

A Nice Way to Dress a Fowl for a Small Dish.—Bone,
singe, and wash a young fowl : make a forcemeat of four ounces
of veal, two ounces of scraped lean of ham, two ounces of fat
bacon, two hard yolks of eggs, a few sweet herbs chopped, two
ounces of beef suet, a tea-spoonful of lemon peel minced quite
fine, an anchovy, salt, pepper, and a very little Cayenne. Beat
all in a mortar, with a tea-cupful of crumbs, and the yolks and
whites of three eggs. Stuff the inside of the fowl, and draw the
legs and wings inwards ; tie the neck and rump close. Stew the
fowl in a white gravy : when it is done through and tender,
add a large cupful of cream, and a bit of butter and flour ;

give it one boil, and serve; the last thing, add the squeeze of a lemon.

**To Force Fowl, &c.,** is to stuff any part with forcemeat, and it is put usually between the skin and the flesh.

**To Braise,** is to put meat into a stew-pan covered with fat bacon, then add six or eight onions, a faggot of herbs, carrots if to be brown, celery, any bones, or trimmings of meat or fowls, and some stock (which you will find among Soups and Gravies). The bacon must be covered with paper, and the lid of the pan must be put down close. Set it on a slow stove, and according to what it is, it will require two or three hours. The meat is then to be taken out; and the gravy very nicely skimmed, and set on to boil very quick till it is thick. The meat is to be kept hot; and if larded, put into the oven for a few minutes; and then put the jelly over it, which is called glazing, and is used for ham, tongue, and many made dishes. White wine is added to some glazing. The glaze should be of a beautiful clear yellow brown, and it is best to put it on with a nice brush.

**Fricassee of Chickens.**—Boil rather more than half, in a small quantity of water: let them cool: then cut up; and put to simmer in a little gravy made of the liquor they were boiled in, and a bit of veal or mutton, onion, mace, and lemon-peel, some white pepper, and a bunch of sweet herbs. When quite tender, keep them hot while you thicken the sauce in the following manner :—Strain it off, and put it back into the saucepan with a little salt, a scrape of nutmeg, and a bit of flour and butter: give it one boil; and when you are going to serve, beat up the yolk of an egg, add half a pint of cream, and stir them over the fire, but do not let it boil. It will be quite as good without the egg.

The gravy may be made (without any other meat) of the necks, feet, small wing-bones, gizzards, and livers; which are called the trimmings of the fowl.

**To Pull Chickens.**—Take off the skin: and pull the flesh off the bone of a cold fowl in as large pieces as you can: dredge it with flour, and fry it of a nice brown in butter. Drain the butter from it: and then simmer the flesh in a good gravy well seasoned, and thickened with a little flour and butter. Add the juice of half a lemon.

**Another way.**—Cut off the legs, and the whole back, of a dressed chicken; if underdone the better. Pull all the white part into little flakes free from skin, toss it up with a little cream thickened with a piece of butter mixed with flour, half a blade of mace in powder, white pepper, salt, and a squeeze of lemon. Cut off the neck-end of the chicken, and broil the back and sidesmen in one piece, and the two legs seasoned. Put the hash in the middle, with the back on it; and the two legs at the end.

**Chicken Currie.**—Cut up the chicken raw, slice onions, and fry both in butter with great care, of a fine light brown; or, if you use chickens that have been dressed, fry only the onions. Lay the joints, cut into two or three pieces each, into a stew-pan, with veal or mutton gravy, and a clove or two of garlic. Simmer till the chicken is quite tender. Half an hour before you serve it, rub smooth a spoonful or two of currie-powder, a spoonful of flour, and an ounce of butter: and add this, with four large spoonfuls of cream, to the stew. Salt to your taste. When serving, squeeze in a little lemon.

Slices of underdone veal, or rabbit, turkey, &c., make excellent currie.

A dish of rice boiled dry must be served. For directions to do this, see the article Rice in the INDEX.

**Another, more easily made.**—Cut up a chicken or young rabbit: if chicken, take off the skin. Roll each piece in a mixture of a large spoonful of flour, and an ounce of currie powder. Slice two or three onions, and fry them in butter, of a light brown: then add the meat, and fry all together till the meat begins to brown. Put it all into a stew-pan, and pour boiling water enough just to cover it. Simmer very gently two or three hours. If too thick, put more water half an hour before serving.

If the meat has been dressed before, a little broth will be better than water: but the currie is richer when made of fresh meat.

**To Braise Chickens.**—Bone them, and fill them with force-meat. Lay the bones, and any other poultry trimmings, into a stew-pan, and the chickens on them. Put to them a few onions, a faggot of herbs, three blades of mace, a pint of stock, and a glass or two of sherry. Cover the chickens with slices of bacon, and then white paper; cover the whole close, and put them on a slow stove for two hours. Then take them up, strain the braise, and skim off the fat carefully : set it on to boil very quick to a glaze, and do the chickens over with it with a brush.

Serve with a brown fricassee of mushrooms. Before glazing, put the chicken into an oven for a few minutes, to give a little colour.

**Ducks Roasted.**—Serve with a fine gravy; and stuff one with sage and onion, a dessert-spoonful of crumbs, a bit of butter, and pepper and salt; let the other be unseasoned.

**To Boil Ducks.**—Choose a fine fat duck, salt it two days, then boil it slowly in a cloth. Serve it with onion sauce, but melt the butter with milk instead of water.

**To Stew Ducks.**—Half-roast a duck; put it into a stew-pan with a pint of beef gravy, a few leaves of sage and mint cut small, pepper and salt, and a small bit of onion shred as fine as possible. Simmer a quarter of an hour, and skim clean; then add near a quart of green peas. Cover close, and simmer near half an hour longer. Put in a piece of butter and a little flour, and give it one boil; then serve in one dish.

**To Hash Ducks.**—Cut a cold duck into joints, and warm it, without boiling, in gravy, and a glass of port wine.

**To Roast Goose.**—After it is picked, the plugs of the feathers pulled out, and the hairs carefully singed, let it be well washed

Pigeon (roast).

Wild Duck (roast).

Turkey (boiled).

Fowl (boiled).

Goose (boiled).

Rabbit, trussed—London mode.

Rabbit, trussed—Country mode.

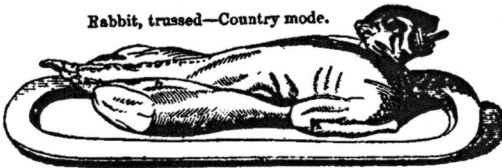

and dried, and a seasoning put in of onion, sage, and pepper and salt. Fasten it tight at the neck and rump, and then roast. Put it first at a distance from the fire, and by degrees draw it nearer. A slip of paper should be skewered on the breast-bone. Baste it very well. When the breast is rising. take off the paper, and be careful to serve it before the breast falls, or it will be spoiled by coming flatted to table. Let a good gravy be sent in the dish. Gravy and apple sauce ; gooseberry sauce for a green goose.

To Stew Giblets.—Do them as will be directed for giblet pie (under the head Pies); season them with salt and pepper and a very small piece of mace. Before serving, give them one boil with a cup of cream, and a piece of butter rubbed in a tea-spoon-ful of flour.

Pigeons may be dressed in so many ways, that they are very useful. The good flavour of them depends very much on their being cropped and drawn as soon as killed. No other bird re-quires so much washing.

Pigeons left from dinner the day before may be stewed or made into a pie ; in either case, care must be taken not to overdo them, which will make them stringy. They need only be heated up in gravy made ready, and forcemeat balls may be fried and added, instead of putting a stuffing into them. If for a pie, let beef steaks be stewed in a little water, and put cold under them, and cover each pigeon with a piece of fat bacon, to keep them moist. Season as usual, and put eggs.

To Stew Pigeons.—Take care that they are quite fresh, and carefully cropped, drawn, and washed ; then soak them half an hour. In the meantime cut a hard white cabbage in slices (as if for pickling) into water; drain it, and then boil it in milk and water; drain it again, and lay some of it at the bottom of a stew-pan. Put the pigeons upon it, but first season them well with pepper and salt, and cover them with the remainder of the cab-bage. Add a little broth, and stew gently till the pigeons are tender ; then put among them two or three spoonfuls of cream, and a piece of butter and flour for thickening. After a boil or two, serve the birds in the middle, and the cabbage placed round them.

Another way.—Stew the birds in a good brown gravy, either stuffed or not ; and seasoned high with spice and mushrooms fresh and a little ketchup.

To Broil Pigeons.—After cleaning, split the backs, pepper and salt them and broil them very nicely ; pour over them either stewed or pickled mushrooms in melted butter, and serve as hot as possible.

Roast Pigeons should be stuffed with parsley, either cut or whole, and seasoned within. Serve with parsley and butter. Peas or asparagus should be dressed to eat with them.

To Pickle Pigeons.—Bone them ; turn the inside out, and lard it. Season with a little allspice and salt, in fine powder ; then turn them again, and tie the neck and rump with thread. Put them into boiling water, let them boil a minute or two to plump take them out, and dry them well: then put them boiling hot into the pickle, which must be made of equal quantities of white wine and white-wine vinegar, with white pepper and allspice, sliced ginger and nutmeg, and two or three bay leaves. When it boils up, put the pigeons in. If they are small, a quarter of an hour will do them; but they will take twenty minutes if large. Then take them out, wipe them, and let them cool. When the pickle is cold, take the fat off from it, and put them in again. Keep them in a stone jar, tied down with a bladder to keep out the air.

Instead of larding, put into some a stuffing made of hard yolks of eggs and marrow in equal quantities, with sweet herbs, pepper, salt, and mace.

**Pigeons in Jelly.**—Save some of the liquor in which a knuckle of veal has been boiled; or boil a calf's or neat's foot; put the broth into a pan with a blade of mace, a bunch of sweet herbs, some white pepper, lemon peel, a slice of lean bacon, and the pigeons. Bake them, and let them stand to get cold. Season as you like, before baking. When done take them out of the liquor, cover them close to preserve the colour, and clear the jelly by boiling it with the whites of two eggs; strain it through a thick cloth dipped in boiling water, and put into a sieve. The fat must be perfectly removed, before it be cleared. Put the jelly over and round them rough.

**The same, a beautiful Dish.**—Pick two very nice pigeons, and make them look as well as possible by singeing, washing, and cleaning the heads well. Leave the heads and the feet on, but clip the nails close to the claws. Roast them of a very nice brown, and when done, put a little sprig of myrtle into the bill of each. Have ready a savoury jelly, as before, and with it half-fill a bowl of a size that is proper to turn down on the dish you mean it to be served in. When the jelly and the birds are cold, see that no gravy hangs to the birds, and then lay them upside down in the jelly. Before the rest of it begins to set, pour it over the birds, so as to be three inches above the feet. This should be done full twenty-four hours before serving.

This dish has a very handsome appearance in the middle range of a second course, or when served with the jelly roughed large, it makes a side or corner dish, its size being then less. The head should be kept up as if alive, by tying the neck with some thread, and the legs bent as if the pigeon sat upon them.

**To Pot Pigeons.**—Let them be quite fresh, clean them carefully, and season them with salt and pepper: lay them close in a small deep pan, for the smaller the surface and the closer they are packed, the less butter will be wanted. Cover them with butter, then with very thick paper tied down, and bake them. When cold, put them dry into pots that will hold two or three in each; and pour butter over them, using that which was baked as part. Observe that the butter should be pretty thick if they are to be kept. If pigeons were boned, and then put in an oval form into the pot, they would lie closer, and require less butter. They may be stuffed with a fine forcemeat made with veal, bacon, &c., and then they will eat excellently. If a high flavour is approved of, add mace, allspice, and a little Cayenne, before baking.

**Larks, and other Small Birds.**—Draw, and spit them on a bird-spit; tie this on another spit, and roast them. Baste gently with butter, and strew bread crumbs upon them till half-done; brown and serve with fried crumbs round.

**GAME, &c.—To Keep Game, &c.**—Game ought not to be thrown away even when it has been kept a very long time; for when it seems to be spoiled, it may often be made fit for eating by nicely cleaning and washing with vinegar and water. If there is any danger of birds not keeping, draw, crop, and pick them, then wash in two or three waters, and rub them with salt. Have ready a large saucepan of boiling water, and plunge them into it one by one, drawing them up and down by the legs, that the water may pass through them. Let them stay five or six minutes in, then hang them up in a cold place. When drained, pepper and salt the insides well Before roasting, wash them well.

The most delicate birds, even grouse, may be preserved thus. Those that live by suction cannot be done this way, as they are never drawn; and pehaps the heat might make them worse, as the water could not pass through them; but they bear being high.

Lumps of charcoal put about birds and meat will preserve them from taint, and restore what is spoiling.

**Pheasants and Partridges.**—Roast them as turkey, and serve with a fine gravy (into which put a small bit of garlic) and bread sauce. When cold, they may be made into excellent patties, but their flavour should not be overpowered by lemon. For the manner of trussing a pheasant or partridge, see page 73.

**To Pot Partridge.**—Clean them nicely; and season with mace, allspice, white pepper, and salt, in fine powder. Rub every part well; then lay the breasts downwards in a pan, and pack the birds as close as you possibly can. Put a good deal of butter on them; then cover the pan with a coarse flour-paste and a paper over, tie it close, and bake. When cold, put the birds into pots, and cover them with butter.

**A very Cheap Way of Potting Birds.**—Prepare them as directed in the last receipt; and when baked and grown cold, cut them into proper pieces for helping, pack them close in a large potting-pot, and (if possible) leave no spaces to receive the butter. Cover them with butter, and one-third part less will be wanted than when the birds are done whole. The butter that has covered potted things will serve for basting, or for paste for meat pies.

**To Clarify Butter for Potted Things.**—Put it into a sauce-boat, and set that over the fire in a stew-pan that has a little water in. When melted, take care not to pour the milky parts over the potted things: they will sink to the bottom.

**To Pot Moor Game.**—Pick, singe, and wash the birds nicely: then dry them; and season, inside and out, pretty high, with pepper, mace, nutmeg, allspice, and salt. Pack them in as small a pot as will hold them, cover them with butter, and bake in a very slow oven. When cold, take off the butter, dry them from the gravy, and put one bird into each pot, which should just fit. Add as much more butter as will cover them, but take care that it does not oil. The best way to melt it is by warming it in a basin set in a bowl of hot water.

**Grouse.**—Roast them like fowls, but the head is to be twisted under the wing. They must not be overdone. Serve with a rich gravy in the dish, and bread sauce. The sauce for wild fowl, as will be described hereafter under the head of Sauces, may be used instead of common gravy.

**To Roast Wild Fowl.**—The flavour is best preserved without stuffing. Put pepper, salt, and a piece of butter into each.

Wild fowl require much less dressing than tame; they should be served of a fine brown colour, and well frothed up. A rich brown gravy should be sent in the dish; and when the breast is cut into slices, before taking off the bone, a squeeze of lemon, with pepper and salt, is a great improvement to the flavour.

To take off the fishy taste which wild fowl sometimes have, put an onion, salt, and hot water, into the dripping-pan, and baste them for the first ten minutes with this: then take away the pan, and baste constantly with butter.

**Wild Ducks, Teale, Widgeon, Dun-Birds, &c.,** should be taken up with the gravy in. Baste them with butter, and sprinkle a little salt before they are taken up; put a good gravy under them, and serve with shalot sauce in a boat.

**Woodcocks, Snipes, and Quails** keep good several days. Roast them without drawing, and serve on toast. Butter only should be eaten with them, as gravy takes off from the fine flavour. The thigh and back are esteemed the most.

**Ruffs and Reeves** are skewered as quails: put bars of bacon over them, and roast them about ten minutes. Serve with a good gravy in the dish.

**To Dress Plovers.**—Roast the green ones in the same way as woodcocks and quails (see above), without drawing; and serve on a toast. Grey plovers may be either roasted or stewed with gravy, herbs, and spice.

**Plovers' Eggs** are a nice and fashionable dish. Boil them ten minutes, and serve either hot or cold on a napkin.

**To Roast Ortolans.**—Pick and singe, but do not draw them. Tie on a bird-spit, and roast them. Some persons like bacon in slices tied between them, but the taste of it spoils the flavour of the ortolan. Cover them with crumbs of bread.

**Guinea and Pea Fowl** eat much like pheasants. Dress them in the same way (see page 80).

**Hares,** if properly taken care of, will keep a great time; and even when the cook fancies them past eating, may be in high perfection, which if eaten when fresh killed they are not. As they are usually paunched in the field, the cook cannot prevent this; but the hare keeps longer, and eats much better, if not opened for four or five days, or according to the weather.

If paunched, as soon as a hare comes in, it should be wiped quite dry, the heart and liver taken out, and the liver scalded to keep for the stuffing. Repeat this wiping every day; mix pepper and ginger, and rub on the inside; and put a large piece of charcoal into it. Apply the spice early to prevent that musty taste which long keeping in the damp occasions, and which also affects the stuffing. An old hare should be kept as long as possible, if to be roasted. It must also be well soaked.

To Roast Hare.—After it is skinned, let it be extremely well washed, and then soaked an hour or two in water: and if old, lard it; which will make it tender, as also will letting it lie in vinegar. If, however, it is put into vinegar, it should be exceedingly well washed in water afterwards. Put a large relishing stuffing into the belly, and then sew it up. Baste it well with milk till half done, and afterwards with butter. If the blood has settled in the neck, soaking the part in warm water, and putting it to the fire warm, will remove it; especially if you also nick the skin here and there with a small knife, to let it out. The hare should be kept at a distance from the fire at first. Serve with a fine froth, rich gravy, melted butter, and currant-jelly sauce; the gravy in the dish. For stuffing use the liver, an anchovy, some fat bacon, a little suet, herbs, pepper, salt, nutmeg, a little onion, crumbs of bread, and an egg to bind it all. The ears must be nicely cleaned and singed. They are reckoned a dainty.

For the manner of trussing a hare, see page 73.

To Jug an Old Hare.—After cleaning and skinning, cut it up, and season it with pepper, salt, allspice, pounded mace, and a little nutmeg. Put it into a jar with an onion, a clove or two, a bunch of sweet herbs, a piece of coarse beef, and the carcase bones over all. Tie the jar down with a bladder and leather or strong paper; and put it into a saucepan of water up to the neck, but no higher. Keep the water boiling five hours. When it is to be served, boil the gravy up with a piece of butter and flour; and if the meat gets cold, warm it in this, but not to boil.

Broiled and Hashed Hare.—The flavour of broiled hare is particularly fine: the legs or wings must be seasoned first, rub with cold butter, and served very hot. The other parts, warmed with gravy and a little stuffing, may be served separately.

To Pot Hare, for which an old one does well, as likewise for soup and pie. After seasoning, bake it with butter. When cold take the meat from the bones, and beat it in a mortar. If not high enough, add salt, mace, pepper, and a piece of the finest fresh butter melted in a spoonful or two of the gravy that came from the hare. When well mixed put it into small pots, and cover with butter. The legs and back should be baked at the bottom of the jar, to keep them moist, and the bones be put over them.

RABBITS may be eaten various ways, as follows:—

Roasted with stuffing and gravy, like hare: or without stuffing;

with sauce of the liver and parsley chopped in melted butter, pepper and salt; or larded. For the manner of trussing a rabbit for either roasting or boiling see page 77.

Boiled and smothered with onion sauce;' the butter to be melted with milk instead of water.

Fried in joints, with dried or fried parsley. The same liver sauce, this way also.

Fricasseed, as before directed (page 75) for chickens.

In a pie, as chicken, with forcemeat, &c. In this way they are excellent when young.

Potted.

**To make a Rabbit Taste much like Hare.**—Choose one that is young, but full grown; hang it in the skin three or four days; then skin it, and lay it without washing, in a seasoning of black pepper and allspice in very fine powder, a glass of port wine, and the same quantity of vinegar. Baste it occasionally for forty hours, then stuff it and roast it as a hare, and with the same sauce. Do not wash off the liquor that it was soaked in.

**To Pot Rabbits.**—Cut up two or three young but full-grown ones, and take the leg-bones off at the thigh; pack them as close as possible in a small pan, after seasoning them with pepper, mace, Cayenne, salt, and allspice, all in very fine powder. Make the top as smooth as you can. Keep out the heads and the carcasses, but take off the meat about the neck. Put a good deal of butter, and bake the whole gently. Keep it two days in the pan, then shift it into small pots, adding butter. The livers also should be added, as they eat well.

**To Blanch Rabbit, Fowl, &c.,** is to set it on the fire in a small quantity of cold water and let it boil; as soon as it boils it is to be taken out and put into cold water for a few minutes.

---

## SOUPS AND GRAVIES.

### *General Directions respecting Soups and Gravies.*

When there is fear of the gravy-meat being spoilt before it is wanted, season well and fry it lightly, which will preserve it two days longer; but the gravy is best when the juices are fresh.

When soups or gravies are to be put by, let them be changed every day into fresh scalded pans. Whatever has vegetables boiled in it will turn sour sooner than the juices of meat. Never keep any gravy, &c., in metal.

When fat remains on any soup a cupful of flour and water, mixed quite smooth, and boiled in, will take it off.

If richness or greater consistency be wanted, a good lump of butter mixed with flour, and boiled in the soup, will give either of these qualities.

Long boiling is necessary to give the full flavour of the ingredients, therefore time should be allowed for soups and gravies ;. and they are best if made the day before they are wanted.

Soups and gravies are far better when the meat is put at the bottom of the pan and stewed, and the herbs, roots, &c., with butter, than when water is put to the meat at first; and the gravy that is drawn from the meat should be almost dried up before the water is put to it. Do not use the sediment of gravies, &c., that have stood to be cold. When onions are strong, boil a turnip with them, if for sauce; this will make them mild.

If soups or gravies are too weak, do not cover them in boiling, that the watery particles may evaporate.

A clear jelly of Cow-Heels is very useful to keep in the house, being a great improvement to soups and gravies.

Truffles and Morels thicken soups and sauces, and give them a fine flavour. Wash half an ounce of each carefully, then simmer them a few minutes in water, and add them with the liquor, to boil in the sauce, &c. till tender.

SOUPS, &c.—Scotch Mutton Broth.—Soak a neck of mutton in water for an hour; cut off the scrag, and put it into a stew-pot with two quarts of water. As soon as it boils skim it well, and then simmer it an hour and a half; then take the best end of the mutton, cut into pieces (two bones in each), take some of the fat off, and put as many as you think proper; skim the moment the fresh meat boils up, and every quarter of an hour afterwards. Have ready four or five carrots, the same number of turnips, and three onions, all cut, but not small, and put them in soon enough to get quite tender: add four large spoonfuls of Scotch barley, first wetted with cold water. The meat should stew three hours. Salt to taste, and serve all together. Twenty minutes before serving put in some chopped parsley. It is an excellent winter dish.

Veal Broth.—Stew a small knuckle in about three quarts of water, two ounces of rice, a little salt, and a blade of mace, till the liquor is half wasted away.

Colouring for Soups and Gravies.—Put four ounces of lump sugar, a gill of water, and half an ounce of the finest butter, into a small tosser, and set it over a gentle fire. Stir it with a wooden spoon till of a bright brown. Then add half a pint of water; boil, skim, and when cold bottle and cork it close. Add to soup or gravy as much of this as will give a proper colour.

A Clear Brown Stock for Gravy Soup or Gravy.— Put a knuckle of veal, a pound of lean beef, and a pound of the lean of a gammon of bacon, all sliced, into a stew-pan, with two or three scraped carrots, two onions, two turnips, two heads of celery sliced, and two quarts of water. Stew the meat quite tender, but do not let it brown. When thus prepared it will serve either for soup, or brown or white gravy; if for brown gravy put some of the above colouring, and boil a few minutes.

An excellent Soup.—Take a scrag or knuckle of veal, slices of undressed gammon of bacon, onions, mace, and a small quantity of water; simmer till very strong, and lower it with a good beef-broth made the day before, and stewed till the meat is done to rags. Add cream, vermicelli, and almonds, as will be directed in the next receipt, and a roll.

**An excellent White Soup.**—Take a scrag of mutton, a knuckle of veal after cutting off as much meat as will make collops, two or three shank-bones of mutton nicely cleaned, and a quarter of a pound of very fine undrest lean gammon of bacon, with a bunch of sweet herbs, a piece of fresh lemon peel, two or three onions, three blades of mace, and a dessert-spoonful of white pepper; boil all in three quarts of water till the meat falls quite to pieces. Next day take off the fat, clear the jelly from the sediment, and put it into a saucepan of the nicest tin. If maccaroni is used, it should be added soon enough to get perfectly tender after soaking in cold water. Vermicelli may be added after the thickening, as it requires less time to do. Have ready the thickening, which is to be made as follows:—Blanch a quarter of a pound of sweet almonds, and beat them to a paste in a marble mortar, with a spoonful of water to prevent their oiling; mince a large slice of dressed veal or chicken, and beat with it a piece of stale white bread; add all this to a pint of thick cream, a bit of fresh lemon peel, and a blade of mace, in the finest powder. Boil it a few minutes; add to it a pint of soup, and strain and pulp it through a coarse sieve; this thickening is then fit for putting to the rest, which should boil for half an hour afterwards.

**A Plainer White Soup.**—Two or three pints of soup may be made of a small knuckle of veal, with seasoning as directed in the last article; and both served together, adding a quarter of a pint of good milk. Two spoonfuls of cream and a little ground rice will give it a proper thickness.

**Giblet Soup.**—Scald and clean three or four sets of goose or duck giblets; set them to stew, with a pound or two of gravy-beef, scrag of mutton, or the bone of a knuckle of veal; an ox-tail, or some shanks of mutton; with three onions, a large bunch of sweet herbs, a tea-spoonful of white pepper, and a large spoonful of salt. Put five pints of water, and simmer till the gizzards (which must be each in four pieces) are quite tender: skim nicely, and add a quarter of a pint of cream, two tea-spoonfuls of mushroom-powder, and an ounce of butter mixed with a dessert-spoonful of flour. Let it boil a few minutes, and serve with the giblets. It may be seasoned, instead of cream, with two glasses of sherry or Madeira, a large spoonful of ketchup, and some Cayenne. When in the tureen, add salt.

**Partridge Soup.**—Take two old partridges, skin them, and cut them into pieces, with three or four slices of ham, a stick of celery, and three large onions cut into slices. Fry them all in butter till brown, but take care not to burn them. Then put them into a stew-pan with five pints of boiling water, a few peppercorns, a shank or two of mutton, and a little salt. Stew it gently two hours, then strain it through a sieve, and put it again into a stew-pan, with some stewed celery and fried bread; when it is near boiling, skim it, pour it into a tureen and serve it up hot.

**Maccaroni Soup.**—Boil a pound of the best maccaroni in a quart of good stock till quite tender; then take out half, and put it into another stew-pot. To the remainder add some more stock, and boil it till you can pulp all the maccaroni through a fine sieve; then add together the two liquors, a pint or more of cream, boiling hot, the maccaroni that was first taken out, and half a pound of grated Parmesan cheese; make it hot, but do not let it boil. Serve it with the crust of a French roll cut into the size of a shilling.

**A Pepper-pot, to be served in a Tureen.**—To three quarts of water put vegetables according to the season; in summer, peas, lettuce, and spinach; in winter, carrots, turnips, celery, and onions in both. Cut small, and stew with two pounds of neck of mutton, or a fowl and a pound of pickled pork, in three quarts of water, till quite tender.

On first boiling, skim. Half an hour before serving, add a lobster or crab, cleared from the shells. Season with salt and Cayenne. A small quantity of rice should be put in with the meat. Some people choose very small suet dumplings boiled with it. Should any fat rise, skim nicely, and put half a cup of water with a little flour.

Pepper-pot may be made of various things, and is understood to be a due proportion of fish, flesh, fowl, vegetables, and pulse.

**Turnip Soup.**—Take off a knuckle of veal all the meat that can be made into cutlets, &c., and set the remainder on to stew with an onion, a bunch of herbs, a blade of mace, and five pints of water; cover it close, and let it do on a slow fire four or five hours. Strain, and set it by till next day; then take the fat and sediment from it, and simmer it with turnips cut into small dice till tender, seasoning it with salt and pepper. Before serving, rub down half a spoonful of flour with half a pint of good cream and the size of a walnut of butter. Let a small roll simmer in the soup till wet through, and serve this with it. It should be as thick as middling cream.

**Old Peas Soup.**—Save the water of boiled pork or beef, and if too salt, put as much fresh water to it, or use fresh water entirely with roast beef bones, a ham or gammon-bone, or an anchovy or two. Simmer these with some good whole or split peas; the smaller the quantity of water at first the better. Simmer till the peas will pulp through a colander; then set the pulp, and more of the liquor that boiled the peas, with two carrots, a turnip, a leek, and a stick of celery cut into bits, to stew till all is quite tender. The last requires less time, an hour will do for it.

When ready, put fried bread cut into dice, dried mint rubbed fine, pepper, and (if wanted) salt into the tureen, and pour the soup in.

**Green Peas Soup.**—In shelling the peas, divide the old from the young; put the old ones, with an ounce of butter, a pint of water, the outside leaves of a lettuce or two, two onions, pepper and salt, to stew till you can pulp the peas; and when you have done so, put to the liquor that stewed them some more water, the hearts and tender stalks of the lettuces, the young peas, a handful of spinach cut small, and salt and pepper to relish properly, and stew till quite soft. If the soup is thin, or not rich enough, either of these faults may be removed by adding an ounce or two of butter, mixed with a spoonful of rice or wheat-flour, and boiled with it half an hour. Before serving, boil some green mint shred fine in the soup.

When there is plenty of vegetables, no meat is necessary; but if meat be preferred, a pig's foot, or ham-bone, &c., may be boiled with the old peas, which is called the stock. More butter than is mentioned above may be used with advantage, if the soup is required to be very rich.

When peas first come in or are very young, the stock may be made of the shells, washed and boiled till they will pulp with the above; more thickening will then be wanted.

**Gravy Soup.**—Wash and soak a leg of beef; break the bone, and set it on the fire with a gallon of water a large bunch of sweet herbs, two large onions sliced and fried a fine brown (but not burnt), two blades of mace, three cloves, twenty berries of allspice, and forty black peppers. Stew till the soup is as rich as you choose; then take out the meat, which will be fit for the servant's table with a little of the gravy. Next day take off the cake of fat; which will serve for basting, or for common piecrust. Have ready such vegetables as you choose to serve. Cut carrots, turnips, and celery small, and simmer till tender: some people do not like them to be sent to table, only the flavour of them. Boil vermicelli a quarter of an hour; and add to it a large spoonful of soy, and one of mushroom ketchup. A French roll should be made hot, put into the soup till moist through, and served in the tureen.

**Vegetable Soup.**—Pare and slice five or six cucumbers; and add to these the inside of as many cos-lettuces, a sprig or two of mint, two or three onions, some pepper and salt, a pint and a half of young peas, and a little parsley. Put these, with half a pound of fresh butter, into a saucepan, to stew in their own liquor, near a gentle fire, half an hour; then pour two quarts of boiling water to the vegetables, and stew them two hours; rub down a little flour into a tea-cupful of water, boil it with the rest fifteen or twenty minutes, and serve it.

**Another way.**—Peel and slice six large onions, six potatoes, six carrots, and four turnips; fry them in half a pound of butter, and pour on them four quarts of boiling water. Toast a crust of bread as brown and hard as possible, but do not burn it: put that, some celery, sweet herbs, white pepper and salt to the above; stew it all gently for four hours, then strain it through a coarse cloth: have ready sliced carrot, celery, and a little turnip, and add to your liking, and stew them tender in the soup. If approved you may add an anchovy, and a spoonful of ketchup.

**Carrot Soup.**—Put some beef-bones, with four quarts of the liquor in which a leg of mutton or beef has been boiled, two large onions, a turnip, pepper, and salt into a saucepan, and stew for three hours. Have ready six large carrots scraped and cut thin, strain the soup on them, and stew them till soft enough to pulp through a hair sieve or coarse cloth, then boil the pulp with the soup, which is to be as thick as peas-soup. Use two wooden spoons to rub the carrots through. Make the soup the day before it is to be used. Add Cayenne. Pulp only the red part of the carrot, and not the yellow.

**Onion Soup.**—Into the water that has boiled a leg or neck of mutton, put carrots, turnips, and (if you have one) a shank-bone, and simmer two hours. Strain it on six onions, first sliced and fried of a light brown; simmer three hours, skim it carefully, and serve. Put into it a little roll, or fried bread.

**Spinach Soup.**—Shred two handfuls of spinach, a turnip, two onions, one head of celery, two carrots, and a little thyme and parsley. Put all into a stew-pot, with a bit of butter the size of a walnut, and a pint of broth, or the water in which meat has been boiled; stew till the vegetables are quite tender; work them through a coarse cloth or sieve with a spoon, then to the pulp of the vegetables and liquor put a quart of fresh water, pepper and salt, and boil all together. Have ready some suet-dumplings, the size of a walnut; and before you put the soup into the tureen, put them into it. The suet must not be shred too fine; and take care that it is quite fresh.

**Scotch Leek Soup.**—Put the water that has boiled a leg of mutton into a stew-pot, with a quantity of chopped leeks, and pepper and salt; simmer them an hour; then mix some oatmeal with a little cold water quite smooth, pour it into the soup, set it on a slow part of the fire, and let it simmer gently; but take care that it does not burn to the bottom.

**Hare Soup.**—Take an old hare that is good for nothing else, cut it into pieces, and put to it a pound and a half of lean beef, two or three shank-bones of mutton well cleaned, a slice of lean bacon or ham, an onion, and a bunch of sweet herbs; pour on it two quarts of boiling water; cover the jar into which you put these, with bladder and paper, and set it in a kettle of water. Simmer till the hare is stewed to pieces; strain off the liquor and give it one boil, with an anchovy cut into pieces; and add a spoonful of soy, a little Cayenne, and salt. A few fine forcemeat-balls, fried of a good brown, should be served in the tureen.

**Ox Rump Soup.**—Two or three rumps of beef will make it stronger than a much larger quantity of meat without these, and form a very nourishing soup.

Make it like gravy soup, and give it what flavour or thickening you like.

**Hessian Soup and Ragout.**—Clean the root of a neat's tongue very nicely, and half an ox head, with salt and water, and soak them afterwards in water only. Then stew them in five or six quarts of water, till quite tender. Let the soup stand to be cold; take off the fat, which will make good paste for hot meat-pies, or will do to baste. Put to the soup a pint of split peas, or a quart of whole ones, twelve carrots, six turnips, six potatoes, six large onions, a bunch of sweet herbs, and two heads of celery,

Simmer them without the meat till the vegetables are done enough
to pulp with the peas through a sieve, and the soup will then be
about the thickness of cream.   Season it with pepper, salt, mace,
allspice, a clove or two, and a little Cayenne, all in fine powder.
If the peas are bad, the soup may not be thick enough; then boil
in it a slice of roll, and put it through the colander, or add a little
rice-flour, mixing it by degrees.

For the Ragout cut the nicest part of the head, the kernels,
and part of the fat of the root of the tongue into small thick pieces.
Rub these with some of the above seasoning as you put them into
a quart of the liquor, kept out for that purpose before the vegetables were added, flour well, and simmer them nicely till tender.
Then put a little mushroom and walnut ketchup, a little soy, a
glass of port wine, and a tea-spoonful of made mustard, and boil
all up together before served.   If for company, small eggs and
forcemeat balls.

This way furnishes an excellent soup and a ragout at a small
expense, and they are not common.   The other part will warm for
the family.

Soup a-la-Sap.—Boil half a pound of grated potatoes, a
pound of beef sliced thin, a pint of grey peas, an onion, and three
ounces of rice in six pints of water to five, strain it through a colander, then pulp the peas to it, and turn it into a saucepan again
with two heads of celery sliced.   Stew it tender, and add pepper
and salt, and when you serve add also fried bread.

Portable Soup.—Boil one or two knuckles of veal, one or two
shins of beef, and three pounds of beef in as much water only as
will cover them.   Take the marrow out of the bones, put any sort
of spice you like, and three large onions.   When the meat is done
to rags strain it off, and put it into a very cold place.   When cold,
take off the cake of fat (which will make crusts for servants' pies),
put the soup into a double-bottomed tin saucepan, and set it on a
pretty quick fire, but do not let it burn.   It must boil fast and
uncovered, and be stirred constantly, for eight hours.   Put it
into a pan and let it stand in a cold place a day; then pour it into
a round china soup-dish, and set the dish into a stew-pan of boiling water on a stove and let it boil, and be now and then stirred,
till the soup is thick and ropy, then it is done enough.   Pour it
into the little round part at the bottom of cups or basins turned
upside down to form cakes, and when cold turn them out on
flannel to dry.   Keep them in tin canisters.   When they are to
be used, melt them in boiling water, and if you wish the flavour of
herbs, or anything else, boil it first, strain off the water, and melt
the soup in it.

This is very convenient in the country, or at sea, where fresh
meat is not always at hand, as by this means a basin of soup may
be made in five minutes.

Soup Maigre.—Melt half a pound of butter into a stew-pan,
shake it round, and throw in six middling onions sliced.   Shake
the pan well for two or three minutes, then put to it five heads of
celery, two handfuls of spinach, two cabbage-lettuces cut small,

and some parsley.  Shake the pan well for ten minutes, then put
in two quarts of water, some crusts of bread, a tea-spoonful of
beaten pepper, three or four blades of mace, and if you have any
white beet leaves, add a large handful of them cut small.

Boil gently an hour.  Just before serving, beat in two yolks of
eggs and a large spoonful of vinegar.

Another.—Flour and fry a quart of green peas, four onions
sliced, the coarse stalks of celery, a carrot, a turnip, and a parsnip;
then pour on them three quarts of water.  Let it simmer till the
whole will pulp through a sieve, then boil in it the best of the
celery cut thin.

Stock for Brown or White Fish Soups.—Take a pound of
skate, four or five flounders, and two pounds of eels.  Clean them
well, and cut them into pieces: cover them with water; and season
them with mace, pepper, salt, an onion stuck with cloves, a head
of celery, two parsley-roots sliced, and a bunch of sweet herbs.
Simmer an hour and a half closely covered, and then strain it off
for use.  If for brown soup, first fry the fish brown in butter,
and then do as above.  It will not keep more than two or three
days.

Eel Soup.—Take three pounds of small eels; put to them two
quarts of water, a crust of bread, three blades of mace, some whole
pepper, an onion, and a bunch of sweet herbs; cover them close,
and stew till the fish is quite broken; then strain it off.  Toast
some bread, cut it into dice, and pour the soup on it boiling.  A
piece of carrot may be put in at first.  This soup will be as rich as
if made of meat.  A quarter of a pint of rich cream, with a
tea-spoonful of flour rubbed smooth in it, is a great improvement.

Skate Soup.—Make it of the stock for fish soup (as directed above); with an ounce of vermicelli boiled in it, a little
before it is served.  Then add half a pint of cream, beaten with
the yolks of two eggs.  Stir it near, but not on, the fire.  Serve it
with a small French roll made hot in a Dutch oven, and then
soaked in the soup an hour,

Excellent Lobster Soup.—Take the meat from the claws,
bodies, and tails, of six small lobsters: take away the brown fur,
and the bag in the head : beat the fins, chine, and small claws, in
a mortar.  Boil it very gently in two quarts of water, with the
crumb of a French roll, some white pepper, salt, two anchovies, a
large onion, sweet herbs, and a bit of lemon-peel, till you have
extracted the goodness of them all.  Strain it off.  Beat the spawn
in a mortar, with a bit of butter, a quarter of a nutmeg, and a tea-
spoonful of flour; mix it with a quart of cream.  Cut the tails
into pieces, and give them a boil up with the cream and soup.
Serve with forcemeat-balls made of the remainder of the lobster, mace, pepper, salt, a few crumbs, and an egg or two.  Let
the balls be made up with a bit of flour, and heated in the
soup.

Crawfish or Prawn Soup.—Boil six whitings, and a large
eel (or the eel and half a thornback, well cleaned), with as much

water as will cover them; skim them clean, and put in whole pepper, mace, ginger, parsley, an onion, a little thyme, and three cloves. Boil to a mash. Pick fifty crawfish, or a hundred prawns; pound the shells, and a little roll; but first boil them with a little water, vinegar, salt, and herbs: put this liquor over the shells in a sieve; then pour the other soup, clear from the sediment. Chop a lobster, and add this to it, with a quart of good beef gravy: add also the tails of the crawfish or the prawns, and some flour and butter: and season as may be liked, if not high enough.

Oyster Soup.—Take two quarts of fish stock, as directed in page 90; beat the yolks of ten hard eggs, and the hard part of two quarts of oysters, in a mortar, and add this to the stock. Simmer it all for half an hour; then strain it off, and put it and the oysters (cleared of the beards, and nicely washed) into the soup. Simmer five minutes: have ready the yolks of six raw eggs well beaten, and add them to the soup. Stir it all well one way on the side of the fire till it is thick and smooth, but do not let it boil. Serve altogether.

Oyster Mouth Soup.—Make a rich mutton broth, with two large onions, three blades of mace, and some black pepper. When strained, pour it on a hundred and fifty oysters, without the beards, and a bit of butter rolled in flour. Simmer gently a quarter of an hour, and serve.

GRAVIES.—General Directions respecting Gravies. —Gravy may be made quite as good of the skirts of beef, and the kidney, as of any other meat, prepared in the same way.

An ox kidney, or milt, makes good gravy, cut all to pieces, and prepared as other meat; and so will the shank end of mutton that has been dressed, if much be not wanted.

The shank bones of mutton are a great improvement to the richness of gravy; but first soak them well, and scour them clean.

Tarragon gives the flavour of French cookery, and in high gravies is a great improvement; but it should be added only a short time before serving.

To Dress Gravy that will keep a week.—Cut lean beef thin, put it into a frying-pan without any butter, and set it on a fire covered, but take care it does not burn; let it stay till all the gravy that comes out of the meat is dried up into it again: put as much water as will cover the meat, and let that stew away. Then put to the meat a small quantity of water, herbs, onions, spice, and a bit of lean ham; simmer till it is rich, and keep it in a cool place. Do not take off the fat till going to be used.

Clear Gravy.—Slice beef thin; broil a part of it over a very clear quick fire, just enough to give colour to the gravy, but not to dress it: put that and the raw into a very nicely tinned stew-pan, with two onions, a clove or two, whole black peppers, berries of allspice, and a bunch of sweet herbs: cover it with hot water, give it one boil, and skim it well two or three times; then cover it, and simmer till quite strong.

**Cullis, or Brown Gravy.**—Lay over the bottom of a stew-pan as much lean veal as will cover it an inch thick; then cover the veal with thin slices of undressed gammon, two or three onions, two or three bay leaves, some sweet herbs, two blades of mace, and three cloves. Cover the stew-pan, and set it over a slow fire; but when the juices come out, let the fire be a little quicker. When the meat is of a fine brown, fill the pan with good beef broth, boil and skim it, then simmer an hour; and add a little water, mixed with as much flour as will make it properly thick; boil it half an hour, and strain it. This will keep a week.

**Bechamel, or White Sauce.**—Cut lean veal into small slices, and the same quantity of lean bacon or ham; put them into a stew-pan with a good piece of butter, an onion, a blade of mace, a few mushroom buttons, a bit of thyme, and a bay leaf; fry the whole over a very slow fire, but do not brown it; thicken it with flour; then put an equal quantity of good broth, and rich cream: let it boil for half an hour, and stir it all the time; strain it through a soup-strainer.

**A Gravy without Meat.**—Put a glass of small beer, a glass of water, some pepper, salt, lemon peel grated, a bruised clove or two, and a spoonful of walnut pickle, or mushroom ketchup, into a basin. Slice an onion, flour and fry it in a piece of butter till it is brown. Then turn all the above into a small tosser with the onion, and simmer it, covered, twenty minutes. Strain it off for use, and when cold take off the fat.

**A Rich Gravy.**—Cut beef into thin slices, according to the quantity wanted; slice onions thin, and flour both; fry them of a light pale brown, but do not on any account suffer them to get black; put them into a stew-pan, pour boiling water on the browning in the frying-pan, boil it up, and pour on the meat. Put to it a bunch of parsley, thyme, and savory, a small bit of knotted marjoram, the same of tarragon, some mace, berries of allspice, whole black peppers, a clove or two, and a bit of ham, or gammon of bacon. Simmer till you have extracted all the juices of the meat; and be sure to skim the moment it boils, and often after. If for a hare, or stewed fish, anchovy should be added.

**Gravy for a Fowl, when there is no Meat to make it of.**—Wash the feet nicely, and cut them and the neck small; simmer them with a little bread browned; a slice of onion, a bit of parsley and thyme, some pepper and salt, and the liver and gizzard, in a quarter of a pint of water, till half-wasted. Take out the liver, bruise it, and strain the liquor to it. Then thicken it with flour and butter, and add a tea-spoonful of mushroom ketchup, and it will be very good.

**Veal Gravy.**—Make it as directed for Cullis as above, but leave out the spice, herbs, and flour. It should be drawn very slowly; and if for white dishes do not let the meat brown.

**Gravy to make Mutton eat like Venison.**—Pick a very stale woodcock, or snipe, cut it to pieces (but first take out the bag from the entrails), and simmer with as much unseasoned meat gravy as you will want. Strain it, and serve in the dish.

**Strong Fish Gravy.**—Skin two or three eels, or some flounders; gut and wash them very clean, cut them into small pieces, and put into a saucepan. Cover them with water, and add a little crust of bread toasted brown, two blades of mace, some whole pepper, sweet herbs, a piece of lemon peel, an anchovy or two, and a tea-spoonful of horse-raddish. Cover close and simmer; add a bit of butter and flour and boil with the above.

**Savoury Jelly, to put over Cold Pies.**—Make it of a small bare knuckle of leg or shoulder of veal, or a piece of scrag of that or mutton; or, if the pie be of fowl or rabbit, the carcasses, necks, and heads, added to any piece of meat, will be sufficient, observing to give consistence by cow-heel or shanks of mutton. Put the meat, a slice of lean ham or bacon, a faggot of different herbs, two blades of mace, an onion or two, a small bit of lemon peel, and a tea-spoonful of Jamaica pepper bruised, and the same of whole pepper, and three pints of water, in a stew-pot that shuts very close. As soon as it boils, skim it well, and let it simmer very slowly till quite strong, strain it, and when cold take off the fat with a spoon first, and then, to remove every particle of grease, lay a clean piece of cap or blotting-paper on it. When cold, if not clear, boil it a few minutes with the whites of two eggs (but do not add the sediment), and pour it through a nice sieve, with a napkin in it, which has been dipped in boiling water to prevent waste.

**Jelly to cover Cold Fish.**—Clean a maid, and put it into three quarts of water, with a calf's-foot, or cow-heel, a stick of horse-raddish, an onion, three blades of mace, some white pepper, a piece of lemon peel, and a good slice of lean gammon. Stew until it will jelly, strain it off; when cold remove every bit of fat; take it up from the sediment, and boil it with a glass of sherry, the whites of four or five eggs, and a piece of lemon. Boil without stirring, and after a few minutes set it by to stand half an hour, and strain it through a bag or sieve with a cloth in it. Cover the fish with it when cold.

---

## SAUCES, &c.

**A very good Sauce, especially to hide the bad Colour of Fowls.**—Cut the livers, slices of lemon in dice, scalded parsley and hard eggs: add salt, and mix them with butter, boil them up, and pour over the fowls.

This will do for roast rabbit.

**White Sauce for Fricassee of Fowls, Rabbits, White Meat, Fish, or Vegetables.**—It is seldom necessary to buy meat for this favourite sauce, as the proportion of that flavour is but small. The water that has boiled fowls, veal, or rabbit; or a little broth, that may be in the house; or the feet and necks of chicken; or raw or dressed veal will suffice. Stew with a little water any of these, with a bit of lemon peel, some sliced onion, some white peppercorns, a little pounded mace or nutmeg, and a bunch of sweet herbs, until the flavour be good, then strain it and add a little good cream, a piece of butter, and a little flour; salt to your taste. A squeeze of lemon may be added after the sauce is taken off the fire, shaking it well. Yolk of egg is often used in fricassee, but if you have any cream it is better, as the former is apt to curdle.

**Sauce for Wild Fowl.**—Simmer a tea-cupful of port wine, the same quantity of good meat gravy, a little shalot, a little pepper, salt, a grate of nutmeg, and a bit of mace for ten minutes; put in a bit of butter and flour, give it all one boil, and pour it through the birds. In general they are not stuffed as tame, but may be done so if liked.

**Another for the same, or for Ducks.**—Serve a rich gravy in the dish; cut the breast into slices, but do not take them off; cut a lemon, and put pepper and salt on it; then squeeze it on the breast, and pour a spoonful of gravy over before you help.

**An excellent Sauce for Carp, or Boiled Turkey.**—Rub half a pound of butter with a tea-spoonful of flour, put to it a little water, melt it, and add near a quarter of a pint of thick cream and half an anchovy chopped fine, not washed; set it over the fire, and as it boils up add a large spoonful of real India soy. If that does not give it a fine colour, put a little more. Turn it into the sauce tureen, and put some salt and half a lemon: stir it well to hinder it from curdling.

**Sauce for Fowls of any sort.**—Boil some veal gravy, pepper, salt, the juice of a Seville orange and a lemon, and a quarter as much of port wine as of gravy: pour it into the dish or a boat.

**Sauce for Cold Fowl or Partridge.**—Rub down in a mortar the yolks of two eggs boiled hard, an anchovy, two dessert spoonfuls of oil, three of vinegar, a shalot, Cayenne if approved, and a tea-spoonful of mustard. All should be pounded before the oil is added. Then strain it. Shalot-vinegar instead of shalot eats well.

**Sauce a-la-Maitre d'Hotel.**—Put a piece of butter into a saucepan with some curled parsley, some tarragon leaves, a shalot, two leaves of balm, a little salt, lemon, or a glass of verjuice, and mix the whole with a spoon until they are well incorporated, and simmer a few minutes.

**A very fine Mushroom Sauce for Fowls or Rabbits.**—Wash and pick a pint of young mushrooms, and rub them with salt to take off the tender skin. Put them into a saucepan with a little salt, some nutmeg, a blade of mace, a pint of cream, and a good piece of butter rubbed in flour. Boil them up and stir them till done; then pour it round the chickens, &c. Garnish with lemon. If you cannot get fresh mushrooms, use pickled ones done white, with a little mushroom powder with the cream, &c.

**Lemon White Sauce for Boiled Fowls.**—Put the peel of a small lemon, cut very thin, into a pint of sweet rich cream, with a sprig of lemon-thyme and ten white pepper-corns. Simmer gently till it tastes well of the lemon; then strain it, and thicken it with a quarter of a pound of butter and a dessert-spoonful of flour rubbed in it. Boil it up, then pour the juice of the lemon strained into it, stirring it well.  Dish the chickens, and then mix a little white gravy, quite hot, with the cream, but do not boil them together: add salt to your taste.

**Liver Sauce.**—Chop boiled liver of rabbits or fowls, and do it as directed for lemon-sauce (page 96), with a very little pepper and salt and some parsley.

**Egg Sauce.**—Boil the eggs hard, and cut them into small pieces; then put them to melted butter.

**Onion Sauce.**—Peel the onions and boil them tender; squeeze the water from them, then chop them and add to them butter that has been melted rich and smooth, as will be hereafter directed, but with a little good milk instead of water; boil it up once, and serve it with boiled rabbits, partridges, scrag or knuckle of veal or roast mutton.  A turnip boiled with the onions makes them milder.

**Clear Shalot Sauce.** — Put a few chopped shalots into a little gravy boiled clear, and near half as much vinegar, season with pepper and salt; boil half an hour.

**To make Parsley Sauce when no Parsley-leaves are to be had.**—Tie up a little parsley-seed in a bit of clean muslin, and boil it a few minutes in some water.  Use this water to melt the butter; and throw into it a little boiled spinach minced, to look like parsley.

**Green Sauce for Green Geese or Ducklings.**—Mix a quarter of a pint of sorrel-juice, a glass of white wine, and some scalded gooseberries.  Add sugar and a bit of butter.  Boil them up.

**Bread Sauce.**—Boil a large onion cut in four, with some black peppers and milk, till the onion is quite a pap.  Pour the milk strained on grated white stale bread, and cover it.  In an hour put it in a saucepan, with a good piece of butter mixed with a little flour: boil the whole up together, and serve.

**Dutch Sauce for Meat or Fish.**—Put six spoonfuls of water, and four of vinegar, into a saucepan, warm, and thicken it with the yolks of two eggs.  Make it quite hot, but do not boil it; squeeze in the juice of half a lemon, and strain it through a sieve.

**Sauce Robert for Rumps or Steaks.**—Put a piece of butter, the size of an egg, into a saucepan, set it over the fire, and when browning throw in a handful of sliced onions cut small; fry them brown, but do not let them burn; add half a spoonful of flour, shake the onions in it and give it another fry; then put four spoonfuls of gravy and some pepper and salt, and boil it gently ten minutes; skim off the fat, and add a tea-spoonful of made mustard, a spoonful of vinegar, and the juice of half a lemon; boil it all, and pour it round the steaks.  They should be of a fine yellow brown, and garnished with fried parsley and lemon.

**Benton Sauce for Hot and Cold Roast Beef.**—Grate, or scrape very fine, some horseradish, a little made mustard, some pounded white sugar, and four large spoonfuls of vinegar.  Serve in a saucer.

**Sauce for Fish Pies where Cream is not ordered.—** Take equal quantities of white wine not sweet, vinegar, oyster liquor and mushroom ketchup: boil them up with an anchovy; strain, and pour it through a funnel into the pie after it is baked.

**Another.**—Chop an anchovy small, and boil it up with three spoonfuls of gravy, a quarter of a pint of cream, and a bit of butter and flour.

**Tomata Sauce for Hot or Cold Meats.**—Put tomatas, when perfectly ripe, into an earthen jar, and set it in an oven, when the bread is drawn, till they are quite soft; then separate the skins from the pulp, and mix this with capsicum vinegar and a few cloves of garlic pounded, which must both be proportioned to the quantity of fruit. Add powdered ginger and salt to your taste. Some white-wine vinegar and Cayenne may be used instead of capsicum vinegar. Keep the mixture in small widemouthed bottles, well corked, and in a dry cool place.

**Apple Sauce for Goose and Roast Pork.**—Pare, core, and slice some apples; and put them in a stone jar, into a saucepan of water, or on a hot hearth. If on a hearth, let a spoonful or two of water be put in to hinder them from burning. When they are done, bruise them to a mash, and put to them a bit of butter the size of a nutmeg, and a little brown sugar. Serve it in a sauce tureen.

**The Old Currant Sauce for Venison.**—Boil an ounce of dried currants in half a pint of water a few minutes; then add a small tea-cupful of bread crumbs, six cloves, a glass of port wine, and a bit of butter. Stir it till the whole is smooth.

**Lemon Sauce.**—Cut thin slices of lemon into very small dice, and put them in melted butter; give it one boil, and pour it over boiled fowls.

**Carrier Sauce for Mutton.**—Chop six shalots fine; and boil them up with a gill of gravy, a spoonful of vinegar, some pepper and salt. Serve in a boat.

**Ham Sauce.**—When a ham is almost done with, pick all the meat clean from the bone, leaving out any rusty part; beat the meat and the bone to a mash with a rolling-pin: put it in a saucepan, with three spoonfuls of gravy; set it over a slow fire, and stir it all the time, or it will stick to the bottom. When it has been on some time, put to it a small bundle of sweet herbs, some pepper, and half a pint of beef gravy; cover it up and let it stew over a gentle fire. When it has a good flavour of the herbs, strain off the gravy. A little of this is an improvement to all gravies.

**A very Fine Fish Sauce.**—Put into a very nice tin saucepan a pint of fine port wine, a gill of mountain, half a pint of fine walnut ketchup, twelve anchovies, and the liquor that belongs to them, a gill of walnut pickle, the rind and juice of a large lemon, four or five shalots, some Cayenne to taste, three ounces of scraped horse-radish, three blades of mace, and two tea-spoonfuls of made mustard; boil it all gently, till the rawness goes off; then put

—it into small bottles for use. Cork them very close, and seal the top.

**Another.**—Chop twenty-four anchovies not washed, and ten shalots, and scrape three spoonfuls of horse-radish, with about ten blades of mace, twelve cloves, two sliced lemons, half a pint of anchovy liquor, a quart of hock, or Rhenish wine, and a pint of water; boil to a quart; then strain off; and when cold, add three large spoonfuls of walnut ketchup, and put into small bottles well corked.

**Fish Sauce without Butter.**—Simmer very gently a quarter of a pint of vinegar and half a pint of water (which must not be hard), with an onion, half a handful of horse-radish, and the following spices lightly bruised; four cloves, two blades of mace, and half a tea-spoonful of black pepper. When the onion is quite tender, chop it small with two anchovies, and set the whole on the fire to boil for a few minutes, with a spoonful of ketchup. In the meantime, have ready and well beaten the yolks of three fresh eggs; strain them, mix the liquor by degrees with them, and when well mixed, set the saucepan over a gentle fire, keeping a basin in one hand, into which toss the sauce to and fro, and shake the saucepan over the fire, that the eggs may not curdle. Do not boil them, only let the sauce be hot enough to give it the thickness of melted butter.

**Fish Sauce a-la-Craster.**—Thicken a quarter of a pound of butter with flour, and brown it; then put to it a pound of the best anchovies cut small, six blades of pounded mace, ten cloves, forty berries of black pepper and allspice, a few small onions, a faggot of herbs (namely, savoury, thyme, basil, and knotted marjoram), and a little parsley and sliced horse-radish; on these pour half a pint of the best sherry, and a pint and a half of very strong gravy. Simmer all gently for twenty minutes, then strain it through a sieve, and bottle it for use: the way of using it is, to boil some of it in the butter while melting.

**An excellent Substitute for Caper Sauce.**—Boil slowly some parsley, to let it become a bad colour, cut, but do not chop it fine; put it to melted butter, with a tea-spoonful of salt, and a dessert-spoonful of vinegar. Boil up and serve.

**Oyster Sauce.**—Save the liquor in opening the oysters; and boil it with the beards, a bit of mace and lemon peel. In the meantime throw the oysters into cold water, and drain it off. Strain the liquor, and put it into a saucepan with them, and as much butter, mixed with a little milk, as will make sauce enough; but first rub a little flour with it. Set them over the fire, and stir all the time; and when the butter has boiled once or twice, take them off, and keep the saucepan near the fire, but not on it; for if done too much, the oysters will be hard. Squeeze a little lemon juice, and serve.

If for company, a little cream is a great improvement. Observe, the oysters will thin the sauce, so put butter accordingly.

**Lobster Sauce.**—Pound the spawn, and two anchovies: pour on them two spoonfuls of gravy: strain all into some

G

butter melted as will be hereafter directed; then put in the meat of the lobster, give it all one boil, and add a squeeze of lemon.

**Another way.**—Leave out the anchovies and gravy; and do it as above, either with or without a little salt and ketchup, as you like. Many prefer the flavour of the lobster and salt only.

**Shrimp Sauce.**—If the shrimps are not picked at home, pour a little water over them to wash them; put them to butter melted thick and smooth, give them one boil and add the juice of a lemon.

**Anchovy Sauce.**—Chop two anchovies without washing, put them to some flour and butter, and a little drop of water; stir it over the fire till it boils once or twice. When the anchovies are good, they will be dissolved; and the colour will be better than by the usual way.

**To Melt Butter, which is rarely well done, though a very essential article.**—Mix in the proportion of a teaspoonful of flour to four ounces of the best butter, on a trencher. Put it into a small saucepan, and two or three table-spoonfuls of hot water, boil quick a minute, shaking it all the time. Milk used instead of water, requires rather less butter, and looks whiter.

**Vingaret, for Cold Fowl or Meat.**—Chop mint, parsley, and shalot, and mix with salt, oil, and vinegar. Serve in a boat.

**Shalot Vinegar.**—Split six or eight shalots; put them into a quart bottle, and fill it up with vinegar, stop it, and in a month it will be fit for use.

**Camp Vinegar.**—Slice a large head of garlic; and put it into a wide-mouthed bottle with half an ounce of Cayenne, two teaspoonfuls of real soy, two of walnut ketchup, four anchovies chopped, a pint of vinegar, and enough cochineal to give it the colour of lavender drops. Let it stand six weeks: then strain off quite clear, and keep in small bottles sealed up.

**Sugar Vinegar.**—To every gallon of water put two pounds of the very coarsest sugar, boil and skim thoroughly, then put one quart of cold water for every gallon of hot. When cool, put into it a toast spread with yeast. Stir it nine days; then barrel, and set in a place where the sun will lie on it, with a bit of slate on the bung-hole. Make it in March, it will be ready in six months.

When sufficiently sour, it may be bottled, or may be used from the cask with a wooden spigot and faucet.

**Gooseberry Vinegar.**—Boil spring water; and when cold, put to every three quarts, a quart of bruised gooseberries in a large tub. Let them remain sixty hours, stirring often, then strain through a hair bag, and to each gallon of liquor, add a pound of the coarsest sugar. Put it into a barrel, and a toast and yeast: cover the bung-hole with a bit of slate, &c., as above. The greater quantity of sugar and fruit the stronger the vinegar.

**Cucumber Vinegar.**—Pare and slice fifteen large cucumbers and put them in a stone jar, with three pints of vinegar, four onions sliced, two or three shalots, a little garlic, two large spoonfuls of salt, three tea-spoonfuls of pepper, and half a tea-spoon-ful of Cayenne. After standing four days, give the whole a boil; when cold, strain and filter the liquor through paper. Keep in small bottles to add to salad, or eat with meat.

**Wine Vinegar.**—After making raisin wine, when the fruit has been strained, lay it on a heap to heat, then to every hundred weight put fifteen gallons of water—set the cask, and put yeast, &c., as before.

As vinegar is so necessary an article in a family, and one on which so great a profit is made, a barrel or two might always be kept preparing, according to what suited. If the raisins of wine were ready, that kind might be made; if a great plenty of goose-berries made them cheap, that sort; or if neither, then the sugar vinegar—so that the cask may not be left empty, and grow musty.

**Nasturtiums for Capers.**—Keep them a few days after they are gathered, then pour boiling vinegar over them, and when cold, cover. They will not be fit to eat for some months, but are then finely flavoured, and by many preferred to capers.

**To make Mustard.**—Mix the best Durham flour of mustard with boiling water till of a proper thickness, rubbing it perfectly smooth; add a little salt, and keep it in a small jar, close covered, and put only as much into the glass as will be used soon, which should be wiped daily round the edges.

**Another way, for immediate use.**—Mix the mustard with new milk by degrees, to be quite smooth, and add a little raw cream. It is much softer this way, is not bitter, and will keep well.

The patent mustard is by many preferred, and it is perhaps as cheap, being always ready; and if the pots are returned, three-pence is allowed for each.

A tea-spoonful of sugar to half a pint of mustard is a great im-provement, and softens it.

**Kitchen Pepper.**—Mix in the finest powder one ounce of gin-ger; of cinnamon, black pepper, nutmeg, and Jamaica pepper, half an ounce each; ten cloves, and six ounces of salt. Keep it in a bottle; it is an agreeable addition to any brown sauces or soups.

Spice in powder, kept in small bottles close stopped, goes much further than when used whole. It must be dried before pounded, and should be done in quantities that may be wanted in three or four months. Nutmeg need not be done, but the others should be kept in separate bottles with a little label on each.

**To Dry Mushrooms.**—Wipe them clean, and of the large take the brown, and peel off the skin. Lay them on paper to dry in a cool oven, and keep them in paper bags in a dry place. When used simmer them in the gravy, and they will swell to near their former size: to simmer them in their own liquor till it dry up into them, shaking the pan, then drying on tin plates, is a good way, with spice or not, as above, before made into powder.

Tie down with bladder, and keep in a dry place, or in paper.

**Mushroom Powder.**—Wash half a peck of large mushrooms

while quite fresh, and free from grit and dirt with flannel: scrape out the black part clean, and do not use any that are worm-eaten; put them into a stew-pan over the fire without water, with two large onions, some cloves, a quarter of an ounce of mace, and two spoonfuls of white pepper, all in powder; simmer and shake them till all the liquor be dried up, but be careful they do not burn. Lay them on tins or sieves in a slow oven till they are dry enough to beat to powder, then put the powder in small bottles, corked and tied closely, and keep in a dry place. A tea-spoonful will give a very fine flavour to any soup or gravy, or any sauce; and it is to be added just before serving, and one boil given to it after it is put in.

**To Choose Anchovies.**— They are preserved in barrels, with bay salt: no other fish has the fine flavour of the anchovy. The best look red and mellow, and the bones moist and oily; the flesh should be high flavoured, the liquor reddish, and have a fine smell.

**Essence of Anchovies.**—Take two dozen of anchovies, chop them, and take out the bone, but with some of their own liquor strained, add them to sixteen large spoonfuls of water; boil gently till dissolved, which will be in a few minutes; when cold, strain and bottle it.

**To Keep Anchovies when the Liquor Dries.**—Pour on them beef brine.

**To Make Sprats Taste like Anchovies.**—Salt them well, and let the salt drain from them. In twenty-four hours wipe them dry, but do not wash them. Mix four ounces of common salt, an ounce of bay salt, an ounce of saltpetre, a quarter of an ounce of sal prunel, and half a tea-spoonful of cochineal, all in the finest powder. Sprinkle it among three quarts of the fish, and pack them in two stone jars. Keep in a cold place fastened down with a bladder.

These are pleasant on bread and butter; but use the best for sauce.

**Forcemeat to Force Fowls or Meat.**—Shred a little ham, or gammon, some cold veal, or fowl, some beef-suet, a small quantity of onion, some parsley, a very little lemon-peel, salt, nutmeg, or pounded mace, and either white pepper or Cayenne, and bread crumbs.

Pound it in a mortar, and bind it with one or two eggs beaten and strained. For forcemeat patties, the mixture as above.

**Forcemeat,** whether in the form of stuffingballs, or for patties, makes a considerable part of good cooking, by the flavour it imparts to whatsoever dish it is added, if properly made.

Exact rules for the quantity cannot easily be given; but the following observations may be useful, and habit will soon give knowledge in mixing it to the taste.

At many tables where everything else is well done, it is common to find very bad stuffing.

According to what it is wanted for, should be the selection from the following list, observing that of the most pungent articles, least must be used. No one flavour should predominate greatly;

yet, if several dishes be served the same day, there should be a marked variety in the taste of the forcemeat, as well as of the gravies. It should be consistent enough to cut with a knife, but not dry and heavy.

### Forcemeat Ingredients.—

| | |
|---|---|
| Cold fowl or veal. | Oysters, |
| Scraped ham. | Anchovy. |
| Fat bacon. | Tarragon. |
| Beef-suet. | Savoury. |
| Crumbs of bread. | Pennyroyal. |
| Parsley. | Knotted Marjoram. |
| White pepper. | Thyme. |
| Salt. | Basil. |
| Nutmeg. | Yolks of hard eggs |
| Yolk and white of eggs well beaten, to bind the mixture. | Cayenne. |
| | Garlic. |
| | Shalot. |
| | Chives. |
| | Jamaica pepper, in fine powder, or two or three cloves. |

The first column contains the articles of which the forcemeat may be made, without any striking flavour; and to those, may be added some of the different ingredients of the second column, to vary the taste.

**For Cold Savoury Pies.**—The same: only substituting fat, or bacon, for suet. The livers (if the pie be of rabbit or fowls) mixed with fat and lean pork, instead of bacon, and seasoned as above, are excellent.

For HARE, see to roast, page 82.
Ditto, for baked PIKE, page 29.
Ditto, for PIKE, HADDOCK, and small COD, page 29.
Ditto, for SOLES, page 29.
Ditto, for MACKEREL, page 28.
Ditto, for FISH PIE, page 103.

**Very fine Forcemeat Balls, for Fish Soups, or Fish Stewed, on Maigre Days.**—Beat the flesh and soft parts of a middling lobster, half an anchovy, a large piece of boiled celery, the yolk of a hard egg, a little Cayenne, mace, salt, and white pepper, with two table-spoonfuls of bread crumbs, one ditto of oyster liquor, two ounces of butter warmed, and two eggs long beaten: make into balls, and fry of a fine brown in butter.

**Forcemeat as for Turtle, at the Bush, Bristol.**—A pound of fresh suet, one ounce of ready dressed veal or chicken, chopped fine, bread crumbs, a little shalot or onion, salt, white pepper, nutmeg, mace, pennyroyal, parsley, and lemon thyme finely shred; beat as many fresh eggs, yolks and whites separately, as will make the above ingredients into a moist paste: roll into small balls, and boil them in fresh lard, putting them in just as it boils up. When of a light brown, take them out, and drain them before the fire. If the suet be moist or stale, a great many more eggs will be necessary.

Balls made this way are remarkably light; but being greasy, some people prefer them with less suet and eggs.

**Little Eggs for Turtle.**—Beat three hard yolks of eggs in a mortar, and make into a paste with the yolk of a raw one, roll it into small balls, and throw them into boiling water for two minutes to harden.

**Browning, to Colour and Flavour Made Dishes.**—Beat to powder four ounces of double-refined sugar, put it into a very nice iron frying-pan, with one ounce of fine fresh butter, mix it well over a clear fire, and when it begins to froth, hold it up higher; when of a very fine dark brown, pour in a small quantity of a pint of port, and the whole by very slow degrees, stirring all the time, Put to the above half an ounce of Jamaica, and the same of black pepper, six cloves of shalots peeled, three blades of mace bruised, three spoonfuls of mushroom, and the same of walnut ketchup, some salt, and the finely pared rind of a lemon; boil gently fifteen minutes, pour it into a basin till cold, take off the scum, and bottle for use.

**Casserol, or Rice, Edging for a Currie, or Fricassee.**—After soaking and picking fine Carolina rice, boil it in water, nd a little salt, until tender, but not to a mash; drain, and put it round the inner edge of the dish, to the height of two inches; smooth it with the back of a spoon, and wash it over with yolk of egg, and put it into the oven for three or four minutes, then serve the meat in the middle.

---

# PIES, PUDDINGS, AND PASTRY.

## SAVOURY PIES.

### (FRUIT PIES WILL BE PLACED UNDER THE HEAD PASTRY.)

*Observations on Savoury Pies.*

THERE are few articles of cookery more generally liked than relishing pies, if properly made; and they may be made so of a great variety of things. Some are best eaten when cold, and, in that case, there should be no suet put into the forcemeat that is used with them. If the pie is either made of meat that will take more dressing, to make it extremely tender, than the baking of the crust will allow; or if it is to be served in an earthen pie-form; observe the following preparation:—

Take three pounds of the veiny piece of beef (for instance) that has fat and lean; wash it, and season it with salt, pepper, mace, and allspice, in fine powder, rubbing them well in. Set it by the side of a slow fire, in a stew-pot that will just hold it; put to it a piece of butter, about two ounces, and cover it quite close; let it just simmer in its own steam till it begins to shrink. When it is cold add more seasoning, forcemeat, and eggs: and if it is in a dish, put some gravy to it before baking; but if it is only in crust, do not put the gravy till after it is cold and in jelly, as has been described in page 93. Forcemeat may be put both under and over the meat, if preferred to balls.

**Eel Pie.**—Cut the eels in lengths of two or three inches, season with pepper, and salt, and place in a dish, with some bits of butter, and a little water; and cover it with paste.

**Cod Pie.**—Take a piece of the middle of a small cod, and salt it well one night: next day wash it; season with pepper, salt, and a very little nutmeg, mixed; place in a dish, and put some butter on it, and a little good broth of any kind into the dish.

Cover it with a crust; and when done, add a sauce of a spoonful of broth, a quarter of a pint of cream, a little flour and butter, a grate of lemon and nutmeg, and give it one boil. Oysters may be added.

**Mackerel** will do well, but do not salt them till used.

Parsley picked and put in, may be used instead of oysters.

**Sole Pie.**—Split some soles from the bones, and cut the fins close; season with a mixture of salt, pepper, a little nutmeg and pounded mace, and put them in layers, with oysters. They eat excellently. A pair of middling-sized ones will do, and half a hundred of oysters. Put in the dish the oyster liquor, two or three spoonfuls of broth, and some butter. When the pie comes home, pour in a cupful of thick cream.

**Shrimp Pie, excellent.**—Pick a quart of shrimps; if they are very salt, season them with only mace and a clove or two. Mince two or three anchovies; mix these with the spice, and then season the shrimps. Put some butter at the bottom of the dish, and cover the shrimps with a glass of sharp white wine. The paste must be light and thin. They do not take long baking.

**Lobster Pie.**—Boil two lobsters, or three small, take out the tails, cut them in two, take out the gut, cut each in four pieces, and lay in a small dish, then put in the meat of the claws and that you have picked out of the body; pick off the furry parts from the latter, and take out the lady; the spawn, beat in a mortar: likewise all the shells: set them on to stew with some water, two or three spoonfuls of vinegar, pepper, salt, and some pounded mace: a large piece of butter, rolled in flour, must be added when the goodness of the shells is obtained; give a boil or two, and pour into the dish strained; strew some crumbs, and put a paste over all; bake slowly, but only till the paste be done.

**A remarkably fine Fish Pie.**—Boil two pounds of small eels; having cut the fins quite close, pick the flesh off, and throw the bones into the liquor, with a little mace, pepper, salt, and a slice of onion; boil till quite rich, and strain it. Make forcemeat of the flesh, an anchovy, parsley, lemon peel, salt, pepper, and crumbs, and four ounces of butter warmed, and lay it at the bottom of the dish. Take the flesh of soles, small cod, or dressed turbot, and lay them on the forcemeat, having rubbed it with salt and pepper; pour the gravy over and bake.

Observe to take off the skin and fins, if cod or soles.

**Pilchard and Leek Pie.**—Clean and skin the white part of some large leeks; scald in milk and water, and put them in layers into a dish, and between the layers, two or three salted pilchards, which have been soaked for some hours the day before. Cover the whole with a good plain crust. When the pie is taken out of the oven, lift up the side crust with a knife, and empty out all the liquor; then pour in half a pint of scalded cream.

**Beef Steak Pie.**—Prepare the steaks as in page 44, and when seasoned and rolled with fat in each, put them in a dish with puff paste round the edges; put a little water in the dish, and cover it with a good crust.

**Veal Pie.**—Take some of the middle, or scrag, of a small neck; season it; and either put to it, or not, a few slices of lean bacon or ham. If it is wanted of a high relish, add mace, Cayenne, and nutmeg, to the salt and pepper; and also forcemeat and eggs: and if you choose, add truffles, morels, mushrooms, sweetbreads cut into small bits, and cock's-combs blanched, if liked. Have a rich gravy ready to pour in after baking. It will be very good without any of the latter additions.

**A Rich Veal Pie.**—Cut steaks from a neck or breast of veal; season them with pepper, salt, nutmeg, and a very little clove in powder. Slice two sweetbreads, and season them in the same manner. Lay a puff paste on the ledge of the dish; then put the meat, yolks of hard eggs, the sweetbreads, and some oysters, up to the top of the dish. Lay over the whole some very thin slices of ham, and fill the dish with water; cover, and when it is taken out of the oven, pour in at the top, through a funnel, a few spoonfuls of good veal gravy, and some cream to fill up; but first boil it up with a tea-spoonful of flour. Truffles, &c. if approved.

**Veal (or Chicken) and Parsley Pie.**—Cut some slices from the leg or neck of veal; if the leg, from about the knuckle. Season them with salt: scald some parsley that is picked from the stems, and squeeze it dry; cut it a little, and lay it at the bottom of the dish; then put the meat, and so on, in layers. Fill the dish with new milk, but not so high as to touch the crust. Cover it, and when baked, pour out a little of the milk, and put in a pint of good scalded cream. Chicken may be cut up skinned, and made in the same way.

**Veal Olive Pie.**—Make the olives as directed in page 53; put them round and round in the dish, making the middle highest. Fill it up almost with water, and cover it. Add gravy, cream, and flour.

**Calf's Head Pie.**—Stew a knuckle of veal till fit for eating with two onions, a few isinglass shavings, a bunch of herbs, a blade of mace, and a few pepper-corns, in three pints of water. Keep the broth for the pie. Take off a bit of the meat for the balls, and let the other be eaten, but simmer the bones in the broth till it is very good. Half boil the head, and cut it in square bits; put a layer of ham at the bottom; then some head, first fat then lean, with balls and hard eggs cut in half, and so on till the dish be full; but be particularly careful not to place the pieces close, or the pie will be too solid, and there will be no space for jelly. The meat must be first pretty well seasoned with pepper and salt, and a scrape or two of nutmeg. Put a little water and a little gravy into the dish, and cover it with a tolerable thick crust; bake it in a slow oven, and when done, pour into it as much gravy as it can possibly hold, and do not cut it till perfectly cold; in doing which, observe to use a very sharp knife, and first cut out a large bit, going down to the bottom of the dish; and when done thus, thinner slices can be cut: the different colours, and the clear jelly, have a beautiful marbled appearance.

A small pie may be made to eat hot, which with high seasoning, oysters, mushrooms, truffles, morels, &c., has a very good appearance.

The cold pie will keep many days. Slices make a pretty side-dish.

Instead of isinglass, use a calf's foot, or a cow-heel, if the jelly is not likely to be stiff enough.

The pickled tongues of former calves' heads may be put in to vary the colour, instead of, or besides ham.

**Excellent Pork Pies, to eat Cold.**—Raise common boiled crust into either a round or oval form, as you choose: have ready the trimming and small bits of pork cut off when a hog is killed; and if these are not enough, take the meat off a sweet bone. Beat it well with a rolling-pin; season with pepper and salt, and keep the fat and lean separate. Put in layers quite close up to the top: lay on the lid: cut the edge smooth round, and pinch it; bake in a slow soaking oven, as the meat is very solid. Directions for raising the crust will be given hereafter. The pork may be put into a common dish, with a very plain crust, and be quite as good. Observe to put no bone or water into pork pie; the outside of the pieces will be hard, unless they are cut small and pressed close.

**Mutton Pie.**—Cut steaks from a loin or neck of mutton that has hung; beat them, and remove some of the fat. Season with salt, pepper, and a little onion; put a little water at the bottom of the dish, and a little paste at the edge; then cover with a moderately thick paste. Or raise small pies, and breaking each bone in two to shorten it, season, and cover it over, pinching the edge. When they come out, pour into each a spoonful of gravy made of a bit of mutton.

**Squab Pie.**—Cut apples as for other pies, and lay them in rows with mutton chops: shred onion, and sprinkle it among them, and also some sugar.

**Lamb Pie.**—Make it of the loin, neck, or breast; the breast of house lamb is one of the most delicate things that can be eaten. It should be very lightly seasoned with pepper and salt; the bone taken out, but not the gristles; and a small quantity of jelly gravy be put in hot; but the pie should not be cut till cold. Put two spoonfuls of water before baking.

Grass lamb makes an excellent pie, and may either be boned or not, but not to bone it is perhaps the best. Season with only pepper and salt; put two spoonfuls of water before baking, and as much gravy when it comes from the oven.

*Note.*—Meat pies being fat, it is best to let out the gravy on one side, and put in again by a funnel, at the centre, and a little may be added.

Chicken Pie.—Cut up two young fowls; season with white pepper, salt, a little mace, and nutmeg, all in the finest powder; likewise a little Cayenne. Put the chicken, slices of ham, or fresh gammon of bacon, forcemeat balls, and hard eggs, by turns in layers. If it is to be baked in a dish, put a little water; but none if in a raised crust. By the time it returns from the oven, have ready a gravy of knuckle of veal, or a bit of the scrag with some shank-bones of mutton, seasoned with herbs, onion, mace, and white pepper. If it is to be eaten hot, you may add truffles, morels, mushrooms, &c., but not if to be eaten cold. If it is made in a dish, put as much gravy as will fill it; but, in a raised crust, the gravy must be nicely strained, and then put in cold as jelly. To make the jelly clear, you may give it a boil with the whites of two eggs, after taking away the meat, and then run it through a fine lawn sieve.

Rabbits, if young and in flesh, do as well: their legs should be cut short, and the breast bones must not go in, but will help to make the gravy.

Green Goose Pie.—Bone two young green geese, of a good size; but first take away every plug, and singe them nicely. Wash them clean; and season them high with salt, pepper, mace, and allspice. Put one inside the other; and press them as close as you can, drawing the legs inwards. Put a good deal of butter over them, and bake them either with or without crust; if the latter, a cover to the dish must fit close to keep in the steam. It will keep long.

Duck Pie.—Bone a full-grown young duck and a fowl; wash them and season with pepper and salt, and a small proportion of mace and allspice, in the finest powder. Put the fowl within the duck, and in the former a calf's tongue pickled red, boiled very tender and peeled. Press the whole close; the skins of the legs should be drawn inwards, that the body of the fowls may be quite smooth. If approved, the space between the sides of the crust may be filled with a fine forcemeat made according to the second receipt given for making forcemeat in page 100. Bake it in a slow oven, either in a raised crust, or pie-dish with a thick crust, ornamented.

The large pies in Staffordshire are made as above: but with a goose outwards, then a turkey, a duck next, then a fowl; and either tongue, small birds, or forcemeat in the middle.

Giblet Pie.—After very nicely cleaning goose or duck giblets, stew them with a small quantity of water, onion, black pepper, and a bunch of sweet herbs, till nearly done. Let them grow cold; and if not enough to fill the dish, lay a beef, veal, or two or three mutton steaks, at bottom. Put the liquor of the stew to bake with the above; and when the pie is baked pour into it a large tea-ful of cream. Sliced potatoes added to it eat extremely well,

**Pigeon Pie.**—Rub the pigeons with pepper and salt, inside and out; in the latter put a little butter, and, if approved, some parsley chopped with the livers, and a little of the same seasoning. Lay a beef steak at the bottom of the dish, and the birds on it; between every two, a hard egg. Put a cup of water in the dish; and if you have any ham in the house, lay a bit on each pigeon; it is a great improvement to the flavour.

Observe, when ham is cut for gravy or pies, to take the under part rather than the prime.

Season the gizzards, and two joints of the wings, and put them in the centre of the pie; and over them, in a hole made in the crust, three feet nicely cleaned, to show what pie it is.

**Partridge Pie in a Dish.**—Pick and singe four partridges; cut off the legs at the knee; season with pepper, salt, chopped parsley, thyme, and mushrooms. Lay a veal steak, and a slice of ham at the bottom of the dish; put the partridges in, and half a pint of good broth. Put puff paste on the ledge of the dish, and cover with the same; brush it over with egg, and bake an hour.

**Hare Pie, to Eat Cold.**—Season the hare after it is cut up; and bake it, with eggs and forcemeat, in a raised crust or dish. When it is to be served, cut off the lid, and cover it with jelly-gravy, as in page 93.

**A French Pie.**—Lay a puff paste round on the ledge of the dish, and put in either veal in slices, rabbits, or chickens jointed, with forcemeat balls, sweetbreads cut in pieces, artichoke bottoms, and a few truffles.

**Vegetable Pie.**—Scald and blanch some broad beans; cut carrots, turnips, artichoke bottoms, mushrooms, peas, onions, lettuce, parsley, celery, or any of them you have; make the whole into a nice stew, with some good veal gravy. Bake a crust over a dish, with a little lining round the edge, and a cup turned up to keep it from sinking. When baked, open the lid and pour in the stew.

**Parsley Pie.**—Lay a fowl, or a few bones of the scrag of veal, seasoned, into a dish; scald a colander-full of picked parsley in milk; season it; and add it to the fowl or meat, with a tea-cupful of any sort of good broth, or weak gravy. When it is baked, pour into it a quarter of a pint of cream scalded, with the size of a walnut of butter and a bit of flour. Shake it round, to mix with the gravy already in.

Lettuces, white mustard leaves, or spinach, may be added to the parsley, and scalded before put in.

**Turnip Pie.**—Season mutton chops with salt and pepper, reserving the end of the neck bones to lay over the turnips, which must be cut into small dice, and put on the steaks.

Put two or three good spoonfuls of milk in. You may add sliced onions. Cover with a crust.

**Potatoe Pie.**—Skin some potatoes, and cut them into slices; season them; and also some mutton, beef, pork, or veal. Put layers of them and of the meat.

**An Herb Pie.**—Pick two handfuls of parsley from the stems, half the quantity of spinach, two lettuces, some mustard and cress, a few leaves of borage, and white beet leaves ; wash, and boil them a little ; then drain, and press out the water ; cut them small : mix, and lay them in a dish, sprinkled with some salt.  Mix a batter of flour, two eggs well beaten, a pint of cream, and half a pint of milk, and pour it on the herbs ; cover with a good crust and bake.

**Raised Crust for Meat Pies or Fowls, &c.**—Boil water with a little fine lard, an equal quantity of fresh dripping, or of butter, but not much of either.  While hot, mix this with as much flour as you will want, making the paste as stiff as you can to be smooth, which you will make it by good kneading and beating it with the rolling-pin.  When quite smooth, put a lump into a cloth, or under a pan, to soak till near cold.

Those who have not a good hand at raising crust may do thus : Roll the paste of a proper thickness, and cut out the top and bottom of the pie, then a long piece for the sides.  Cement the bottom to the sides with egg, bringing the former rather farther out, and pinching both together ; put egg between the edges of the paste, to make it adhere at the sides.  Fill your pie, and put on the cover, and pinch it and the side crust together.  The same mode of uniting the paste is to be observed if the sides are pressed into a tin form, in which the paste must be baked, after it shall be filled and covered ; but in the latter case the tin should be buttered, and carefully taken off when done enough ; and as the form usually makes the sides of a lighter colour than is proper, the paste should be put into the oven again for a quarter of an hour.  With a feather, put egg over at first.

**PUDDINGS, &c.**—Observations on making Puddings and Pancakes.—The outside of a boiled pudding often tastes disagreeably, which arises from the cloth not being nicely washed, and kept in a dry place.  It should be dipped in boiling water, squeezed dry, and floured when to be used.

If bread, it should be tied loose ; if batter, tight over.

The water should boil quick when the pudding is put in ; and it should be moved about for a minute, lest the ingredients should not mix.

Batter pudding should be strained through a coarse sieve, when all is mixed.  In others the eggs separately.

The pans and basins must be always buttered.

A pan of cold water should be ready and the pudding dipt in as soon as it comes out of the pot, and then it will not adhere to the cloth.

Very good puddings may be made without eggs ; but they must have as little milk as will mix, and must boil three or four hours. A few spoonfuls of fresh small beer, or one of yeast, will answer instead of eggs.

Or snow is an excellent substitute for eggs, either in puddings or pancakes.  Two large spoonfuls will supply the place of one egg, and the article it is used in will be equally good.  This is a ful piece of information, especially as snow often falls at the season when eggs are dearest. Fresh small beer, or bottled malt liquors, likewise serve instead of eggs. The snow may be taken up from any clean spot before it is wanted, and will not lose its virtue, though the sooner it is used the better.

· *Note.*—The yolks and whites beaten separately, make the articles they are put into much lighter.

**Almond Puddings.**—Beat half a pound of sweet and a few bitter almonds with a spoonful of water; then mix four ounces of butter, four eggs, two spoonfuls of cream, warm with the butter, one of brandy, a little nutmeg, and sugar to taste. Butter some cups, half fill, and bake the puddings.

Serve with butter, wine, and sugar.

**Baked Almond Pudding.**—Beat fine four ounces of almonds, four or five bitter ditto, with a little wine, the yolks of six eggs, peel of two lemons grated, six ounces of butter, near a quart of cream, and juice of one lemon. When well mixed, bake it half an hour, with paste round the dish.

**Small Almond Pudding.**—Pound eight ounces of almonds, and a few bitter, with a spoonful of water; mixed with four ounces of butter warmed, four yolks and two whites of eggs; sugar to taste; two spoonfuls of cream, and one of brandy; mix well, and bake in little cups buttered. Serve with pudding-sauce.

**Sago Pudding.**—Boil a pint and a half of new milk with four spoonfuls of sago nicely washed and picked, lemon peel, cinnamon, and nutmeg; sweeten to taste, then mix four eggs, put a paste round the dish and bake slowly.

**Bread and Butter Pudding.**—Slice bread spread with butter, and lay it in a dish with currants between each layer, and sliced citron, orange, or lemon, if to be very nice. Pour over an unboiled custard of milk, two or three eggs, a few pimentos, and a very little ratafia, two hours at least before it is to be baked, and lade it over to soak the bread.

A paste round the edge makes all puddings look better, but it is not necessary.

**Orange Pudding.**—Grate the rind of a Seville orange, put to it six ounces of fresh butter, six or eight ounces of lump sugar pounded; beat them all in a marble mortar, and add as you do it the whole of eight eggs well beaten and strained; scrape a raw apple and mix with the rest; put a paste at the bottom and sides of the dish, and over the orange mixture put cross bars of paste. Half an hour will bake it.

**Another.**—Mix two spoonfuls of orange paste with four of sugar, six eggs, four ounces of butter warm, and put into a shallow dish with a paste lining. Bake twenty minutes.

**An excellent Lemon Pudding.**—Beat the yolks of four eggs; add four ounces of white sugar, the rind of a lemon being rubbed with some lumps of it to take the essence; then peel, and beat it in a mortar with the juice of a large lemon, and mix all with four or five ounces of butter warmed. Put a crust into a shallow dish, nick the edges, and put the above into it. When served, turn the pudding out of the dish.

**A very fine Amber Pudding.**—Put a pound of butter into a saucepan, with three quarters of a pound of loaf sugar finely powdered: melt the butter, and mix well with it; then add the yolks of fifteen eggs well beaten, and as much fresh candied orange as will add colour and flavour to it, being first beaten to a fine paste. Line the dish with paste for turning out; and when well filled with the above, lay a crust over, as you would a pie, and bake in a slow oven.

It is as good cold as hot.

**Baked Apple Pudding.**—Pare and quarter four large apples, boil them tender with the rind of a lemon, in so little water that, when done, none may remain; beat them quite fine in a mortar, and add the crumb of a small roll, four ounces of butter melted, the yolks of five and whites of three eggs, juice of half a lemon, and sugar to taste; beat all together, and lay it in a dish with paste to turn out.

**Oatmeal Pudding.**—Pour a quart of boiling milk over a pint of the best fine oatmeal; let it soak all night; next day beat two eggs, and mix a little salt; butter a basin that will just hold it: cover it tight with a floured cloth, and boil it an hour and a half. Eat it with cold butter and salt.

When cold, slice and toast it, and eat it as oatcake buttered.

**Dutch Pudding, or Souster.**—Melt one pound of butter in half a pint of milk; mix it into two pounds of flour, eight eggs, four spoonfuls of yeast, add one pound of currants, and a quarter of a pound of sugar beaten and sifted.

This is a very good pudding hot, and equally so as a cake when cold. If for the latter, caraways may be used instead of currants. An hour will bake it in a quick oven.

**A Dutch Rice Pudding.**—Soak four ounces of rice in warm water half an hour; drain the latter from it, and throw it into a stewpan, with half a pint of milk, half a stick of cinnamon, and simmer till tender. When cold, add four whole eggs well beaten, two ounces of butter melted in a tea-cupful of fresh cream, and put three ounces of sugar, a quarter of a nutmeg, and a good piece of lemon peel.

Put a light puff paste into a mould or dish, or grated tops and bottoms, and bake in a quick oven.

**Light or German Puddings or Puffs.**—Melt three ounces of butter in a pint of cream; let it stand till nearly cold; then mix two ounces of fine flour, and two ounces of sugar, four yolks and two whites of eggs, and a little rose or orange-flower water. Bake in little cups, buttered, half an hour. They should be served the moment they are done, and only when going to be eaten, or they will not be light.

Turn out of the cups, and serve with white wine and sugar.

**Little Bread Puddings.**—Steep the crumb of a penny loaf grated, in about a pint of warm milk; when soaked, beat six eggs, whites and yolks, and mix with the bread and two ounces of butter warmed, sugar, orange-flower water, a spoonful of brandy, a little nutmeg, and a tea-cupful of cream. Beat all well, and bake in tea-cups buttered. If currants are chosen, a quarter of a pound is sufficient, if not, they are good without; or you may put orange or lemon candy. Serve with pudding sauce.

**Puddings in haste.**—Shred suet, and put with grated bread, a few currants, the yolks of four eggs and the whites of two, some grated lemon peel, and ginger. Mix, and make into little balls about the size and shape of an egg, with a little flour.

Have ready a skillet of boiling water, and throw them in. Twenty minutes will boil them, but they will rise to the top when done.

Pudding sauce.

**New College Puddings.**—Grate the crumb of a twopenny loaf, shred suet eight ounces, and mix with eight ounces of currants, one of citron mixed fine, one of orange, a handful of sugar, half a nutmeg, three eggs beaten, yolk and white separately. Mix, and make into the size and shape of a goose-egg. Put half a pound of butter into a frying-pan, and when melted and quite hot, stew them gently in it over a stove; turn them two or three times till of a fine light brown. Mix a glass of brandy with the butter. Serve with pudding-sauce.

**Boiled Bread Pudding.**—Grate white bread, pour boiling milk over it, and cover close. When soaked an hour or two, beat it fine, and mix it with two or three eggs well beaten.

Put it into a basin that will just hold it; tie a floured cloth over it, and put it into boiling water. Send it up with melted butter poured over.

It may be eaten with salt or sugar.

Prunes, or French plums, make a fine pudding instead of raisins, either with suet or bread pudding.

**Another and Richer.**—On half a pint of crumbs of bread pour half a pint of scalding milk; cover for an hour. Beat up four eggs, and when strained add to the bread, with a tea-spoonful of flour, an ounce of butter, two ounces of sugar, half a pound of currants, an ounce of almonds beaten, with orange-flower water, half an ounce of orange-peel, and the same of lemon and citron. Butter a basin that will exactly hold it, flour the cloth, tie tight over, and boil one hour.

**Brown Bread Pudding.**—Half a pound of stale brown bread grated, ditto of currants, ditto of suet, sugar, and nutmeg; mix with four eggs, a spoonful of brandy, and two spoonfuls of cream; boil in a cloth or basin that exactly holds it three or four hours.

**Nelson Puddings.**—Put into a Dutch oven six small cakes called Nelson balls, or rice cakes made in small tea-cups. When quite hot, pour over them boiling melted butter, white wine and sugar; and serve.

**Eve's Pudding.**—Grate three quarters of a pound of bread; mix it with the same quantity of shred suet, the same of apples, and also of currants; mix with these the whole of four eggs, and the rind of half a lemon shred fine. Put it into a shape; boil three hours; and serve with pudding sauce, the juice of half a lemon, and a little nutmeg.

**Quaking Pudding.**—Scald a quart of cream; when almost cold put to it four eggs well beaten, a spoonful and a half of flour, some nutmegs and sugar; tie it close in a buttered cloth; boil it an hour, and turn it out with care, lest it should crack. Serve with melted butter, a little wine, and sugar.

**Duke of Cumberland's Pudding.**—Mix six ounces of grated bread, the same quantity of currants well cleaned and picked, the same of beef suet finely shred, the same of chopped apples and also of lump sugar, six eggs, half a nutmeg, a pinch of salt, the rind of a lemon minced as fine as possible; and citron, orange and lemon, a large spoonful of each cut thin. Mix thoroughly, and put into a basin, cover very close with floured cloths, and boil three hours.

Serve it with pudding sauce, and the juice of half a lemon, boiled together.

**Transparent Pudding.**—Beat eight eggs very well; put them into a stew-pan, with half a pound of sugar pounded fine, the same quantity of butter, and some nutmeg grated. Set it on the fire, and keep stirring it till it thickens. Then set it into a basin to cool; put a rich puff paste round the edge of the dish; pour in your pudding, and bake it in a moderate oven. It will cut light and clear. You may add candied orange and citron, if you like.

**Batter Pudding.**—Rub three spoonfuls of fine flour extremely smooth by degrees into a pint of milk; simmer till it thickens; stir in two ounces of butter; set it to cool; then add the yolks of three eggs: flour a cloth that has been wet, or butter a basin, and put the batter into it; tie it tight, and plunge it into boiling water, the bottom upwards. Boil it an hour and a half, and serve it with plain butter. If approved, a little ginger, nutmeg, and lemon peel may be added. Serve with sweet sauce.

**Batter Pudding with Meat.**—Make a batter with flour, milk, and eggs; pour a little into the bottom of a pudding dish; then put seasoned meat of any kind into it, and a little shred onion; pour the remainder of the batter over, and bake in a slow oven.

Some like a loin of mutton baked in batter, being first cleared of most of the fat.

**Rice Small Pudding.**—Wash two large spoonfuls of rice, and simmer it with half a pint of milk till thick, then put the size of an egg of batter, and near half a pint of thick cream, and give it one boil. When cold mix four yolks and two whites of eggs well beaten, sugar and nutmeg, to taste; and add grated lemon, and a little cinnamon.

Butter little cups, and fill three parts full, putting at bottom some orange or citron. Bake three quarters of an hour in a slowish oven. Serve the moment before to be eaten, with sweet sauce in the dish, or a boat.

**Plain Rice Pudding.**—Wash and pick some rice; throw among it some pimento finely pounded, but not much; tie the rice

RICE PUDDING—POTATO PUDDING.     113

in a cloth, and leave plenty of room for it to swell. Boil it in a quantity of water for an hour or two. When done, eat it with butter and sugar, or milk. Put lemon peel if you please.

It is very good without spice, and eaten with salt and butter.

**A Rich Rice Pudding.**—Boil half a pound of rice in water, with a little bit of salt, till quite tender ; drain it dry, mix it with the yolks and whites of four eggs, a quarter of a pint of cream, with two ounces of fresh butter melted in the latter, four ounces of beef-suet or marrow, or veal-suet taken from a fillet of veal, finely shred, three quarters of a pound of currants, two spoonfuls of brandy, one of peach-water, or ratafia, nutmeg, and grated lemon peel. When well mixed, put a paste round the edge, and fill the dish. Slices of candied orange, lemon, and citron, if approved. Bake in a moderate oven.

**Rice Pudding with Fruit.**—Swell the rice with a very little milk over the fire; then mix fruit of any kind with it (currants, gooseberries scalded, pared and quartered apples, raisins, or black currants) ; with one egg in the rice, to bind it; boil it well, and serve with sugar.

**Baked Rice Pudding.**—Swell rice as above ; then add some more milk, an egg, sugar, allspice, and lemon peel. Bake in a deep dish.

**Another, for the Family.**—Put into a very deep pan half a pound of rice washed and picked ; two ounces of butter, four ounces of sugar, a few allspice pounded, and two quarts of milk. Less butter will do, or some suet. Bake in a slow oven.

**A George Pudding.**—Boil very tender a handful of whole rice in a small quantity of milk, with a large piece of lemon peel. Let it drain ; then mix with it a dozen of good-sized apples, boiled to pulp as dry as possible : add a glass of white wine, the yolks of five eggs, two ounces of orange and citron cut thin ; make it pretty sweet. Line a mould or basin with a very good paste : beat the five whites of the eggs to a very strong froth, and mix with the other ingredients ; fill the mould, and bake it of a fine bright colour. Serve it with the bottom upward with the following sauce : two glasses of wine, a spoonful of sugar, the yolks of two eggs, and a bit of butter as large as a walnut ; simmer without boiling, and pour to and from the saucepan, till of a proper thickness; and put in the dish.

**An excellent Plain Potato Pudding.**—Take eight ounces of boiled potatoes, two ounces of butter, the yolks and whites of two eggs, a quarter of a pint of cream, one spoonful of white wine, a morsel of salt, the juice and rind of a lemon ; beat all to froth ; sugar to taste. A crust or not, as you like. Bake it. If wanted richer, put three ounces more butter, sweet-meats and almonds, and another egg.

**Potato Pudding with Meat.**—Boil them till fit to mash ; rub through a colander, and make into a thick batter with milk and two eggs. Lay some seasoned steaks in a dish, then some batter, and over the last layer put the remainder of the batter. Bake a fine brown.

H

**Steak or Kidney Pudding.**—If kidney, split and soak it, and season that or the meat. Make a paste of suet, flour, and milk; roll it, and line a basin with some; put the kidney or steaks in, cover with paste and pinch round the edge. Cover with a cloth, and boil a considerable time.

**Beef Steak Pudding.**—Prepare some fine steaks as in page 44; roll them with fat between, and if you approve shred onion, add a very little. Lay a paste of suet in a basin, and put in the rollers of steaks; cover the basin with a paste, and pinch the edges to keep the gravy in. Cover with a cloth tied close, and let the pudding boil slowly, but for a length of time.

**Baked Beef Steak Pudding.**—Make a batter of milk, two eggs and flour, or, which is much better, potatoes boiled and mashed through a colander; lay a little of it at the bottom of the dish, then put in the steaks prepared as above, and very well seasoned; pour the remainder of the batter over them, and bake it.

**Mutton Pudding.**—Season with salt, pepper, and a bit of onion; lay one layer of steaks at the bottom of the dish, and pour a batter of potatoes boiled and pressed through a colander, and mixed with milk and an egg over them; then putting the rest of the steaks and batter, bake it.

Batter with flour, instead of potatoes, eats well, but requires more egg, and is not so good.

**Another.**—Cut slices off a leg that has been underdone, and put them into a basin lined with a fine suet crust. Season with pepper, salt, and finely-shred onion or shalot.

**Suet Pudding.**—Shred a pound of suet, mix with a pound and a quarter of flour, two eggs beaten separately, a little salt, and as little milk as will make it. Boil four hours. It eats well next day cut in slices and broiled.

The outward fat of loins or necks of mutton finely shred, makes a more delicate pudding than suet.

**Veal Suet Pudding.**—Cut the crumb of a threepenny loaf into slices; boil and sweeten two quarts of new milk and pour over it. When soaked, pour out a little of the milk, and mix with six eggs well beaten, and half a nutmeg. Lay the slices of bread into a dish, with layers of currants and veal-suet shred, a pound of each. Butter the dish well, and bake; or you may boil it in a basin, if you prefer it.

**Hunter's Pudding.**—Mix a pound of suet, ditto flour, ditto currants, ditto raisins stoned and a little cut, the rind of half a lemon shred as fine as possible, six Jamaica peppers in fine powder, four eggs, a glass of brandy, a little salt, and as little milk as will make it of a proper consistence; boil it in a floured cloth, or a melon mould, eight or nine hours. Serve with sweet sauce. Add sometimes a spoonful of peach-water for change of flavour.

This pudding will keep, after it has been boiled, six months, if kept tied up in the same cloth, and hung up folded in a sheet of cap-paper to preserve it from dust, being first cold. When to be used it must boil a full hour.

**Common Plum Pudding.**—The same proportions of flour and suet, and half the quantity of fruit, with spice, lemon, a glass of wine or not, and one egg and milk, will make an excellent pudding if long boiled.

**Custard Pudding.**—Mix by degrees a pint of good milk with a large spoonful of flour, yolks of five eggs, some orange-flower water, and a little pounded cinnamon. Butter a basin that will exactly hold it, pour the batter in, and tie a floured cloth over. Put in boiling water over the fire, and turn it about a few minutes to prevent the egg going to one side. Half an hour will boil it. Put currant jelly on it, and serve with sweet sauce.

**Maccaroni Pudding.**—Simmer an ounce or two of the pipe sort in a pint of milk, with a bit of lemon and cinnamon till tender; put it into a dish, with milk, two or three eggs, but only one white, sugar, nutmeg, a spoonful of peach-water, and half a glass of raisin-wine. Bake with a paste round the edge.

A layer of orange-marmalade, or raspberry-jam, in a maccaroni pudding, for change, is a great improvement; in which case omit the almond-water, or ratafia, which you would otherwise flavour it with.

**Millet Pudding.**—Wash three spoonfuls of the seed; put it into the dish with a crust round the edges; pour over it as much new milk as will nearly fill the dish, two ounces of butter warmed with it, sugar, shred lemon, and a little scrape of ginger and nutmeg. As you put it in the oven, stir in two eggs beaten, and a spoonful of shred suet.

**Carrot Pudding.**—Boil a large carrot tender; then bruise it in a marble mortar, and mix with it a spoonful of biscuit-powder, or three or four little sweet biscuits without seeds, four yolks and two whites of eggs, a pint of cream either raw or scalded, a little ratafia, a large spoonful of orange or rosewater, a quarter of a nutmeg, and two ounces of sugar. Bake it in a shallow dish lined with paste, and turn it out to serve, with a little sugar dusted over.

**An excellent Apricot Pudding.**— Halve twelve large apricots, give them a scald till they are soft; meantime pour on the grated crumbs of a penny loaf, a pint of boiling cream; when half cold, four ounces of sugar, the yolks of four beaten eggs, and a glass of white wine. Pound the apricots in a mortar with some or all of the kernels; then mix the fruit and other ingredients together; put a paste round a dish, and bake the pudding half an hour.

**Baked Gooseberry Pudding.**—Stew gooseberries in a jar over a hot hearth, or in a saucepan of water till they will pulp. Take a pint of the juice pressed through a coarse sieve, the yolks and whites of three eggs beaten and strained, and one ounce and a half of butter; sweeten it well, and put a crust round the dish. A few crumbs of rolls should be mixed with the above to give a little consistence, or four ounces of Naples biscuits.

**A Green Bean Pudding.**—Boil and blanch old beans, beat them in a mortar, with very little pepper and salt, some cream, and the yolk of an egg. A little spinach juice will give a finer colour, but it is as good without. Boil it in a basin that will just hold it, an hour, and pour parsley and butter over. Serve bacon to eat with it.

**Shelford Pudding.**—Mix three quarters of a pound of currants or raisins, one pound of suet, one pound of flour, six eggs, a little good milk, some lemon peel, a little salt. Boil it in a melon-shape six hours.

**Brandy Pudding.**—Line a mould with jar-raisins stoned, or dried cherries, then with thin slices of French roll, next to which put ratafias or macaroons; then the fruit, rolls, and cakes in succession, until the mould be full; sprinkling in at times two glasses of brandy. Beat four eggs, yolks and whites; put to a pint of milk or cream, lightly sweetened, half a nutmeg, and the rind of half a lemon finely grated. Let the liquor sink into the solid part; then flour a cloth, tie it tight over, and boil one hour; keep the mould the right side up. Serve with pudding-sauce.

**Buttermilk Pudding.**—Warm three quarts of new milk; turn it with a quart of buttermilk; drain the curd through a sieve; when dry pound it in a marble mortar, with near half a pound of sugar, a lemon boiled tender, the crumb of a roll grated, a nutmeg grated, six bitter almonds, four ounces of warm butter, a tea-cupful of good cream, the yolks of five and whites of three eggs, a glass of sweet wine, and ditto of brandy.

When well incorporated, bake it in small cups or bowls well buttered; if the butter be not brown, use a salamander; but serve as quick as possible, and with pudding sauce.

**Curd Puddings or Puffs.**—Turn two quarts of milk to curd, press the whey from it, rub through a sieve, and mix four ounces of butter, the crumb of a penny loaf, two spoonfuls of cream, and half a nutmeg, a small quantity of sugar, and two spoonfuls of white wine. Butter little cups, or small patty-pans, and fill them three parts. Orange flower water is an improvement. Bake them with care. Serve with sweet sauce in a boat.

**Boiled Curd Pudding.**—Rub the curd of two gallons of milk, when drained, through a sieve. Mix it with six eggs, a little cream, two spoonfuls of orange-flower water, half a nutmeg, flour and crumbs of bread, each three spoonfuls, currants and raisins half a pound of each. Boil an hour in a thick well floured cloth.

**Pippin Pudding.**—Coddle six pippins in vine leaves covered with water, very gently, that the inside be done without breaking the skins. When soft, skin, and with a tea-spoon take the pulp from the core. Press it through a colander; add two spoonfuls of orange-flower water, three eggs beaten, a glass of raisin wine, a pint of scalded cream, sugar and nutmeg to taste. Lay a thin puff paste at the bottom and sides of the dish: shred very thin
non peel as fine as possible, and put it into the dish; likewise

lemon, orange, and citron, in small slices, but not so thin as to dissolve in the baking.

**Yorkshire Pudding.**—Mix five spoonfuls of flour, with a quart of milk, and three eggs well beaten. Butter the pan. When quite brown by baking under the meat, turn the other side upwards, and brown that. It should be made in a square pan, and cut into pieces to come to table. Set it over a chafing-dish at first, and stir it some minutes,

**A quick-made Pudding.**—Flour and suet, half a pound of each, four eggs, a quarter of a pint of new milk, with a little mace and nutmeg, a quarter of a pound of raisins, ditto of currants; mix well, and boil three quarters of an hour with the cover of the pot on, or it will require longer.

**Russian Seed, or Ground Rice Pudding.**—Boil a large spoonful heaped, of either, in a pint of new milk, with lemon peel and cinnamon. When cold, add sugar, nutmeg, and two eggs well beaten. Bake with a crust round the dish.

**A Welsh Pudding.**—Let half a pound of fine butter melt gently, beat with it the yolks of eight, and whites of four eggs, mix in six ounces of loaf sugar, and the grated rind of a lemon. Put a paste into a dish for turning out, and pour the above in, and nicely bake it.

**Oxford Dumplings.**—Of grated bread two ounces, currants and shred suet four ounces each, two large spoonfuls of flour, a great deal of grated lemon peel, a bit of sugar, and a little pimento in fine powder. Mix with two eggs and a little milk into five dumplings, and fry of a fine yellow brown. Made with flour instead of bread, but with half the quantity, they are excellent. Serve with sweet sauce.

**Suet Dumplings.**—Make as pudding (page 114), and drop into boiling water, or into the boiling of beef: or you may boil them in a cloth.

**Apple, Currant, or Damson Dumplings, or Puddings.**—Make as above, and line a basin with the paste tolerably thin; fill with the fruit, and cover it; tie a cloth over tight, and boil till the fruit shall be done enough.

**Yeast, or Suffolk Dumplings.**—Make a very light dough with yeast, as for bread, but with milk instead of water, and put salt. Let it raise an hour before the fire.

Twenty minutes before you are to serve, have ready a large stew-pan of boiling water; make the dough into balls, the size of a middling apple; throw them in, and boil twenty minutes. If you doubt when done enough, stick a clean fork into one, and if it come out clear, it is done.

The way to eat them is to tear them apart on the top with two forks, for they become heavy by their own steam. Eat immediately with meat, or sugar and butter, or salt.

**A Charlotte.**—Cut as many very thin slices of white bread as will cover the bottom and line the sides of a baking dish, but first rub it thick with butter. Put apples, in thin slices, into the dish, in layers, till full, strewing sugar between, and bits of butter. In the meantime, soak as many thin slices of bread as will cover the whole, in warm milk, over which lay a plate, and a weight to keep the bread close on the apples. Bake slowly three hours. To a middling-sized dish use half a pound of butter in the whole.

**Common Pancakes.**—Make a light batter of eggs, flour, and milk. Fry in a small pan, in hot dripping or lard. Salt, or nutmeg, and ginger, may be added.

Sugar and lemon should be served to eat with them. Or, when eggs are scarce, make the batter with flour, and small beer, ginger, &c., or clean snow, with flour, and a very little milk, will serve as well as egg.

**Fine Pancakes, fried without Butter or Lard.**—Beat six fresh eggs extremely well, and mix, when strained, with a pint of cream, four ounces of sugar, a glass of wine, half a nutmeg grated, and as much flour as will make it almost as thick as ordinary pancake batter, but not quite. Heat the frying-pan tolerably hot, wipe it with a clean cloth; then pour in the batter, to make thin pancakes.

**Pancakes of Rice.**—Boil half a pound of rice to a jelly in a small quantity of water; when cold, mix it with a pint of cream, eight eggs, a bit of salt and nutmeg: stir in eight ounces of butter just warmed, and add as much flour as will make the batter thick enough. Fry in as little lard or dripping as possible.

**Irish Pancakes.**—Beat eight yolks and four whites of eggs, strain them into a pint of cream, put a grated nutmeg, and sugar to your taste; set three ounces of fresh butter on the fire, stir it, and as it warms pour it to the cream, which should be warm when the eggs are put to it: then mix smooth almost half a pint of flour. Fry the pancakes very thin; the first with a bit of butter, but not the others.

Serve several, one on another.

**New England Pancakes.**—Mix a pint of cream, five spoonfuls of fine flour, seven yolks and four whites of eggs, and a very little salt; fry them very thin in fresh butter, and between each strew sugar and cinnamon. Send up six or eight at once.

**Fritters.**—Make them of any of the batters directed for pancakes, by dropping a small quantity into the pan; or make the plainer sort, and put pared apple sliced and cored into the batter, and fry some of it with each slice. Currants or sliced lemon as thin as paper, make an agreeable change. Fritters for company should be served on a folded napkin in the dish. Any sort of sweetmeat or ripe fruit may be made into fritters.

**Spanish Fritters.**—Cut the crumb of a French roll into lengths, as thick as your finger, in what shape you will. Soak in some cream, nutmeg, sugar, pounded cinnamon, and an egg. When well soaked, fry of a nice brown, and serve with butter, wine, and sugar sauce.

**Potato Fritters.**—Boil two large potatoes, scrape them fine: beat four yolks and three whites of eggs, and add to the above one large spoonful of cream, another of sweet wine, a squeeze of lemon, and a little nutmeg. Beat this batter half an hour at least. It will be extremely light. Put a good quantity of fine lard in a stew-pan, and drop a spoonful of the batter at a time into it. Fry them: and serve as a sauce a glass of white wine, the juice of a lemon, one dessert-spoonful of peach leaf or almond water, and some white sugar warmed together, not to be served in the dish.

**Another way.**—Slice potatoes thin, dip them in a fine batter, and fry them. Serve with white sugar sifted over them. Lemon peel, and a spoonful of orange-flower water should be added to the butter.

**Bookings.**—Mix three ounces of buck-wheat flour with a tea-cupful of warm milk, and a spoonful of yeast; let it rise before the fire about an hour; then mix four eggs well beaten, and as much milk as will make the batter the usual thickness for pan-cakes, and fry them the same.

**PASTRY.—Rich Puff Paste.**—Puffs may be made of any sort of fruit, but it should be prepared first with sugar.

Weigh any quantity of butter with as much fine flour as you judge necessary; mix a little of the former with the latter, and wet with as little water as will make it into a stiff paste. Roll it out, and put all the butter over it in slices, turn in the ends, and roll it thin; do this twice, and touch it no more than can be avoided. The butter may be added at twice; and to those who are not accustomed to make paste it may be better to do so.

A quicker oven than for a short crust.

**A less rich Paste.**—Weigh a pound of flour, and a quarter of a pound of butter, rub them together, and mix into a paste with a little water, and an egg well beaten—of the former as little as will suffice, or the paste will be tough. Roll, and fold it three or four times.

Rub extremely fine in one pound of dried flour, six ounces of butter, and a spoonful of white sugar; work up the whole into a stiff paste with as little hot water as possible.

**Crust for Venison Pasty.**—To a quarter of a peck of fine flour use two pounds and a half of butter, and four eggs; mix into paste with warm water, and work it smooth and to a good con-sistence. Put a paste round the inside, but not to the bottom of the dish, and let the cover be pretty thick, to bear the long con-tinuance in the oven.

**Rice Paste for Sweets.**—Boil a quarter of a pound of ground rice in the smallest quantity of water: strain from it all the mois-ture as well as you can; beat it in a mortar with half an ounce of butter, and one egg well beaten, and it will make an excellent paste for tarts, &c.

**Rich Paste for relishing things.**—Clean, and put some rice, with an onion and a little water and milk, or milk only, into a saucepan, and simmer till it swell. Put seasoned chops into a dish, and cover it with the rice; by the addition of an egg the rice will adhere better.

Rabbits fricasseed, and covered thus, are very good.

**Potato Paste.**—Pound boiled potatoes very fine, and add, while warm, a sufficiency of butter to make the mash hold together, or you may mix with it an egg; then, before it gets cold, flour the board pretty well to prevent it from sticking, and roll it to the thickness wanted.

If it has become quite cold before it be put on the dish, it will be apt to crack.

**Raised Crusts for Custards or Fruit.**—Put four ounces of butter into a saucepan with water, and when it boils pour it into as much flour as you choose; knead and beat it till smooth; cover it, as at page 108. Raise it; and if for custard, put a paper within to keep out the sides till half done, then fill with a cold mixture of milk, egg, sugar, and add a little peach water, lemon peel, or nutmeg. By cold is meant that the egg is not to be warmed, but the milk should be warmed by itself—not to spoil the crust.

The above butter will make a great deal of raised crust, which must not be rich, or it will be difficult to prevent the sides from falling.

**Excellent Short Crusts.**—Take two ounces of fine white sugar, pounded and sifted, quite dry, then mix it with a pound of flour well dried; rub into it three ounces of butter so fine as not to be seen—into some cream put the yolks of two eggs, beaten, and mix the above into a smooth paste; roll it thin, and bake it in a moderate oven.

**Another.**—Mix with a pound of fine flour dried, an ounce of sugar pounded and sifted; then crumble three ounces of butter in it till it looks all like flour, and with a gill of boiling cream work it up to a fine paste.

**Another, not sweet but rich.**—Rub six ounces of butter in eight ounces of fine flour; mix into a stiffish paste, with as little water as possible; beat it well, and roll it thin. This, as well as the former, is fit for tarts of fresh or preserved fruits. Bake in a moderate oven.

**A very fine Crust for Orange Cheesecakes, or Sweet-meats, when to be particularly nice.**—Dry a pound of fine flour, mix with it three ounces of refined sugar; then work half a pound of butter with your hand till it come to froth; put the flour into it by degrees, and work into it, well beaten and strained, the yolks of three, and whites of two eggs. If too limber, put some flour and sugar to make it fit to roll. Line your patty-pans, and fill. A little above fifteen minutes will bake them. Against they come out, have ready some refined sugar beat up with the white of an egg as thick as you can; ice them all over, set them in the oven to harden, and serve cold. Use fresh butter.

Salt butter will make a very fine flaky crust; but if for mince-pies, or any sweet things, should be washed.

**Observations on Pastry.**—An adept in pastry never leaves any part of it adhering to the board or dish used in making. It is best when rolled on marble, or a very large slate. In very hot weather the butter should be put into cold water to keep it as firm as possible, and if made early in the morning, and preserved from the air until it is to be baked, the cook will find it much better. A good hand at pastry will use much less butter, and produce lighter crust than others. Salt butter, if very good and well washed, makes a fine flaky crust.

**Remarks on Using Preserved Fruits in Pastry.**—Preserved fruits should not be baked long; those that have been done with their full proportion of sugar, need no baking; the crust should be baked in a tin shape, and the fruit be afterwards added; or it may be put into a small dish, or tart-pans, and the covers be baked on a tin cut out according to your taste.

**Apple Pie.**—Pare and core the fruit, having wiped the outside, which, with the cores, boil with a little water till it tastes well; strain, and put a little sugar and a bit of bruised cinnamon, and simmer again. In the meantime place the apples in a dish, a paste being put round the edge; when one layer is in, sprinkle half the sugar, and shred lemon peel, and squeeze some juice, or a glass of cyder if the apples have lost their spirit; put in the rest of the apples, sugar, and the liquor that you have boiled. Cover with paste. You may add some butter when cut, if eaten hot, or put quince-marmalade, orange-paste, or cloves, to flavour.

**Hot Apple Pie.**—Make with the fruit, sugar, and a clove, and put a bit of butter in when cut open.

**Cherry Pie** should have a mixture of other fruit,—currants or raspberries, or both.

**Currant Pie,** with or without raspberries.

**Mince Pie.**—Of scraped beef free from skin and strings, weigh two pounds, four pounds of suet picked and chopped, then add six pounds of currants nicely cleaned and perfectly dry, three pounds of chopped apples, the peel and juice of two lemons, a pint of sweet wine, a nutmeg, and a quarter of an ounce of cloves, ditto mace, ditto pimento, in finest powder; press the whole into a deep pan when well mixed, and keep it covered in a dry cool place.

Half the quantity is enough, unless for a very large family.

Have citron, orange, and lemon peel ready, and put some of each in the pies when made.

**Mince Pies without Meat.**—Of best apples six pounds, pared, cored, and minced; of fresh suet and raisins stoned, each three pounds, both likewise minced: to these add of mace and cinnamon a quarter of an ounce each, and eight cloves, in finest powder, three pounds of the finest powdered sugar, three quarters of an ounce of salt, the rinds of four and juice of two lemons, half a pint of port, the same of brandy. Mix well and put into a deep pan.

Have ready washed and dried four pounds of currants, and add as you make the pies, with candied fruit.

**Lemon Mince Pies.**—Squeeze a large lemon, boil the outside till tender enough to beat to a mash, add to it three large apples chopped, and four ounces of suet, half a pound of currants, four ounces of sugar; put the juice of the lemon, and candied fruit as for other pies. Make a short crust, and fill the patty-pans as usual.

**Egg Mince Pies.**—Boil six eggs hard, shred them small; shred double the quantity of suet; then put currants washed and picked one pound, or more, if the eggs were large; the peel of one lemon shred very fine, and the juice, six spoonfuls of sweet wine, mace, nutmeg, sugar, a very little salt: orange, lemon, and citron, candied. Make a light paste for them.

**Currant and Raspberry.**—For a tart, line the dish, put sugar and fruit, lay bars across, and bake.

**Light Paste for Tarts and Cheesecakes.**—Beat the white of an egg to a strong froth; then mix with it as much water as will make three quarters of a pound of fine flour into a very stiff paste; roll it very thin, then lay the third part of half a pound of butter upon it in little bits; dredge it with some flour left out at first, and roll it up tight. Roll it out again, and put the same proportion of butter; and so proceed till all be worked up.

**Icing for Tarts.**—Beat the yolk of an egg and some melted butter well together, wash the tarts with a feather, and sift sugar over as you put them in the oven. Or beat white of egg, wash the paste, and sift white sugar.

**Pippin Tarts.**—Pare in two Seville or China oranges, boil the peel tender, and shred it fine; pare and core twenty apples, put them in a stew-pan, and as little water as possible: when half done, add half a pound of sugar, the orange peel and juice; boil till pretty thick. When cold, put it in a shallow dish, or patty-pans lined with paste, to turn out, and be eaten cold.

**Prune Tart.**—Give prunes a scald, take out the stones and break them; put the kernels into a little cranberry juice, with the prunes and sugar; simmer; and, when cold, make a tart of the sweetmeat.

**Orange Tart.**—Squeeze, pulp, and boil two Seville oranges tender, weigh them, and double of sugar; beat both together to a paste, and then add the juice and pulp of the fruit, and the size of a walnut of fresh butter, and beat together. Choose a very shallow dish, line it with a light puff crust, and lay the paste of orange in it. You may ice it.

**Codlin Tart.**—Scald the fruit as will be directed under that article: when ready take off the thin skin, and lay them whole in a dish, put a little of the water the apples were boiled in at bottom, strew them over with lump sugar or fine Lisbon; when cold, put a paste round the edges and over the tart.

You may wet it with white of egg, and strew sugar over, which looks very well: or cut the lid in quarters, without touching the paste on the edge of the dish: and either put the broad end downwards, and make the point stand up, or remove the lid altogether.  Pour a good custard over it when cold, and sift sugar over.

Or, line the bottom of a shallow dish with paste, lay the apples in it, sweeten, and lay little twists of paste over in bars.

**Rhubarb Tart.**—Cut the stalks in lengths of four or five inches, and take off the thin skin.  If you have a hot hearth, lay them in a dish, and put over a thin syrup of sugar and water, cover with another dish, and let it simmer very slowly an hour ; or do them in a block-tin saucepan.

When cold, make into a tart, as codlin.  When tender, the baking the crust will be sufficient.

**Raspberry Tart with Cream.**—Roll out some thin puff paste, and lay it in a patty-pan of what size you choose ; put in raspberries ; strew over them fine sugar ; cover with a thin lid, and then bake.  Cut it open, and have ready the following mixture warm : half a pint of cream, the yolks of two or three eggs well beaten, and a little sugar ; and when this is added to the tart, return it to the oven for five or six minutes.

**Orange Tart.**—Line a tart-pan with thin puff paste ; put into it orange marmalade that is made with apple jelly ; lay bars of paste, or a croquant cover over, and bake in a moderate oven.

**Fried Patties.**—Mince a bit of cold veal, and six oysters, mixed with a few crumbs of bread, salt, pepper, nutmeg, and a very small bit of lemon peel—add the liquor of the oysters ; warm all in a tosser, but do not boil ; let it cool ; have ready a good puff paste, roll thin, and cut it in round or square bits ; put some of the above between two of them, twist the edges to keep in the gravy, and fry them of a fine brown.

This is a very good thing ; and baked, is a fashionable dish.

Wash all patties over with egg before baking.

**Oyster Patties.**—Put a fine puff paste into small patty-pans, and cover with paste, with a bit of bread in each ; and against they are baked have ready the following to fill with, taking out the bread.  Take off the beards of the oysters, cut the other parts into small bits, put them in a small tosser, with a grate of nutmeg, the least white pepper, and salt, a morsel of lemon peel, cut so small that you can scarcely see it, a very little cream, and a little of the oyster liquor.  Simmer for a few minutes before you fill.

Observe always to put a bit of crust into patties, to keep them hollow while baking.

**Oyster Patties, or Small Pies.**—As you open the oysters separate them from the liquor, which strain ; parboil them, after taking off the beards.  Parboil sweetbreads, and cutting them in slices, lay them and the oysters in layers, season very lightly with salt, pepper and mace.  Then put half a teacup of liquor, and the same of gravy.  Bake in a slow oven ; and before you serve, put a teacup of cream, a little more oyster liquor, and a cup of white gravy, all warmed, but not boiled.  If for patties, the oysters should be cut in small dice, gently stewed, and seasoned as above, and put into the paste when ready for table.

**Lobster Patties.**—Make with the same seasoning, a little cream, and the smallest bit of butter.

**Podovies, or Beef Patties.**—Shred underdone dressed beef with a little fat, season with pepper, salt, and a little shalot or onion. Make a plain paste, roll it thin, and cut it in shape like an apple puff, fill it with the mince, pinch the edges, and fry them of a nice brown. The paste should be made with a small quantity of butter, egg, and milk.

**Veal Patties.**—Mince some veal that is not quite done with a little parsley, lemon peel, a scrape of nutmeg, and a bit of salt; add a little cream, and gravy just to moisten the meat; and if you have any ham scrape a little, and add to it. Do not warm it till the patties are baked.

**Turkey Patties.**—Mince some of the white part, and with grated lemon, nutmeg, salt, a very little white pepper, cream, and a very little bit of butter warmed, fill the patties.

**Sweet Patties.**—Chop the meat of a boiled calf's foot, of which you use the liquor for jelly, with two apples, one ounce of orange and lemon peel candied, and some fresh peel and juice; mix with them half a nutmeg grated, the yolk of an egg, a spoonful of brandy, and four ounces of currants washed and dried.

Bake in small patty-pans.

**Patties resembling Mince Pies.**—Chop the kidney and fat of cold veal, apple, orange, and lemon peel candied, and fresh currants, a little wine, two or three cloves, a little brandy, and a bit of sugar. Bake as before.

**Apple Puffs.**—Pare the fruit, and either stew them in a stone jar on a hot hearth, or bake them. When cold, mix the pulp of the apple with sugar and lemon peel shred fine, taking as little of the apple juice as you can. Bake them in thin paste, in a quick oven: a quarter of an hour will do them, when small. Orange, or quince marmalade, is a great improvement. Cinnamon pounded, or orange-flower water, in change.

**Lemon Puffs.**—Beat and sift a pound and a quarter of double refined sugar; grate the rind of two large lemons, and mix it well with the sugar; then beat the whites of three new-laid eggs a great while, add them to the sugar and peel, and beat it for an hour; make it up in any shape you please, and bake it on paper put on tin plates, in a moderate oven. Do not remove the paper till cold. Oiling the paper will make it come off with ease.

**Cheese Puffs.**—Cream cheese-curd from the whey, and beat half a pint basin of it fine in a mortar, with a spoonful and a half of flour, three eggs, but only one white, a spoonful of orange-flower water, a quarter of a nutmeg, and sugar to make it pretty sweet. Lay a little of this paste, in small very round cakes, on a tin plate. If the oven is hot, a quarter of an hour will bake them. Serve with pudding sauce.

**Excellent Light Puffs.**—Mix two spoonfuls of flour, a little grated lemon peel, some nutmeg, half a spoonful of brandy, a little loaf sugar, and one egg; then fry it enough, but not brown; beat it in a mortar with five eggs, whites and yolks: put a quantity of lard in a frying-pan, and when quite hot drop a dessert-spoonful of batter at a time: turn as they brown. Serve them immediately with sweet sauce.

**To prepare Venison for Pasty.**—Take the bones out, then season and beat the meat, lay it into a stone jar in large pieces, pour upon it some plain drawn-beef gravy, but not a strong one; lay the bones on the top, then set the jar in a water-bath, that is, a saucepan of water over the fire, simmer three or four hours—then leave it in a cold place till next day. Remove the cake of fat, lay the meat in handsome pieces on the dish; if not sufficiently seasoned, add more pepper, salt, or pimento, as necessary. Put some of the gravy, and keep the remainder for the time of serving. If the venison be thus prepared, it will not require so much time to bake, or such a very thick crust as is usual, and by which the under part is seldom done through.

**Venison Pasty.**—A shoulder boned makes a good pasty, but it must be beaten and seasoned, and the want of fat supplied by that of a fine well-hung loin of mutton, steeped twenty-four hours in equal parts of rape, vinegar and port. The shoulder being sinewy, it will be of advantage to rub it well with sugar for two or three days, and when to be used, wipe it perfectly clean from it, and the wine.

A mistake used to prevail, that venison could not be baked too much; but, as above directed, three or four hours in a slow oven will be quite sufficient to make it tender, and the flavour will be preserved. Either in a shoulder or side, the meat must be cut in pieces, and laid with fat between, that it may be proportioned to each person without breaking up the pasty to find it. Lay some pepper and salt at the bottom of the dish, and some butter; then the meat nicely packed, that it may be sufficiently done, but not lie hollow to harden at the edges.

The venison bones should be boiled with some fine old mutton —of this gravy put half a pint cold into the dish, then lay butter on the venison, and cover as well as line the sides with a thick crust, but do not put one under the meat. Keep the remainder of the gravy till the pasty comes from the oven; put it into the middle by a funnel, quite hot, and shake the dish to mix well. It should be seasoned with pepper and salt.

**To make a Pasty of Beef or Mutton, to eat as well as Venison.**—Bone a small rump or a piece of sirloin of beef, or a fat loin of mutton, after hanging several days. Beat it very well with a rolling-pin; then rub ten pounds of meat with four ounces of sugar, and pour over it a glass of port, and the same of vinegar. Let it lie five days and nights; wash and wipe the meat very dry, and season it very high with the best Jamaica pepper, nutmeg, and salt. Lay it in your dish, and to ten pounds put about a pound of butter, spreading it over the meat. Put a crust round the edges, and cover with a thick one, or it will be overdone before the meat be soaked. It must be done in a slow oven.

Set the bones in a pan in the oven, with no more water than will cover them, and one glass of port, a little pepper and salt, that you may have a little rich gravy to add to the paste when drawn.

*Note.*—Sugar gives a greater shortness, and better flavour to meats than salt, too great a quantity of which hardens, and it is quite as great a preservative.

**Potato Pasty.**—Boil, peel, and mash potatoes as fine as possible, mix them with salt, pepper, and a good bit of butter. Make a paste; roll it out thin like a large puff, and put in the potato: fold over one half, pinching the edges. Bake in a moderate oven.

**Cheap and Excellent Custards.**—Boil three pints of new milk, with a bit of lemon peel, a bit of cinnamon, two or three bay leaves, and sweeten it. Meanwhile rub down smooth a large spoonful of rice flour into a cup of cold milk, and mix with it two yolks of eggs well beaten. Take a basin of the boiling milk, and mix with the cold, and then pour that to the boiling; stirring it one way till it begins to thicken, and is just going to boil up; then pour it into a pan, and stir it some time; add a large spoonful of peach water, two tea-spoonfuls of brandy, or a little ratafia. Marbles boiled in custard or anything likely to burn, will, by shaking them in the sauce-pan, prevent it from catching.

**Rich Custards.**—Boil a pint of milk with lemon peel and cinnamon; mix a pint of cream, and the yolks of five eggs well beaten; when the milk tastes of the seasoning, sweeten it enough for the whole; pour it into the cream, stirring it well; then give the custard a simmer till of a proper thickness. Do not let it boil; stir the whole time one way; season as above. If to be extremely rich, put no milk, but a quart of cream to the eggs.

**Baked Custard.**—Boil one pint of cream and half a pint of milk, with mace, cinnamon, and lemon peel, a little of each. When cold, mix the yolks of three eggs; sweeten and make your cups or paste nearly full. Bake them ten minutes.

**Lemon Custards.**—Beat the yolks of eight eggs till they are as white as milk: then put to them a pint of boiling water, the rinds of two lemons grated, and the juice sweetened to your taste. Stir it on the fire till thick enough; then add a large glass of rich wine, and half a glass of brandy; give the whole one scald, and put it in cups, to be eaten cold.

**Almond Custard.**—Blanch and beat four ounces of almonds fine with a spoonful of water; then beat a pint of cream with two spoonfuls of rose water, and put them to the yolks of four eggs, and as much sugar as will make it pretty sweet; then add the almonds; stir it all over a slow fire till it is of a proper thickness; but do not boil. Pour it into cups.

**Cheesecakes.**—Strain the whey from the curd of two quarts of milk; when rather dry, crumble it through a coarse sieve, and mix with six ounces of fresh butter, one ounce of pounded blanched almonds, a little orange-flower water, half a glass of raisin wine, a grated biscuit, four ounces of currants, some nutmeg, and cinnamon in fine powder, and beat all the above with three eggs, and half a pint of cream, till quite light; then fill the patty-pans three parts full.

**A Plainer Sort.**—Turn three quarts of milk to curd, break it and drain the whey; when dry, break it up in a pan, with two ounces of butter, till perfectly smooth; put to it a pint and a half of thin cream, or good milk, and add sugar, cinnamon, nutmeg, and three ounces of currants.

**Cheesecakes, another way.**—Mix the curd of three quarts of milk, a pound of currants, twelve ounces of Lisbon sugar, a quarter of an ounce of cinnamon, ditto of nutmeg, the peel of one lemon chopped so fine that it becomes a paste, the yolks of eight and whites of six eggs, a pint of scalded cream, and a glass of brandy. Put a light thin puff paste in the patty-pans, and three parts fill them.

**Lemon Cheesecakes.**— Mix four ounces of sifted lump sugar, with four ounces of butter, and gently melt it; then add the yolks of two and the white of one egg, the rind of three lemons shred fine, and the juice of one and a half, with one Savoy biscuit, some blanched almonds pounded, and three spoonfuls of brandy; mix well: put in paste made as follows :—Eight ounces of flour, six ounces of butter, two-thirds of which mix with the flour first, then wet it with six spoonfuls of water, and roll the remainder in.

**Another way.**—Boil two fine large lemons, or three small ones, and after squeezing, pound them well together in a mortar, with four ounces of loaf sugar, the yolks of six eggs, and eight ounces of fresh butter.

Fill the patty-pans half full.

Orange Cheesecakes are done the same way, only you must boil the peel in two or three waters to take out the bitterness, or make them of orange marmalade well beaten in a mortar.

**Orange Cheesecakes.**— When you have blanched half a pound of almonds, beat them very fine with orange-flower water, and half a pound of fine sugar beaten and sifted, a pound of butter that has been melted carefully without oiling, and which must be nearly cold before you use it; then beat the yolks of ten, and whites of four eggs; pound two candied oranges, and a fresh one with the bitterness boiled out, in a mortar till as tender as marmalade, without any lumps; and beat the whole together and put into patty-pans.

**Potato Cheesecakes.**—Boil six ounces of potatoes, and four ounces of lemon peel; beat the latter in a marble mortar with four ounces of sugar: then add the potatoes, beaten, and four ounces of butter melted in a little cream. When well mixed, let it stand to grow cold. Put crust in patty-pans, and rather more than half fill them. Bake in a quick oven half an hour, sifting some double-refined sugar on them when going to the oven.— This quantity will make a dozen.

**Almond Cheesecakes.**—Blanch and pound four ounces of sweet almonds, and a few bitter, with a spoonful of water; then add four ounces of sugar pounded, a spoonful of cream, and the whites of two eggs well beaten ; mix all as quick as possible : put into very small patty-pans, and bake in a pretty warm oven under twenty minutes.

**Another way.**—Blanch and pound four ounces of almonds, with a little orange-flower, or rose water ; then stir in the yolks of six and whites of three eggs, well beaten, five ounces of butter warmed, the peel of a lemon grated, and a little of the juice : sweeten with fine Lisbon sugar. When well mixed, bake in a delicate paste, in small pans.

**Another way.**—Press the whey from as much curd as will make two dozen small ones : then put it on the back of a sieve, and with half an ounce of butter rub it through with the back of a spoon ; put to it six yolks, and three whites of eggs, and a few bitter almonds pounded with as much sugar as will make the curd properly sweet : mix with it the rind of a lemon grated, and a glass of brandy. Put a puff paste into the pans, and ten minutes will bake them.

**Dough Nuts.**—Rub a quarter of a pound of butter into a pound of flour, then add six ounces of sugar, three eggs, about a dessert spoonful of yeast, and sufficient milk to make it into a stiff paste. Let it stand to rise, then roll it out, and cut it into shapes with a paste cutter, and boil them in lard, till they are of a nice brown colour.

**A Tippling Cake.**—Put a sponge cake into a deep china or glass dish, pour round it some white wine (raisin is very suitable), and a wine glass of brandy. Let the cake soak up the wine, and then strew sifted sugar over it, and pour in the dish a rich thick custard, according to your fancy.

**Royal Paste, called "Au Choux."**—This paste is the basis of many sorts of pastry : it is used to mix an infinite number of second-course dishes of various forms, and of different denominations.

Take a stew-pan large enough to contain four quarts of water, pour half a pint of water into it, with a quarter of a pound or a little more of fresh butter, two ounces of sugar, a little salt, and the peel of a lemon ; let the whole boil till the butter is entirely melted. Then take some very fine dry flour and shake through a sieve. Take the lemon peel out with a ladle, and throw a handful of flour into the preparation while boiling ; take care, however, not to put more flour than the liquor can soak up. Stir with a wooden spoon till the paste can easily be detached from the stew-pan, and then take it off the fire. Next break an egg into this paste, and mix it well : then break a second, which also mix ; do not put more eggs than the paste can absorb, but you must be careful not to make this preparation too liquid. It is almost certain, that about five or six eggs will be wanted for the above quan-tity ; then form them *en choux*, by which is meant in the shape of a ball an inch in circumference. As this paste swells very much, you must dress it accordingly, putting the choux on a baking sheet, at an inch distant from each other, in order that they may undergo a greater effect in the oven. Brush them over as usual with the dorure or egg-wash, to which has been added a little milk. Put them into an oven moderately hot, but do not open the oven till they are quite baked, otherwise they would flatten, and all attempts to make them rise again would be found to be useless: next dry them. Sometimes you may glaze them; at other times you may send them up without being glazed.

To detach them from the baking sheet, apply the sharp edge of your knife, and take them off gently. Then make a small opening on the side, into which put with a tea-spoon such sweetmeats as you think proper, and send them up dished *en buisson*.

N.B.—Be cautious to smell every egg before you use it, for a bad one would spoil the whole.

\*\*\* This elegant receipt is extracted from " The French Cook," by Mr. Ude.

## VEGETABLES.

### *Observations on Dressing Vegetables.*

VEGETABLES should be carefully cleaned from insects and nicely washed. Boil them in plenty of water, and drain them the moment they are done enough. If overboiled, they will lose their beauty and crispness. Bad cooks sometimes dress them with meat, which is wrong, except carrots with boiling beef.

To Boil Vegetables Green.—Be sure the water boils when you put the vegetables in. Make them boil very fast. Do not cover, but watch them; and if the water has not slackened, you may be sure they are done when they begin to sink. Then take them out immediately, or the colour will change. Hard water, especially if chalybeate, spoils the colour of such vegetables as should be green.

To boil them green in hard water, put a tea-spoonful of salt of wormwood into the water when it boils, before the vegetables are put in.

Vegetable Marrow, to Boil or Stew.—This excellent vegetable may be boiled as asparagus. When boiled, divide it lengthways into two, and serve it up on toast accompanied by melted butter; or when nearly boiled divide it as above, and stew gently in gravy like cucumbers. Care should be taken to choose young ones not exceeding six inches in length.

To Keep Green Peas.—Shell, and put them into a kettle of water when it boils; give them two or three warms only, and pour them into a colander. When the water drains off, turn them out on a dresser covered with cloth, and pour them on another cloth to dry perfectly. Then bottle them in wide-mouthed bottles, leaving only room to pour clarified mutton-suet upon them an inch thick, and for the cork. Rosin it down, and keep it in the cellar or in the earth, as will be directed for gooseberries under the head of " Keeping for Winter." When they are to be used, boil them

I

till tender, with a bit of butter, a spoonful of sugar, and a bit of mint.

**Another way** (as practised in the Emperor of Russia's kitchen). Shell, scald, and dry them as above; put them on tins or earthen dishes in a cool oven, once or twice to harden. Keep them in paper bags hung up in the kitchen. When they are to be used, let them lie an hour in water; then set them on with cold water and a bit of butter, and boil them till ready. Put a sprig of dried mint to boil with them.

**Boiled Peas** should not be overdone, nor in much water. Chop some scalded mint to garnish them, and stir a piece of butter in with them.

**To Stew Green Peas.**—Put a quart of peas, a lettuce and an onion, both sliced, a bit of butter, pepper, salt, and no more water than hangs round the lettuce from washing. Stew them two hours very gently. When to be served, beat up an egg, and stir it into them, or a bit of flour and butter.

Some think a tea-spoonful of white powdered sugar is an improvement. Gravy may be added, but then there will be less of the flavour of the peas. Chop a bit of mint and stew in them.

**To Stew Old Peas.**—Steep them in water all night, if not fine boilers, otherwise half an hour will do; put them into water just enough to cover them, with a good bit of butter or a piece of beef or pork. Stew them very gently till the peas are soft, and the meat is tender; if it is not salt meat, add salt and a little pepper. Serve them round the meat.

**To Dress Artichokes.**—Trim a few of the outside leaves off, and cut the stalk even. If young, half an hour will boil them. They are better for being gathered two or three days first. Serve them with melted butter, in as many small cups as there are artichokes, to help with each.

**Artichoke Bottoms.**—If dried they must be soaked, then stewed in weak gravy, and served with or without forcemeat in each; or they may be boiled in milk, and served with cream sauce, or added to ragouts, French pies, &c.

**Jerusalem Artichokes** must be taken up the moment they are done, or they will be too soft.

They may be boiled plain, or served with white fricassee sauce.

**To Stew Cucumbers.**—Slice them thick, or halve and divide them into two lengths; strew some salt and pepper and sliced onions; add a little broth or a bit of butter. Simmer very slowly, and before serving, if no butter was in before, put some and a little flour, or if there was butter in, only a little flour, unless it wants richness.

**Another way.**—Slice the onions, and cut the cucumbers large; flour them, and fry them in some butter; then pour on some good broth or gravy, and stew them till done enough. Skim off the fat.

**To Stew Onions.**—Peel six large onions; fry gently of a fine brown, but do not blacken them; then put them into a small stew-pan with a little weak gravy, pepper, and salt; cover and stew two hours gently. They should be lightly floured at first.

Roast Onions should be done with all the skins on. They eat well alone with only salt and cold butter, or with roast potatoes or beetroots.

To Stew Celery.—Wash six heads and strip off their outer leaves, either halve or leave them whole, according to their size; cut into lengths of four inches. Put them into a stew-pan with a cup of broth or weak white gravy, stew till tender; then add two spoonfuls of cream and a little flour and butter, seasoned with pepper, salt, and nutmeg, and simmer all together.

To Boil Cauliflowers.—Choose those that are close and white, cut off the green leaves, and look carefully that there are no caterpillars about the stalk. Soak an hour in cold water, then boil them in milk and water, and take care to skim the saucepan that not the least foulness may fall on the flower. It must be served very white and rather crisp.

Cauliflower in White Sauce.—Half boil it, then cut it into handsome pieces, and lay them in a stew-pan with a little broth, a bit of mace, a little salt, and a dust of white pepper; simmer half an hour, then put a little cream, butter, and flour; shake and simmer a few minutes, and serve.

To Dress Cauliflowers and Parmesan.—Boil a cauliflower, drain it on a sieve, and cut the stalk so that the flower will stand upright about two inches above the dish. Put it into a stew-pan with a little white sauce, let it stew till done enough, which will be but a few minutes, then dish it with the sauce round, and put Parmesan grated over it. Brown it with a salamander.

To Dress Broccoli.—Cut the heads with short stalks, and pare the tough skin off them. Tie the small shoots into bunches, and boil them a shorter time than the heads. Some salt must be put into the water. Serve with or without toast.

Spinach requires great care in washing and picking it. When that is done, throw it into a saucepan that will just hold it, sprinkle it with a little salt, and cover close. The pan must be set on the fire, and well shaken. When done, beat the spinach well with a small bit of butter: it must come to table pretty dry, and looks well if pressed into a tin mould in the form of a large leaf, which is sold at the tin shops. A spoonful of cream is an improvement.

To Dress Beans.—Boil tender with a bunch of parsley, which must be chopped to serve with them. Bacon or pickled pork must be served to eat with, but not boiled with them.

Fricasseed Windsor Beans.—When grown large, but not mealy, boil, blanch, and lay them in a white sauce ready hot; just heat them through in it, and serve. If any are not of a fine green, do not use them for this dish.

French Beans.—String, and cut them into four or eight; the last looks best. Lay them in salt and water, and when the saucepan boils put them in with some salt. As soon as they are done serve them immediately, to preserve the green colour. Or when half-done drain the water off, and put them into two spoonfuls of broth strained; and add a little cream, butter, and flour, to finish doing them.

**To Stew Red Cabbage.**—Slice a small, or half a large red cabbage, wash and put it into a saucepan with pepper, salt, no water but what hangs about it, and a piece of butter. Stew till quite tender; and when going to serve, add two or three spoonfuls of vinegar, and give one boil over the fire. Serve it for cold meat, or with sausages on it.

**Another way.**—Shred the cabbage, wash it, and put it over a slow fire, with slices of onion, pepper and salt, and a little plain gravy. When quite tender, and a few minutes before serving, add a bit of butter rubbed with flour, and two or three spoonfuls of vinegar and boil up.

**Another.**—Cut the cabbage very thin, and put it into the stew-pan with a small slice of ham, and half an ounce of butter at the bottom, half a pint of broth, and a gill of vinegar. Let it stew covered three hours. When it is very tender add a little more broth, salt, pepper, and a table-spoonful of pounded sugar. Mix these well, and boil them all till the liquor is wasted; then put it into the dish, and lay fried sausages on it.

**Mushrooms.**—The cook should be perfectly acquainted with the different sorts of things called by this name by ignorant people, as the death of many persons has been occasioned by carelessly using the poisonous kinds.

The eatable mushrooms first appear very small, and of a round form, on a little stalk. They grow very fast, and the upper part and stalk are white. As the size increases the under part gradually opens, and shows a fringy fur of a very fine salmon-colour, which continues more or less till the mushroom has gained some size, and then turns to a dark brown. These marks should be attended to, and likewise whether the skin can be easily parted from the edges and middle. Those that have a white or yellow fur should be carefully avoided, though many of them have the same smell (but not so strong) as the right sort.

**To Stew Mushrooms.**—The large buttons are best, and the small flaps while the fur is still red. Rub the large buttons with salt and a bit of flannel, cut out the fur, and take off the skin from the others. Sprinkle them with salt, and put into a stew-pan with some pepper-corns; simmer slowly till done, then put a small bit of butter and flour, and two spoonfuls of cream: give them one boil, and serve with sippets of bread.

**To Stew Sorrel for Fricandeau and Roast Meat.**—Wash the sorrel, and put it into a silver vessel, or stone jar, with no more water than hangs to the leaves. Simmer it as slow as you can, and when done enough put a bit of butter, and beat it well.

**French Salad.**—Chop three anchovies, a shalot, and some parsley, small; put them into a bowl with two table-spoonfuls of vinegar, one of oil, a little mustard, and salt. When well mixed, add by degrees some cold roast or boiled meat in very thin slices;

put in a few at a time, not exceeding two or three inches long. Shake them in the seasoning, and then put more; but cover the bowl close, and let the salad be prepared three hours before it is to be eaten. Garnish with parsley, and a few slices of the fat.

**Lobster Salad.**—Make a salad, and put some of the red part of the lobster to it, cut. This forms a pretty contrast to the white and green of the vegetables. Do not put much oil, as shell-fish absorb the sharpness of the vinegar. Serve in a dish, not a bowl.

**To Boil Potatoes.**—Set them on a fire, without paring them, in cold water; let them half boil, then throw some salt in and a pint of cold water, and let them boil again till almost done. Pour off the water, and put a clean cloth over them, and then the sauce-pan cover, and set them by the fire to steam till ready. Many persons prefer steamers. Potatoes look best when the skin is peeled, not cut. Do new potatoes the same; but be careful they are taken off in time, or they will be watery. Before dressing, rub off the skin with a cloth and salt, and then wash.

**To Broil Potatoes.**—Parboil, then slice and broil them. Or parboil, and then set them whole on the gridiron over a very slow fire, and when thoroughly done send them up with their skins on. This last way is practised in many Irish families.

**To Roast Potatoes.**—Half-boil, take off the thin peel, and roast them of a beautiful brown.

**To Fry Potatoes.**—Take the skin off raw potatoes, slice and fry them, either in butter or thin batter.

**To Mash Potatoes.**—Boil the potatoes, peel them, and break them to paste; then to two pounds of them add a quarter of a pint of milk, a little salt, and two ounces of butter, and stir it all well over the fire. Either serve them in this manner, or place them on the dish in a form, and then brown the top with a sala-mander, or in scallops.

**Carrots** require a good deal of boiling. When young, wipe off the skin after they are boiled; when old, boil them with the salt meat, and scrape them first.

**To Stew Carrots.**—Half-boil, then nicely scrape, and slice them into a stew-pan. Put to them half a tea-cupful of any weak broth, some pepper and salt, and half a cupful of cream; simmer them till they are very tender, but not broken. Before serving, rub a very little flour with a bit of butter, and warm up with them. If approved, chopped parsley may be added, ten minutes before-served.

**To Mash Parsnips.**—Boil them tender, scrape, then mash them into a stew-pan with a little cream, a good piece of butter, and pepper and salt.

**Fricassee of Parsnips.**—Boil in milk till they are soft, then cut them lengthways into bits two or three inches long, and sim-mer in a white sauce made of two spoonfuls of broth, a bit of mace, half a cupful of cream, a bit of butter, and some flour, pepper, and salt.

**To dress Chardoons.**—Cut them into pieces of six inches long, and put on a string; boil till tender, and have ready a piece of butter in a pan; flour, fry them brown, and serve.

Or, tie them up in bundles, and serve as asparagus boiled, on toast, and pour butter over them.

Or boil in salt and water, dry, then dip them into butter, and fry them. Serve with melted butter.

Or stew them: boil as directed in last page; toss them up with a brown or white gravy, add Cayenne, ketchup, and salt. Thicken with a bit of butter and flour.

**Beet-roots.**—Make a very pleasant addition to winter-salad, of which they may agreeably form a full half, instead of being only used to ornament it. This root is cooling and very wholesome.

It is extremely good boiled, and sliced with a small quantity of onion; or stewed with whole onions, large or small, as follows:—

Boil the beet tender with the skin on, slice it into a stew-pan with a little broth, and a spoonful of vinegar; simmer till the gravy is tinged with the colour, then put it into a small dish, and make a round of the button-onions, first boiled till tender; take off the skin just before serving, and mind they are quite hot and clear.

Or, roast three large onions, and peel off the outer skins till they look clear, and serve the beet-root stewed round them.

If beet-root is in the least broken before dressed, it parts with its colour, and looks ill.

**Frying Herbs, as dressed in Staffordshire.**—Clean and drain a good quantity of spinach leaves, two large handfuls of parsley, and a handful of green onions. Chop the parsley and onions, and sprinkle them among the spinach. Set them all on to stew with some salt, and a bit of butter the size of a walnut, shake the pan when it begins to grow warm, and let it be closely covered over a slow stove till done enough. It is served with slices of broiled calves' liver, small rashers of bacon, and eggs fried: the latter on the herbs, the other in a separate dish.

**Sea Kale** must be boiled very white, and served on toast like asparagus.

**Laver.**—This is a plant that grows on the rocks near the sea in the west of England, and is sent in pots prepared for eating.

Set some of it on a dish over a lamp, with a bit of butter, and the squeeze of a Seville orange. Stir it till hot. It is eaten with roast meat, and is a great sweetener of the blood. It is seldom liked at first, but people become extremely fond of it by habit.

**To Preserve several Vegetables to eat in Winter.**—For

French beans, pick them young, and throw into a little wooden keg a layer of them three inches deep; then sprinkle them with salt, put another layer of beans, and do the same as high as you think proper, alternately with salt, but not too much of this. Lay over them a plate, or cover of wood, that will go into the keg, and put a·heavy stone on it. A pickle will rise from the beans and salt. If they are too salt, the soaking and boiling will not be sufficient to make them pleasant to the taste. When they are to be eaten, cut, soak, and boil them as if fresh.

**Carrots, Parsnips, and Beet-roots,** should be kept in layers of dry sand for winter use; and neither they nor potatoes should be cleared from the earth. Potatoes should be carefully kept from frost.

**Store Onions** keep best hung up in a dry cold room.

**Parsley** should be cut close to the stalks, and dried in a warm room, or on tins in a very cold oven; it preserves its flavour and colour, and is very useful in winter.

**Artichoke Bottoms,** slowly dried, should be kept in paper-bags; and **Truffles, Morels, Lemon Peel,** &c., in a dry place, ticketed.

Small close **Cabbages,** laid on a stone floor before the frost sets in, will blanch and be very fine after many weeks' keeping.

**PICKLES.—Rules to be observed with Pickles.—** Keep them closely covered, and have a wooden spoon, with holes, tied to each jar; all metals being improper. They should be well kept from the air, the large jars be seldom opened, and small ones for the different pickles in use, should be kept for common supply, into which what is not eaten may be returned, and the top closely covered.

Acids dissolve the lead that is in the tinning of saucepans. When necessary to boil vinegar, do it in a stone jar on the hot hearth. Pickles should never be put into glazed jars, as salt and vinegar penetrate the glaze, which is poisonous.

**Lemon Pickle.—** Wipe six lemons, cut each into eight pieces; put on them a pound of salt, six large cloves of garlic, two ounces of horse-radish sliced thin, likewise of cloves, mace, nutmeg, and Cayenne, a quarter of an ounce each, and two ounces of flour of mustard; to these put two quarts of vinegar. Boil a quarter of an hour in a well-tinned saucepan; or, which is better, do it in a stone jar, in a kettle of boiling water; or set the jar on the hot hearth till done. Set the jar by, and stir it daily for six weeks; keep the jar close covered. Put it into small bottles.

**Indian Pickle.—** Lay a pound of white ginger in water one night; then scrape, slice, and lay it in salt in a pan till the other ingredients shall be ready.

Peel, slice, and salt a pound of garlic three days, then put it in the sun to dry. Salt and dry long pepper in the same way.

Prepare various sorts of vegetables thus:

Quarter some small white cabbages, salt three days, squeeze, and set them in the sun to dry.

Cauliflowers cut in the branches; take off the green from

radishes; cut celery in three-inch lengths; ditto young French beans whole, likewise the shoots of elder, which will look like bamboo. Apples and cucumbers, choose of the least seedy sort; cut them in slices, or quarters if not too large. All must be salted, drained, and dried in the sun, except the latter, over which you must pour boiling vinegar, and in twelve hours drain them, but no salt must be used.

Put the spice, garlic, a quarter of a pound of mustard-seed, and as much vinegar as you think enough for the quantity you are to pickle, into a large stone jar, and one ounce of turmeric, to be ready against the vegetables shall be dried. When they are ready, observe the following directions:—Put some of them into a two-quart stone jar, and pour over them one quart of boiling vinegar. Next day take out those vegetables, and when drained, put them into a large stock jar, and boiling the vinegar pour it over some more of the vegetables; let them lie a night, and do as before. Thus proceed till you have cleansed each set from the dust which must inevitably fall on them by being so long in doing; then, to every gallon of vinegar put two ounces of flour of mustard, mixing, by degrees, with a little of it boiling hot. The whole of the vinegar should have been previously scalded, but set to be cool before it was put to the spice. Stop the jar tight.

This pickle will not be ready for a year, but you may make a small jar for eating in a fortnight, only by giving the cauliflower one scald in water after salting and drying as above, but without the preparative vinegar; then pour the vinegar that has the spice and garlic, boiling hot over. If at any time it be found that the vegetables have not swelled properly, boiling the pickle and pouring it over them hot, will plump them.

**English Bamboo.**—Cut the large young shoots of elder, which put out in the middle of May (the middle stalks are most tender); peel off the outward peel or skin, and lay them in salt and water, very strong, one night. Dry them piece by piece in a cloth. Have in readiness a pickle thus made and boiled: to a quart of vinegar put an ounce of white pepper, an ounce of sliced ginger, a little mace and pimento, and pour boiling on the elder shoots in a stone jar; stop close, and set by the fire two hours, turning the jar often to keep it scalding hot. If not green when cold, strain off the liquor, and pour it boiling hot again; keep it hot as before. Or, if you intend to make Indian pickle, the above shoots are a great improvement to it, in which case you need only pour boiling vinegar and mustard seed on them, and keep them till your jar of pickles shall be ready to receive them. The cluster of elder-flowers before it opens, makes a delicious pickle to eat with boiled mutton. It is only done by pouring boiling vinegar over.

**Melon Mangoes.**—There is a particular sort for this purpose which the gardeners all know. Cut a small square piece from one side, and through that take out the seeds, and mix with them mustard-seeds and shred garlic; stuff the melon as full as the space will allow, and replace the square small piece. Bind it up with a pack-thread. Boil a good quantity of vinegar, to allow for wasting, with pepper, salt, ginger, and pour boiling hot over the mangoes four successive days; the last, put flour of mustard and scraped horse-radish into the vinegar just as it boils up. Stop close. Observe that there is plenty of vinegar. All pickles are spoiled if not well covered. Mangoes should be done soon after they are gathered. Large cucumbers, called Green Turley, prepared as mangoes, are excellent, and come sooner into eating.

Mark, the greater number of times boiling vinegar is poured over either sort, the sooner it will be ready.

**Pickled Lemons.**—They should be small and with thick rinds; rub them with a piece of flannel, then slit them half down in four quarters, but not through to the pulp: fill the slits with salt hard pressed in, set them upright in a pan for four or five days until the salt melts, turn them thrice a day in their own liquid until tender, make enough pickle to cover them of rape vinegar, the brine of the lemons, Jamaica pepper, and ginger; boil and skim it; when cold put it to the lemons, with two ounces of mustard-seed and two cloves of garlic to six lemons. When the lemons are used, the pickle will be useful in fish or other sauces.

**Olives** are of three kinds, Italian, Spanish, and French, of different sizes and flavour; each sort should be firm, though some are most fleshy.

Preserve them from the air.

**Pickled Onions.**—In the month of September, choose the small white round onions, take off the brown skin, have a very nice tin stew-pan of boiling water ready, throw in as many onions as will cover the top; as soon as they look clear on the outside, take them up as quick as possible with a slice, and lay them on a clean cloth; cover them close with another, and scald more, and so on. Let them lie to be cold, then put them in a jar, or glass, or wide-mouth bottles, and pour over them the best white wine vinegar, just hot but not boiling. When cold cover them; should the outer skin shrivel, peel it off. They must look quite clear.

**To Pickle Cucumbers and Onions Sliced.**—Cut them in slices, and sprinkle salt over them: next day drain them for five or six hours; then put them into a stone jar, pour boiling vinegar over them, and keep them in a warm place. The slices should be thick. Repeat the boiling vinegar, and stop them up again instantly; and so on till green; the last time put pepper and ginger. Keep in small stone jars.

**To Pickle young Cucumbers.**—Choose young gherkins, spread them on dishes, salt them, and let them lie a week; drain them, and putting them in a jar, pour boiling vinegar over them. Set them near the fire, covered with plenty of vine leaves; if they do not become a tolerable good green, pour the vinegar into another jar, set it over the hot hearth, and when it boils pour it over them again, covering with fresh leaves; and thus do till they are of as good a colour as you wish: but as it is now known that the very fine green pickles are made so by using brass or bell-metal vessels, which, when vinegar is put into them, become highly poisonous, few people like to eat them.

**To Pickle Walnuts.**—When they will bear a pin to go into them, put a brine of salt and water boiled, and strong enough to bear an egg, on them, being quite cold first. It must be well skimmed while boiling. Let them soak six days; then change the brine, let them stand six more; then drain them, and pour over them in the jar a pickle of the best white wine vinegar, with a good quantity of pepper, pimento, ginger, mace, cloves, mustard-seed, and horse-radish; all boiled together, but cold. To every hundred of walnuts put six spoonfuls of mustard-seed, and two or three heads of garlic or shalot; but the latter is least strong.

Thus done, they will be good for several years, if kept close covered. The air will soften them. They will not be fit to eat under six months.

The pickle will serve as good ketchup, when all the walnuts are used.

**Another way.**—Put them into a jar, cover them with the best vinegar cold, let them stand four months; then pour off the pickle, and boil as much fresh vinegar as will cover the walnuts, adding to every three quarts of vinegar one quarter pound of best Durham mustard, a stick of horse-radish sliced, one half ounce of black pepper, one half ounce of cloves, one ounce of ginger, one half ounce of allspice, and a good handful of salt; pour the whole, boiling hot, upon the walnuts, and cover them close; they will be fit for use in three or four months. You may add two ounces of garlic, or shalot, but not boiled in the vinegar.

Of the pickle in which the walnuts stood for the first four months, you may make excellent ketchup.

**An excellent Way to Pickle Mushrooms, to preserve the Flavour.**—Buttons must be rubbed with a bit of flannel and salt; and from the larger take out the red inside, for when they are black they will not do, being too old. Throw a little salt over, and put them in a stew-pan, with some mace and pepper; as the liquor comes out shake them well, and keep them over a gentle fire till all of it be dried into them again; then put as much vinegar into the pan as will cover them, give it one warm, and turn all into a glass or stone jar. They will keep two years, and are delicious.

**To Pickle Red Cabbage.**—Slice it into a colander, and sprinkle each layer with salt; let it drain two days, then put it into a jar, and pour boiling vinegar enough to cover, and put a few slices of red beet-root. Observe to choose the purple red cabbage. Those who like the flavour of spice will boil it with the vinegar. Cauliflower cut in branches, and thrown in after being salted, will look of a beautiful red.

**Mushroom Ketchup.**—Take the largest broad mushrooms, break them into an earthen pan, strew salt over, and stir them now and then for three days. Then let them stand for twelve, till there is a thick scum over; strain, and boil the liquor with

Jamaica and black peppers, mace, ginger, a clove or two, and some mustard-seed. When cold, bottle it, and tie a bladder over the cork; in three months boil it again with some fresh spice, and it will then keep a twelvemonth.

**Mushroom Ketchup another way.**—Take a stew-pan full of large-flap mushrooms that are not worm-eaten, the skins and fringe of those you have pickled, throw a handful of salt among them, and set them by a slow fire; they will produce a great deal of liquor, which you must strain; and put to it four ounces of shalots, two cloves of garlic, a good deal of pepper, ginger, mace, cloves, and a few bay leaves—boil and skim very well. When cold, cork close. In two months boil it up again with a little fresh spice and a stick of horse-radish, and it will then keep the year, which mushroom ketchup rarely does, if not boiled a second time.

**Walnut Ketchup of the finest sort.**—Boil or simmer a gallon of the expressed juice of walnuts when they are tender, and skim it well; then put in two pounds of anchovies, bones and liquor, ditto of shalots, one ounce of cloves, ditto of mace, ditto of pepper and one clove of garlic. Let all simmer till the shalots sink; then put the liquor into a pan till cold; bottle and share the spice with each. Cork closely, and tie a bladder over. It will keep twenty years, and is not good the first. Be very careful to express the juice at home; for it is rarely unadulterated, if bought. Some people make liquor of the outside shell when the nut is ripe; but neither the flavour nor the colour is then so fine.

**Cockle Ketchup.**—Open the cockles, scald them in their own liquor; add a little water when the liquor settles, if you have not enough; strain through a cloth, then season with every savoury spice: and if for brown sauce, add port, anchovies, and garlic; if for white, omit these, and put a glass of sherry, lemon-juice and peel, mace, nutmeg, and white pepper. If for brown, burn a bit of sugar for colouring. It is better to have cockles enough than to add water; and they are cheap.

**To Keep Capers.**—Add fresh vinegar that has been scalded, and become cold, and tie them close, to keep out the air, which makes them soft.

-------

# SWEET DISHES, PRESERVES, SWEETMEATS, ETC.

**SWEET DISHES.—Buttered Rice.**—Wash and pick some rice, drain, and put it with some new milk, enough just to swell it, over the fire; when tender, pour off the milk, and add a bit of butter, a little sugar, and pounded cinnamon. Shake it, that it do not burn, and serve.

**Souffle of Rice and Apple.**—Blanch Carolina rice, strain it, and set it to boil in milk, with lemon peel and a bit of cinnamon. Let it boil till the rice is dry; then cool it, and raise a rim three inches high round the dish; having egged it where it is put to make it stick. Then egg the rice all over. Fill the dish half way up with a marmalade of apples; have ready the whites of four eggs beaten to a fine froth, and put them over the marmalade; then sift fine sugar over it, and set it in the oven, which should be warm enough to give it a beautiful colour.

**Snow Balls.**—Swell rice in milk, and strain it off, and having pared and cored apples, put the rice round them, tying each up in a cloth. Put a bit of lemon peel, a clove, or cinnamon in each, and boil them well.

**Lent Potatoes.**—Swell three or four ounces of almonds, and three or four bitter, when blanched, putting some orange-flower water to prevent oiling; add eight ounces of butter, four eggs well beaten and strained, half a glass of raisin wine, and sugar to your taste. Bent all well till quite smooth, and grate in three Savoy biscuits. Make balls of the above with a little flour, the size of a chestnut; throw them into a stew-pan of boiling lard, and boil them of a beautiful yellow brown. Drain them on a sieve. Serve sweet sauce in a boat to eat with them.

**A Tansey.**—Beat seven eggs, yolks and whites separately; add a pint of cream, the same of spinach-juice, and a little tansey-juice gained by pounding in a stone mortar, a quarter of a pound of Naples biscuits, sugar to taste, a glass of white wine, and some nutmeg. Set all in a saucepan, just to thicken, over the fire; then put it into a dish, lined with paste, to turn out, and bake it.

**Puits d'Amour.**—Cut a fine rich puff-paste rolled thin, with tin shapes made on purpose, one size less than another, in a pyramidical form, and lay them so; then bake in a moderate oven, that the paste may be done sufficiently, but very pale. Lay different coloured sweetmeats on the edges.

**A very nice Dish of Maccaroni dressed Sweet.**—Boil two ounces in a pint of milk, with a bit of lemon peel, and a good bit of cinnamon, till the pipes are swelled to their utmost size without breaking. Lay them on a custard dish, and pour a custard over them hot. Serve cold.

**Floating Island.**—Mix three half-pints of thin cream with a quarter of a pint of raisin wine, a little lemon-juice, orange-flower water, and sugar: put it into a dish for the middle of the table, and put on the cream a froth, as will be directed in page 146, which may be made of raspberry or currant jelly.

**Another way.**—Scald a codlin before it is ripe, or any sharp apple; pulp it through a sieve. Beat the whites of two eggs with sugar, and a spoonful of orange-flower water; mix in by degrees the pulp, and beat all together until you have a large quantity of froth; serve it on a raspberry cream; or you may colour the froth with beet-root, raspberry, or currant jelly, and set it on a white cream, having given it the flavour of lemon; sugar and wine, as above; or, put the froth on a custard.

**Flummery.**—Put three large handfuls of very small white oatmeal to steep a day and night in cold water; then pour it off clear, and add as much more water, and let it stand the same time.

Strain it through a fine hair sieve, and boil till it be as thick as hasty pudding; stirring it well all the time. When first strained, put in one large spoonful of white sugar, and two of orange-flower water. Put it into shallow dishes, and serve to eat with wine, cyder milk, or cream and sugar. It is very good.

**Dutch Flummery.**—Boil two ounces of isinglass in a pint and a half of water very gently half an hour; add a pint of white wine, the juice of three, and the thin rind of one lemon, and rub a few lumps of sugar on another lemon to obtain the essence, and with them add as much more sugar as shall make it sweet enough; and having beaten the yolks of seven eggs, give them and the above, when mixed, one scald; stir all the time, and pour it into a basin; stir it till half cold; then let it settle, and put it into a melon shape.

**Rice Flummery.**—Boil with a pint of new milk, a bit of lemon peel, and cinnamon; mix with a little cold milk as much rice-flour as will make the whole of a good consistence; sweeten, and add a spoonful of peach-water, or a bitter almond beaten; boil it, observing it do not burn; pour it into a shape or pint basin, taking out the spice. When cold, turn the flummery into a dish, and serve with cream, milk, or custard round; or put a tea-cupful of cream into half a pint of new milk, a glass of white wine, half a lemon squeezed, and sugar.

**Somersetshire Firmity.**—To a quart of ready-boiled wheat, put by degrees two quarts of new milk, breaking the jelly, and then four ounces of currants picked clean and washed; stir them and boil till they are done. Beat the yolks of three eggs, and a little nutmeg, with two or three spoonfuls of milk; add this to the wheat; stir them together while over the fire; then sweeten, and serve cold in a deep dish. Some persons like it best warm.

**Curds and Cream.**—Put three or four pints of milk into a pan a little warm, and then add rennet or gallino. When the curd is come, lade it with a saucer into an earthen shape perforated, of any form you please. Fill it up as the whey drains off, without breaking or pressing the curd. If turned only two hours before wanted, it is very light; but those who like it harder may have it so, by making it earlier, and squeezing it. Cream, milk, or a whip of cream, sugar, wine, and lemon, to be put in the dish, or into a glass bowl, to serve with the curd.

**Another Way.**—To four quarts of new milk warmed, put from a pint to a quart of buttermilk strained, according to its sourness; keep the pan covered until the curd be of firmness to cut three or four times across with a saucer; as the whey leaves it, put it into a shape, and fill up until it be solid enough to take the form. Serve with cream plain, or mixed with sugar, wine, and lemon.

**A Curd Star.**—Set a quart of new milk upon the fire with two or three blades of mace; and, when ready to boil, put to it the yolks and whites of nine eggs well beaten, and as much salt as will lie upon a small knife's point. Let it boil till the whey is clear; then drain it in a thin cloth, or hair sieve; season it with sugar, or a little cinnamon, rose-water, orange-flower water, or white wine, to your taste; and put it into a star form, or any other. Let it stand some hours before you turn it into a dish; then put round it thick cream or custard.

**Blanc-mange or Blamange.**—Boil two ounces of isinglass in three half-pints of water half an hour; strain it to a pint and a half of cream; sweeten it, and add some peach-water, or a few bitter almonds; let it boil once up, and put it into what forms you please. If not to be very stiff, a little less isinglass will do. Observe to let the blamange settle before you turn it into the forms, or the blacks will remain at the bottom of them, and be on the top of the blamange when taken out of the moulds.

**Jaune-mange.**—Pour a pint of boiling water over three ounces of isinglass, and when it is dissolved, add a pint of white wine, the juice of three oranges, and two lemons, the peel of a lemon shred fine; sweeten this to your taste, and add the yolks of eight eggs; let it simmer gently, strain, and pour into moulds. Turn out next day.

**An excellent Trifle.**—Lay macaroons and ratafia-drops over the bottom of your dish, and pour in as much raisin wine as they will suck up, which, when they have done, pour on them cold rich custard made with more eggs than directed in the foregoing pages, and some rice flour. It must stand two or three inches thick; on that put a layer of raspberry jam, and cover the whole with a very high whip, made the day before, of rich cream, the whites of two well-beaten eggs, sugar, lemon peel, and raisin wine, well beat up with a whisk kept only to whip syllabubs and creams. If made the day before used it has quite a different taste, and is solid and far better.

**Gooseberry or Apple Trifle.**—Scald such a quantity of either of these fruits as, when pulped through a sieve, will make a thick layer at the bottom of your dish; if of apples, mix the rind of half a lemon grated fine, and to both as much sugar as will be pleasant.

Mix half a pint of milk, half a pint of cream, and the yolk of one egg; give it a scald over the fire, and stir it all the time; do not let it boil; add a little sugar only, and let it grow cold. Lay it over the apples with a spoon, and then put on it a whip made the day before, as for other Trifle.

**Chantilly Cake, or Cake Trifle.**—Bake a rice cake in a mould. When cold, cut it round about two inches from the edge with a sharp knife, taking care not to perforate the bottom. Put in a thick custard and some tea-spoonfuls of raspberry jam, and then put on a high whip.

**Gooseberry Fool.**—Put the fruit into a stone jar, and some good Lisbon sugar; set the jar on a stove or in a saucepan of water over the fire; if the former, a large spoonful of water should be added to the fruit. When it is done enough to pulp, press it through a colander; have ready a sufficient quantity of new milk and a tea-cup of raw cream, boiled together; or an egg instead of the latter, and left to be cold; then sweeten it pretty well with fine Lisbon sugar, and mix the pulp by degrees with it.

**Apple Fool.**—Stew apples as directed for gooseberries, and then peel and pulp them. Prepare the milk, &c., and mix as before.

**Orange Fool.**—Mix the juice of three Seville oranges, three eggs well beaten, a pint of cream, a little nutmeg and cinnamon, and sweeten to your taste. Set the whole over a slow fire, and stir it till it becomes as thick as good melted butter, but it must not be boiled; then pour it into a dish for eating cold.

**A Cream.**—Boil half a pint of cream and half a pint of milk, with two bay-leaves, a bit of lemon-peel, a few almonds beaten to paste, with a drop of water, a little sugar, orange-flower water, and a tea-spoonful of flour, having been rubbed down with a little cold milk, and mixed with the above. When cold, put a little lemon-juice to the cream, and serve it in cups or lemonade glasses.

**An excellent Cream.**—Whip up three-quarters of a pint of very rich cream to a strong froth, with some finely-scraped lemon peel, a squeeze of the juice, a glass of sweet wine, and sugar, to make it pleasant, but not too sweet; lay it in a sieve or in a form, and next day put it on a dish, and ornament it with very light puff-paste biscuits, made in tin shapes the length of a finger, and about two inches thick, over which sugar may be strewed, or a light glaze with isinglass. Or you may use macaroons to line the edge of the dish.

**Burnt Cream.**—Boil a pint of cream with a stick of cinnamon and some lemon peel; take it off the fire, and pour it very slowly into the yolks of four eggs, stirring till half cold; sweeten, and take out the spice, &c.; pour it into the dish; when cold, strew white pounded sugar over, and brown it with a salamander.

**Another way.**—Make a rich custard without sugar, boiling lemon peel in it. When cold, sift a good deal of sugar over the whole, and brown the top with a salamander.

**Sack Cream.**—Boil a pint of raw cream, the yolk of an egg well beaten, two or three spoonfuls of white wine, sugar, and lemon peel; stir it over a gentle fire till it be as thick as rich cream, and afterwards till cold; then serve it in glasses, with long pieces of dry toast.

**Brandy Cream.**—Boil two dozen of almonds blanched, and pounded bitter almonds, in a little milk. When cold, add to it the yolks of five eggs beaten well in a little cream, sweeten, and put to it two glasses of the best brandy; and when well mixed, pour to it a quart of thin cream; set it over the fire, but do not let it boil; stir one way till it thickens, then pour it into cups, or low glasses. When cold it will be ready. A ratafia-drop may be put in each, if you choose it. If you wish it to keep, scald the cream previously.

**Ratafia Cream.**—Boil three or four laurel, peach, or nectarine leaves, in a full pint of cream; strain it, and when cold add the yolks of three eggs beaten and strained, sugar, and a large spoonful of brandy stirred quick into it.  Scald till thick, stirring it all the time.

**Another way.**—Mix half a quarter of a pint of ratafia, the same quantity of mountain wine, the juice of two or three lemons, a pint of rich cream, and as much sugar as will make it pleasantly flavoured.  Beat it with a whisk, and put it into glasses.  This cream will keep eight or ten days.

**Lemon Cream.**—Take a pint of thick cream, and put to it the yolks of two eggs well beaten, four ounces of fine sugar, and the thin rind of a lemon; boil it up, then stir it till almost cold; put the juice of a lemon in a dish or bowl and pour the cream upon it, stirring it till quite cold.

**Yellow Lemon Cream without Cream.**—Pare four lemons very thin into twelve large spoonfuls of water, and squeeze the juice on seven ounces of finely-pounded sugar: beat the yolks of nine eggs well; add the peels and juice beaten together for some time; then strain it through a flannel into a silver or very nice block-tin saucepan; set it over a gentle fire, and stir it one way till pretty thick and scalding hot, but not boiling or it will curdle.  Pour it into jelly-glasses.  A few lumps of sugar should be rubbed hard on the lemons before they are pared, or after, as the peel will be so thin as not to take all the essence, and the sugar will attract it, and give a better colour and flavour.

**White Lemon Cream** is made the same as the above, only put the whites of the eggs in lieu of the yolks, whisking it extremely well to froth.

**Imperial Cream.**—Boil a quart of cream with the thin rind of a lemon, then stir it till nearly cold; have ready in a dish or bowl that you are to serve in, the juice of three lemons strained with as much sugar as will sweeten the cream, which pour into the dish from a large teapot, holding it high and moving it about to mix with the juice.  It should be made at least six hours before it be served, and will be still better if a day.

**Almond Cream.**—Beat four ounces of sweet almonds, and a few bitter, in a mortar, with a tea-spoonful of water to prevent oiling, both having been blanched.  Put the paste to a quart of cream, and add the juice of three lemons sweetened; beat it up with a whisk to a froth, which take off on the shallow part of a sieve; fill glasses with some of the liquor and the froth.

**Snow Cream.**—Put to a quart of cream the whites of three eggs well beaten, four spoonfuls of sweet wine, sugar to your taste, and a bit of lemon peel; whip it to a froth, remove the peel, and serve in a dish.

**Coffee Cream, much admired.**—Boil a calf's foot in water till it wastes to a pint of jelly, clear of sediment and fat.  Make a tea-cup of very strong coffee; clear it with a bit of isinglass to be perfectly bright; pour to it the jelly, and add a pint of very good cream, and as much fine Lisbon sugar as is pleasant; give one boil up, and pour into the dish.

It should jelly, but not be stiff.  Observe that your coffee be fresh.

**Chocolate Cream.**—Scrape into one quart of thick cream, one ounce of the best chocolate, and a quarter of a pound of sugar; boil and mill it; when quite smooth take it off, and leave it to be cold; then add the whites of nine eggs.  Whisk; and take up the froth, on sieves, as others are done; and serve the froth in glasses, to rise above some of the cream.

**Codlin Cream.**—Pare and core twenty good codlins; beat them in a mortar, with a pint of cream; strain it into a dish; and put sugar, bread crumbs, and a glass of wine, to it.  Stir it well.

**Excellent Orange Cream.**—Boil the rind of a Seville orange very tender; beat it fine in a mortar; put to it a spoonful of the best brandy, the juice of a Seville orange, four ounces of loaf sugar, and the yolks of four eggs; beat all together for ten minutes; then, by gentle degrees, pour in a pint of boiling cream; beat till cold; put into custard cups set into a deep dish of boiling water, and let them stand till cold again.  Put at the top small strips of orange-paring cut thin, or preserved chips.

**Raspberry Cream.**—Mash the fruit gently, and let them drain; then sprinkle a little sugar over, and that will produce more juice; then put the juice to some cream, and sweeten it; after which, if you choose to lower it with some milk it will not curdle; which it would, if put to the milk before the cream; but it is best made of raspberry jelly, instead of jam, when the fresh fruit cannot be obtained.

**Another way.**—Boil one ounce of isinglass shavings in three pints of cream and new milk mixed, for fifteen minutes, or until the former be melted, and strain it through a hair-sieve into a basin; when cool put about half a pint of raspberry-juice, or syrup, to the milk and cream: stir it till well incorporated; sweeten and add a glass of brandy, whisk it about till three parts cold; then put it into a mould till quite cold.  In summer use the fresh juice; in winter, syrup of raspberries.

**Spinach Cream.**—Beat the yolks of eight eggs with a wooden spoon or a whisk; sweeten them a good deal; and put to them a stick of cinnamon, a pint of rich cream, three quarters of a pint of new milk; stir it well; then add a quarter of a pint of spinach-juice; set it over a gentle stove, and stir it one way constantly till it is as thick as a hasty pudding.  Put into a custard dish some Naples biscuits, or preserved orange, in long slices, and pour the mixture over them.  It is to be eaten cold; and is a dish either for supper, or for a second course.

**Pistachio Cream.**—Blanch four ounces of pistachio nuts; beat them fine with a little rose water, and add the paste to a pint of cream; sweeten; let it just boil, and put it into glasses.

**Clouted Cream.**—String four blades of mace on a thread; put them to a gill of new milk, and six spoonfuls of rose water; simmer a few minutes; then by degrees stir this liquor strained

K

into the yolks of two new eggs well beaten. Stir the whole into
a quart of very good cream, and set it over the fire : stir it till hot,
but not boiling hot; pour it into a deep dish, and let it stand
twenty-four hours. Serve it in a cream dish, to eat with fruits.
Many people prefer it without any flavour but that of the cream ;
in which case use a quart of new milk and the cream, or do it as
the Devonshire scalded cream.

When done enough, a round mark will appear on the surface of
the cream, the size of the bottom of the pan it is done in, which
in the country they call the ring; and when that is seen, remove
the pan from the fire.

**A Froth to set on Cream, Custard, or Trifle, which
looks and eats well.**—Sweeten half a pound of the pulp of
damsons, or any other sort of scalded fruit, put to it the whites of
four eggs beaten, and beat the pulp up with them until it will
stand as high as you choose; and being put on the cream, &c.,
with a spoon, it will take any form; it should be rough, to imitate
a rock.

**A Carmel Cover for Sweetmeats.**—Dissolve eight ounces
of double-refined sugar in three or four spoonfuls of water, and three
or four drops of lemon-juice ; then put it into a copper untinned
skillet ; when it boils to be thick, dip the handle of a spoon in it,
and put that in a pint basin of water, squeeze the sugar from the
spoon into it, and so on till you have all the sugar. Take a bit
out of the water, and if it snaps, and is brittle when cold, it is
done enough; but only let it be three parts cold; then pour the
water from the sugar, and having a copper form well oiled, run
the sugar on it, in the manner of a maze, and when cold you may
put it on the dish it is to cover ; but if, on trial, the sugar is not
brittle, pour off the water, and return it into the skillet and boil
it again. It should look thick, like treacle, but of a bright light
gold colour. It is a most elegant cover.

**Calf's Feet Jelly.**—Boil two feet in two quarts and a pint of
water till the feet are broken, and the water half wasted; strain
it ; when cold take off the fat, and remove the jelly from the sediment ; then put it into a saucepan, with sugar, raisin wine, lemon-
juice to your taste, and some lemon-peel. When the flavour is
rich, put it to the whites of five eggs well beaten and their shells
broken. Set the saucepan on the fire, but do not stir the jelly
after it begins to warm. Let it boil twenty minutes after it rises
to a head ; then pour it through a flannel jelly bag, first dipping
the bag into hot water to prevent waste, and squeezing it quite
dry. Rub the jelly through and through till clear ; then put it
into glasses or forms.

The following mode will greatly facilitate the clearing of jelly :
When the mixture has boiled twenty minutes, throw in a tea-
cupful of cold water : let it boil five minutes longer ; then take
the saucepan off the fire covered close, and keep it half an hour ;
after which it will be so clear as to need only once running through
the bag, and much waste will be saved.

Observe, feet for all jellies are boiled so long by the people who sell them that they are less nutritious: they should be only scalded to take off the hair. The liquor will require greater care in removing the fat; but the jelly will be far stronger, and, of course, allow more water.

*Note.*—Jelly is equally good made of cow-heels nicely cleaned; and as they bear a less price than those of calves, and make a stronger jelly, this observation may be useful.

**Another way.**—Boil four quarts of water with three calf's feet, or two cow-heels that have been only scalded, till half wasted; take the jelly from the fat and sediment: mix with it the juice of a Seville orange, and twelve lemons, the peels of three ditto, the whites and shells of twelve eggs, brown sugar to taste, near a pint of raisin wine, one ounce of coriander seeds, a quarter of an ounce of allspice, a bit of cinnamon and six cloves, all bruised, after having previously mixed them cold. The jelly should boil fifteen minutes without stirring; then clear it through a flannel bag. While running, take a little jelly, and mix with a tea-cupful of water, in which a bit of beet-root has been boiled, and run it through the bag when all the rest is run out; and this is to garnish the other jelly, being cooled on a plate; but this is matter of choice. The jelly has a very fine high colour and flavour.

**Orange Jelly.**—Grate the rind of two Seville and two China oranges, and two lemons; squeeze the juice of three of each, and strain, and add the juice of a quarter of a pound of lump sugar, and a quarter of a pint of water, and boil till it almost candies. Have ready a quart of isinglass-jelly made with two ounces; put to it the syrup, and boil it once up; strain off the jelly, and let it stand to settle as above, before it is put into the mould.

**Hartshorn Jelly.**—Simmer eight ounces of hartshorn shavings with two quarts of water to only one; strain it, and boil it with the rinds of four China oranges and two lemons pared thin; when cold; add the juice of both, half a pound of sugar, and the whites of six eggs beaten to a froth; let the jelly have three or four boils without stirring, and strain it through a jelly bag.

**Cranberry Jelly.**—Make a very strong isinglass jelly. When cold, mix it with a double quantity of cranberry juice pressed, sweeten and boil it up; then strain it into a shape.

The sugar must be good loaf, or the jelly will not be clear.

**Cranberry and Rice Jelly.**—Boil and press the fruit, strain the juice and by degrees mix into it as much ground rice as will, when boiled, thicken to a jelly; boil it gently, stirring it, and sweeten to your taste. Put it in a basin or form, and serve to eat as the afore-directed jelly, with milk or cream.

**Apple Jelly to serve at Table.**—Prepare twenty golden pippins; boil them in a pint and a half of water from the spring, till quite tender; then strain the liquor through a colander, and to every pint put a pound of fine sugar; add grated orange or lemon; then boil to a jelly.

**Another.**—Prepare apples as before by boiling and straining; have ready half an ounce of isinglass boiled in half a pint of water

K 2

to a jelly; put this to the apple water and apple, as strained through a coarse sieve; add sugar, a little lemon juice and peel; boil all together, and put into a dish.  Take out the peel.

**To Scald Codlins.**—Wrap each in a vine-leaf, and pack them close in a nice saucepan; and when full, pour as much water as will cover them.  Set it over a gentle fire, and let them simmer slowly till done enough to take the thin skin off when cold.  Place them in a dish, with or without milk, cream, or custard; if the latter, there should be no ratafia.  Dust fine sugar over the apples.

**Stewed Golden Pippins.**—Scoop out the core, pare them very fine, and as you do it, throw them in water.  For ever pound of fruit make half a pound of single refined sugar into syrup with a pint of water; when skimmed, put the pippins in, and stew till clear; then grate lemon over, and serve in the syrup.  Be careful not to let them break.

They are an elegant and good dish for a corner or dessert.

**Black Caps.**—Halve and core some fine large apples, put them in a shallow pan, strew white sugar over, and bake them.  Boil a glass of wine, the same of water, and sweeten it for sauce.

**Another way.**—Take off a slice from the stalk end of some apples, and core without paring them.  Make ready as much sugar as may be sufficient to sweeten them, and mix it with some grated lemon, and a few cloves in fine powder.  Stuff the holes as close as possible with this, and turn the flat end down on a stew-pan; set them on a very slow fire, with half a pint of raisin wine, and the same of water: cover them close, and now and then baste them with the liquor; when done enough, black the tops with a salamander.

**Stewed Pears.**—Pare and halve, or quarter, large pears, according to their size; throw them into water, as the skin is taken off before they are divided, to prevent their turning black.  Pack them round a block-tin stew-pan, and sprinkle as much sugar over as will make them pretty sweet, and add lemon peel, a clove or two, and some allspice cracked; just cover them with water, and put some of the red liquor, as directed in another article.  Cover them close, and stew three or four hours; when tender, take them out, and pour the liquor from them.

**Baked Pears.**—These need not be of a fine sort; but some taste better than others, and often those that are least fit to eat raw.  Wipe, but do not pare, and lay them on tin plates, and bake them in a slow oven.  When done enough to bear it, flatten them with a silver spoon.  When done through, put them on a dish.  They should be baked three or four times, and very gently.

**Orange Butter.**—Boil six hard eggs, beat them in a mortar with two ounces of fine sugar, three ounces of butter, and two ounces of blanched almonds beaten to a paste.  Moisten with orange-flower water, and when all is mixed, rub it through a colander on a dish, and serve sweet biscuits between.

**Wine Rolls.**—Soak a penny French roll in raisin wine till it will hold no more; put it in the dish, and pour round it a custard;

or cream, sugar, and lemon juice. Just before it be served, sprinkle over it some nonpareil comfits; or stick a few blanched split almonds into it.

Sponge biscuits may be used instead of the roll.

**To Prepare Fruit for Children, a far more wholesome way than in Pies and Puddings.**—Put apples or pears, sliced, plums, currants, gooseberries, &c., into a stone jar, and sprinkle as much Lisbon sugar as is necessary among them; set the jar on a hot hearth, or in a saucepan of water, and let it remain till the fruit is perfectly done.

Slices of bread, or rice, may be either stewed with the fruit, or added, when eaten: the rice being plain boiled.

**To Prepare Ice for Icing.**—Get a few pounds of ice, break it almost to powder, throw a large handful and a half of salt among it. You must prepare it in a part of the house where as little of the warm air comes as you can possibly contrive. The ice and salt being in a bucket, put your cream into an ice-pot, and cover it; immerse it in the ice, and draw that round the pot, so as to touch every possible part.

In a few minutes put a spatula or spoon in, and stir it well, removing the parts that ice round the edges to the centre. If the ice-cream or water be in a form, shut the bottom close, and move the whole in the ice, as you cannot use a spoon to that without danger of waste. There should be holes in the bucket, to let off the ice as it thaws.

*Note.*—When any fluid tends towards cold, the mere moving it quickly accelerates the cold; and likewise, when any fluid is tending to heat, stirring it will facilitate its boiling.

**Ice Waters.**—Rub some fine sugar on lemon or orange, to give the colour and flavour, then squeeze the juice of either on its respective peel; add water and sugar to make a fine sherbet, and strain it before it be put into the ice-pot. If orange, the greater proportion should be of the China juice, and only a little of Seville, and a small bit of the peel grated by the sugar.

**Currant or Raspberry Water Ice.**—The juice of these, or any other sort of fruit, being gained by squeezing, sweetened and mixed with water, will be ready for icing.

**Ice Creams.**—Mix the juice of the fruits with as much sugar as will be wanted, before you add cream, which should be of a middling richness.

**Brown Bread Ice.**—Grate as fine as possible stale brown bread, soak a small proportion in cream two or three hours, sweeten and ice it.

**Ratafia Cream.**—Blanch a quarter ounce of bitter almonds, beat them with a tea-spoonful of water in a marble mortar; then rub with the paste two ounces of lump sugar, and simmer ten minutes with a tea-cupful of cream, which add to a quart more of cream, and having strained, ice it.

**Colourings to stain Jellies, Ices, or Cakes.**—For a beautiful *red*, boil fifteen grains of cochineal in the finest powder, with a dram and a half of cream of tartar, in half a pint of water, very slowly, half an hour; add in boiling a bit of alum the size of a pea. Or use beet-root sliced, and some liquor poured over.

For *white*, use almonds finely powdered, with a little drop of water; or use cream.

For *yellow*, yolks of eggs, or a bit of saffron, steeped in the liquor and squeezed.

For *green*, pounded spinach leaves or beet leaves, express the juice, and boil in a tea-cupful in a saucepan of water to take off the rawness.

**London Syllabub.**—Put a pint and a half of port or white wine into a bowl, nutmeg grated, and a good deal of sugar, then milk into it near two quarts of milk, frothed up. If the wine be not rather sharp, it will require more for this quantity of milk.—In Devonshire, clouted cream is put on the top, and pounded cinnamon and sugar.

**Staffordshire Syllabub.**—Put a pint of cider, and a glass of brandy, sugar, and nutmeg, into a bowl and milk into it; or pour warm milk from a large teapot some height into it.

**A very fine Somersetshire Syllabub.**—In a large china bowl put a pint of port, and a pint of sherry, or other white wine; sugar to taste. Milk the bowl full. In twenty minutes' time cover it pretty high with clouted cream; grate over it nutmeg, put pounded cinnamon and nonpareil comfits.

**Devonshire Junket.**—Put warm milk into a bowl; turn it with rennet; then put some scalded cream, sugar, and cinnamon on the top, without breaking the curd.

**Everlasting, or Solid Syllabubs.**—Mix a quart of thick raw cream, one pound of refined sugar, a pint and a half of fine raisin wine in a deep pan; put to it the grated peel and the juice of three lemons. Beat or whisk it one way half an hour: then put it on a sieve with a bit of thin muslin laid smooth in the shallow end till next day. Put it in glasses. It will keep good, in a cool place, ten days.

**Lemon Honeycomb.**—Sweeten the juice of a lemon to your taste, and put it in the dish that you serve it in. Mix the white of an egg that is beaten with a pint of rich cream, and a little sugar; whisk it, and as the froth rises, put it on the lemon juice. Do it the day before it is to be used.

**Rice and Sago Milks** are made by washing the seeds nicely, and simmering with milk over a slow fire till sufficiently done. The former sort requires lemon, spice, and sugar; the latter is good without anything to flavour it.

**A very Pretty Supper Dish.**—Boil a tea-cupful of rice, having first washed it, in milk, till tender: strain off the milk, lay the rice in little heaps on a dish, strew over them some finely powdered sugar and cinnamon, and put warm wine and a little butter into the dish.

**Savory Rice.**—Wash and pick some rice, stew it very gently in a small quantity of veal or rich mutton broth, with an onion, a blade of mace, pepper and salt. When swelled, but not boiled to mash, dry it on the shallow end of a sieve before the fire, and either serve it dry, or put it in the middle of a dish, and pour the gravy round, having heated it.

**Carrole of Rice.**—Take some well-picked rice, wash it well and boil it five minutes in water, strain it, and put it into a stew-pan, with a bit of butter, a good slice of ham, and an onion. Stew it over a very gentle fire till tender; have ready a mould lined with very thin slices of bacon; mix the yolks of two or three eggs with the rice, and then line the bacon with it about half an inch thick; put into it a ragout of chicken, rabbit, veal, or of anything else. Fill up the mould, and cover it close with rice. Bake it in a quick oven an hour, turn it over, and send it to table in a good gravy or curry-sauce.

**Casserol**, or Rice Edging, see page 102.

**Salmagundy** is a beautiful small dish, if in nice shape, and if the colours of the ingredients are varied. For this purpose chop separately the white parts of cold chicken or veal, yolks of eggs boiled hard, the whites of eggs, parsley, half a dozen anchovies, beet-root, red pickled cabbage, ham and grated tongue, or anything well flavoured, and of a good colour. Some people like a small proportion of onion, but it may be better left out. A saucer, large tea-cup, or any other base, must be put into a small dish; then make rows round it wide at bottom, and growing smaller towards the top; choosing such of the ingredients for each row as will most vary the colours. At the top a little sprig of curled parsley may be stuck in; or, without anything on the dish, the salmagundy may be laid in rows, or put into the half-whites of eggs, which may be made to stand upright by cutting off a bit at the round end. In the latter case, each half egg has but one ingredient. Curled butter and parsley may be put as garnish between.

**Macaroni as usually served.**—Boil it in milk, or a weak veal broth, pretty well flavoured with salt. When tender, put it into a dish without the liquor, and among it put some bits of butter and grated cheese, and over the top grate more, and a little more butter. Set the dish into a Dutch oven a quarter of an hour, but do not let the top become hard.

**Another way.**—Wash it well, and simmer it in half milk, and half broth of veal or mutton, till it is tender. To a spoonful of this liquor, put the yolk of an egg beaten in a spoonful of cream; just make it hot to thicken but not boil; put it over the macaroni, and then grate some fine old cheese all over, and bits of butter. Brown with the salamander.

**Another.**—Wash the macaroni, then simmer it in a little broth, with a little pounded mace and salt. When quite tender, take it out of the liquor, lay it in a dish, grate a good deal of cheese over, then cover that with bread grated fine. Warm some butter without oiling, and pour it from a boat through a little earthen colander over the crumbs, then put the dish in a Dutch oven, to roast the cheese, and brown the bread of a fine colour. The bread should be in separated crumbs, and look light.

**Omelet.**—Make a batter of eggs and milk and a very little flour; put to it chopped parsley, green onions, or chives (th latter is best), or a very small quantity of shalot, a little pepper, salt. and a scrape or two of nutmeg. Make some butter boil in a small frying-pan, and pour the above batter into it; when one side is of a fine yellow-brown, turn it and do the other. Double it when served. Some scraped lean ham, or grated tongue, put in at first, is a very pleasant addition. Four eggs will make a pretty sized omelet; but many cooks will use eight or ten. A small proportion of flour should be used.

If the taste be approved, a *little* tarragon gives a fine flavour. A good deal of parsley should be used.

Ramakins and omelet, though usually served in the course, would be much better if they were sent up after, that they might be eaten as hot as possible.

**Butter to serve as a little dish.**—Roll butter in different forms; either like a pine and make the marks with a tea-spoon, or rolling it in crimping rollers, work it through a colander, or scoop with a tea-spoon, and mix with grated beef, tongue, or anchovies. Make a wreath of curled parsley to garnish.

**Ramakins.**—Scrape a quarter of a pound of Cheshire, and ditto of Gloucester cheese, ditto of good fresh butter; then beat all in a mortar with the yolks of four eggs, and the inside of a small French roll boiled in cream till soft; mix the paste with the whites of the eggs previously beaten, and put into small paper pans made rather long than square, and bake in a Dutch oven till of a fine brown. They should be eaten quite hot. Some like the addition of a glass of white wine.—The batter for ramakins is equally good over macaroni when boiled tender; or on stewed brocoli, celery, or cauliflower, a little of the gravy they have been stewed in being put in the dish with them, but not enough to make the vegetable swim.

**Potted Cheese.**—Cut and pound four ounces of Cheshire cheese, one ounce and a half of fine butter, a tea-spoonful of white pounded sugar, a little bit of mace, and a glass of white wine. Press it down in a deep pot.

**Roast Cheese to come up after Dinner.**—Grate three ounces of fat Cheshire cheese, mix it with the yolks of two eggs, four ounces of grated bread, and three ounces of butter; beat the whole well in a mortar, with a dessert-spoonful of mustard, and a little salt and pepper. Toast some bread, cut it into proper pieces, lay the paste as above thick upon them into a Dutch oven covered with a dish, till hot through, remove the dish, and let the cheese brown a little. Serve as hot as possible.

**Melted Cheese.**—Take two ounces of good Cheshire, and two ditto of Parmesan cheese, grate them, and add about double the weight of each in beaten yolks of eggs and melted butter, mix them well together, add pepper and salt to your taste, and then put to it the white of the eggs, which have been beaten separately; stir them lightly in, and bake it in a deep dish, filled but half full, as it will rise very much. Serve when quite hot.

**Welsh Rabbit.**—Toast a slice of bread on both sides, and butter it; toast a slice of Gloucester cheese on one side, and lay that next the bread, and toast the other with a salamander; rub mustard over, and serve very hot, and covered.

**Cheese Toast.**—Mix some fine butter, made mustard, and salt, into a mass; spread it on fresh-made thin toasts, and grate or scrape Gloucester cheese upon them.

.**Anchovy Toast.**—Bone and skin six or eight anchovies; pound them to a mass with an ounce of fine butter till the colour is equal, and then spread it on toasts or rusks.

**Another way.**—Cut thin slices of bread into any form, and fry them in clarified butter. Wash three anchovies, split, pound them in a mortar with some fresh butter, rub them through a hair sieve, and spread it on the toast when cold. Then quarter and wash some anchovies, and lay them on the toast. Garnish with parsley or pickles.

**To Poach Eggs.**—Set a stew-pan of water on the fire; when boiling, slip an egg, previously broken in a cup, into the water; when the white looks done enough, slide an egg-slice under the egg, and lay it on toast and butter, or spinach. As soon as enough are done, serve hot. If not fresh laid, they will not poach well, and without breaking. Trim the ragged parts of the whites, and make them look round.

**Buttered Eggs.**—Beat four or five eggs, yolk and white together, put a quarter of a pound of butter in a basin, and then put that in boiling water, stir it till melted; then pour that butter and the eggs into a saucepan: keep a basin in your hand, just hold the saucepan in the other, over a slow part of the fire, shaking it one way, as it begins to warm; pour it into a basin and back; then hold it again over the fire, stirring it constantly in the saucepan, and pouring it into the basin, more perfectly to mix the egg and butter, until they shall be hot without boiling.

Serve on toasted bread: or in a basin, to eat with salt fish, or red herrings.

**Scotch Eggs.**—Boil hard five pullets' eggs, and without removing the white, cover completely with a fine relishing forcemeat, in which let scraped ham, or chopped anchovy, bear a due proportion. Fry of a beautiful yellow brown, and serve with a good gravy in the dish.

**A Pepper-pot.**—To three quarts of water, put such vegetables as you choose; in summer, peas, lettuce, spinach, and two or three onions; in winter, carrot, turnip, onions, and celery. Cut them very small, and stew them with two pounds of neck of mutton, and a pound of pickled pork, till quite tender. Half an hour before serving, clear a lobster or crab from the shell, and put it into the stew. Some people choose very small suet-dumplings boiled in the above. Season it with salt and Cayenne.

Instead of mutton you may put a fowl. Pepper-pot may be made of various things, and is understood to be a proper mixture of fish, flesh, fowl, vegetables, and pulse. A small quantity of rice should be boiled with the whole.

**The Staffordshire Dish of Frying Herbs and Liver.** —Prepare the frying herbs as has been directed among the vegetables, page 134: on which lay slices of liver fried a beautiful brown, and slices of bacon just warmed at the fire, and laid on each. On the outside part of the herbs lay eggs fried very nicely, and then trimmed round; or they may be served on the herbs, and the liver garnished with the bacon separately.

**To Preserve Suet a Twelvemonth.**—As soon as it comes in, choose the firmest part, and pick free from skin and veins. In a very nice saucepan, set it at some distance from the fire, that it may melt without frying, or it will taste.

When melted, pour into a pan of cold water. When in a hard cake, wipe it very dry, fold it in fine paper, and then in a linen bag, and keep it in a dry but not hot place. When used, scrape it fine, and it will make a fine crust, either with or without butter.

**SWEETMEATS.—To Green Fruits for Preserving or Pickling.**—Take pippins, apricots, pears, plums, peaches while green for the first, or radish-pods, French beans for the latter, and cucumbers for both processes; and put them, with vine-leaves under and over, into a *block-tin* preserving-pan, with spring-water to cover them, and then the tin cover to exclude all air. Set it on the side of a fire, and when they begin to simmer, take them off, pour off the water, and if not green, put fresh leaves when cold, and repeat the same. Take them out carefully with a slice; they are to be peeled, and then done according to the receipts for the several modes.

**To Clarify Sugar for Sweetmeats.**—Break as much as required in large lumps, and put a pound to half a pint of water in a bowl, and it will dissolve better than when broken small. Set it over the fire, with the well-whipt white of an egg; let it boil up, and, when ready to run over, pour a little cold water in to give it a check; but when it rises a second time, take it off the fire, and set it by in the pan for a quarter of an hour, during which the foulness will sink to the bottom, and leave a black scum on the top, which take off gently with a skimmer, and pour the syrup into a vessel very quickly from the sediment.

**To Candy any Sort of Fruit.**—When finished in the syrup, put a layer into a new sieve, and dip it suddenly into hot water to take off the syrup that hangs about it; put it on a napkin before the fire to drain, and then do some more in the sieve. Have ready sifted double-refined sugar, which sift over the fruit on all sides till quite white. Set it on the shallow end of sieves in a slightly warm oven, and turn it two or three times. It must not be cold till dry. Watch it carefully, and it will be beautiful.

**To prepare Barberries for Tartlets.**—Pick barberries that have no stones, from the stalks, and to every pound weigh three quarters of a pound of lump sugar; put the fruit into a stone jar, and either set it on a hot hearth or in a saucepan of water, and let them simmer very slowly till soft; put them and the sugar into a preserving-pan, and boil them gently fifteen minutes. Use no metal but silver.

**Barberries in Bunches.**—Have ready bits of flat white

wood three inches long and a quarter of an inch wide. Tie the stalks of the fruit on the stick from within an inch of one end to beyond the other, so as to make them look handsome. Simmer them in some syrup two successive days, covering them each time with it when cold. When they look clear, they are simmered enough. The third day do them like other candied fruit. See receipt for it p. 154.

**A Beautiful Preserve of Apricots.**—When ripe choose the finest apricots; pare them as thin as possible, and weigh them. Lay them in halves on dishes, with the hollow part upwards. Have ready an equal weight of good loaf-sugar finely pounded, and strew it over them; in the meantime break the stones and blanch the kernels. When the fruit has lain twelve hours, put it, with the sugar and juice and also the kernels, into a preserving-pan. Let it simmer very gently till clear; then take out the pieces of apricots singly as they become so, put them into small pots and pour the syrup and kernels over them. The scum must be taken off as it rises. Cover with brandy paper.

**To Preserve Apricots in Jelly.**—Pare the fruit very thin and stone it; weigh an equal quantity of sugar in fine powder and strew over it. Next day boil very gently till they are clear, move them into a bowl and pour the liquor over. The following day pour the liquor to a quart of codlin-liquor, made by boiling and straining, and a pound of fine sugar; let it boil quickly till it will jelly; put the fruit into it, and give one boil, skim well, and put into small pots.

**To Preserve Green Apricots.**—Lay vine or apricot leaves at the bottom of your pan, then fruit, and so alternately till full, the upper layer being thick with leaves; then fill with spring-water, and cover down, that no steam may come out. Set the pan at a distance from the fire, that in four or five hours they may be only soft, but not cracked. Make a thin syrup of some of the water, and drain the fruit. When both are cold, put the fruit into the pan and the syrup to it; put the pan at a proper distance from the fire till the apricots green, but on no account boil or crack; remove them very carefully into a pan with the syrup for two or three days; then pour off as much of it as will be necessary, and boil with more sugar to make a rich syrup, and put a little sliced ginger into it. When cold, and the thin syrup has all been drained from the fruit, pour the thick over it. The former will serve to sweeten pies.

**Apricots or Peaches in Brandy.**—Wipe, weigh, and pick the fruit, and have ready a quarter of the weight of fine sugar in fine powder. Put the fruit into an ice-pot that shuts very close; throw the sugar over it, and then cover the fruit with brandy. Between the top and the cover of the pot put a piece of double-cap paper. Set the pot into a saucepan of water till the brandy be as hot as you can possibly bear to put your finger in, but it must not boil. Put the fruit into a jar, and pour the brandy on it. When cold put a bladder over, and tie it down tight.

**To Dry Apricots in Half.**—Pare thin and halve four pounds of apricots, weighing them ·after; put them in a dish; strew among them three pounds of sugar in the finest powder. When it melts, set the fruit over a stove to do very gently ; as each piece becomes tender, take it out and put it into a china bowl. When all are done. and the boiling heat a little abated, pour the syrup over them. In a day or two remove the syrup, leaving only a little in each half. After about a day or two more turn them, and so continue daily till quite dry, in the sun or a warm place. Keep in boxes with layers of paper.

**Apricot Cheese.**—Weigh an equal quantity of pared fruit and sugar, wet the latter a very little, and let it boil quickly or the colour will be spoiled; blanch the kernels, and add to it. Twenty or thirty minutes will boil it. Put it in small pots or cups half filled.

**Orange Marmalade.**—Rasp the oranges, cut out the pulp, then boil the rinds very tender, and beat fine in a marble mortar. Boil three pounds of loaf-sugar in a pint of water, skim it, and add a pound of the rind ; boil fast till the syrup is very thick, but stir it carefully ; then put a pint of the pulp and juice, the seeds having been removed, and a pint of apple-liquor; boil all gently until well jellied, which it will be in about half an hour. Put it into small pots.

**Lemon Marmalade** do in the same way ; they are very good and elegant sweetmeats.

**Transparent Marmalade.**—Cut the palest Seville oranges in quarters, take the pulp out and put it in a basin, pick out the seeds and skins. Let the outsides soak in water with a little salt all night, then boil them in a good quantity of spring-water till tender ; drain and cut them in very thin slices, and put them to the pulp ; and to every pound, a pound and a half of double-refined sugar beaten fine; boil them together twenty minutes, but be careful not to break the slices. If not quite clear, simmer five or six minutes longer. It must be stirred all the time very gently. When cold, put it into glasses.

**To Butter Oranges Hot.**—Grate off a little of the outside rind of four Seville oranges, and cut a round hole at the blunt end, opposite the stalk, large enough to take out the pulp, seeds, and juice ; then pick the seeds and skin from the pulp; rub the oranges with a little salt, and lay them in water for a short time. You are to save the bits cut out. Set the fruit on to boil in fresh water till they are tender, shifting the water to take out the bitterness. In the meantime make a thin syrup with fine sugar, and put the oranges into it and boil them up, turning them round that each part may partake of the syrup, as there need not be enough to cover them, and let them remain in it hot till they are to be served. About half an hour before you want them put some sugar to the pulp, and set over the fire ; mix it well, and let it boil ; then add a spoonful of white wine for every orange, give it a boil, and then put in a bit of fresh butter, and stir over the fire to thicken it ; fill the ·oranges with it, and serve them with some of ᵗʰe syrup in the dish. Put the bits on the top.

**To Fill Preserved Oranges** (a Corner Dish).—For five, take a pound of Naples biscuits, some blanched almonds, the yolks of four eggs well beaten, sugar to your taste, and four ounces of butter warmed, grate the biscuits, and mix well with the above some orange-flower water. Fill preserved oranges, and bake in a very slow oven. If you like them frosted, sift sugar over them as soon as filled, otherwise wipe them. Custard to fill will do as well; if so, you need not bake the oranges, but put it in when become cold.

**Whole Oranges Carved.**—Cut on the rinds any shapes you please with a penknife, cut a bit off near and round the stalk, and with an apple-scoop take all the pulp carefully out; put them into salt and water two days, changing it daily; boil them an hour or more in fresh water and salt, drain them quite dry; let them stand a night more in plain water, and then another night in a thin syrup, in which boil them the next day a few minutes. Do this four days successively. Let them stand six or seven weeks, observing often whether they keep well, otherwise boil the syrup again. Then make a rich syrup.

**Buttered Orange Juice** (a Cold Dish).—Mix the juice of seven Seville oranges with four spoonfuls of rosewater, and add the whole to the yolks of eight and whites of four eggs, well beaten; then strain the liquor to half a pound of sugar pounded, stir it over a gentle fire, and when it begins to thicken, put about the size of a small walnut of butter: keep it over the fire a few minutes longer, then pour it into a flat dish, and serve it to eat cold.

If you have no silver saucepan, do it in a china basin in a saucepan of boiling water, the top of which will just receive the basin.

**Orange Chips.**—Cut oranges in halves, squeeze the juice through a sieve; soak the peel in water; next day boil it in the same till tender, drain them, and slice the peels, put them to the juice, weigh as much sugar, and put all together into a broad earthen dish, and place over the fire at a moderate distance, often stirring till the chips candy; then set them in a cool room to dry. They will not be so under three weeks.

**Orange Biscuits, or Little Cakes.**—Boil whole Seville oranges in two or three waters, till most of the bitterness is gone; cut them, and take out the pulp and juice; then beat the outside very fine in a mortar, and put to it an equal weight of double-refined sugar beaten and sifted. When extremely well mixed to a paste, spread it thin on china dishes, and set them in the sun or before the fire; when half dry, cut it into what form you please, turn the other side up, and dry that. Keep them in a box, with layers of paper.

They are for desserts; and are also useful as a stomachic, to carry in the pocket on journeys, or for gentlemen when shooting, and for gouty stomachs.

**Orange-flower Cakes.**—Put four ounces of the leaves of the flowers into cold water for an hour; drain, and put between napkins, and roll with a rolling-pin till they are bruised; then have ready boiled one pound of sugar to add to it in a thick syrup, give them a simmer until the syrup adheres to the sides of the pan, drop in little cakes on a plate, and dry as before directed.

To Preserve Oranges or Lemons in Jelly.—Cut a hole in the stalk part, the size of a shilling, and with a blunt small knife scrape out the pulp quite clear without cutting the rind. Tie each separately in muslin, and lay them in spring water two days, changing twice a day; on the last boil them tender on a slow fire. Observe that there is enough at first to allow for wasting, as they must be covered to the last. To every pound of fruit weigh two pounds of double-refined sugar and one pint of water; boil the two latter together with the juice of the orange to a syrup, and clarify it; skim well, and let it stand to be cold; then boil fruit in the syrup half an hour; if not clear do this daily till they are so.

Pare and core some green pippins and boil in water till it tastes strong of them; do not break them, only gently press them with the back of a spoon; strain the water through a jelly-bag till quite clear; then to every pint put a pound of double-refined sugar, the peel and juice of a lemon, and boil to a strong syrup. Drain off the syrup from the fruit, and turning each orange with the hole upwards in a jar, pour the apple jelly over it. The bits cut out must go through the same process with the fruit. Cover with brandy paper.

To Keep Oranges or Lemons for Puddings, &c.— When you squeeze the fruit, throw the outside in water, without the pulp; let them remain in the same a fortnight, adding no more: boil them therein till tender, strain it from them, and when they are tolerably dry, throw them into any jar of candy you may have remaining from old sweetmeats; or if you have none, boil a small quantity of syrup of common loaf-sugar and water and put over them: in a week or ten days, boil them gently in it till they look clear; and that they may be covered with it in the jar, you may cut each half of the fruit in two, and they will occupy but small space.

To Preserve Strawberries Whole.—Take equal weights of the fruit and double-refined sugar; lay the former in a large dish, and sprinkle half the sugar in fine powder over; give a gentle shake to the dish, that the sugar may touch the under side of the fruit. Next day make a thin syrup with the remainder of the sugar, and, instead of water, allow one pound of red currant juice to every pint of strawberries; in this simmer them until sufficiently jellied. Choose the largest scarlets, or others, when not dead ripe. In either of the above ways they eat well served in thin cream, in glasses.

To Preserve Strawberries in Wine.—Put a quantity of the finest large strawberries into a gooseberry-bottle, and strew in three large spoons of fine sugar; fill up with Madeira wine, or fine sherry.

To Dry Cherries with Sugar.—Stone six pounds of

Kentish; put them into a preserving-pan, with two pounds of loaf-sugar pounded and strewed among them; simmer till they begin to shrivel; then strain them from the juice; lay them on a hot hearth, or in an oven, when either is cool enough to dry without baking them.

The same syrup will do another six pounds of fruit.

**To Dry Cherries without Sugar.**—Stone, and set them over the fire in the preserving-pan; let them simmer in their own liquor, and shake them in the pan. Put them by in common china dishes; next day give them another scald, and put them, when cold, on sieves to dry, in an oven of a temperate heat as above. Twice heating, an hour each time, will do them.

Put them in a box, with a paper between each layer.

**To Dry Cherries the best way.**—To every five pounds of cherries stoned, weigh one of sugar double-refined. Put the fruit into the preserving-pan with very little water; make both scalding hot; take the fruit immediately out and dry them; put them into the pan again, strewing the sugar between each layer of cherries; let it stand to melt; then set the pan on the fire, and make it scalding hot, as before; take it off, and repeat this thrice with the sugar. Drain them from the syrup, and lay them singly to dry on dishes, in the sun or on a stove. When dry, put them into a sieve, dip it into a pan of cold water, and draw it instantly out again, and pour them on a fine soft cloth; dry them, and set them once more in the hot sun, or on a stove. Keep them in a box, with layers of white paper, in a dry place. This way is the best to give plumpness to the fruit, as well as colour and flavour.

**Cherries in Brandy.**—Weigh the finest morellas, having cut off half the stalk prick them with a new needle, and drop them into a jar or wide-mouthed bottle. Pound three quarters the weight of sugar or white candy; strew over; fill up with brandy, and tie a bladder over.

**Cherry Jam.**—To twelve pounds of Kentish or duke cherries, when ripe, weigh one pound of sugar; break the stones of part, and blanch the kernels; then put them to the fruit and sugar, and boil all gently till the jam comes clear from the pan. Pour it into china plates to come up dry to table. Keep in boxes with white paper between.

**Currant Jam, Black, Red, or White.**—Let the fruit be very ripe, pick it clean from the stalks, bruise it, and to every pound put three quarters of a pound of loaf-sugar; stir it well, and boil half an hour.

**Currant Jelly, Red or Black.**—Strip the fruit, and strew them in a stone jar in a saucepan of water, or boil them on the hot hearth; strain off the liquor, and to every pint weigh a pound of loaf-sugar; put the latter in large lumps into it, in a stone or china vessel, till nearly dissolved; then put it in a preserving-pan; simmer and skim as necessary. When it will jelly on a plate, put it in small jars or glasses.

**Apple Marmalade.**—Scald apples till they will pulp from

the core; then take an equal weight of sugar in large lumps; just dip them in water, and boiling it up till it can be well skimmed, and is a thick syrup, put it to the pulp, and simmer it on a quick fire a quarter of an hour. Grate a little lemon peel before boiled, but if too much it will be bitter.

**Apple Jelly for Preserving Apricots, or for any sort of Sweetmeats.**—Let apples be pared, quartered, and cored; put them into a stew-pan with as much water as will cover them; boil as fast as possible; when the fruit is all in a mash, add a quart of water: boil half an hour more, and run through a jelly-bag.

If in summer, codlins are best; in September, golden rennets or winter pippins.

**Red Apples in Jelly.**—Pare and core some well-shaped apples, pippins or golden rennets, if you have them, but others will do; throw them into water as you do them: put them in a preserving pan, and with as little water as will only half cover them; let them coddle, and when the lower side is done, turn them. Observe that they do not lie too close when first put in. Mix some pounded cochineal with the water, and boil with the fruit. When sufficiently done, take them out on the dish they are to be served in, the stalk downwards. Take the water, and make a rich jelly of it with loaf sugar, boiling the thin rind and juice of a lemon. When come to a jelly, let it grow cold, and put it on and among the apples; cut the peel of the lemon in narrow strips, and put it across the eye of the apple.

Observe that the colour be fine from the first, or the fruit will not afterwards gain it, and use as little of the cochineal as will serve, lest the syrup taste bitter.

**Dried Apples.**—Put them in a cool oven six or seven times, and flatten them by degrees, and gently, when soft enough to bear it. If the oven be too hot, they will waste and     first it should be very cool.

The biffin, the minshul crab, o any tart apple   are the sorts for drying.

**To Preserve Jargonel Pears most beautifully.**—Pare them very thin, and simmer in a thin syrup; let them lie a day or two. Make the syrup richer, and simmer again, and repeat this till they are clear; then drain, and dry them in the sun or a cool oven a very little time. They may be kept in syrup, and dried as wanted, which makes them more moist and rich.

**Gooseberry Jam for Tarts.**—Put twelve pounds of the red hairy gooseberries, when ripe, and gathered in dry weather, into a preserving-pan, with a pint of currant juice, drawn as for jelly; let them boil pretty quick, and beat them with the spoon; when they begin to break, put to them six pounds of pure white Lisbon sugar, and simmer slowly to a jam. It requires long boiling, or will not keep, but is an excellent and reasonable thing for tarts or puffs. Look at it in two or three days, and if the syrup and fruit separate, the whole must be boiled longer. Be careful it does not burn to the bottom.

**Another.**—Gather your gooseberries (the clear white or green sort) when ripe; top and tail, and weigh them, a pound to three quarters of a pound of fine sugar, and half a pint of water; boil and skim the sugar and water, then put the fruit, and boil gently till clear; then break, and put into small pots.

**White Gooseberry Jam.**—Gather the finest white gooseberries, or green if you choose, when just ripe; top and tail them. To each pound put three quarters of a pound of fine sugar, and half a pint of water. Boil and clarify the sugar in the water, as directed in page 154, then add the fruit; simmer gently till clear, then break it, and in a few minutes put the jam into small pots.

**Gooseberry Hops.**—Of the largest green walnut kind, take and cut the bud end in four quarters, leaving the stalk end whole; pick out the seeds, and with a strong needle and thread fasten five or six together, by running the thread through the bottoms, till they are of the size of a hop. Lay vine leaves at the bottom of a tin preserving pan, cover them with the hops, then a layer of leaves, and so on; lay a good many on the top, then fill the pan with water. Stop it so close down that no steam can get out; set it by a slow fire till scalding hot; then take it off till cold, and so do till on opening while cold the gooseberries are of a good green. Then drain them on sieves, and make a thin syrup of a pound of sugar to a pint of water, boil, and skim it well; when half cold, put in the fruit; next day give it one boil, and do this thrice. If the hops are to be dried, which way they eat best, and look well, they may be set to dry in a week; but if to be kept wet, make a syrup in the above proportions, adding a slice of ginger in boiling; when skimmed and clear, give the gooseberries one boil, and when cold, pour it over them. If the first syrup be found too sour, a little sugar may be added and boiled in it, before the hops that are for drying have their last boil.

The extra-syrup will serve for pies, or go towards other sweet-meats.

**Raspberry Jam.**—Weigh equal quantities of fruit and sugar; put the former into a preserving pan, boil and break it; stir constantly, and let it boil very quickly. When most of the juice is wasted, add the sugar, and simmer half an hour.

This way the jam is greatly superior in colour and flavour to that which is made by putting the sugar in at first.

**Another way.**—Put the fruit into a jar in a kettle of water, or on a hot hearth, till the juice will run from it, then take away a quarter of a pint from every pound of fruit; boil and bruise it half an hour, then put in the weight of the fruit in sugar, and adding the same quantity of currant-juice, boil it to a strong jelly.

The raspberry-juice will serve to put into brandy, or may be boiled with its weight in sugar for making the jelly for raspberry-ice or cream.

**To Preserve Greengages.**—Choose the largest, when they begin to soften; split them without paring, and strew a part of the sugar, of which you have previously weighed an equal quantity. Blanch the kernels with a small sharp knife. Next day, pour the syrup from the fruit, and boil it with the other sugar, six or eight minutes, but very gently; skim, and add the plums and kernels. Simmer till clear, taking off any scum that rises: put the fruit singly into small pots, and pour the syrup and kernels to it. If you would candy it, do not add the syrup, but observe the directions that will be given for candying fruit; some may be done each way.

**Damson Cheese.**—Bake or boil the fruit in a stone-jar in a saucepan of water, or on a hot hearth. Pour off some of the juice, and for every two pounds of fruit weigh half a pound of sugar. Set the fruit over a fire in the pan, let it boil quickly till it begins to look dry; take out the stones, and add the sugar, stir it well in, and simmer two hours slowly; then boil it quickly half an hour, till the sides of the pan candy: then pour the jam into potting-pans or dishes, about an inch thick, so that it may cut firm. If the skins be disliked, then the juice is not to be taken out; but after the first process, the fruit is to be pulped through a very coarse sieve with the juice, and managed as above. The stones are to be cracked, or some of them, and the kernels boiled in the jam. All the juice may be left in, and boiled to evaporate, but do not add the sugar until it has done so. The above looks well in shapes.

**Muscle-plum Cheese.**—Weigh six pounds of the fruit, bake it in a stone jar, remove the stones, and take out the kernels to put in. Pour half the juice on two pounds and a half of good Lisbon; when melted and simmered a few minutes, skim it, and add the fruit. Keep it doing very gently till the juice is much evaporated, taking care to stir it constantly, lest it burn. Pour it into small moulds, patty-pans, or saucers. The remaining juice may serve to colour cream, or be added to a pie.

**Biscuits of Fruit.**—To the pulp of any scalded fruits, put of sifted sugar an equal weight; beat it two hours, then put it into little white paper forms, dry in a cool oven, turn, the next day, and in two or three days box them.

**Quince Marmalade.**—Pare and quarter quinces, weigh an equal quantity of sugar; to four pounds of the latter, put a quart of water, boil and skim, and have ready against four pounds of quinces are tolerably tender by the following mode: lay them into a stone jar, with a tea-cup of water at the bottom, and pack them with a little sugar strewed between: cover the jar close, and set it on a stove or cool oven, and let them soften till the colour becomes red; then pour the fruit syrup and a quart of quince-juice into a preserving-pan, and boil all together till the marmalade be completed, breaking the lumps of fruit with the preserving ladle.

This fruit is so hard, that if it be not done as mentioned, it requires a great deal of time.

Stewing quinces in a jar, and then squeezing them through a cheese-cloth, is the best method of obtaining the juice to add as above, but dip the cloth in boiling water first and wring it.

**To Preserve Whole or Half Quinces.**—Into two quarts

of boiling water put a quantity of the fairest golden pippins, in slices not very thin, and not pared, but wiped clean. Boil them very quick, close covered, till the water becomes a thick jelly; then scald the quinces. To every pint of pippin-jelly put a pound of the finest sugar; boil it, and skim it clear. Put those quinces that are to be done whole into the syrup at once, and let it boil very fast; and those that are to be in halves by themselves; skim it, and when the fruit are clear, put some of the syrup into a glass to try whether it jellies before taking off the fire. The quantity of quinces is to be a pound to a pound of sugar, and a pound of jelly already boiled with the sugar.

**Excellent Sweetmeats for Tarts, when Fruit is plentiful.**—Divide two pounds of apricots when just ripe, and take out and break the stones; put the kernels without their skin to the fruit; add to it three pounds of greengage plums, and two pounds and a half of lump sugar; simmer until the fruit be a clear jam. The sugar should be broken in large pieces, and just dipped in water, and added to the fruit over a slow fire. Observe that it does not boil, and skim it well. If the sugar be clarified, it will make the jam bitter.

Put it into small pots, which keep sweetmeats best.

**Magnum Bonum Plums: excellent as a Sweetmeat, or in Tarts, though very bad to eat raw.**—Prick them with a needle to prevent bursting, simmer them very gently in a thin syrup, put them in a china bowl, and when cold pour it over. Let them lie three days; then make a syrup of three pounds of sugar to five of fruit, with no more water than hangs to large lumps of the sugar dipped quickly, and instantly brought out. Boil the plums in this fresh syrup, after draining the first from them. Do them very gently till they are clear, and the syrup adheres to them. Put them one by one into small pots, and pour the liquor over. Those you may like to dry, keep a little of the syrup for, longer in the pan, and boil it quickly; then give the fruit one warm more; drain, and put them to dry on plates in a cool oven. These plums are apt to ferment, if not boiled in two syrups; the former will sweeten pies, but will have too much acid to keep. You may reserve part of it, and add a little sugar to do those that are to dry, for they will not require to be so sweet as if kept wet, and will eat very nicely if only boiled as much as those. Do not break them. One parcel may be done after another, and save much sugar.

**Lemon Drops.**—Grate three fine large lemons, with a large piece of double-refined sugar; then scrape the sugar into a plate, add half a tea-spoonful of flour, mix well, and beat it into a light paste with the white of an egg. Drop it upon white paper, and put them into a moderate oven on a tin plate.

**Barberry Drops.**—The black tops must be cut off: then roast the fruit before the fire, till soft enough to pulp with a silver spoon through a sieve into a china basin: then set the basin in a saucepan of water, the top of which will just fit it, or on a hot hearth, and stir it till it grows thick. When cold, put to every

L 2

pint a pound and a half of sugar, the finest double-refined, pounded and sifted through a lawn sieve, which must be covered with a fine linen, to prevent its wasting while sifting. Beat the sugar and juice together three hours and a half if a large quantity, but two and a half for less; then drop it on sheets of thick white paper, the size of the drops sold in the shops.

Some fruit is not so sour, and then less sugar is necessary. To know if there be enough, mix till well incorporated, and then drop; if it run, there is not enough sugar, and if there is too much it will be rough. A dry room will suffice to dry them. No metal must touch the juice but the point of a knife, just to take the drop off the erd of a wooden spoon, and then as little as possible.

**Ginger Drops: a good Stomachic.**—Beat two ounces of fresh candied orange in a mortar, with a little sugar, to a paste; then mix one ounce of powder of white ginger with one pound of loaf-sugar. Wet the sugar with a little water, and boil altogether to a candy, and drop it on paper the size of mint drops.

**Peppermint Drops.**—Pound and sift four ounces of double-refined sugar, beat it with the whites of two eggs till perfectly smooth; then add sixty drops of oil of peppermint, beat it well, and drop on white paper, and dry at a distance from the fire.

**Ratafia Drops.**—Blanch and beat in a mortar four ounces of bitter, and two of sweet almonds, with a little of a pound of sugar sifted, and add the remainder of the sugar, and the whites of two eggs, making a paste; of which put little balls, the size of a nutmeg, on wafer-paper, and bake gently on tin-plates.

**Raspberry Cakes.**—Pick out any bad raspberries that are among the fruit, weigh and boil what quantity you please, and when mashed, and the liquor is wasted, put to it sugar the weight of the fruit you first put into the pan, mix it well off the fire until perfectly dissolved, then put it on china-plates, and dry it in the sun. As soon as the top part dries, cut, with the cover of a canister, into small cakes, turn them on fresh plates, and, when dry, put them in boxes with layers of paper. ●

**TO PRESERVE FRUITS FOR WINTER USE.**— Observations on Sweetmeats.—Sweetmeats should be kept carefully from the air, and in a very dry place. Unless they have a very small proportion of sugar, a warm one does not hurt; but when not properly boiled, that is, long enough, but not quick, heat makes them ferment; and damp causes them to grow mouldy. They should be looked at two or three times in the first two months, that they may be gently boiled again, if not likely to keep.

It is necessary to observe, that the boiling of sugar, more or less, constitutes the principal art of the confectioner, and those who are not practised in this knowledge, and only preserve in a plain way for family use, are not aware that, in two or three minutes, a syrup over the fire will pass from one gradation to another, called by the confectioners degrees of boiling, of which there are six, and those subdivided. But I am not versed in the minutiæ, and only make the observation to guard against under-boiling, which prevents sweetmeats from keeping; and quick boiling and long, which brings them to a candy.

Attention, without much practice, will enable a person to do any of the following sort of sweetmeats, &c., and they are as much as is wanted in a private family; the higher articles of preserved fruits may be bought at less expense than made.

Jellies of fruit made with an equal quantity of sugar, that is, a pound to a pint, require no very long boiling.

A pan should be kept for the purpose of preserving, of double block tin, with a bow-handle opposite the straight one, for safety, will do very well; and if put by nicely cleaned, in a dry place, when done with, will last for several years. Those of copper or brass are improper, as the tinning wears out by the scraping of the sweetmeat ladle. There is a new sort of iron, with a strong tinning, which promises to wear long. Sieves and spoons should be kept for sweet things.

Sweetmeats keep best in drawers that are not connected with a wall. If there be -the least damp, cover them only with paper dipped in brandy, laid quite close; putting a little fresh over in spring, to prevent insect mould. When any sweetmeats are directed to be dried in the sun or in a stove, it will be best in private families, where there is not a regular stove for the purpose, to put them in the sun on flag-stones, which reflect the heat, and place a garden glass over them to keep insects off; or if put in an oven, to take care not to let it be too warm, and watch that they do properly and slowly.

**To Keep Currants.**—The bottles being perfectly clean and dry, let the currants be cut from the large stalks with the smallest bit of stalk to each, that the fruit not being wounded no moisture may be among them. It is necessary to gather them when the weather is quite dry, and if the servant can be trusted, it is best to cut them under the trees, and let them drop gently into the bottles.

Stop up the bottles with cork and resin, and put them into the trench in the garden with the neck downwards; stocks should be placed opposite to where each sort of fruit begins.

**Cherries** and **Damsons** keep in the same way.

Currants may be scalded, as directed for gooseberries, the first method.

**To Keep Codlins for several months.**—Gather codlins at Midsummer of a middling size, put them into an earthen pan, pour boiling water over them, and cover the pan with cabbage-leaves. Keep them by the fire till they would peel, but do not peel them; then pour the water off till they are both quite cold. Place the codlins then in a stone jar with a smallish mouth, and pour on them the water that scalded them. Cover the pot with bladder wetted, and tied very close, and then over it coarse paper tied again.

It is best to keep them in small jars, such as will be used at once when opened.

**To Keep Gooseberries.**—Before they become too large, let

them be gathered ; and take care not to cut them in taking off the
stalks and buds. Fill wide-mouthed bottles ; put the corks loosely
in, and set the bottles up to the neck in a boiler of water. When
the fruit looks scalded, take them out ; and when perfectly cold,
cork close and resin the top. Dig a trench in a part of the garden
less used, sufficiently deep for all the bottles to stand, and let the
earth be thrown over to cover them a foot and a half. When a
frost comes on, a little fresh litter from the stable will prevent the
ground from hardening so that the fruit cannot be dug up. Or,
scald as above ; when cold, fill the bottles with cold water, cork
them, and keep them in a damp or dry place ; they will not be
spoiled.

Another way.—In the size and preparations as above ; when
done, have boiling water ready, either in a boiler or large kettle ;
and put into it as much roach-alum as will, when dissolved, harden
the water, which you will taste by a little roughness ; if there be
too much it will spoil the fruit. Put as many gooseberries into a
large sieve as will lie at the bottom without covering one another.
Hold the sieve in the water till the fruit begins to look scalded on
the outside ; then turn them gently out of the sieve on a cloth on
the dresser, cover them with another cloth, and put some more to
be scalded, and so on till all be finished. Observe not to put one
quantity on another, or they will become too soft. The next day
pick out any bad or broken ones, bottle the rest, and fill up the
bottles with alum water in which they were scalded ; which must
be kept in the bottles, for if left in the kettle, or in a glazed pan,
it will spoil. Stop them close.

The water must boil all the time the process is carrying on.
Gooseberries done this way make as fine tarts as those gathered
fresh off the bushes.

Another way.—In dry weather pick the gooseberries that are
full grown, but not ripe ; top and tail, and put them into open-
mouthed bottles ; gently cork them with new velvet corks ; put
them in the oven when the bread is drawn, and let them stand till
shrunk a quarter part ; take them out of the oven, and immediately
beat the corks in tight, cut off the tops, and resin down close ; set
them in a dry place, and if well secured from the air, they will
keep the year round.

If gathered in the damp, or the gooseberries' skins are the least
cut in taking off the stalks and buds, they will mould. The hairy
sort only must be used for keeping, and do them before the seeds
become large.

Currants and damsons may be done the same way.

To Keep Damsons for Winter Pies.—Put them in small
stone jars, or wide-mouthed bottles ; set them up to their necks
in a boiler of cold water, and lighting a fire under, scald them.
Next day, when perfectly cold, fill up with spring water ; cover
them.

Another way.—Boil one-third as much sugar as fruit with it,
over a slow fire, till the juice adheres to the fruit, and forms a jam.

Keep it in small jars in a dry place.  If too sweet, mix with it some of the fruit that is done without sugar.

**Another way.**—Choose stean pots, if you can get them, which are of equal size top and bottom (they should hold eight or nine pounds); put the fruit in about a quarter up, then strew in a quarter of the sugar; then another quantity of fruit, and so till all of both are in.  The proportion of sugar is to be three pounds to nine pounds of fruit.  Set the jars in the oven, and bake the fruit quite through.   When cold, put a piece of clean scraped stick into the middle of the jar, and let the upper part stand above the top; then put melted mutton suet over the top full half an inch thick, having previously covered the fruit with white paper.  Keep the jars in a cool dry place, and use the suet as a cover, which you will draw up by the stick, minding to leave a little forked branch to it to prevent its slipping out.

**To Preserve Fruit for Tarts, or Family Desserts.**— Cherries, plums of all sorts, and American apples, gather when ripe, and lay them in small jars that will hold a pound; strew over each jar six ounces of good loaf-sugar pounded: cover with two bladders each, separately tied down; then set the jars in a large stew-pan of water up to the neck, and let it boil three hours gently.  Keep these and all other sorts of fruit free from damp,

**To Keep Lemon Juice.**—Buy the fruit when cheap, keep it in a cool place two or three days, if too unripe to squeeze at once; cut the peel off some, and roll them under your hand to make them part with the juice more readily; others you may leave unpared for grating, when the pulp shall be taken out and dried.   Squeeze the juice into a china basin; then strain it through some muslin, which will not permit the least pulp to pass.  Have ready half and quarter-ounce phials perfectly dry; fill them with the juice so near the top as only to admit half a tea-spoonful of sweet oil into each; or a little more, if for larger bottles.   Cork the bottles, and set them upright in a cool place.

When you want lemon-juice, open such a sized bottle as you shall use in two or three days; wind some clean cotton round a skewer, and dipping it in, the oil will be attracted; and when all shall be removed, the juice will be as fine as when first bottled.

Hang the peels up till dry; then keep them from the dust.

**China Orange Juice.** (A very useful thing to mix with Water in Fevers, when the fresh Juice cannot be procured).— Squeeze from the finest fruit a pint of juice strained through fine muslin, and gently simmer with three quarters of a pound of double-refined sugar for twenty minutes; when cold put it in small bottles.

**Different ways of Dressing Cranberries.**—For pies and puddings, with a good deal of sugar.

Stew in a jar with the same: which way they eat well with bread, and are very wholesome.

Thus done, pressed and strained, the juice makes a fine drink for people in fevers.

**Orgeat.**—Boil a quart of new milk with a stick of cinnamon, sweeten to your taste, and let it grow cold ; then pour it by degrees to three ounces of almonds, and twenty bitter that have been blanched and beaten to a paste, with a little water to prevent oiling ; boil all together, and stir till cold, then add half a glass of brandy.

**Another way.**—Blanch and pound three quarters of a pound of almonds, and thirty bitter, with a spoonful of water. Stir in by degrees two pints of water, and three of milk, and strain the whole through a cloth. Dissolve half a pound of fine sugar in a pint of water, boil and skim it well ; mix it with the other, as likewise two spoonfuls of orange-flower water, and a tea-cupful of the best brandy.

**Lemonade, to be made the day before wanted.**—Pare two dozen of tolerably sized lemons as thin as possible, put eight of the rinds into three quarts of hot, not boiling, water, and cover it over for three or four hours. Rub some fine sugar on the lemons to attract the essence, and put it into a china bowl, into which squeeze the juice of the lemons. To it add one pound and a half of fine sugar, then put the water to the above, and three quarts of milk made boiling hot ; mix, and pour through a jelly-bag till perfectly clear.

**Another way.**—Pare a number of lemons according to the quantity you are likely to want ; on the peels pour hot water, but more juice will be necessary than you need use the peels of. While infusing, boil sugar and water to a good syrup with the white of an egg whipt up ; when it boils, pour a little cold water into it ; set it on again, and when it boils up, take the pan off, and put it to settle. If there is any scum, take it off, and pour it clear from the sediment to the water the peels were infused in, and the lemon-juice ; stir and taste it, and add as much more water as shall be necessary to make a very rich lemonade. Wet a jelly-bag, and squeeze it dry, then strain the liquor, which is uncommonly fine.

**Lemonade that has the Flavour and Appearance of Jelly.**—Pare two Seville oranges and six lemons as thin as possible, and steep them four hours in a quart of hot water. Boil a pound and a quarter of loaf-sugar in three pints of water, and skim it. Add the two liquors to the juice of six China oranges and twelve lemons ; stir the whole well, and run it through a jelly-bag till clear. Then add a little orange-water, if you like the flavour, and if wanted, more sugar. It will keep well if corked.

**Raspberry Vinegar.**—Put a pound of fine fruit into a china bowl, and pour upon it a quart of the best white-wine vinegar ; next day strain the liquor on a pound of fresh raspberries, and the following day do the same, but do not squeeze the fruit, only drain the liquor as dry as you can from it. The last time pass it through a canvas previously wet with vinegar to prevent waste. Put it into a stone jar, with a pound of loaf sugar to every pint of juice broken into large lumps; stir it when melted, then put the jar into a saucepan of water, or on a hot hearth, let it simmer, and skim it. When cold, bottle it.

This is one of the most useful preparations that can be kept in a house, not only as affording the most refreshing beverage, but being of singular efficacy in complaints of the chest. A large spoonful or two in a tumbler of water. Be careful to use no glazed nor metal vessel for it.

The fruit, with an equal quantity of sugar, makes excellent **Raspberry Cakes,** without boiling.

---

## CAKES, BREAD, &c.

### Observations on Making and Baking Cakes.

CURRANTS should be very nicely washed, dried in a cloth, and then set before the fire. If damp they will make cakes or puddings heavy. Before they are added, a dust of dry flour should be thrown among them, and a shake given to them, which causes the thing that they are put to to be lighter.

Eggs should be very long beaten, whites and yolks apart, and always strained.

Sugar should be rubbed to a powder on a clean board, and sifted through a very fine hair or lawn sieve.

Lemon peel should be pared very thin, and with a little sugar beaten in a marble mortar to a paste, and then mixed with a little wine, or cream, so as to divide easily among the other ingredients.

After all the articles are put into the pan, they should be thoroughly and long beaten, as the lightness of the cake depends much on their being well incorporated.

Whether black or white plum-cakes, they require less butter and eggs for having yeast, and eat equally light and rich. If the leaven be only of flour, milk, water, and yeast, it becomes more tough and is less easily divided than if the butter be first put with those ingredients, and the dough afterwards set to rise by the fire.

The heat of the oven is of great importance for cakes, especially those that are large. If not pretty quick, the batter will not rise. Should you fear its catching, by being too quick, put some paper over the cake to prevent its being burnt. If not long enough lighted to have a body of heat, or it is become slack, the cake will be heavy. To know when it is soaked, take a broad-bladed knife that is very bright, and plunge into the very centre; draw it instantly out, and if the least stickiness adheres, put the cake immediately in, and shut up the oven.

If the heat was sufficient to raise but not to soak, I have with great success had fresh fuel quickly put in, and kept the cakes hot until the oven was fit to finish the soaking, and they turned out extremely well. But those who are employed ought to be particularly careful that no mistake occur from negligence when large cakes are to be baked.

**Iceing for Cakes.**—For a large one, beat and sift eight ounces of fine sugar; put into a mortar with four spoonfuls of rose-water and the whites of two eggs, beaten and strained, whisk it well, and when the cake is almost cold, dip a feather in the ice-ing, and cover the cake well; set it in the oven to harden, but do not let it stay to discolour. Put the cake into a dry place.

**To Ice a very large Cake.**—Beat the whites of twenty fresh eggs; then, by degrees, beat a pound of double-refined sugar sifted through a lawn sieve; mix these well in a deep earthen pan, add orange-flower water and a piece of fresh lemon peel of the former, enough to flavour, and no more. Whisk it for three hours, till the mixture is thick and white; then with a thin broad bit of board spread it all over the top and sides, and set it in a cool oven, and an hour will harden it.

**A Common Cake.**—Mix three quarters of a pound of flour with half a pound of butter, four ounces of sugar, four eggs, half an ounce of caraways, and a glass of raisin wine. Beat it well, and bake in a quick oven. Use fine Lisbon sugar.

**A very good Common Cake.**—Rub eight ounces of butter into two pounds of dried flour; mix it with three spoonfuls of yeast that is not bitter, to a paste. Let it rise an hour and a half, then mix in the yolks and whites of four eggs beaten apart, one pound of sugar, some milk to make it a proper thickness (about a pint will be sufficient), a glass of sweet wine, the rind of a lemon, and a tea-spoonful of ginger. Add either a pound of currants, or some caraways, and beat well.

**An excellent Cake.**—Rub two pounds of dry fine flour with one of butter, washed in plain rose-water, and mix it with three spoonfuls of yeast in a little warm milk and water. Set it to rise an hour and a half before the fire, then beat into it two pounds of currants, one pound of sugar sifted, four ounces of almonds, six ounces of stoned raisins chopped fine, half a nutmeg, cinnamon, allspice, and a few cloves, the peel of a lemon chopped as fine as possible, a glass of wine, ditto of brandy, twelve yolks and whites of eggs beat separately and long, orange, citron, and lemon. Beat exceedingly well, and butter the pan. A quick oven.

**A very fine Cake.**—Wash two pounds and a half of fresh butter in water first, and then in rose-water; beat the butter to a cream; beat twenty eggs, yolks and whites separately, half an hour each. Have ready two pounds and a half of the finest flour, well dried and kept hot, likewise a pound and a half of sugar pounded and sifted, one ounce of spice in finest powder, three pounds of currants nicely cleaned and dried, half a pound of almonds blanched, and three quarters of a pound of sweetmeats cut, not too thin. Let all be kept by the fire; mix all the dry ingredients; pour the eggs strained to the butter; mix half a pint of sweet wine with a large glass of brandy, pour it to the butter nd eggs, mix well, then have all the dry things put in by degrees, eat them very thoroughly, you can hardly do it too much.

Having half a pound of stoned jar-raisins chopped as fine as possible, mix them carefully so that there shall be no lumps, and add a tea-cupful of orange-flower water. Beat the ingredients together a full hour at least. Have a hoop well buttered, or, if you have none, a tin or copper cake-pan; take a white paper doubled and buttered, and put in the pan, round the edge, if the cake batter fill it more than three parts, for space should be allowed for rising. Bake in a quick oven. It will require three hours.

**Rout Drop Cakes.**—Mix two pounds of flour, one ditto butter, one ditto sugar, one ditto currants, clean and dry; then wet into a stiff paste with two eggs, and a large spoonful of orange-flower water, ditto rose-water, ditto sweet wine, ditto brandy; drop on a tin plate floured: a very short time bakes them.

**Flat Cakes, that will keep long in the house good.**—Mix two pounds of flour, one pound of sugar, and one ounce of caraways, with four or five eggs, and a few spoonfuls of water, to make a stiff paste; roll it thin, and cut it into any shape. Bake on tins lightly floured. While baking, boil a pound of sugar in a pint of water to a thin syrup; while both are hot, dip each cake into it, and put them on tins into the oven to dry for a a short time, and when the oven is cooler still, return them there again, and let them stay four or five hours.

**Little White Cakes.**—Dry half a pound of flour; rub into it a very little pounded sugar, one ounce of butter, one egg, a few caraways, and as much milk and water as to make a paste; roll it thin, and cut it with the top of a canister or glass. Bake fifteen minutes on tin plates.

**Little Short Cakes.**—Rub into a pound of dried flour four ounces of butter, four ounces of white powder-sugar, one egg, and a spoonful or two of thin cream to make into a paste. When mixed, put currants into one half, and caraways into the rest. Cut them as before, and bake on tins.

**Plum Cakes.**—Mix thoroughly a quarter of a peck of fine flour, well dried, with a pound of dry and sifted loaf sugar, three pounds of currants washed, and very dry, half a pound of raisins stoned and chopped, a quarter of an ounce of mace and cloves, twenty Jamaica peppers, a grated nutmeg, the peel of a lemon cut as fine as possible, and half a pound of almonds blanched and beaten with orange-flower water. Melt two pounds of butter in a pint and quarter of cream, but not hot, put to it a pint of sweet wine, a glass of brandy, the whites and yolks of twelve eggs beaten apart, and half a pint of good yeast. Strain this liquid by degrees into the dry ingredients, beating them together a full hour, then butter the hoop, or pan, and bake it. As you put the batter in the hoop, or pan, throw in plenty of citron, lemon, and orange-candy.

If you ice the cake, take half a pound of double-refined sugar sifted, and put a little with the white of an egg, beat it well, and by degrees pour in the remainder. It must be whisked near an hour, with the addition of a little orange-flower water, but mind not to put much. When the cake is done, pour the iceing over, and return it to the oven for fifteen minutes ; but if the oven be very warm, keep it near the mouth, and the door open, lest the colour be spoiled.

**Another.**—Flour dried, and currants washed and picked, four pounds ; sugar pounded and sifted, one pound and a half; six orange, lemon, and citron-peels, cut in slices : mix these.

Beat ten eggs, yolks and whites separately ; then melt a pound and a half of butter in a pint of cream ; when lukewarm, put it to half a pint of ale-yeast, near half a pint of sweet wine, and the eggs ; then strain the liquid to the dry ingredients, beat them well, and add of cloves, mace, cinnamon, and nutmeg, half an ounce each.  Butter the pan, and put it into a quick oven.  Three hours will bake it.

**Very good common Plum Cakes.**—Mix five ounces of butter in three pounds of dry flour, and five ounces of fine Lisbon sugar ; then add six ounces of currants, washed and dried, and some pimento finely powdered.  Put three spoonfuls of yeast into a Winchester pint of new milk warmed, and mix into a light dough with the above.  Make it into twelve cakes, and bake on a floured tin half an hour.

**Little Plum Cakes, to keep long.**—Dry one pound of flour, and mix six ounces of finely-pounded sugar ; beat six ounces of butter to a cream, and add to three eggs, well beaten, half a pound of currants, washed and nicely dried, and the flour and sugar ; beat all for some time, then dredge flour on tin-plates, and drop the batter on them the size of a walnut.  If properly mixed, it will be a stiff paste.  Bake in a brisk oven.

**A good Pound Cake.**—Beat a pound of butter to a cream, and mix with it the whites and yolks of eight eggs beaten apart. Have ready warm by the fire, a pound of flour, and the same of sifted sugar, mix them and a few cloves, a little nutmeg and cinnamon in fine powder together ; then by degrees work up all the dry ingredients into the butter and eggs.  When well beaten, add a glass of wine and some caraways.  It must be beaten a full hour. Butter a pan, and bake it a full hour in a quick oven.

The above proportions, leaving out four ounces of the butter, and the same of sugar, make a less luscious cake, and to most tastes a more pleasant one.

**A cheap Seed Cake.**—Mix a quarter of a peck of flour with half a pound of sugar, a quarter of an ounce of allspice, and a little ginger ; melt three quarters of a pound of butter, with half a pint of milk ; when just warm, put to it a quarter of a pint of yeast, and work up to a good dough.  Let it stand before the fire a few minutes before it goes to the oven ; add seeds, or currants, and bake an hour and a half.

**Another.**— Mix a pound and a half of flour, and a pound of common lump-sugar, eight eggs beaten separately, an ounce of seeds, two spoonfuls of yeast, and the same of milk and water.

*Note.*—Milk alone causes cake and bread soon to dry.

**Common Bread Cake.**—Take the quantity of a quartern loaf from the dough, when making white bread, and knead well into it two ounces of butter, two of Lisbon sugar, and eight of currants. Warm the butter in a tea-cupful of good milk.

By the addition of an ounce of butter, or sugar, or an egg or two, you may make the cake better. A tea-cupful of raw cream improves it much. It is best to bake it in a pan, rather than as a loaf, the outside being less hard.

**Queen Cakes.**—Mix a pound of dried flour, the same of sifted sugar, and of currants washed clean. Wash a pound of butter in rose-water, beat it well, then mix with it eight eggs, yolks and whites beaten separately, and put in all the dry ingredients by degrees; beat the whole an hour; butter little tins, teacups, or saucers, and bake the batter in, filling only half. Sift a little fine sugar over just as you put into the oven.

**Another way.**—Beat eight ounces of butter, and mix with two well-beaten eggs, strained; mix eight ounces of dried flour, and the same of lump sugar, and the grated rind of a lemon, then add the whole together, and beat full half an hour with a silver-spoon. Butter small pattypans, half fill, and bake twenty minutes in a quick oven.

**Shrewsbury Cakes.**—Sift one pound of sugar, some pounded cinnamon, and a nutmeg grated, into three pounds of flour, the finest sort; add a little rose-water to three eggs, well beaten, and mix these with the flour, &c., then pour into it as much melted butter as will make it a good thickness to roll out.

Mould it well, and roll thin, and cut it into such shapes as you like.

**Tunbridge Cakes.**—Rub six ounces of butter quite fine, into a pound of flour, then mix six ounces of sugar, beat and strain two eggs, and make with the above into a paste. Roll it very thin, and cut it with the top of a glass; prick them with a fork, and cover with caraways, or wash with the white of an egg, and dust a little white sugar over.

**Rice Cake.**—Mix ten ounces of ground rice, three ounces of flour, eight ounces of pounded sugar; then sift by degrees into eight yolks and six whites of eggs, and the peel of a lemon shred so fine that it is quite mashed; mix the whole well in a tin stew-pan over a very slow fire with a whisk, then put it immediately into the oven in the same and bake forty minutes.

**Another.**—Beat twelve yolks and six whites of eggs with the peels of two lemons grated. Mix one pound of flour of rice, eight ounces of flour, and one pound of sugar pounded and sifted; then beat it well with the eggs, by degrees, for an hour, with a wooden spoon. Butter a pan well, and put in at the oven's mouth.

A gentle oven will bake it in an hour and a half.

**Water Cakes.**—Dry three pounds of fine flour, and rub into it one pound of sugar sifted, one pound of butter, and one ounce of caraway seeds. Make it into a paste with three quarters of a pint of boiling new milk, roll very thin, and cut into the size you choose; punch full of holes, and bake on tin-plates in a cool oven.

**Sponge Cake.**—Weigh ten eggs, and add their weight in very fine sugar, and that of six in flour; beat the yolks with the flour and the whites alone, to a very stiff froth; then by degrees mix the whites and the flour with the other ingredients, and beat them well half an hour. Bake in a quick oven an hour.

**Another, without Butter.**—Dry one pound of flour, and one and a quarter of sugar; then beat seven eggs, yolks and whites apart; grate a lemon, and, with a spoonful of brandy, beat the whole together with your hand for an hour. Bake in a buttered pan in a quick oven.

Sweetmeats may be added if approved.

**Tea Cakes.**—Rub fine four ounces of butter into eight ounces of flour; mix eight ounces of currants and six of fine Lisbon sugar, two yolks and one white of eggs, and a spoonful of brandy. Roll the paste the thickness of an Oliver biscuit, and cut with a wine glass. You may beat the other white and wash over them, and either dust sugar or not, as you like.

**Benton Tea Cakes.**—Mix a paste of flour, a little bit of butter and milk; roll as thin as possible, and bake on a back-stone over the fire, or on a hot hearth.

**Another sort, as Biscuits.**—Rub into a pound of flour six ounces of butter, and add three large spoonfuls of yeast and make into a paste, with a sufficient quantity of new milk; make into biscuits, and prick them with a clean fork.

**Another sort.**—Melt six or seven ounces of butter with a sufficiency of new milk warmed to make seven pounds of flour into a stiff paste; roll thin, and make into biscuits.

**A Biscuit Cake.**—One pound of flour, five eggs well beaten and strained, eight ounces of sugar, a little rose or orange-flower water; beat the whole thoroughly and bake one hour.

**Macaroons.**—Blanch four ounces of almonds, and pound with four spoonfuls of orange-flower water; whisk the whites of four eggs to a froth, then mix it and a pound of sugar sifted, with the almonds, to a paste; and laying a sheet of wafer-paper on a tin, put it on in different little cakes, the shape of macaroons.

**Wafers.**—Dry the flour well which you intend to use, mix a little pounded sugar and finely-pounded mace with it; then make it into a thick batter with cream; butter the wafer irons, let them be hot: put a tea-spoonful of the batter into them, so bake them carefully, and roll them off the iron with a stick.

**Crack Nuts.**—Mix eight ounces of flour and eight ounces of sugar; melt four ounces of butter in two spoonfuls of raisin wine; then, with four eggs beaten and strained, make into a paste; add caraways, roll out as thin as paper, cut with the top of a glass, wash with the white of an egg, and dust sugar over.

**Cracknels.**—Mix with a quart of flour half a nutmeg grated, the yolks of four eggs beaten, with four spoonfuls of rose-water, into a stiff paste, with cold water; then roll in a pound of butter, and make them into cracknel shapes; put them into a kettle of boiling water and boil them till they swim, then take out and put them into cold water; when hardened, lay them out to dry, and bake them on tin plates.

**A good Plain Bun, that may be eaten with or without Toasting and Butter.**—Rub four ounces of butter into two pounds of flour, four ounces of sugar, a nutmeg, or not, as you like, a few Jamaica peppers, a dessert spoonful of caraways; put a spoonful or two of cream into a cup of yeast, and as much good milk as will make the above into a light paste. Set it to rise by a fire till the oven be ready. They will quickly bake on tins.

**Richer Buns.**—Mix one pound and a half of dried flour with half a pound of sugar; melt a pound and two ounces of butter in a little warm water; add six spoonfuls of rose-water, and knead the above into a light dough, with half a pint of yeast; then mix five ounces of caraway-comfits in, and put some on them.

**Gingerbread.**—Mix with two pounds of flour, half a pound of treacle, three quarters of an ounce of caraways, one ounce of ginger finely sifted, and eight ounces of butter.

Roll the paste into what form you please, and bake on tins, after having worked it very much and kept it to rise.

If you like sweetmeats add orange candied; it may be added in small bits.

**Another sort.**—To three quarters of a pound of treacle beat one egg strained; mix four ounces of brown sugar, half an ounce of ginger sifted; of cloves, mace, allspice and nutmeg a quarter of an ounce, beaten as fine as possible; coriander and caraway seeds each a quarter of an ounce; melt one pound of butter and mix with the above, and add as much flour as will knead into a pretty stiff paste; then roll it out and cut into cakes.

Bake on tin plates in a quick oven. A little time will bake them.

Of some, drops may be made.

**A Good Plain Sort.**—Mix three pounds of flour with half a pound of butter, four ounces of brown sugar, half an ounce of pounded ginger; then make into a paste with one pound and a quarter of treacle, warm.

**A Good Sort without Butter.**—Mix two pounds of treacle, of orange, lemon, and citron, and candied ginger, each four ounces, all thinly sliced; one ounce of coriander seeds, one ounce of caraways, and one ounce of beaten ginger, in as much flour as will make a soft paste; lay it in cakes on tin plates, and bake it in a quick oven. Keep it dry in a covered earthen vessel, and it will be good for some months.

*Note.*—If cakes or biscuits be kept in paper, or a drawer, the taste will be disagreeable. A pan and cover, or tureen, will preserve them long and moist. —Or, if to be crisp, laying them before the fire will make them so.

**Rusks.**—Beat seven eggs well, and mix with half a pint of new milk, in which have been melted four ounces of butter; add to it a quarter of a pint of yeast and three ounces of sugar, and put them by degrees into as much flour as will make a very light paste rather like batter, and let it rise before the fire half an hour; then add some more flour to make it a little stiffer, but not stiff. Work it well, and divide it into small loaves or cakes, about five or six inches wide, and flatten them. When baked and cold, slice them the thickness of rusks, and put them in the oven to brown a little.

*Note.*—The cakes, when first baked, eat deliciously buttered for tea ; or, with caraways, to eat cold.

**To make Yeast.**— Thicken two quarts of water with fine flour, about three spoonfuls ; boil half an hour, sweeten with near half a pound of brown sugar ; when near cold, put into it four spoonfuls of fresh yeast in a jug, shake it well together, and let it stand one day to ferment near the fire, without being covered. There will be a thin liquor on the top, which must be poured off ; shake the remainder, and cork it up for use. Take always four spoonfuls of the old to ferment the next quantity, keeping it always in succession.

A half-peck loaf will require about a gill.

**Another way.**—Boil one pound of potatoes to a mash ; when half cold, add a cupful of yeast, and mix it well. It will be ready for use in two or three hours, and keeps well.

Use double the quantity of this, to what you do of beer yeast.

To take off the bitter of yeast, put bran into a sieve, and pour it through, having first mixed a little warm water with it.

**To make Bread.**—Let flour be kept four or five weeks before it is begun to bake with. Put half a bushel of good flour into a trough, or kneading-tub ; mix with it between four and five quarts of warm water, and a pint and a half of good yeast ; put it into the flour, and stir it well with your hands till it becomes tough. Let it rise about an hour and twenty minutes, or less, if it rises fast ; then, before it falls, add four more quarts of warm water, and half a pound of salt ; work it well, and cover it with a cloth. Put the fire into the oven, and by the time it is warm enough, the dough will be ready. Make the loaves about five pounds each ; sweep out the oven very clean and quick, and put in the bread ; shut it up close and two hours and a half will bake it. In summer the water should be milk-warm, in winter a little more, and in frosty weather as hot as you can bear your hand in, but not scalding, or the whole will be spoiled. If baked in tins, the crust will be very nice.

The oven should be round, not long ; the roof from twenty to twenty-four inches high, the mouth small, and the door of iron, to shut close. This construction will save firing and time, and bake better than long and high-roofed ovens.

Rolls, muffins, or any sort of bread, may be made to taste new, when two or three days old, by dipping them, uncut, in water, and baking afresh, or toasting.

**American Flour** requires almost twice as much water to make it into bread as is used for English flour, and therefore it is more profitable ; for a stone of the American, which weighs fourteen pounds, will make twenty-one pounds and a half of bread ; but the best sort of English flour produces only eighteen pounds and a half.

**The Reverend Mr. Hagget's Economical Bread.—** Only the coarse flake bran is to be removed from the flour; of this take five pounds, and boil it in rather more than four gallons of water, so that when perfectly smooth, you may have three gallons and three quarts of bran-water clear. With this knead fifty-six pounds of the flour, adding salt and yeast in the same way and proportion as for other bread. When ready to bake, divide it into loaves, and bake them two hours and a half.

Thus made, flour will imbibe three quarts more of bran-water than of plain, so that it not only produces a more nutritious and substantial food, but makes an increase of one-fifth the usua. quantity of bread, which is a saving of one day's consumption out of six; and if this was adopted throughout the kingdom, it would effect a saving of ten millions sterling a year, when wheat was at the price it stood in the scarcity, reckoning the consumption to be two hundred thousand bushels a day. The same quantity of flour, which, kneaded with water, produces sixty-nine pounds eight ounces of bread, will, in the above way, make eighty-three pounds eight ounces, and gain fourteen pounds. At the ordinary price of flour four millions would be saved. When ten days old, if put into the oven for twenty minutes, this bread will appear quite new again.

**Rice and Wheat Bread.—**Simmer a pound of rice in two quarts of water till it becomes perfectly soft; and when it is of a proper warmth, mix it extremely well with four pounds of flour, and yeast and salt as for other bread; of yeast about four large spoonfuls; knead it extremely well; then set it to rise before the fire. Some of the flour should be reserved to make up the loaves. The whole expense, including baking, will not exceed three shillings, for which eight pounds and a half of exceeding good bread will be produced. If the rice should require more water it must be added, as some rice swells more than other.

**French Bread.—**With a quarter of a peck of fine flour mix the yolks of three, and whites of two eggs, beaten and strained, a little salt, half a pint of good yeast that is not bitter, and as much milk, made a little warm, as will work into a thin light dough. Stir it about, but do not knead it. Have ready three quart wooden dishes, divide the dough among them. Set to rise, then turn them out into the oven, which must be quick. Rasp when done.

**To Discover whether Bread has been Adulterated with Whiting or Chalk.—**Mix it with lemon-juice, or strong vinegar, and if this puts it into a state of fermentation, you may be certain it has a mixture of alkaline particles, and these are sometimes in large quantities in bakers' bread.

**To Detect Bones, Jalap, Ashes, &c., in Bread.—**Slice a large loaf very thin, the crumb only; set it over the fire with water, and let it boil gently a long time; take it off, and pour the water into a vessel; let it stand till nearly cold, then pour it gently

M

out, and in the sediment will be seen the ingredients which have been mixed. The alum will be dissolved in the water, and may be extracted from it. If jalap has been used, it will form a thick film at top, and the heavy ingredients will sink to the bottom.

**Excellent Rolls.**—Warm one ounce of butter in half a pint of milk, put to it a spoonful and a half of yeast of small beer, and a little salt. Put two pounds of flour into a pan, and mix in the above. Let it rise an hour, knead it well, make into seven rolls, and bake in a quick oven.

If made in cakes three inches thick, sliced and buttered, they resemble Sally Lunns, as made at Bath. The foregoing receipt, with the addition of a little saffron boiled in half a tea-cupful of milk, makes them remarkably good.

**French Rolls.**—Rub an ounce of butter into a pound of flour; mix one egg beaten, a little yeast that is not bitter, and as much milk as will make the dough of a middling stiffness. Beat it well, but do not knead; let it rise and bake on tins.

**Brentford Rolls.**—Mix with two pounds of flour a little salt, two ounces of sifted sugar, four ounces of butter, and two eggs beaten with two spoonfuls of yeast, and about a pint of milk. Knead the dough well, and set it to rise before the fire. Make twelve rolls, butter tin plates, and set them before the fire to rise, till they become of a proper size; then bake half an hour.

**Potato Rolls.**—Boil three pounds of potatoes, bruise and work them with two ounces of butter, and as much milk as will make them pass through a colander. Take half or three quarters of a pint of yeast, and half a pint of warm water to mix with the potatoes; then pour the whole upon five pounds of flour, and add some salt. Knead it well: if not of a proper consistence, put a little more milk and water warm; let it stand before the fire an hour to rise; work it well, and make it into rolls. Bake about half an hour in an oven not quite so hot as for bread. They eat well toasted and buttered.

**Muffins.**—Mix two pounds of flour with two eggs, two ounces of butter melted in a pint of milk, and four or five spoonfuls of yeast; beat it thoroughly, and set it to rise two or three hours. Bake on a hot hearth in flat cakes. When done on one side turn them.

*Note.*—Muffins, rolls, or bread, if stale, may be made to taste new, by dipping in cold water, and toasting, or heating in an oven, or Dutch oven, till the outside be crisp.

**Yorkshire Cakes.**—Take two pounds of flour, and mix with it four ounces of butter melted in a pint of good milk, three spoonfuls of yeast, and two eggs; beat all well together and let it rise; then knead it, and make into cakes; let them rise on tins before you bake, which do in a slow oven. Another sort is made as above, leaving out the butter. The first is a shorter sort; the last lighter.

**Hard Biscuits.**—Warm two ounces of butter in as much

skimmed milk as will make a pound of flour into a very stiff paste, beat it with a rolling-pin, and work it very smooth. Roll it thin, and cut it into round biscuits; prick them full of holes with a fork. About six minutes will bake them.

**Plain and very Crisp Biscuits.**—Make a pound of flour, the yolk of an egg, and some milk, into a very stiff paste; beat it well, and knead till quite smooth; roll very thin, and cut into biscuits. Bake them in a slow oven till quite dry and crisp.

---

## HOME BREWERY, WINES, &c.

**To Brew very fine Welsh Ale.**—Pour forty-two gallons of water hot, but not quite boiling, on eight bushels of malt, cover and let it stand three hours. In the meantime infuse four pounds of hops in a little hot water, and put the water and hops into the tub, and run the wort upon them, and boil them together three hours. Strain off the hops, and keep for the small beer. Let the wort stand in a high tub till cool enough to receive the yeast, of which put two quarts of ale, or if you cannot get it, of small-beer yeast. Mix it thoroughly and often. When the wort has done working the second or third day, the yeast will sink rather than rise in the middle, remove it then, and tun the ale as it works out; pour a quart in at a time, and gently, to prevent the fermentation from continuing too long, which weakens the liquor. Put a bit of paper over the bung-hole two or three days before stopping up.

**Strong Beer or Ale.**—Twelve bushels of malt to the hogshead for beer (or fourteen if you wish it of a very good body), eight for ale; for either pour the whole quantity of water hot, but not boiling, on at once, and let it infuse three hours close covered; mash it in the first half hour, and let it stand the remainder of the time. Run it on the hops previously infused in water; for strong beer three quarters of a pound to a bushel; if for ale, half a pound. Boil them with the wort two hours from the time it begins to boil. Cool a pailful—add two quarts of yeast to, which will prepare it for putting to the rest when ready next day; but if possible put together the same night. Tun as usual. Cover the bung-hole with paper when the beer has done working; and when it is to be stopped, have ready a pound and a half of hops dried before the fire, put them into the bung-hole, and fasten it up. Let it stand twelve months in casks, and twelve in bottles, before it be drunk. It will keep and be very fine eight or ten years. It should be brewed in the beginning of March.

Great care must be taken that the bottles are perfectly prepared, and that the corks are of the best sort.

The ale will be ready in three or four months; and if the vent-peg never be removed, it will have spirit and strength to the very last. Allow two gallons of water at first for waste.

After the beer or ale has run from the grains, pour a hogshead and half for the twelve bushels, and a hogshead of water if eight were brewed; mash, and let stand, and then boil, &c.   Use some of the hops for this table-beer that were boiled for the strong.

When thunder or hot weather causes beer to turn sour, a tea-spoonful, or more if required, of salt of wormwood put into the jug, will rectify it.   Let it be drawn just before it is drunk, or it will taste flat.

**Excellent Table Beer.**—On three bushels of malt pour of hot water the third of the quantity you are to use, which is to be thirty-nine gallons.   Cover it warm half an hour, then mash, and let it stand two hours and a half more, then set it to drain. When dry, add half the remaining water, mash, and let it stand half an hour, run that into another tub, and pour the rest of the water on the malt, stir it well, and cover it, letting it infuse a full hour.   Run that off, and mix all together,   A pound and a half of hops should be infused in water, as in the former receipt, and be put into the tub for the first running.

Boil the hops with the wort an hour from the time it first boils. Strain off and cool.   If the whole be not cool enough that day to add to the yeast, a pail or two of wort may be prepared, and a quart of yeast put to it over night.   Before tunning, all the wort should be added together, and thoroughly mixed with the lade-pail. When the wort ceases to work, put a bit of paper on the bunghole for three days, when it may be safely fastened close.   In three or four weeks the beer will be fit for drinking.

Servants should be directed to put a cork into every barrel as soon as the cock is taken out, and to fasten in the vent-peg, the air causing casks to become musty.

**To Refine Beer, Ale, Wine, or Cyder.**—Put two ounces of isinglass shavings to soak in a quart of the liquor that you want to clear, beat it with a whisk every day till dissolved.   Draw off a third part of the cask, and mix the above with it: likewise a quarter of an ounce of pearl-ashes, one ounce of salt of tartar cal-cined, and one ounce of burnt alum powdered.   Stir it well, then return the liquor into the cask, and stir it with a clean stick.   Stop it up, and in a few days it will be fine.

**Extract of Malt for Coughs.**—Over half a bushel of pale ground malt, pour as much hot, not boiling water, as will just cover it.   In forty-eight hours drain off the liquor entirely, but without squeezing the grains; put the former into a large sweetmeat-pan, or saucepan, that there may be room to boil as quick as possible, without boiling over: when it begins to thicken, stir constantly. It must be as thick as treacle.   A dessert-spoonful thrice a day.

**To Preserve Yeast.**—When you have plenty of yeast, begin to save it in the following manner:—Whisk it until it becomes thin, then take a new large wooden dish, wash it very nicely, and when quite dry, lay a layer of yeast over the inside with a soft brush; let it dry, then put another layer in the same manner and so do until you have a sufficient quantity, observing that each coat dry thoroughly before another be added.   It may be put on two or three inches thick, and will keep several months; when to be used, cut a piece out and stir it in warm water.   If to be used for brewing, keep it by dipping large handfuls of birch tied together; and when dry, repeat the dipping once. You may thus do as many as you please; but take care that no dust comes to them or the vessel in which it has been prepared as before. When the wort is set to work, throw into it one of these bunches, and it will do as well as fresh yeast; but if mixed with a small quantity first, and then added to the whole, it will work sooner.

**Remarks on English Wines.**—English wines would be found particularly useful, now foreign are so high priced; and though sugar is dear, they may be made at a quarter of the expense. If carefully made, and kept three or four years, a proportionable strength being given, they would answer the purpose of foreign wines for health, and cause a very considerable reduction in the expenditure.

**A Rich and Pleasant Wine.**—Take new cider from the press, mix it with as much honey as will support an egg, boil gently fifteen minutes, but not in an iron, brass, or copper pot. Skim it well; when cool let it be tunned, but do not quite fill. In March following bottle it, and it will be fit to drink in six weeks; but will be less sweet if kept longer in the cask. You will have a rich and strong wine, and it will keep well. This will serve for any culinary purposes which sack, or sweet wine, is directed for.

Honey is a fine ingredient to assist, and render palatable new crabbed austere cyder.

**Raspberry Wine.**—To every quart of well-picked raspberries put a quart of water; bruise, and let them stand two days; strain off the liquor, and to every gallon put three pounds of lump sugar; when dissolved, put the liquor into a barrel, and when fine, which will be in about two months, bottle it, and to each bottle put a spoonful of brandy, or a glass of wine.

**Raspberry or Currant Wine.**—To every three pints of fruit, carefully cleared from mouldy or bad, put one quart of water; bruise the former. In twenty-four hours strain the liquor, and put to every quart a pound of Lisbon sugar, of good middling quality. If for white currants, use lump-sugar. It is best to put the fruit, &c., in a large pan, and when in three or four days the scum rises, take that off before the liquor be put into the barrel: those who make from their own gardens may not have a sufficiency to fill the barrel at once; the wine will not hurt if made in the pan, in the above proportions, and added as the fruit ripens, and can be gathered in dry weather. Keep an account of what is put in each time.

**Another way.**—Put five quarts of currants, and a pint of raspberries, to every two gallons of water; let them soak a night; then squeeze and break them well. Next day rub them well on a fine wire sieve, till all the juice is obtained, washing the skins again with some of the water; then, to every gallon, put four pounds of very good Lisbon sugar, but not white, which is often adulterated; tun it immediately, and lay the bung lightly on. Do not use anything to work it. In two or three days put :

bottle of brandy to every four gallons; bung it close, but leave the peg out at top a few days: keep it three years, and it will be a very fine agreeable wine; four years would make it still better:

**Black Currant Wine, very fine.**—To every three quarts of juice, put the same of water unboiled; and to every three quarts of the liquor, add three pounds of very pure moist sugar. Put it into a cask, preserving a little for filling up. Put the cask in a warm dry room, and the liquor will ferment of itself. Skim off the refuse when the fermentation shall be over, and fill up with the reserved liquor. When it has ceased working, pour three quarts of brandy to forty quarts of wine. Bung it close for nine months, then bottle it, and drain the thick part through a jelly-bag until it be clear, and bottle that. Keep it ten or twelve months.

**Excellent Ginger Wine.**—Put into a very nice boiler ten gallons of water, fifteen pounds of lump sugar, with the whites of six or eight eggs well beaten and strained; mix all well while cold; when the liquor boils skim it well; put in half a pound of common white ginger bruised, boil it twenty minutes. Have ready the very thin rinds of seven lemons, and pour the liquor on them; when cool, tun it with two spoonfuls of yeast; put a quart of the liquor to two ounces of isinglass shavings while warm, whisk it well three or four times, and pour all together into the barrel. Next day stop it up; in three weeks bottle, and in three months it will be a delicious and refreshing liquor; and though very cool, perfectly safe.

**Another.**—Boil nine quarts of water with six pounds of lump-sugar, the rinds of two or three lemons very thinly pared, with two ounces of bruised white ginger, half an hour; skim. Put three quarters of a pound of raisins into the cask; when the liquor is lukewarm, tun it with the juice of two lemons strained, and a spoonful and a half of yeast. Stir it daily, then put in half a pint of brandy, and half an ounce of isinglass shavings; stop it up, and bottle it six or seven weeks. Do not put the lemon-peel in the barrel.

**Orange Wine.**—To six gallons of spring water, put fifteen pounds of loaf-sugar, and the whites of four eggs well beaten; let it boil for a quarter of an hour, and as the scum rises take it off; when cold, add the juice of fifty Seville oranges and five lemons; pare twelve oranges and five lemons as thin as possible, put them on thread, and suspend them in the barrel for one month, then take them out, and put in two pounds of loaf-sugar and bung it up.

**Excellent Cowslip Wine.**—To every gallon of water weigh three pounds of lump sugar, boil the quantity half an hour, taking off the scum as it rises. When cool enough, put to it a crust of toasted bread dipped in thick yeast, let the liquor ferment in the tub thirty-six hours: then into the cask put, for every gallon, the juice of two and rind of one lemon, and both of one Seville orange, and one gallon of cowslip pips, then pour on them the liquor. It must be carefully stirred every day for a week; then to every five gallons put in a bottle of brandy. Let the cask be closely stopped, and stand only six weeks before you bottle off. Observe to use the best corks.

**Elder Wine.**—To every quart of berries put two quarts of water, boil half an hour, run the liquor, and break the fruit through a hair sieve; then to every quart of juice, put three quarters of a pound of Lisbon sugar, coarse, but not the very coarsest. Boil the whole a quarter of an hour with some Jamaica peppers, ginger, and a few cloves. Pour it into a tub, and when of a proper warmth, into the barrel, with toast and yeast to work, which there is more difficulty to make it do than most other liquors. When it ceases to hiss, put a quart of brandy to eight gallons, and stop up. Bottle in the spring or at Christmas. The liquor must be in a warm place to make it work.

**White Elder Wine, very much like Frontinac.**—Boil eighteen pounds of white powder sugar, with six gallons of water, and two whites of eggs well beaten; then skim it, and put in a quarter of a peck of elder-flowers from the tree that bears white berries; do not keep them on the fire. When near cold, stir it, and put in six spoonfuls of lemon-juice, four or five of yeast, and beat well into the liquor; stir it every day; put six pounds of the best raisins, stoned, into the cask, and tun the wine. Stop it close, and bottle in six months. When well kept this wine will pass for Frontinac.

**Clary Wine.**—Boil fifteen gallons of water with forty-five pounds of sugar, skim it; when cold put a little to a quarter of a pint of yeast, and so by degrees add a little more. In an hour pour the small quantity to the large, pour the liquor on clary-flowers, picked in the dry: the quantity for the above is twelve quarts. Those who gather from their own garden may not have sufficient to put in at once, and may add as they can get them, keeping account of each quart. When it ceases to hiss, and the flowers are all in, stop it up for four months. Rack it off, empty the barrel of the dregs, and, adding a gallon of the best brandy, stop it up, and let it stand six or eight weeks, then bottle it.

**Excellent Raisin Wine.**—To every gallon of spring water put eight pounds of fresh Smyrnas in a large tub; stir it thoroughly every day for a month; then press the raisins in a horse-hair bag as dry as possible; put the liquor into a cask, and, when it has done hissing, pour in a bottle of the best brandy; stop it close for twelve months, then rack it off, but without the dregs; filter them through a bag of flannel of three or four folds; add the clear to the quantity, and pour one or two quarts of brandy, according to the size of the vessel. Stop it up, and, at the end of three years, you may either bottle it, or drink it fresh from the cask. Raisin wine would be extremely good, if made rich of the fruit and kept long, which improves the flavour greatly.

**Raisin Wine with Cyder.**—Put two hundredweight of Malaga raisins into a cask, and pour upon them a hogshead of good sound cyder that is not rough: stir it well two or three days; stop it, and let it stand six months; then rack it into a cask that it will fill, and put in a gallon of the best brandy. If raisin wine be much used, it would answer well to keep a cask always for it, and bottle off one year's wine just in time to make the next, which, allowing the six months of infusion, would make the wine to be eighteen months old. In cyder counties this way is very economical; and even if not thought strong enough, the addition of another quarter of a hundred of raisins would be sufficient, and the wine would still be very cheap. When the raisins are pressed through a horse-hair bag, they will either produce a good spirit by distillation, and must be sent to a chemist who will do it (but if for that purpose, they must be very little pressed), or they will make excellent vinegar, on which article see page 98. The stalks should be picked out for the above, and may be thrown into any cask of vinegar that is making, being very acid.

**Raisin Wine without Cyder.**—On four hundredweight of Malagas pour one hogshead of spring-water, stir well daily for fourteen days, then squeeze the raisins in a horse-hair bag in a press, and tun the liquor; when it ceases to hiss, stop it close. In six months rack it off into another cask, or into a tub, and after clearing out the sediment, return it into the same, but do not wash it; add a gallon of the best brandy, stop it close, and in six months bottle it. Take care of the pressed fruit, for the uses of which refer to the preceding receipt.

**Sack Mead.**—To every gallon of water put four pounds of honey, and boil it three quarters of an hour, taking care to skim it. To every gallon add an ounce of hops, then boil it half an hour and let it stand till next day; put it into your cask, and to thirteen gallons of the liquor add a quart of brandy. Let it be lightly stopped till the fermentation is over, and then stop it very close. If you make a large cask, keep it a year in cask.

**Cowslip Mead.**—Put thirty pounds of honey into fifteen gallons of water, and boil till one gallon is wasted; skim it, take it off the fire, and have ready a dozen and a half of lemons quartered; pour a gallon of the liquor boiling hot upon them; put the remainder of the liquor into a tub with seven pecks of cowslip-pips; let them remain there all night, and then put the liquor and the lemons to eight spoonfuls of new yeast and a handful of sweet-brier; stir all well together and let it work three or four days. Strain it, and put into the cask: let it stand six months, and then bottle it for keeping.

**Imperial.**—Put two ounces of cream of tartar and the juice and paring of two lemons into a stone-jar, pour on them seven quarts of boiling water, stir and cover close. When cold sweeten with loaf-sugar, and straining it, bottle and cork it tight. This is a very pleasant liquor and very wholesome; but from the latter consideration was at one time drank in such quantities as to become injurious. Add, in bottling, half a pint of rum to the whole quantity.

**Ratafia.**—Blanch two ounces of peach and apricot kernels, bruise and put them into a bottle, and fill nearly up with brandy. Dissolve half a pound of white sugar-candy in a cup of cold water, and add to the brandy after it has stood a month on the kernels, and they are strained off; then filter through paper, and bottle for use. The leaves of peach and nectarines, when the trees are cut in the spring, being distilled, are an excellent substitute for ratafia in puddings.

**Raspberry Brandy.**—Pick fine dry fruit, put into a stone jar, and the jar into a kettle of water, or on a hot hearth, till the juice will run; strain, and to every pint add half a pound of sugar, give one boil, and skim it; when cold put equal quantities of juice and brandy, shake well and bottle. Some people prefer it stronger of the brandy.

**An excellent Method of making Punch.**—Take two large fresh lemons with rough skins, quite ripe, and some large lumps of double-refined sugar. Rub the sugar over the lemons till it has absorbed all the yellow part of the skins. Then put into the bowl these lumps, and as much more as the juice of the lemons may be supposed to require; for no certain weight can be mentioned, as the acidity of a lemon cannot be known till tried, and therefore this must be determined by the taste. Then squeeze the lemon juice upon the sugar, and with a bruiser press the sugar and the juice particularly well together, for a great deal of the richness and fine flavour of the punch depends on this rubbing and mixing process being thoroughly performed. Then mix this up very well with boiling water (soft water is best) till the whole is rather cool. When this mixture (which is now called the sherbet) is to your taste, take brandy and rum in equal quantities, and put them to it, mixing the whole well together again. The quantity of liquor must be according to your taste: two good lemons are generally enough to make four quarts of punch, including a quart of liquor, with half a pound of sugar; but this depends much on taste and on the strength of the spirit.

As the pulp is disagreeable to some persons, the sherbet may be strained before the liquor is put in. Some strain the lemon before they put it to the sugar, which is improper; as, when the pulp and sugar are well mixed together, it adds much to the richness of the punch.

When only rum is used, about half a pint of porter will soften the punch; and even when both rum and brandy are used, the porter gives a richness, and to some a very pleasant flavour.

This receipt has never been in print before, but is greatly admired among the writer's friends. It is impossible to take too much pains in all the processes of mixing, and in minding to do them extremely well, that all the different articles may be most thoroughly incorporated together.

**Vendor, or Milk Punch.**—Pare six oranges and six lemons as thin as you can, grate them after with sugar to get the flavour. Steep the peels in a bottle of rum or brandy, stopped close, twenty-four hours. Squeeze the fruit on two pounds of sugar, and add to it four quarts of water and one of new milk boiling hot; stir the rum into the above, and run it through a jelly-bag till perfectly clear. Bottle, and cork close immediately.

**Norfolk Punch.**—In twenty quarts of French brandy put the peels of thirty lemons and thirty oranges, pared so thin that not the least of the white is left. Infuse twelve hours. Have ready thirty quarts of cold water that has boiled, put to it fifteen pounds of double-refined sugar, and when well mixed pour it upon the brandy and peels, adding the juice of the oranges and of twenty-four lemons; mix well, then strain through a very fine hair-sieve into a very clean barrel that has held spirits, and put two quarts of new milk. Stir, and then bung it close; let it stand six weeks in a warm cellar; bottle the liquor for use, observing great care that the bottles are perfectly clean and dry, and the corks of the best quality and well put in. This liquor will keep many years and improves by age.

**Another way.**—Pare six lemons and three Seville oranges very thin, squeeze the juice into a large tea-pot, put to it two quarts of brandy, one of white-wine, and one of milk, and one pound and a quarter of sugar. Let it be mixed and then covered for twenty-four hours, strain through a jelly-bag till clear, then bottle it.

**White Currant Shrub.**—Strip the fruit, and prepare in a jar as for jelly; strain the juice, of which put two quarts to one gallon of rum and two pounds of lump-sugar; strain through a jelly-bag.

---

## DAIRY, AND POULTRY YARD.

**DAIRY.**—The servants of each country are generally acquainted with the best mode of managing the butter and cheese of that country; but the following hints may not be unacceptable, to give information to the mistress.

**On the Management of Cows, &c.**—Cows should be carefully treated; if their teats are sore, they should be soaked in warm water twice a day, and either be dressed with soft ointment, or done with spirits and water. If the former, great cleanliness is necessary. The milk, at these times, should be given to the pigs.

When the milk is brought into the dairy, it should be strained and emptied into clean pans immediately in winter, but not till cool in summer. White ware is preferable, as the red is porous, and cannot be so thoroughly scalded.

The greatest possible attention must be paid to great cleanliness in a dairy; all the utensils, shelves, dressers, and the floor, should be kept with the most perfect neatness, and cold water thrown over every part very often. There should be shutters to keep out sun and the hot air. Meat hung in a dairy will spoil milk.

The cows should be milked at a regular and early hour, and the udders emptied, or the quantity will decrease. The quantity of milk depends on many causes; as the goodness, breed, and health of the cow, the pasture, the length of time from calving, the having plenty of clean water in the field she feeds in, &c. A change of pasture will tend to increase it. People who attend properly to the dairy will feed the cows particularly well two or three weeks before they calve, which makes the milk more abundant after. In gentlemen's dairies more attention is paid to the size and beauty of the cows than to their produce, which dairymen look most to.

For making cheese the cows should calve from Lady-Day to May, that the large quantity of milk may come into use about the same time; but in gentlemen's families one or two should calve in August or September for a supply in winter. In good pastures, the average produce of a dairy is about three gallons a day each cow from Lady-Day to Michaelmas, and from thence to Christmas one gallon a day. Cows will be profitable milkers to fourteen or fifteen years of age, if of a proper breed.

When a calf is to be reared, it should be taken from the cow in a week at farthest, or it will cause great trouble in rearing, because it will be difficult to make it take milk in a pan. Take it from the cow in the morning, and keep it without food till the next morning: and then, being hungry, it will drink without difficulty. Skimmed milk and fresh whey, just as warm as new milk, should be given twice a day in such quantity as may be required. If milk runs short, smooth gruel mixed with milk will do. At first, let the calf be out only by day, and feed it at night, and morning.

When the family is absent, or there is not a great call for cream, a careful dairy-maid seizes the opportunity to provide for a good winter store: she should have a book to keep an account, or get some one to write down for her the produce of every week, and set down what butter she pots. The weight the pot will hold should be marked on each in making at the pottery. In another part of the book should be stated the poultry reared, in one leaf, and the weekly consumption in another part.

**Observations respecting Cheese.**—This well-known article differs according to the pasture in which the cows feed. Various modes of preparing may effect a great deal; and it will be bad or good of its kind, by being in unskilful hands or the contrary; but much will still depend on the former circumstance. The same land rarely makes very fine butter, and remarkably fine cheese; but yet due care may give one pretty good, when the other excels in quality.

When one is not as fine as the other, attention and change of method may amend the inferior. There is usually, however, too much prejudice in the minds of dairy people, to make them give up an old custom for one newly recommended. This calls for the eye of the superior. A gentleman has been at the expense of procuring cattle from every county noted for good cheese, and it is affirmed that the Cheshire, double Gloucester, North Wiltshire, Chedder, and many other sorts, are so excellent as not to discredit their names. As the cows are all on one estate, it should seem that the mode of making must be a principal cause of the difference in flavour: besides, there is much in the size and manner of keeping.

Cheese made on the same ground, of new skimmed, or mixed milk, will differ greatly, not in richness only, but also in taste. Those who direct a dairy in a gentleman's family should consider in which way it can be managed to the best advantage. Even with few cows, cheeses of value may be made from a tolerable pasture, by taking the whole of two meals of milk, and proportioning the thickness of the vat to the quantity, rather than having a wide and flat one, as the former will be most mellow. The addition of a pound of fresh-made butter, of a good quality, will cause the cheese made on poor land to be of a very different quality from that usually produced by it.

A few cheeses thus made, when the weather is not extremely hot, and when the cows are in full feed, will be very advantageous for the use of the parlour. Cheese for common family use will be very well produced by two meals of skim, and one of new milk ; or on good land, by skim milk only. Butter likewise should be made, and potted down for winter use, but not to interfere with the cheese as above, which will not take much time.

**To Prepare Rennet, to Turn the Milk.**—Take out the stomach of a calf as soon as killed, and well scour it inside and out with salt, after it is cleared of the curd always found in it. Let it drain a few hours ; then sew it up with two good handfuls of salt in it, or stretch it on a stick well salted ; or keep it in the salt wet, and soak a bit, which will do over and over by fresh water.

**Another way.**—Clean the maw as above ; next day take two quarts of fresh spring water, and put into it a handful of hawthorn tops, a handful of sweet-briar, a handful of rose-leaves, a stick of cinnamon, forty cloves, four blades of mace, a sprig of knotted marjoram, and two large spoonfuls of salt. Let them boil gently to three pints of water ; strain it off ; and when only milk-warm, pour it on the vell (that is, the maw). Slice a lemon into it ; let it stand two days ; strain it again, and bottle it for use. It will keep good at the least twelve months, and has a very fine flavour. You may add any sweet aromatic herbs to the above. It must be pretty salt, but not brine. A little will do for turning. Salt the vell again for a week or two, and dry it stretched on sticks crossed, and it will be near as strong as ever. Do not keep it in a hot place when dry.

**To Make Cheese.**—Put the milk into a large tub, warming a part till it is of a degree of heat quite equal to new ; if too hot, the cheese will be tough. Put in as much rennet as will turn it, and cover it over. Let it stand till completely turned ; then strike the curd down several times with the skimming dish, and let it separate, still covering it. There are two modes of breaking the curd ; and there will be a difference in the taste of the cheese, according as either is observed ; one is, to gather it with the hands very gently towards the side of the tub, letting the whey pass through the fingers till it is cleared, and lading it off as it collects. The other is, to get the whey from it by early breaking the curd ;

the last method deprives it of many of its oily particles, and is therefore less proper.

Put the vat on a ladder over the tub, and fill it with curd by the skimmer; press the curd close with your hands, and add more as it sinks; and it must be finally left two inches above the edge. Before the vat is filled, the cheese-cloth must be laid at the bottom; and when full, drawn smooth over on all sides.

There are two modes of salting cheese; one by mixing it in the curd while in the tub, after the whey is out; and the other by putting it into the vat and crumbling the curd all to pieces with it, after the first squeezing with the hands has dried it. The first method appears best on some accounts, but not on all, and therefore the custom of the country must direct. Put a board under and over the vat, and place it in the press; in two hours turn it out and put a fresh cheese-cloth; press it again for eight or nine hours; then salt it all over, and turn it again in the vat, and let it stand in the press fourteen or sixteen hours, observing to put the cheeses last made undermost. Before putting them the last time into the vat pare the edges if they do not look smooth. The vat should have holes at the sides and at bottom, to let all the whey pass through. Put on clean boards, and change and scald them.

**To Preserve Cheese Sound.**—Wash in warm whey, when you have any, and wipe it once a month, and keep it on a rack. If you want to ripen it quick, a damp cellar will bring it forward. When a whole cheese is fresh cut, the larger quantity should be spread with butter inside, and the outside wiped to preserve it. To keep those in daily use moist, let a clean cloth be wrung out from cold water, and wrapt round them when carried from table. Dry cheese may be used to advantage to grate for serving with macaroni or eating without. These observations are made with a view to make the above articles less expensive, as in most families where much is used there is waste.

**To Make Sage Cheese.**—Bruise the tops of young red sage in a mortar, with some leaves of spinach, and squeeze the juice; mix it with the rennet in the milk, more or less according as you like for colour and taste. When the curd is come, break it gently, and put it in with the skimmer, till it is pressed two inches above one vat. Press it eight or ten hours. Salt it, and turn every day.

**Cream Cheese.**—Put five quarts of strippings, that is, the last of the milk, into a pan with two spoonfuls of rennet. When the curd is come, strike it down two or three times with the skimming dish just to break it. Let it stand two hours, then spread a cheese-cloth on a sieve, put the curd on it, and let the whey drain; break the curd a little with your hand, and put it into a vat with a two-pound weight upon it. Let it stand twelve hours, take it out and bind a fillet round. Turn every day till dry, from one board to another; cover them with nettles, or clean dock-leaves, and place between two pewter plates to ripen. If the weather be warm, it will be ready in three weeks.

**Another.**—Have ready a kettle of boiling water, put five quarts of new milk into a pan, and five pints of cold water, and five of hot; when of a proper heat, put in as much rennet as will bring it in twenty minutes, likewise a bit of sugar. When come, strike the skimmer three or four times down, and leave it on the curd. In an hour or two lade it into the vat without touching it; put a two-pound weight on it when the whey has run from it, and the vat is full.

**Another Sort.**—Put as much salt to three pints of raw cream as shall season it; stir it well, and pour it into a sieve in which you have folded a cheese-cloth three or four times, and laid at the bottom. When it hardens, cover it with nettles on a pewter plate.

**Rush Cream Cheese.**—To a quart of fresh cream put a pint of new milk, warm enough to make the cream a proper warmth, a bit of sugar, and a little rennet.

Set near the fire till the curd comes; fill a vat made in the form of a brick, of wheat straw or rushes sewed together. Have ready a square of straw, or rushes sewed flat, to rest the vat on, and another to cover it; the vat being open at top and bottom. Next day take it out, and change it as above, to ripen. A half pound weight will be sufficient to put on it.

**Another way.**—Take a pint of very thick sour cream from the top of the pan for gathering butter, lay a napkin on two plates, and pour half into each; let them stand twelve hours, then put them on a fresh wet napkin in one plate, and cover with the same; this do every twelve hours until you find the cheese begins to look dry, then ripen it with nut leaves; it will be ready in ten days.

Fresh nettles, or two pewter plates will ripen cream cheese very well.

**Observations respecting Butter.**—There is no one article of family consumption more in use, of great variety in goodness, or that is of more consequence to have of a superior quality, than this, and the economising of which is more necessary. The sweetness of butter is not affected by the cream being turned, of which it is made. When cows are in turnips, or eat cabbages, the taste is very disagreeable; and the following ways have been tried with advantage to obviate it:—

When the milk is strained into the pans, put to every six gallons one gallon of boiling water. Or dissolve one ounce of nitre in a pint of spring water, and put a quarter of a pint to every fifteen gallons of milk. Or, when you churn, keep back a quarter of a pint of the sour cream, and put it into a well-scalded pot, into which you are to gather the next cream; stir that well, and do so with every fresh addition.

**To Make Butter.**—During summer, skim the milk when the sun has not heated the dairy; at that season it should stand for butter twenty-four hours without skimming, and forty-eight in ·

winter.  Deposit the cream-pot in a very cold cellar, if your dairy
is not more so.  If you cannot churn daily, change it into fresh
scalded pots; but never omit turning twice a week.  If possible,
put the churn in a thorough air; and if not a barrel one, set it in
a tub of water two feet deep, which will give firmness to the
butter.  When the butter is come, pour off the buttermilk, and
put the butter into a fresh-scalded pan, or tubs, which have afterwards been in cold water.  Pour water on it, and let it lie to
acquire some hardness before you work it; then change the water,
and beat it with flat boards so perfectly that not the least taste of
the buttermilk remain, and that the water, which must be often
changed, shall be quite clear in colour.  Then work some salt into
it, weigh, and make it into forms; throw them into cold water in
an earthen pan and cover of the queen's ware.  You will then
have very nice and cool butter in the hottest weather.  It requires
more working in hot than in cold weather; but neither should be
left with the least particle of buttermilk, or a sour taste, as is sometimes done.

**To Preserve Butter.**—Take two parts of the best common
salt, one part good loaf-sugar, and one part saltpetre; beat them
well together.  To sixteen ounces of butter thoroughly cleansed
from the milk, put one ounce of this composition; work it well,
and pot down, when it has become firm and cold.

The butter thus preserved is the better for keeping, and should
not be used under a month.  This article should be kept from the
air, and is best in pots of the best glazed earth, that will hold from
ten to fourteen pounds each.

**To Preserve Butter for Winter, the best Way.**—When
the butter has been prepared as above directed, take two parts of
the best common salt, one part of good loaf-sugar, and one part of
saltpetre, beaten and blended well together.  Of this composition
put one ounce to sixteen ounces of butter, and work it well together
in a mass.  Press it into the pans after the butter is become cool;
for friction, though it be not touched by the hands, will soften it.
The pans should hold ten or twelve pounds each.  On the top put
some salt; and when that is turned to brine, if not enough to
cover the butter entirely, add some strong salt and water.  It requires only then to be covered from the dust.

**To Manage Cream for Whey Butter.**—Set the whey one
day and night, skim it, and so till you have enough; then boil it
and pour it into a pan or two of cold water.  As the cream rises,
skim it till no more comes; then churn it.  Where new milk
cheese is made daily, whey-butter for common and present use
may be made to advantage.

**To Scald Cream, as in the West of England.**—In winter
let the milk stand twenty-four hours.  In the summer twelve at
least; then put the milk-pan on a hot hearth, if you have one; if
not, set it in a clean brass kettle of water, large enough to receive
the pan.  It must remain on the fire till quite hot, but on no
account boil, or there will be a skin instead of cream upon the
milk.  You will know when done enough, by the undulations on

the surface looking thick, and having a ring round the pan the size of the bottom. The time required to scald cream depends on the size of the pan and the heat of the fire ; the slower the better. Remove the pan into the dairy when done, and skim it next day. In cold weather it may stand thirty-six hours, and never less than two meals. The butter is usually made in Devonshire of cream thus prepared, and if properly done it is very firm.

**Buttermilk.**—If made of sweet cream, is a delicious and most wholesome food. Those who can relish sour buttermilk, find it still more light ; and it is reckoned more beneficial in consumptive cases. Buttermilk, if not very sour, is also as good as cream to eat with fruit, if sweetened with white sugar and mixed with a very little milk. It likewise does equally for cakes and rice-puddings, and of course it is economical to churn before the cream is too stale for anything but to feed pigs.

**To Keep Milk and Cream.**—In hot weather, when it is difficult to preserve milk from becoming sour, and spoiling the cream, it may be kept perfectly sweet by scalding the new milk very gently, without boiling, and setting it by in the earthen dish or pan that it is done in. This method is pursued in Devonshire, for butter and eating, and would equally answer in small quantities for coffee, tea, &c. Cream already skimmed may be kept twenty-four hours if scalded without sugar ; and by adding to it as much powdered lump-sugar as shall make it pretty sweet, will be good two days, keeping it in a cool place.

**´Syrup of Cream** may be preserved as above in the proportion of a pound and a quarter of sugar to a pint of perfectly fresh cream ; keep it in a cool place two or three hours ; then put it in one or two ounce phials, and cork it close. It will keep good thus for several weeks, and will be found very useful on long voyages.

**Gallino Curds and Whey, as in Italy.**—Take a number of the rough coats that line the gizzards of turkeys and fowls ; clean them from the pebbles they contain ; rub them well with salt, and hang them to dry. This makes a more tender and delicate curd than common rennet. When to be used, break off some bits of the skin, and put on it some boiling water : in eight or nine hours use the liquor as you do other rennet.

**To Choose Butter at Market.**—Put a knife into the butter if salt, and smell it when drawn out ; if there is anything rancid or unpleasant, it is bad. Being made at different times, the layers in casks will vary greatly, and you will not easily come at the goodness but by unhooping the cask, and trying it between the staves. Fresh butter ought to smell like a nosegay, and be of an equal colour all through : if sour in smell, it has not been sufficiently washed ; if veiny and open, it is probably mixed with staler or an inferior sort.

**POULTRY-YARD.—Management of Fowls.**—In order to have fine fowls, it is necessary to choose a good breed, and have proper care taken of them. The Dartford sort is thought highly of, and it is desirable to have a fine large kind, but people differ in their opinion of which is best. The black are very juicy, but do not answer so well for boiling, as their legs partake of their colour. They should be fed as nearly as possible at the same hour and place. Potatoes boiled, unskinned, in a little water, and then cut, and either wet with skimmed milk or not, form one of the best foods. Turkeys and fowls thrive amazingly on them. The milk must not be sour.

The best age for setting a hen is from two to five years; and you should remark which hens make the best brooders, and keep those to laying who are giddy and careless of their young. In justice to the animal creation, however, it must be observed, there are but few instances of bad parents for the time their nursing is necessary.

Hens sit twenty days. Convenient places should be provided for their laying, as these will be proper for sitting likewise. If the hen-house is not secured from vermin, the eggs will be sucked, and the fowls destroyed.

Those hens are usually preferred which have tufts of feathers on their heads; those that crow are not looked upon as profitable. Some fine young fowls should be reared every year, to keep up a stock of good breeders; and by this attention and removing bad layers and careless nurses, you will have a chance of a good stock.

Let the hens lay some time before you set them, which should be done from the end of February to the beginning of May. While hens are laying, feed them well, and sometimes with oats.

Broods of chickens are hatched all through the summer, but those that come out very late require much care till they have gained some strength.

If the eggs of any other sort are put under the hen with some of her own, observe to add her own as many days after the others as there is a difference in the length of their sitting. A turkey and duck sit thirty days. Choose large clear eggs to put her upon, and such a number as she can properly cover. If the eggs are large, there are sometimes two yolks, and of course neither will be productive. Ten or twelve are quite enough.

A hen-house should be large and high, and should be frequently cleaned out, or the vermin of fowls will increase greatly. But hens must not be disturbed while sitting, for, if frightened, they sometimes forsake their nests. Wormwood and rue should be planted plentifully about their houses; boil some of the former, and sprinkle it about the floor, which should be of smooth earth, not paved. The windows of the house should be open to the rising sun, and a hole must be left at the door to let the smaller fowls go in; the larger may be let in and out by opening the door. There should be a small sliding board to shut down when the fowls are gone to roost, which would prevent the smaller beasts of prey from committing ravages; and a good strong door and lock may possibly, in some measure, prevent the depredations of human enemies.

When some of the chickens are hatched long before the others,

N

it may be necessary to keep them in a basket of wool till the others come forth. The day after they are hatched give them some crumbs of white bread, and small (or rather cracked) grits soaked in milk. As soon as they have gained a little strength, feed them with curd, cheese-parings, cut small, or any soft food, but nothing sour, and give them clean water twice a day. Keep the hen under a pen till the young have strength to follow her about, which will be in two or three weeks; and be sure to feed her well.

The food of fowls goes first into their crop, which softens it, and then passes into the gizzard, which by constant friction macerates it; and this is facilitated by small stones, which are generally found there, and which help to digest the food.

If a sitting hen is troubled with vermin, let her be well washed with a decoction of white lupins. The pip in fowls is occasioned by their drinking dirty water, or taking filthy food. A white thin scale on the tongue is the symptom. Pull the scale off with your nail, and rub the tongue with some salt; and the complaint will be removed.

It answers well to pay some boy employed in the farm or stable, so much a score for the eggs he brings in. It will be his interest then to save them from being purloined, which nobody but one in his situation can prevent; and sixpence or eightpence a score will be buying eggs cheap.

**To Make Hens Lay.**—Dissolve an ounce of Glauber's salts in a quart of water; mix the meal of potatoes with a little of the liquor, and feed the hens two days, giving them plenty of clean water to drink. The above quantity is sufficient for six or eight hens. They should have plenty of clean water in reach. In a few days they will produce eggs.

**To Fatten Fowls or Chickens in Four or Five Days.**—Set rice over the fire with skimmed milk, only as much as will serve one day. Let it boil till the rice is quite swelled out; you may add a tea-spoonful or two of sugar, but it will do well without. Feed them three times a day, in common pans, giving them only as much as will quite fill them at once. When you put fresh, let the pans be set in water, that no sourness may be conveyed to the fowls, as that prevents them from fattening. Give them clean water, or the milk of the rice, to drink; but the less wet the latter is when perfectly soaked the better. By this method the flesh will have a clear whiteness which no other food gives; and when it is considered how far a pound of rice will go, and how much time is saved by this mode, it will be found to be as cheap as barley-meal, or more so. The pen should be daily cleaned, and no food given for sixteen hours before poultry be killed.

**To Choose Eggs at Market, and Preserve them.**—Put the large end of the egg to your tongue; if it feels warm it is new. In new-laid eggs there is a small division of the skin from the shell, which is filled with air, and is perceptible to the eye at the end. On looking through them against the sun or a candle, if fresh, eggs will be pretty clear. If they shake they are not fresh.

Eggs may be bought cheapest when the hens first begin to lay in the spring, before they sit; in Lent and at Easter they become dear. They may be preserved fresh by dipping them in boiling water and instantly taking them out, or by oiling the shell, either of which ways is to prevent the air passing through it; or kept on shelves with small holes to receive one in each, and be turned every other day; or close packed in a keg, and covered with strong lime-water.

**Feathers.**—In towns, poultry being usually sold ready picked, the feathers, which may occasionally come in small quantities, are neglected; but orders should be given to put them into a tub free from damp, and as they dry to change them into paper bags, a few in each; they should hang in a dry kitchen to season: fresh ones must not be added to those in part dried, or they will occasion a musty smell, but they should go through the same process. In a few months they will be fit to add to beds, or to make pillows, without the usual mode of drying them in a cool oven, which may be pursued if they are wanted before five or six months.

**Ducks** generally begin to lay in the month of February. Their eggs should be daily taken away except one, till they seem inclined to sit; then leave them, and see that there are enough. They require no attention while sitting, except to give them food at the time they come out to seek it; and there should be water placed at a moderate distance from them, that their eggs may not be spoiled by their long absence in seeking it. Twelve or thirteen eggs are enough. In an early season it is best to put them under a hen; and then they can be kept from water till they have a little strength to bear it, which in very cold weather they cannot do so well. They should be kept under cover, especially in a wet season; for though water is the natural element of ducks, yet they are apt to be killed by the cramp before they are covered with feathers to defend them.

Ducks should be accustomed to feed and rest at one place, which would prevent their straggling too far to lay. Places near the water to lay in are advantageous, and these might be small wooden houses, with a partition in the middle, and door at each end. They eat anything, and when to be fattened must have plenty, however coarse, and in three weeks they will be fat.

**Geese** require little expense, as they chiefly support themselves, on commons or in lanes, where they can get water. The largest are esteemed best, as also are the white and grey. The pied and dark-coloured are not so good. Thirty days is generally the time the goose sits, but in warm weather she will sometimes hatch sooner. Give them plenty of food, such as scalded bran and light oats; and as soon as the goslings are hatched, keep them housed for eight or ten days, and feed them with barley-meal, bran, curds, &c. For green geese, begin to fatten them at six or seven weeks old, and feed them as above. Stubble geese require no fattening if they have the run of good fields.

**Turkeys** are very tender when young. As soon as hatched,

put three pepper-corns down their throat. Great care is necessary to their well-being, because the hen is so careless that she will walk about with one chick, and leave the remainder, or even tread upon and kill them. Turkeys are violent eaters, and must therefore be left to take charge of themselves in general, except one good feed a day. The hen sits twenty-five or thirty days; and the young ones must be kept warm, as the least cold or damp kills them. They must be fed often, and at a distance from the hen, who will eat everything from them. They should have curds, green-cheese parings cut small, and bread and milk with chopped wormwood in it; and their drink milk and water, but not left to be sour. All young fowls are a prey for vermin, therefore they should be kept in a safe place where none can come; weasels, stoats, ferrets, &c., creep in at very small crevices.

Let the hen be under a coop, in a warm place exposed to the sun, for the first three or four weeks; and the young should not be suffered to go out in the dew at morning or evening. Twelve eggs are enough to put under a turkey, and when she is about to lay, lock her up till she has laid every morning. They usually begin to lay in March, and sit in April. Feed them near the hen-house; and give them a little meat in the evening, to accustom them to roosting there. Fatten them with sodden oats or barley for the first fortnight; and the last fortnight give them as above, and rice swelled with warm milk over the fire, twice a day. The flesh will be beautifully white and fine flavoured. The common way is to cram them; but they are so ravenous that it seems unnecessary, if they are not suffered to go far from home, which makes them poor.

**Pea Fowl.**—Feed them as you do turkeys. They are so shy that they are seldom found for some days after hatching; and it is very wrong to pursue them, as many ignorant people do, in the idea of bringing them home; for it only causes the hen to carry the young ones through dangerous places, and by hurrying she treads upon them. The cock kills all the young chickens he can get at, by one blow on the centre of the head with his bill; and he does the same by his own brood before the feathers of the crown come out. Nature therefore impels the hen to keep them out of his way till the feathers rise.

**Guinea Hens** lay a great number of eggs; and if you can discover the nest it is best to put them under common hens, which are better nurses. They require great warmth, quiet, and careful feeding with rice swelled with milk, or bread soaked in it. Put two peppercorns down their throat when first hatched.

**Pigeons** bring two young ones at a time, and breed every month, if well looked after and plentifully fed. They should be kept very clean, and the bottom of the dovecote be strewed with sand, once a month at least. Tares, beans, and peas, are their proper food. They should have plenty of fresh water in their house. Starlings and other birds are apt to come among them, and suck the eggs. Vermin likewise are their great enemies, and destroy them. If the breed should be too small, put a few tame pigeons of the common kind and of their own colour among them. Observe not to have too large a proportion of cock birds; for they are quarrelsome, and will soon thin the dovecote.

Pigeons are fond of salt, and it keeps them healthy. Lay a large heap of clay near the house; and let the salt brine that may be done with in the family be poured upon it.

Bay salt and cummin seeds mixed are a universal remedy for the diseases of pigeons. The backs and breasts are sometimes scabby; in which case, take a quarter of a pound of bay salt, and as much common salt, a pound of fennel seed, a pound of dill seed, as much cummin seed, and an ounce of assafœtida; mix all with a little wheaten flour, and some fine-worked clay; when all are well beaten together, put it into two earthen pots, and bake them in the oven. When cold, put them on the table in the dovecote; the pigeons will eat it, and thus be cured.

**Rabbits.**—The wild ones have the finest flavour, unless great care is taken to keep the tame delicately clean. The tame one brings forth every month, and must be allowed to go with the buck as soon as she has kindled. The sweetest hay, oats, beans, sow-thistle, parsley, carrot tops, cabbage leaves, and bran, fresh and fresh, should be given to them. If not very well attended, their stench will destroy themselves, and be very unwholesome to all who live near them; but attention will prevent this inconvenience.

---

## COOKERY FOR THE SICK, AND FOR THE POOR.

THE following pages will contain cookery for the sick; it being of more consequence to support those whose bad appetite will not allow them to take the necessary nourishment, than to stimulate that of persons in health.

It may not be unnecessary to advise that a choice be made of the things most likely to agree with the patient; that a change be provided; that some one at least be always ready; that not too much of those be made at once, which are not likely to keep, as invalids require variety; and that they should succeed each other in different forms and flavours.

**A clear Broth that will keep long.**—Put the mouse round of beef, a knuckle bone of veal, and a few shanks of mutton, into a deep pan, and cover close with a dish or coarse crust: bake till the beef is done enough for eating, with only as much water as will cover. When cold, cover it close in a cool place. When to be used, give what flavour may be approved.

**A Quick-made Broth.**—Take a bone or two of a neck or loin of mutton, take off the fat and skin, set it on the fire in a small tin saucepan that has a cover, with three quarters of a pint of water, the meat being first beaten, and cut in thin bits; put a bit of thyme and parsley, and if approved a slice of onion. Let it boil very quick, skim it nicely; take off the cover, if likely to be too weak; else cover it. Half an hour is sufficient for the whole process.

**A very Supporting Broth against any kind of Weakness.**—Boil two pounds of loin of mutton, with a very large handful of chervil, in two quarts of water to one. Take off part of the fat. Any other herb or roots may be added. Take half a pint three or four times a day.

**A very Nourishing Veal Broth.**—Put the knuckle of a leg or shoulder of veal, with very little meat to it, an old fowl, and four shank-bones of mutton extremely well soaked and bruised, three blades of mace, ten pepper corns, an onion, and a large bit of bread, and three quarts of water, into a stew-pot that covers close, and simmer in the slowest manner after it has boiled up, and been skimmed: or bake it; strain, and take off the fat. Salt as wanted. It will require four hours.

**Broth of Beef, Mutton, and Veal.**—Put two pounds of lean beef, one pound of scrag of veal, one pound of scrag of mutton, sweet herbs, and ten peppercorns, into a nice tin saucepan, with five quarts of water; simmer to three quarts; and clear from the fat when cold. Add one onion if approved.

Soup and broth made of different meats are more supporting, as well as better flavoured.

To remove the fat, take it off when cold as clean as possible; and if there be still any remaining, lay a bit of clean blotting or cap paper on the broth when in the basin, and it will take up every particle.

**Calves' Feet Broth.**—Boil two feet in three quarts of water to half; strain and set it by; when to be used, take off the fat, put a large tea-cupful of the jelly into a saucepan, with half a glass of sweet wine, a little sugar and nutmeg, and beat it up till it be ready to boil, then take a little of it, and beat by degrees to the yolk of an egg, and adding a bit of butter, the size of a nutmeg, stir it all together, but do not let it boil. Grate a bit of fresh lemon-peel into it.

**Another.**—Boil two calves' feet, two ounces of veal, and two of beef, the bottom of a penny loaf, two or three blades of mace, half a nutmeg sliced, and a little salt, in three quarts of water, to three pints; strain, and take off the fat.

**Chicken Broth.**—Put the body and legs of the fowl that chicken panada was made of, as in page 200, after taking off the skin and rump, into the water it was boiled in, with one blade of mace, one slice of onion, and ten white pepper-corns. Simmer till the broth be of a pleasant flavour. If not water enough, add a little. Beat a quarter of an ounce of sweet almonds, with a teaspoonful of water, fine, boil it in the broth, strain, and, when cold, remove the fat.

**Eel Broth.**—Clean half a pound of small eels, and set them on with three pints of water, some parsley, one slice of onion, a few pepper-corns; let them simmer till the eels are broken, and the broth good. Add salt, and strain it off.

The above should make three half-pints of broth.

**Tench Broth.**—Make as eel broth above. They are both very nutritious, and light of digestion.

**Beef Tea.**—Cut a pound of fleshy beef into thin slices; simmer with a quart of water twenty minutes, after it has once boiled, and been skimmed. Season, if approved; but it has generally only salt.

**Dr. Ratcliff's Restorative Pork-jelly.**—Take a leg of well-fed pork, just as cut up, beat it, and break the bone. Set it over a gentle fire, with three gallons of water, and simmer to one. Let half an ounce of mace, and the same of nutmegs, stew in it. Strain through a fine sieve. When cold, take off the fat. Give a chocolate cup the first and last thing, and at noon, putting salt to taste.

**Shank Jelly.**—Soak twelve shanks of mutton four hours, then brush and scour them very clean. Lay them in a saucepan with three blades of mace, an onion, twenty Jamaica, and thirty or forty black peppers, a bunch of sweet herbs, and a crust of bread made very brown by toasting. Pour three quarts of water to them, and set them on a hot hearth close-covered; let them simmer as gently as possible for five hours, then strain it off, and put it in a cold place.

This may have the addition of a pound of beef, if approved, for flavour. It is a remarkably good thing for people who are weak.

**Arrow-root Jelly.**—Of this beware of having the wrong sort, for it has been counterfeited with bad effect. If genuine, it is very nourishing, especially for weak bowels. Put into a saucepan half a pint of water, a glass of sherry, or a spoonful of brandy, grated nutmeg, and fine sugar; boil once up, then mix by degrees into a dessert-spoonful of arrow-root, previously rubbed smooth, with two spoonfuls of cold water; then return the whole into the saucepan; stir and boil it three minutes.

**Tapioca Jelly.**—Choose the largest sort, pour cold water on to wash it two or three times, then soak it in fresh water five or six hours, and simmer it in the same until it become quite clear; then put lemon-juice, wine, and sugar. The peel should have been boiled in it. It thickens very much.

**Gloucester Jelly.**—Take rice, sago, pearl-barley, hartshorn shavings, and eringo-root, each an ounce; simmer with three pints of water to one, and strain it. When cold it will be a jelly; of which give, dissolved in wine, milk, or broth, in change with other nourishment.

**Panada, made in five minutes.**—Set a little water on the fire with a glass of white wine, some sugar, and a scrape of nutmeg and lemon-peel; meanwhile grate some crumbs of bread. The moment the mixture boils up, keeping it still on the fire, put the crumbs in, and let it boil as fast as it can. When of a proper thickness just to drink, take it off.

Another.—Make as above, but instead of a glass of wine, put in a tea-spoonful of rum, and a bit of butter; sugar as above. This is a most pleasant mess.

Another.—Put to the water a bit of lemon peel, mix the crumbs in, and when nearly boiled enough, put some lemon or orange syrup. Observe to boil all the ingredients; for if any be added after, the panada will break, and not jelly.

Chicken Panada.—Boil it till about three parts ready, in a quart of water, take off the skin, cut the white meat off when cold, and put into a marble-mortar; pound it to a paste with a little of the water it was boiled in, season with a little salt, a grate of nutmeg, and the least bit of lemon-peel. Boil gently for a few minutes to the consistency you like; it should be such as you can drink, though tolerably thick.

This conveys great nourishment in small compass.

Sippets, when the Stomach will not receive Meat.—On an extremely hot plate put two or three sippets of bread, and pour over them some gravy from beef, mutton, or veal, if there is no butter in the dish. Sprinkle a little salt over.

Eggs.—An egg broken into a cup of tea, or beaten and mixed with a basin of milk, makes a breakfast more supporting than tea solely.

An egg divided, and the yolk and white beaten separately, then mixed with a glass of wine, will afford two very wholesome draughts, and prove lighter than when taken together.

Eggs very little boiled, or poached, taken in small quantity, convey much nourishment: the yolk only, when dressed, should be eaten by invalids.

A great Restorative.—Bake two calves' feet in two pints of water, and the same quantity of new milk, in a jar closely covered, three hours and a half. When cold remove the fat.

Give a large tea-cupful the last and first thing. Whatever flavour is approved, give it by baking in it lemon-peel, cinnamon, or mace. Add sugar after.

Another.—Simmer six sheep's trotters, two blades of mace, a little cinnamon, lemon-peel, a few hartshorn shavings, and a little isinglass, in two quarts of water to one; when cold, take off the fat, and give near half a pint twice a-day, warming with it a little new milk.

Another.—Boil an ounce of isinglass-shavings, forty Jamaica peppers, and a bit of brown crust of bread in a quart of water to a pint, and strain it.

This makes a pleasant jelly to keep in the house; of which a large spoonful may be taken in wine and water, milk, tea, soup, or any way.

Another, a most pleasant Draught.—Boil a quarter of an ounce of isinglass-shavings with a pint of new milk, to half: add a bit of sugar, and. for change, a bitter almond.

Give this at bed-time, not too warm.

Dutch flummery, blancmange, and jellies, as directed in pages 141, 142, and 147, or less rich according to judgment.

**Caudle.**—Make a fine smooth gruel of half-grits; strain it when boiled well, stir it at times till cold. When to be used, add sugar, wine, and lemon-peel, with nutmeg. Some like a spoonful of brandy besides the wine; others like lemon-juice.

**Another.**—Boil up half a pint of fine gruel, with a bit of butter the size of a large nutmeg, a large spoonful of brandy, the same of white wine, one of capillaire, a bit of lemon-peel and nutmeg.

**Another.**—Into a pint of fine gruel, not thick, put, when it is boiling hot, the yolk of an egg beaten with sugar, and mixed with a large spoonful of cold water, a glass of wine, and nutmeg. Mix by degrees. It is very agreeable and nourishing. Some like gruel, with a glass of table beer, sugar, &c., with or without a tea-spoonful of brandy.

**Cold Caudle.**—Boil a quart of spring water; when cold, add the yolk of an egg, the juice of a small lemon, six spoonfuls of sweet wine, sugar to your taste, and syrup of lemons one ounce.

**A Flour Caudle.**—Into five large spoonfuls of the purest water rub smooth one dessert-spoonful of fine flour. Set over the fire five spoonfuls of new milk, and put two bits of sugar into it; the moment it boils, pour into it the flour and water, and stir it over a slow fire twenty minutes. It is a nourishing and gently astringent food. This is an excellent food for babies who have weak bowels.

**Rice Caudle.**—When the water boils, pour into it some grated rice mixed with a little cold water; when of a proper con-sistence add sugar, lemon peel, and cinnamon, and a glass of brandy to a quart. Boil all smooth.

**Another.**—Soak some Carolina rice in water an hour, strain it, and put two spoonfuls of the rice into a pint and a quarter of milk; simmer till it will pulp through a sieve; then put the pulp and milk into the saucepan with a bruised clove and a bit of white sugar. Simmer ten minutes; if too thick, add a spoonful or two of milk, and serve with thin toast.

**To Mull Wine.**—Boil some spice in a little water till the flavour is gained, then add an equal quantity of port, some sugar, and nutmeg; boil together, and serve with toast.

**Another way.**—Boil a bit of cinnamon and some grated nut-meg a few minutes in a large cupful of water; then pour to it a pint of port wine, and add sugar to your taste: heat it up and it will be ready.

Or, it may be made of good British wine.

**To Make Coffee.**—Put two ounces of fresh ground coffee, of the best quality, into a coffee-pot, and pour eight coffee-cups of boiling water on it; let it boil six minutes, pour out a cupful two or three times, and return it again, then put two or three isin-glass-chips into it, and pour one large spoonful of boiling water on it; boil it five minutes more, and set the pot by the fire to keep hot for ten minutes, and you will have coffee of a beautiful clear-ness.

Fine cream should always be served with coffee, and either pounded sugar-candy or fine Lisbon sugar.

If for foreigners, or those who like it extremely strong, make only eight dishes from three ounces. If not fresh roasted, lay it before a fire until perfectly hot and dry; or you may put the smallest bit of fresh butter into a preserving pan of a small size, and when hot, throw the coffee in it and toss it about until it be freshened, letting it be cold before ground.

Coffee Milk. — Boil a dessert-spoonful of ground coffee in nearly a pint of milk a quarter of an hour; then put into it a shaving or two of isinglass and clear it; let it boil a few minutes, and set it on the side of the fire to grow fine.

This is a very fine breakfast; it should be sweetened with real Lisbon sugar of a good quality.

Chocolate.—Those who use much of this article will find the following mode of preparing it both useful and economical.

Cut a cake of chocolate in very small bits; put a pint of water into the pot, and when it boils put in the above; mill it off the fire until quite melted, then on a gentle fire till it boils; pour it into a basin, and it will keep in a cool place eight or ten days, or more. When wanted, put a spoonful or two into milk, boil it with sugar, and mill it well.

This, if not made thick, is a very good breakfast or supper.

Patent Cocoa is a light wholesome breakfast.

Saloop.—Boil a little water, wine, lemon peel, and sugar together; then mix with a small quantity of the powder, previously rubbed smooth, with a little cold water; stir it altogether, and boil it a few minutes.

Milk Porridge.—Make a fine gruel of half-grits, long boiled; strain off; either add cold milk, or warm with milk, as may be approved. Serve with toast.

French Milk Porridge.—Stir some oatmeal and water together, let it stand to be clear, and pour off the latter; pour fresh upon it, stir it well, let it stand till next day; strain through a fine sieve, and boil the water, adding milk while doing. The proportion of water must be small.

This is much ordered, with toast, for the breakfast of weak persons, abroad.

Ground-rice Milk.—Boil one spoonful of ground-rice rubbed down smooth, with three half pints of milk, a bit of cinnamon, lemon peel, and nutmeg. Sweeten when nearly done.

Sago.—To prevent the earthy taste soak it in cold water an hour; pour that off, and wash it well; then add more, and simmer gently till the berries are clear, with lemon peel and spice, if approved. Add wine and sugar, and boil all up together.

Sago Milk.—Cleanse as above, and boil it slowly and wholly with new milk. It swells so much that a small quantity will be sufficient for a quart, and when done it will be diminished to about a pint. It requires no sugar or flavouring.

Asses' Milk far surpasses any imitation of it that can be made. It should be milked into a glass that is kept warm by being in a basin of hot water.

The fixed air that it contains gives some people a pain in the stomach. At first a tea-spoonful of rum may be taken with it, but should only be put in the moment it is to be swallowed.

**Artificial Asses' Milk.**—Boil together a quart of water, a quart of new milk, an ounce of white sugar-candy, half an ounce of eringo-root, and half an ounce of conserve of roses, till half be wasted.

This is astringent, therefore proportion the doses to the effect and the quantity to what will be used while sweet.

**Another.**—Mix two spoonfuls of boiling water, two of milk, and an egg well beaten; sweeten with pounded white sugar-candy. This may be taken twice or thrice a day.

**Another.**—Boil two ounces of hartshorn-shavings, two ounces of pearl-barley, two ounces of candied eringo-root, and one dozen of snails that have been bruised, in two quarts of water, to one. Mix with it an equal quantity of new milk, when taken twice a day.

**Water Gruel.**—Put a large spoonful of oatmeal by degrees into a pint of water, and when smooth boil it.

**Another way.**—Rub smooth a large spoonful of oatmeal, with two of water, and pour it into a pint of water boiling on the fire; stir it well, and boil it quick, but take care it does not boil over. In a quarter of an hour strain it off, and add salt and a bit of butter when eaten. Stir until the butter be incorporated.

**Barley Gruel.**—Wash 4 oz. of pearl-barley, boil it in two quarts of water and a stick of cinnamon, till reduced to a quart; strain and return it into the saucepan with sugar, and three-quarters of a pint of port wine. Heap up, and use as wanted.

**A very agreeable Drink.**—Into a tumbler of fresh cold water, pour a table-spoonful of capillaire, and the same of good vinegar.

Tamarinds, currants, fresh or in jelly, or scalded currants or cranberries, make excellent drinks; with a little sugar, or not, as may be agreeable.

**A Refreshing Drink in a Fever.**—Put a little tea-sage, two sprigs of balm, and a little wood-sorrel into a stone jug, having first washed and dried them; peel thin a small lemon, and clear from the white; slice it, and put a bit of the peel in, then pour in three pints of boiling water, sweeten, and cover it close.

**Another Drink.**—Wash extremely well an ounce of pearl-barley; shift it twice, then put to it three pints of water, an ounce of sweet almonds beaten fine, and a bit of lemon peel; boil till you have a smooth liquor, then put in a little syrup of lemons and capillaire.

**Another.**—Boil three pints of water with an ounce and a half of tamarinds, three ounces of currants, and two ounces of stoned raisins, till near a third be consumed. Strain it on a bit of lemon peel, which remove in an hour, as it gives a bitter taste if left long.

**A most pleasant Drink.**—Put a tea-cupful of cranberries into a cup of water, and mash them. In the meantime boil two quarts of water with one large spoonful of oatmeal and a bit of lemon peel; then add the cranberries, and as much fine Lisbon sugar as shall leave a smart flavour of the fruit; and about a quarter of a pint of sherry, or less, as may be proper; boil the whole for half an hour, and strain off.

**Soft and Fine Draught for those who are weak and have a Cough.**—Beat a fresh-laid egg, and mix it well with a quarter of a pint of new milk warmed, a large spoonful of capillaire, the same of rose-water, and a little nutmeg, scraped. Do not warm it after the egg is put in. Take it the first and last thing.

**Toast and Water.**—Toast slowly a thin piece of bread till extremely brown and hard, but not the least black; then plunge it into a jug of cold water, and cover it over an hour before used. This is of particular use to weak bowels. It should be of a fine brown colour before drinking.

**Barley Water.**—Wash a handful of common barley, then simmer it gently in three pints of water with a bit of lemon peel. This is less apt to nauseate than pearl-barley; but the other is a very pleasant drink.

**Another way.**—Boil an ounce of pearl-barley a few minutes, to cleanse, then put on it a quart of water, simmer an hour; when half done, put into it a bit of fresh lemon peel, and one bit of sugar. If likely to be too thick, you may put another quarter of a pint of water. Lemon juice may be added if chosen.

**Lemon Water, a Delightful Drink.**—Put two slices of lemon thinly pared into a tea-pot, a little bit of the peel, and a bit of sugar, or a large spoonful of capillaire; pour in a pint of boiling water, and stop it close two hours.

**Apple Water.**—Cut two large apples in slices, and pour a quart of boiling water on them, or on roasted apples; strain it two or three hours, and sweeten lightly.

**Raspberry Vinegar Water.**—(See page 168.) This is one of the most delightful drinks that can be made.

**Whey.**—That of cheese is a very wholesome drink, especially when the cows are in fresh herbage.

**White Wine Whey.**—Put half a pint of new milk on the fire; the moment it boils up, pour in as much sound raisin wine as will completely turn it, and look clear; let it boil up, then set the saucepan aside till the curd subsides, and do not stir it. Pour the whey off, and add to it half a pint of boiling water, and a bit of white sugar. Thus you will have a whey perfectly cleared of milky particles, and as weak as you choose to make it.

**Vinegar and Lemon Wheys.**—Pour into boiling milk as much vinegar or lemon juice as will make a small quantity quite clear, dilute with hot water to an agreeable smart acid, and put a bit or two of sugar. This is less heating than if made of wine; and if only to excite perspiration, answers as well.

**Buttermilk, with or without Bread.**—It is most wholesome when sour, as being less likely to be heavy; but most agreeable when made of sweet cream.

**Dr. Boerhaave's Sweet Buttermilk.**—Take the milk from the cow into a small churn, of about 6s. price; in about ten minutes begin churning, and continue so to do till the flakes of butter swim about pretty thick, and the milk has discharged all the greasy particles, and appears thin and blue.  Strain it through a sieve, and drink it as frequently as possible.

·. It should form the whole of the patient's drink, and the food should be biscuits and rusks, in every way and sort; ripe and dried fruits, of various kinds, when a decline is apprehended.

Baked and dried fruits, raisins in particular, make excellent suppers for invalids, with biscuits or common cake.

**Orgeat.**—Beat two ounces of almonds with a tea-spoonful of orange-flower water, and a bitter almond or two; then pour a quart of milk and water to the paste.  Sweeten with sugar, or capillaire.  This is a fine drink for those who have a tender chest; and in the gout it is highly useful, and, with the addition of half an ounce of gum arabic, has been found to allay the painfulness of the attendant heat.  Half a glass of brandy may be added if thought too cooling in the latter complaints, and the glass of orgeat may be put into a basin of warm water.

Another orgeat, for company, is in page 168.

**Orangeade, or Lemonade.**—Squeeze the juice from a dozen of the fruit; pour boiling water on a little of the peel, and cover close.  Boil water and sugar to a thin syrup, and skim it.  When all are cold, mix the juice, the infusion, and the syrup, with as much more water as will make a rich sherbet; strain through a jelly-bag.  Or squeeze the juice, and strain it, and add water and capillaire.

**Egg Wine.**—Beat an egg, mix it with a spoonful of cold water; set on the fire a glass of white wine, half a glass of water, sugar, and nutmeg.  When it boils pour a little of it to the egg by degrees till the whole be in, stirring it well; then return the whole into the saucepan, put it on a gentle fire, stir it one way for not more than a minute: for if it boil, or the egg be stale, it will curdle.  Serve with toast.

Egg wine may be made as above, without warming the egg, and it is then lighter on the stomach, though not so pleasant to the taste.

**COOKERY FOR THE POOR.—General Remarks and Hints.**—I promised a few hints, to enable every family to assist the poor of their neighbourhood at a very trivial expense: and these may be varied or amended at the discretion of the mistress.

Where cows are kept, a jug of skimmed milk is a valuable present, and a very common one.

When the oven is hot, a large pudding may be baked, and given to a sick or young family; and thus made, the trouble is little:—Into a deep coarse pan put half a pound of rice, four ounces of coarse sugar or treacle, two quarts of milk, and two ounces of dripping; set it cold into the oven.  It will take a good while, but be an excellent solid food.

A very good meal may be bestowed in a thing called brewis, which is thus made:—Cut a very thick upper crust of bread, and put it into the pot where salt beef is boiling and near ready: it will attract some of the fat, and when swelled out, will be no unpalatable dish to those who rarely taste meat.

A Baked Soup.—Put a pound of any kind of meat cut in slices; two onions, two carrots, ditto; two ounces of rice, a pint of split peas, or whole ones, if previously soaked, pepper and salt, into an earthen jug or pan, and pour one gallon of water. Cover it very close, and bake it with the bread.

The cook should be charged to save the boiling of every piece of meat, ham, tongue, &c., however salt: as it is easy to use only a part of that, and the rest of fresh water, and by the addition of more vegetables, the bones of the meat used in the family, the pieces of meat that come from table on the plates, and rice, Scotch barley, or oatmeal, there will be some gallons of nutritious soup two or three times a week. The bits of meat should be only warmed in the soup, and remain whole; the bones, &c., boiled till they yield their nourishment. If the things are ready to put in the boiler as soon as the meat is served, it will save lighting fire, and second cooking.

Take turnips, carrots, leeks, potatoes, the outer leaves of lettuce, celery, or any sort of vegetable that is at hand; cut them small, and throw in with the thick part of peas, after they have been pulped for soup, and grits, or coarse oatmeal, which have been used for gruel.

Should the soup be poor of meat, the long boiling of the bones, and different vegetables, will afford better nourishment than the laborious poor can obtain; especially as they are rarely tolerable cooks, and have not fuel to do justice to what they buy. But in every family there is some superfluity; and if it be prepared with cleanliness and care, the benefit will be very great to the receiver, and the satisfaction no less to the giver.

I found, in the time of scarcity, ten or fifteen gallons of soup could be dealt out weekly, at an expense not worth mentioning, though the vegetables were bought. If in the villages about London, abounding with opulent families, the quantity of ten gallons were made in ten gentlemen's houses, there would be a hundred gallons of wholesome agreeable food given weekly for the supply of forty poor families, at the rate of two gallons and a half each.

What a relief to the labouring husband, instead of bread and cheese, to have a warm comfortable meal! To the sick, aged, and infant branches, how important an advantage! nor less to the industrious mother whose forbearance from the necessary quantity of food, that others may have a larger share, frequently reduces that strength upon which the welfare of her family essentially depends.

It very rarely happens that servants object to seconding the kindness of their superiors to the poor; but should the cook in any family think the adoption of this plan too troublesome, a gratuity at the end of the winter might repay her, if the love of her fellow-creatures failed of doing it a hundredfold. Did she readily enter into it, she would never wash away, as useless, the peas or grits of which soup or gruel had been made; broken potatoes, the green heads of celery, the necks and feet of fowls, and particularly the shanks of mutton, and various other articles which in preparing dinner for the family are thrown aside.

Fish affords great nourishment, and that not by the part eaten only, but the bones, heads, and fins, which contain isinglass. When the fish is served, let the cook put by some of the water, and stew in it the above; as likewise add the gravy that is in the dish, until she obtain all the goodness. If to be eaten by itself, when it makes a delightful broth, she should add a very small bit of onion, some pepper, and a little rice flour rubbed down smooth with it.

But strained, it makes a delicious improvement to the meat soup, particularly for the sick; and when such are to be supplied, the milder parts of the spare bones and meat should be used for them, with little, if any, of the liquor of the salt meats.

The fat should not be taken off the broth or soup, as the poor like it, and are nourished by it.

An excellent Soup for the Weakly.—Put two cow-heels, and a breast of mutton, into a large pan, with four ounces of rice, one onion, twenty Jamaica peppers, and twenty black, a turnip, a carrot, and four gallons of water; cover with brown paper, and bake six hours.

Sago.—Put a tea-cupful of sago into a quart of water, and a bit of lemon peel; when thickened, grate some ginger, and add half a pint of raisin wine, brown sugar and two spoonfuls of Geneva; boil all up together.

It is a most supporting thing for those whom disease has left very feeble.

Caudle for the Sick and Lying-in.—Set three quarts of water on the fire; mix smooth as much oatmeal as will thicken the whole, with a pint of cold water; when boiling pour the latter in, and twenty Jamaica peppers in fine powder; boil to a good middling thickness; then add sugar, half a pint of well-fermented table-beer, and a glass of gin. Boil all.

This mess twice, and once or twice of broth, will be of incalculable service.

There is not a better occasion for charitable commiseration than when a person is sick. A bit of meat or pudding sent unexpectedly has often been the means of recalling long-lost appetite.

Nor are the indigent alone the grateful receivers; for in the highest houses a real good sick cook is rarely met with; and many who possess all the goods of fortune have attributed the first return of health to an appetite excited by good kitchen physic, as it is called.

## VARIOUS RECEIPTS, AND DIRECTIONS FOR SERVANTS.

**VARIOUS RECEIPTS.—To Make Soft Pomatum.—** Beat half a pound of unsalted fresh lard in common water; then soak and beat it in two rose-waters, drain it, and beat it with two spoonfuls of brandy; let it drain from this, add to it some essence of lemon, and keep it in small pots.

**Another way.—** Soak half a pound of clear beef-marrow and a pound of unsalted fresh lard, in water two or three days, changing and beating it every day. Put it into a sieve, and when dry, into a jar, and the jar into a saucepan of water. When melted, pour it into a basin, and beat it with two spoonfuls of brandy: drain off the brandy, and then add essence of lemon, begamot, or any other scent that is liked.

**Hard Pomatum.—** Prepare equal quantities of beef-marrow and mutton-suet as before, using the brandy to preserve it, and adding the scent; then pour it into moulds, or, if you have none, into phials of the size you choose the rolls to be of. When cold, break the bottles, clear away the glass carefully, and put paper round the rolls.

**Pomade Divine.—** Clear a pound and a half of beef-marrow from the strings and bone, put it into an earthen pan, or vessel of water fresh from the spring, and change the water night and morning for ten days; then steep it in rose-water twenty-four hours, and drain it in a cloth till quite dry. Take an ounce of each of the following articles—namely, storax, gum-benjamin, odoriferous cypress-powder, or of Florence: half an ounce of cinnamon, two drams of cloves, and two drams of nutmeg, all finely powdered; mix them with the marrow above prepared, then put all the ingredients into a pewter pot that holds three pints; make a paste of white of egg and flour, and lay it upon a piece of rag. Over that must be another piece of linen to cover the top of the pot very close that none of the steam may evaporate. Put the pot into a large copper pot, with water, observing to keep it steady, that it may not reach to the covering of the pot that holds the marrow. As the water shrinks, add more boiling hot, for it must boil four hours without ceasing a moment. Strain the ointment through a linen cloth into small pots, and, when cold, cover them. Do not touch it with anything but silver. It will keep many years.

A fine pomatum may be made by putting half a pound of fresh marrow, prepared as above, and two ounces of hog's-lard, on the ingredients: and then observing the same process as before.

**Pot Pourri.—** Put into a large china jar the following ingredients in layers, with bay-salt strewed between the layers; two pecks of damask roses, part in buds and part blown, violets, orange-flowers, and jasmine, a handful of each; orris-root sliced, benjamin and storax, two ounces of each; a quarter of an ounce of musk, a quarter of a pound of angelica-root sliced, a quart of the red parts of clove-gillyflowers, two handfuls of lavender-flowers, half a handful of rosemary-flowers, bay and laurel leaves, half a handful of each; three Seville oranges, stuck as full of cloves as possible, dried in a cool oven, and pounded; half a handful of knotted marjoram, and two handfuls of balm of Gilead dried. Cover all quite close. When the pot is uncovered the perfume is very fine.

**A quicker Sort of Sweet Pot.**—Take three handfuls of orange-flowers, three of clove-gillyflowers, three of damask roses, one of knotted marjoram, one of lemon-thyme, six bay-leaves, a handful of rosemary, one of myrtle, half a one of mint, one of lavender, the rind of a lemon, and a quarter of an ounce of cloves. Chop all, and put them in layers, with pounded bay salt between up to the top of the jar.

If all the ingredients cannot be got at once, put them in as you get them, always throwing in salt with every new article.

**To Make Wash-Balls.**—Shave thin two pounds of new white soap into about a tea-cupful of rose-water; then pour as much boiling water on it as will soften it. Put into a brass pan a pint of sweet oil, four penny-worth of oil of almonds, half a pound of spermaceti, and set all over the fire till dissolved; then add the soap, and half an ounce of camphor that has first been reduced to powder by rubbing it in a mortar with a few drops of spirits of wine or lavender-water, or any other scent. Boil ten minutes, then pour it into a basin, and stir it till it is quite thick enough to roll up into hard balls, which must then be done as soon as possible. If essence is used, stir it in quick after it is taken off the fire that the flavour may not fly off.

**Paste for Chapped Hands,** and which will preserve them smooth by constant use.—Mix a quarter of a pound of unsalted hog's lard, which has been washed in common and then rose-water, with the yolks of two new-laid eggs and a large spoonful of honey. Add as much fine oatmeal, or almond-paste, as will work into a paste.

**For Chapped Lips.**—Put a quarter of an ounce of gum benjamin, storax, and spermaceti, twopenny-worth of alkanet-root, a large juicy apple chopped, a bunch of black grapes bruised, a quarter of a pound of unsalted butter, and two ounces of bees-wax into a new tin saucepan. Simmer gently till the wax, &c., are dissolved, and then strain it through a linen cloth. When cold melt it again, and pour it into small pots or boxes, or if to make cakes, use the bottoms of tea-cups.

**Hungary Water.**—To one pint of highly rectified spirit of wine put an ounce of oil of rosemary and two drams of essence of ambergris; shake the bottle well several times, then let the cork remain out twenty-four hours. After a month, during which time shake it daily, put the water into small bottles.

**Honey Water.**—Take a pint of spirit as above, and three drams of essence of ambergris; shake them well daily.

o

**Lavender Water.**—Take a pint of spirit as above, essential oil of lavender one ounce, essence of ambergris two drams; put all into a quart bottle, and shake it extremely well.

**An excellent Water to prevent Hair from Falling-off and to Thicken it.**—Put four pounds of unadulterated honey into a still, with twelve handfuls of the tendrils of vines, and the same quantity of rosemary-tops. Distil as cool and as slowly as possible. The liquor may be allowed to drop till it begins to taste sour.

**Black Paper for Drawing Patterns.**—Mix and smooth lamp-black and sweet-oil: with a bit of flannel cover a sheet or two of large writing-paper with this mixture; then dab the paper dry with a bit of fine linen, and keep it by for using in the following manner.

Put the black side on another sheet of paper, and fasten the corners together with a small pin. Lay on the back of the black paper the pattern to be drawn, and go over it with the point of a steel pencil; the black paper will then leave the impression of the pattern on the under sheet, on which you must now draw it with ink.

If you draw patterns on cloth or muslin, do it with a pen dipped in a bit of stone blue, a bit of sugar, and a little water, mixed smooth in a tea-cup, in which it will be always ready for use; if fresh, wet to a due consistence as wanted.

**Black Ink.**—Take a gallon of rain or soft water, and three quarters of a pound of blue galls, bruised; infuse them three weeks, stirring daily. Then add four ounces of green copperas, four ounces of logwood chips, six ounces of gum arabic, and a wine-glassful of brandy.

**Another way.**—The ink-powder sold in Shoe-lane is one of the best preparations for this useful article. Directions are given with it how to mix it; in addition to which, a large cup of sweet wort to two papers of the powder, gives it the brightness of the japan ink. If a packet of six papers is bought together, it costs only eighteen-pence, and that quantity will last a long time.

**To Cement Broken China.**—Beat lime into the most impalpable powder, sift it through fine muslin; then tie some into a thin muslin, put on the edges of the broken china some white of egg, then dust some lime quickly on the same, and unite them exactly.

**An excellent Stucco, which will adhere to Woodwork.**—Take a bushel of the best stone-lime, a pound of yellow ochre, and a quarter of a pound of brown umber, all in fine powder. Mix them with a sufficient quantity of hot (but not boiling) water, to a proper thickness; and lay it on with a whitewasher's brush, which should be new. If the wall be quite smooth, one or two coats will do; but each must be dry before the next is put on. The month of March is the best season for doing this.

**Mason's Washes for Stucco—Blue.**—To four pounds of blue vitriol, and a pound of the best whiting, put a gallon of water, in an iron or brass pot. Let it boil an hour, stirring it all the time. Then pour it into an earthen pan; and set it by for a day or two, till the colour is settled. Pour off the water, and mix the colour with whitewasher's size. Wash the walls three or four times, according as is necessary.

**Yellow.**—Dissolve in soft water, over the fire, equal quantities separately of umber, bright ochre, and blue black. Then put it into as much whitewash as you think sufficient for the work, some of each, and stir it all together. If either cast predominates, add more of the others till you have the proper tint.

The most beautiful whitewash is made by mixing the lime and size with skim milk, instead of water.

**Roman Cement, or Mortar for outside Plastering, or Brick-work.**—This will resist all weather; and may be used to great advantage to line reservoirs, as no water can penetrate it.

Take eighty-four pounds of drift-sand, twelve pounds of un-slacked lime and four pounds of the poorest cheese grated through an iron grater. When well mixed, add enough hot (but not boiling) water to make into a proper consistence for plastering, such a quantity of the above as is wanted. It must have good and quick working. One hod of this mortar will go a great way, as it is to be laid on in a thin smooth coat, without the least space being left uncovered. The wall or lath-work should be covered first with hair and lime-mortar, and well dried. This was used by the ancients, and is now adopted among us. The Suffolk cheese does better than any other of this country.

**TO TAKE STAINS OF ANY KIND OUT OF LINEN.**—Stains caused by Acids.—Wet the part and lay on it some salt of wormwood. Then rub it without diluting it with more water.

**Another.**—Let the cloth imbibe a little water without dipping, and hold the part over a lighted match at a due distance. The spots will be removed by the sulphureous gas.

**Another way.**—Tie up in the stained part some pearlash; then scrape some soap into cold soft water to make a lather, and boil the linen till the stain disappears.

**Stains of Wine, Fruit, &c., after they have been long in the Linen.**—Rub the part on each side with yellow soap. Then lay on a mixture of starch in cold water very thick; rub it well in, and expose the linen to the sun and air till the stain comes out. If not removed in three or four days, rub that off, and renew the process. When dry it may be sprinkled with a little water.

**Many other Stains** may be taken out by dipping the linen in sour butter-milk, and drying in a hot sun.—Then wash it in cold water, and dry it, two or three times a day.

**Ironmoulds** should be wetted; then laid on a hot water-plate, and a little essential salt of lemons put on the part. If the linen becomes dry, wet it and renew the process; observing that the plate is kept boiling hot. Much of the powder sold under the name of salt of lemons is a spurious preparation; and therefore it is necessary to dip the linen in a good deal of water, and wash it as soon as the stain is removed to prevent the part from being worn into holes by the acid.

**To Take out Mildew.**—Mix soft soap with starch powdered, half as much salt, and the juice of a lemon; lay it on the part of both sides with a painter's brush. Let it lie on the grass day and night till the stain comes out.

**To Make Flannels Keep their Colour, and not Shrink.** —Put them into a pail, and pour boiling water on, letting them lie till cold the first time of washing.

**To Preserve Furs and Woollen from Moths.**—Let the former be occasionally combed while in use, and the latter be brushed and shaken. When not wanted, dry them first, let them be cool, then mix among them bitter apples from the apothecary's, in small muslin bags, sewing them in several folds of linen, carefully turned in at the edges, and keep from damp.

**TO DYE THE LININGS OF FURNITURE, &c.— Buff or Salmon Colour, according to the Depth of the Hue.**—Rub down on a pewter plate twopenny-worth of Spanish arnatta, and then boil it in a pail of water a quarter of an hour. Put into it two ounces of potash, stir it round, and instantly put in the lining; stir it about all the time it is boiling, which must be five or six minutes; then put it into cold pump water, and hang the articles up singly without ringing. When almost dry, fold and mangle it.

**Pink.**—The calico must be washed extremely-clean and be dry. Then boil it in two gallons of soft water, and four ounces of alum: take it out, and dry in the air. In the meantime boil in the alum-water two handfuls of wheat-bran till quite slippery, and then strain it. Take two scruples of cochineal, and two ounces of argall finely pounded and sifted; mix it with the liquor by little at a time. Then put into the liquor the calico, and boil till it is almost wasted, moving it about. Take out the calico, and wash it in chamber-lye first, and in cold water after; then rinse it in water-starch strained, and dry it quick without hanging it in folds. Mangle it very highly, unless you have it calendered, which is best.

**Blue.**—Let the calico be washed clean and dried; them mix some of Scot's liquid blue in as much water as will be sufficient to cover the things to be dyed, and put some starch to it, to give a light stiffness. Dry a bit, to see whether the colour is deep enough; then set the linen, &c., into it, and wash it; then dry the articles singly, and mangle or calender them.

**To Dye Gloves to look like York Tan or Limerick, according to the Deepness of the Dye.**—Put some saffron into a pint of soft water boiling hot, and let it infuse all night; next morning wet the leather over with a brush. The tops should be sewn close to prevent the colour from getting in.

**To Dye White Gloves a beautiful Purple.**—Boil four ounces of logwood and two ounces of roche-alum in three pints of soft water till half wasted. Let it stand to be cold, after straining. Let the gloves be nicely mended; then with a brush do it over them, and when dry repeat it. Twice is sufficient, unless the colour is to be very dark. When dry, rub off the loose dye with a coarse cloth. Beat up the white of an egg, and with a sponge rub it over the leather. The dye will stain the hands, but wetting them with vinegar will take it off, before they are washed.

**A Liquor to Wash Old Deeds, &c. on Paper or Parchment, when the Writing is Obliterated, or when Sunk, to make it Legible.**—Take five or six galls, bruise them, and put them into a pint of strong white wine : let it stand in the sun two days. Then dip a brush into the wine, and wash the part of the writing which is sunk ; and by the colour you will see whether it is strong enough of the galls.

**To Prevent the Rot in Sheep.**—Keep them in the pens till the dew is off the grass.

**To Prevent Green Hay from Firing.**—Stuff a sack as full of straw or hay as possible ; tie the mouth with a cord ; and make the rick round the sack, drawing it up as the rick advances in height, and quite out when finished. The funnel thus left in the centre preserves it.

**To Preserve a Granary from Insects and Weasels.**— Make the floor of Lombardy poplars.

**To Destroy Crickets.**—Put Scotch snuff upon the holes where they come.

**DIRECTIONS TO SERVANTS.—To Clean Calico Furniture when taken down for the Summer.**—Shake off the loose dust, then lightly brush with a small long-haired furniture brush ; after which wipe it closely with clean flannels, and rub it with dry bread.

If properly done, the curtains will look nearly as well as at first, and if the colour be not light, they will not require washing for years.

Fold in large parcels, and put carefully by.

While the furniture remains up, it should be preserved from the sun and air as much as possible, which injure delicate colours ; and the dust may be blown off with bellows.

By the above mode curtains may be kept clean, even to use with the linings newly dipped.

**To Clean Plate.**—Boil an ounce of prepared hartshorn-powder in a quart of water ; while on the fire, put into it as much plate as the vessel will hold ; let it boil a little, then take it out, drain it over the saucepan, and dry it before the fire. Put in more, and serve the same, till you have done. Then put into the water some clean linen rags till all be soaked up. When dry, they will serve to clean the plate, and are the very best things to clean the brass looks and finger-plates of doors. When the plate is quite dry, it must be rubbed bright with leather. This is a very nice mode. In many plate-powders there is a mixture of quicksilver, which is very injurious ; and, among other disadvantages, it makes silver so brittle that from a fall it will break.

**To Clean Looking-glasses.**—Remove the fly-stains, and other soil, by a damp rag; then polish with woollen cloth and powder blue.

**To Preserve Gilding, and Clean it.**—It is not possible to prevent flies from staining the gilding without covering it; before which, blow off the light dust, and pass a feather or clean brush over it; then, with strips of paper cover the frames of your glasses, and do not remove it till the flies are gone.

Linen takes off the gilding, and deadens its brightness: it should therefore never be used for wiping it.

Some means should be used to destroy the flies, as they injure furniture of every kind, and the paper likewise. Bottles hung about with sugar and vinegar, or beer, will attract them; or fly-water put into little shells placed about the room, but out of the reach of children.

**To Clean Paint.**—Never use a cloth, but take off the dust with a little long-haired brush, after blowing off the loose part with the bellows. With care, paint will look well for a length of time. When soiled, dip a sponge or a bit of flannel into soda and water, wash it off quickly, and dry immediately, or the strength of the soda will eat off the colour.

When wainscot requires scouring, it should be done from the top downwards, and the soda be prevented from running on the unclean part as much as possible, or marks will be made which will appear after the whole is finished. One person should dry with old linen as fast as the other has scoured off the dirt and washed the soda off.

**To Clean Paper Hangings.**—First blow off the dust with the bellows. Divide a white loaf of eight days old into eight parts. Take the crust into your hand, and, beginning at the top of the paper, wipe it downwards in the lightest manner with the crumb. Do not cross nor go upwards. The dirt of the paper and the crumbs will fall together. Observe, you must not wipe above half a yard at a stroke and after doing all the upper part, go round again, beginning a little above where you left off. If you do not do it extremely lightly, you will make the dirt adhere to the paper.

It will look like new if properly done.

**To Give a Fine Gloss to Oak Wainscot.**—If greasy, it must be washed with warm beer; then boil two quarts of strong beer, a bit of bees'-wax as large as a walnut, and a large spoonful of sugar; wet it all over with a large brush, and when dry rub it till bright.

**To Give a Fine Colour to Mahogany.**—Let the tables be washed perfectly clean with vinegar, having first taken out any ink stains there may be with spirit of salt; but it must be used with the greatest care, and only touch the part affected, and be instantly washed off. Use the following liquid:—Into a pint of cold-drawn linseed oil, put four pennyworth of alkanet-root, and two pennyworth of rose-pink, in an earthen vessel; let it remain all night, then stirring well, rub some of it all over the tables with a linen rag; when it has lain some time, rub it bright with linen cloths.

Eating-tables should be covered with mat, oil-cloth, or baize, to prevent staining, and be instantly rubbed when the dishes are taken off, while still warm.

**To Take Ink out of Mahogany.**—Dilute half a tea-spoonful of oil of vitriol with a large spoonful of water, and touch the part with a feather; watch it, for if it stays too long it will leave a white mark. It is, therefore, better to rub it quick, and repeat if not quite removed.

**Floor Cloths** should be chosen that are painted on a fine cloth, that is well covered with the colour, and the flowers on which do not rise much above the ground, as they wear out first. The durability of the cloth will depend much on these two particulars, but more especially on the time it has been painted, and the goodness of the colours. If they have not deen allowed sufficient space for becoming hardened, a very little use will injure them; and as they are very expensive articles, care in preserving them is necessary. It answers to keep them some time before they are used, either hung up in a dry barn where they will have air, or laid down in a spare room. When taken up for the winter, they should be rolled round a carpet roller, and observe not to crack the paint by turning the edges in too suddenly. Old carpets answer extremely well, painted and seasoned some months before laid down. If for passages, the width must be directed when they are sent to the manufactory, as they are cut before painting.

**To Clean Floor-cloths.**—Sweep, then wipe them with a flannel; and when all dust and spots are removed, rub with a waxed flannel, and then with a dry plain one; use but little wax, and rub only enough with the latter to give a little smoothness, or it may endanger your falling. Washing now and then with milk after the above sweeping, and dry-rubbing them, give as beautiful a look, and they are less slippery.

**To Dust Carpets and Floors.**—Sprinkle tea-leaves on them, then sweep carefully. The former should not be swept frequently with a whisk brush, as it wears them fast; only once a week, and the other times with leaves and a hair brush. Fine carpets should be gently done with a hair hand-brush, such as for cloths, on the knees.

**To Clean Old Carpets.**—Take up the carpet, let it be well beaten, then laid down, and brushed on both sides with a hand-brush: turn it the right side upwards, and scour it with ox-gall, and soap and water, very clean, and dry it with linen cloths. Then lay it on the grass, or hang it up to dry.

**To Give to Boards a Beautiful Appearance.**—After washing them very nicely clean with soap and warm water and a brush, wash them with a very large sponge and clean water: Both times observe to leave no spot untouched; and clean straight up and down, not crossing from board to board; then dry with clean cloths, rubbing hard up and down in the same way.

The floors should not be often wetted, but very thoroughly

when done ; and once a week dry rubbed with hot sand, and a heavy brush the right way of the boards.

The sides of stairs or passages on which are carpets, or floor-cloth, should be washed with sponge instead of linen or flannel, and the edges will not be soiled. Different sponges should be kept for the two above uses ; and those and the brushes should be well washed when done with, and kept in dry places.

**To Extract Oil from Boards or Stone.**—Make a strong lye of pearl-ashes and soft water ; and add as much unslacked lime as it will take up ; stir it together, and let it settle a few minutes ; bottle it, and stop close ; have ready some water to lower it as used, and scour the part with it. If the liquor should lie long on the boards, it will draw out the colour of them ; there-fore do it with care and expedition.

**To Clean Stone Stairs and Halls.**—Boil a pound of pipe-makers' clay, with a quart of water, a quart of small beer, and put in a pit of stone blue. Wash with this mixture, and, when dry, rub the stones with flannel and a brush.

**To Blacken the Fronts of Stone Chimney-pieces.**—Mix oil-varnish with lamp black, and a little spirit of turpentine to thin it to the consistence of paint. Wash the stone with soap and water very clean ; then sponge it with clear water ; and when perfectly dry, brush it over twice with this colour, letting it dry between the times. It looks extremely well. The lamp black must be sifted first.

**To Take Stains out of Marble.**—Mix unslacked lime, in finest powder, with the strongest soap lye, pretty thick ; and in-stantly with a painter's brush, lay it on the whole of the marble. In two months' time wash it off perfectly clean ; then have ready a fine thick lather of soft soap, boiled in soft water ; dip a brush in it, and scour the marble with powder, not as common cleaning. This will, by very good rubbing, give a beautiful polish. Clear off the soap, and finish with a smooth hard brush till the end be effected.

**To Take Iron Stains out of Marble.**—An equal quantity of fresh spirit of vitriol and lemon-juice being mixed in a bottle, shake it well ; wet the spots, and in a few minutes rub with soft linen till they disappear.

**To Preserve Irons from Rust.**—Melt fresh mutton suet, smear over the iron with it while hot ; then dust well with un-slacked lime pounded, and tied up in a muslin. Irons so prepared will keep many months. Use no oil for them at any time, except salad oil, there being water in all other.

Fire-irons should be kept wrapt in baize, in a dry place, when not used.

**Another way.**—Beat into three pounds of unsalted hogs' lard, two drams of camphor sliced thin, till it is dissolved ; then take as much black lead as will make it of the colour of broken steel. Dip a rag into it, and rub it thick on the stove, &c., and the steel will never rust, even if wet. When it is to be used, the grease must be washed off with hot water, and the steel be dried before polishing.

**To Take Rust out of Steel.**—Cover the steel with sweet oil well rubbed on it, and in forty-eight hours use unslacked lime finely powdered, and rub until all the rust disappears.

**To Clean the Back of the Grate, the Inner Hearth, and the Fronts of Cast-iron Stoves.**—Boil about a quarter of a pound of the best black lead, with a pint of small beer and a bit of soap the size of a walnut. When that is melted, dip a painter's brush, and wet the grate, having first brushed off all the soot and dust; then take a hard brush, and rub it till of a beautiful brightness.

**Another way to Clean Cast Iron, and Black Hearths.** —Mix black lead and whites of eggs well beaten together; dip a painter's brush, and wet all over, then rub it bright with a hard brush.

**To Take the Black off the Bright Bars of Polished Stoves in a few Minutes.**—Rub them well with some of the following mixture on a bit of broadcloth; when the dirt is removed, wipe them clean, and polish with glass, not sand-paper.

**The Mixture.**—Boil slowly one pound of soft soap in two quarts of water, to one. Of this jelly take three or four spoonfuls, and mix to a consistence with emery, No. 3.

**To Clean Tin Covers, and Patent Pewter Porter Pots.**—Get the finest whiting, which is only sold in large cakes, the small being mixed with sand: mix a little of it powdered, with the least drop of sweet oil, and rub well and wipe clean; then dust some dry whiting in a muslin bag over, and rub bright with dry leather. The last is to prevent rust, which the cook must be careful to guard against by wiping dry, and putting by the fire when they come from the parlour; for if but once hung up without, the steam will rust the inside.

**To Prevent the Creaking of a Door.**—Rub a bit of soap on the hinges.

**A Strong Paste for Paper.**—To two large spoonfuls of fine flour, put as much pounded resin as will lie on a shilling; mix with as much strong beer as will make it of a due consistence, and boil half an hour. Let it be cold before it is used.

**Fine Blacking for Shoes.** —Take four ounces of ivory black, three ounces of the coarsest sugar, a table-spoonful of oil, and a pint of small beer; mix them gradually cold.

## BILLS OF FARE, FAMILY DINNERS, &c.

### BILLS OF FARE, ETC.

*List of various Articles in Season in different Months.*

#### JANUARY.

**Poultry.**—Game; Pheasants, Partridges, Hares, Rabbits, Woodcocks, Snipes, Turkeys, Capons, Pullets, Fowls, Chickens, Tame Pigeons.

**Fish.**—Carp, Tench, Perch, Lampreys, Eels, Crayfish, Cod, Soles, Flounders, Plaice, Turbot, Thornback, Skate, Sturgeon; Smelts, Whitings, Lobsters, Crabs, Prawns, Oysters.

**Vegetables.**—Cabbage, Savoys, Colewort, Sprouts, Brocoli, Leeks, Onions, Beet, Sorril, Chervil, Endive, Spinach, Celery, Garlic, Scorzonera, Potatoes, Parsnips, Turnips, Brocoli, white and purple; Shalots, Lettuces, Cresses, Mustard, Rape, Salsafy, Herbs of all sorts, dry and some green; Cucumbers, Asparagus and Mushrooms to be had, though not in season.

**Fruit.**—Apples, Pears, Nuts, Walnuts, Medlars, Grapes.

#### FEBRUARY AND MARCH.

Meat, Fowls, and Game, as in January, with the addition of Ducklings and Chickens; which last are to be bought in London most, if not all the year, but very dear.

**Fish.**—As the last two months, except that Cod is not thought so good from February to July, but may be bought.

**Vegetables.**—The same as the former months, with the addition of Kidney Beans.

**Fruit.**—Apples, Pears, Forced Strawberries.

#### SECOND QUARTER—APRIL, MAY, AND JUNE.

**Meat.**—Beef, Mutton, Veal, Lamb; Venison in June.

**Poultry.** — Pullets, Fowls, Chickens, Ducklings, Pigeons, Rabbits; Leverets.

**Fish.**—Carp, Tench, Sole, Smelts, Eels, Trout, Turbot, Lobsters, Chub, Salmon, Herrings, Crayfish, Mackerel, Crabs, Prawns, Shrimps.

**Vegetables.**—As before, and in May early Potatoes, Peas, Radishes, Kidney Beans, Carrots, Turnips, Early Cabbages, Cauliflowers, Asparagus, Artichokes. All sorts of Salads forced.

**Fruits.**—In June—Strawberries, Cherries, Melons, Green Apricots, Currants and Gooseberries, for Tarts. In July—Cherries, Strawberries, Pears, Melons, Gooseberries, Currants, Apricots, Grapes, Nectarines, and some Peaches; but most of these are forced.

#### THIRD QUARTER.—JULY, AUGUST, AND SEPTEMBER.

Meat as before.

**Poultry.**—Pullets, Fowls, Chickens, Rabbits, Pigeons, Green Geese, Leverets, Turkey Poults. Two former months, Plovers, Wheatears; Geese in September.

**Fish.**—Cod, Haddock, Flounders, Plaice, Skates, Thornback, Mullets, Pike, Carp, Eels, Shell-fish, except Oysters. Mackerel the first two months of the quarter, but not good in August.

Partridge shooting begins the 1st of September; what is therefore used before is poached.

**Vegetables** of all sorts.—Beans, Peas, French Beans, &c.

**Fruit.** — In July—Strawberries, Gooseberries, Pine Apples, Plums various, Cherries, Apricots, Raspberries, Melons, Currants, Damsons.

In August and September—Peaches, Plums, Figs, Filberts, Mulberries, Cherries, Apples, Pears, Nectarines, Grapes. Latter months, Pines, Melons, Strawberries. Medlars and Quinces in the latter month. Morella Cherries, Damsons, and various Plums.

## OCTOBER.

**Meat** as before and Doe Venison.

**Poultry and Game.**—Domestic Fowls as in former quarter. Pheasants from the 1st of October. Partridges, Larks, Hares, Dotterels. At the end of the month Wild Ducks, Teal, Snipes, Widgeon, Grouse.

**Fish.**—Dories, Smelts, Pike, Peach, Halibut, Brills, Carp, Salmon Trout, Barbel, Gudgeons, Tench, Shell Fish.

**Vegetables.**—As in January—French Beans, last crops of Beans, &c.

**Fruit.**—Peaches, Peas, Figs, Bullace, Grapes, Apples, Medlars, Damsons, Filberts, Walnuts, Nuts, Quinces, Services.

## NOVEMBER.

**Meat.**—Beef, Mutton, Veal, Pork, House Lamb, Doe Venison, Poultry and Game as in last month.

**Fish** as the last month.

**Vegetables.**—Carrots, Turnips, Parsnips, Potatoes, Skirrets, Scorzonera, Onion, Leeks, Shalots, Cabbage, Savoys, Colewort, Spinach, Chard-Beets, Cardoons, Cresses, Endive, Celery, Lettuces, Salad, Herbs, Pot-Herbs.

**Fruit.**—Pears, Apples, Nuts, Walnuts, Bullace, Chesnuts, Medlars, Grapes.

## DECEMBER.

**Meat.**—Beef, Mutton, Veal, House Lamb, Pork, and Venison.

**Poultry and Game.**—Geese, Turkeys, Pullets, Pigeons, Capons, Fowls, Chickens, Rabbits, Hares, Snipes, Woodcocks, Larks, Pheasants, Partridges, Sea-Fowls, Guinea-Fowls, Wild Ducks, Teal, Widgeon, Dotterels, Dun-Birds, Grouse.

**Fish.**—Cod, Turbot, Halibut, Soles, Gurnets, Sturgeon, Carp, Gudgeons, Codlins, Eels, Dories, Shell Fish.

**Vegetables** as in last month. Asparagus forced, &c.

**Fruit** as the last, except Bullace.

## FAMILY DINNERS.

### FIVE DISHES.

| Apple-sauce. | Knuckle of Veal stewed with Rice.<br>Bread-and-Butter Pudding,<br>Loin of Pork roasted. | Potatoes. |

| Potatoes. | Peas Soup.<br>(*Remove—Boiled Fowl.*)<br>Oyster Sauce.<br>Apple-pie.<br>Roasted Beef.<br>Benton Sauce. | Brocoli. |

| Potatoes. | Pigs' Souse fried in Batter.<br>(*Remove—Yorkshire Pudding.*)<br>Peas Soup.<br>Roast Veal. | Salads. |

| Stewed Beef<br>and Onions. | Hessian Ragout.<br>Hessian Soup,<br>of the above.<br>Leg of Lamb roasted. | Potatoes. |

| Mashed Potatoes<br>grilled. | Beef Podovies.<br>(*Remove—Curd Puddings.*)<br>Mutton Broth.<br>Neck of Mutton. | Carrots<br>and Turnips. |

| Potatoes. | Broiled Haddocks stuffed.<br>Light Suet<br>Dumplings.<br>Round of Beef. | Carrots<br>and Greens, |

| Salad. | Crimp Cod.<br>Gooseberry<br>Pudding.<br>Leg of Mutton. | Jerusalem<br>Artichokes. |

| Potatoes. | Spitchcock Eels.<br>(*Remove—Chine of Lamb in Cresses.*)<br>Damson Pudding.<br>Cold Beef. | Stewed Carrots. |

| Mashed Potatoes rim-<br>med with small slices<br>of Bacon. | Scrag of Veal smothered with Onions.<br>(*Remove—a Fruit Pie.*)<br>Peas Soup.<br>Hashed Hare. | Brocoli. |

Half Calf's Head, grilled.
(*Remove—Pie or Pudding.*)

Tongue
and Brains.

Carrot Soup.

Bacon.
Greens round.

Saddle of Mutton.
*Potatoes and Salad, at side table.*

---

Boiled Neck of Mutton.
Young Greens,     Baked Plum Pudding.     Turnips.
Currie of dressed Meat, in Casserole of Rice.

---

Aitchbone of Beef.
Carrots.     Vegetable Soup.     Greens.
Pulled Turkey or Fowl.
Leg broiled.

---

Boiled Fowls.
(*Remove—Snowballs.*)
Potatoes.     Patties of     Greens, and
dressed Meat.     mashed Turnips.
Chine of Bacon Pork, boiled.

---

SEVEN DISHES.
Salmon and fried Smelts.
Macaroni Pudding.     Stewed Celery.
Giblet Soup.
Potatoes.     Veal Patties.
Roast Beef.

---

Leg of Pork, boiled.
Peas Pudding.     Bread Sauce.
Onion Soup.
Turnips and Potatoes.     Plum Pudding, baked.
Large Fowl, dressed as Turkey.

---

Minced Veal, garnished with fried Crumbs.
Small Meat     Hot Apple Pie     Potatoes in
Pie.     in change for Soup.     a form.
Stewed Onions.     Beans and Bacon.
Saddle of Mutton.

---

FOUR AND FIVE.
(FIRST COURSE.)
Soup.
Carrots.     Mashed Turnips.
Bouillie.

(SECOND COURSE.)
Fricassee of Sweetbreads.
Mushrooms, stewed.    Lemon Pudding.        Peas.

---

(FIRST COURSE.)
Mackerel broiled, with Herbs.
Bacon.       Butter.     Greens and Carrots.
Boiled Chickens.
(SECOND COURSE.)
Beef Cecils.
Salad.       Fruit Pie.     Potatoes in a shape.
Fore-quarter of Lamb, roasted.

---

SEVEN AND SEVEN.
(FIRST COURSE.)
Broiled Salmon.
(*Remove—Chine of Pork.*)
Stewed Spinach.        Mince-Pies.
Peas Soup.
Oxford Dumplings.        Peas Pudding.
Fillet of Veal.
(*Potatoes and Mashed Turnips, on side table.*)
(SECOND COURSE.)
Ragout of Palates.
Orange Fool.        Potted Beef.
Curd Star with whip.
Collared Eel.        Stewed Pears.
Pheasant.
(*Bread Sauce, on side table.*)

---

(FIRST COURSE.)
Cod's Head and Shoulders.
(*Remove—Boiled Turkey.*)
Curric of Rabbit.        Patties.
Giblet Soup.
Eel Pie.       Boiled Neck of Mutton,
7 Bones.
Small Leg of Pork.
*Four small dishes of Vegetables may be put round the Soup,*
*or two served at the side table.*
(SECOND COURSE.)
Fricandeau.
Orange Pudding.        Scraped Beef.
Lemon Creams.
Anchovy Toast.        Tarts.
Teal, or other wild Fowls.

SEVEN AND NINE.

(FIRST COURSE.)

Pepper Pot.

Brocoli.

Tongue braised.

Hunter's Pudding.

Chickens, boiled.

Celery, dishes in a
Pyramid.

Saddle of Mutton.

(*Greens and Potatoes on the side table.*)

(SECOND COURSE.)

Roasted Partridges.

Almond Cheesecakes.
Celery in
White Sauce.
Collared Beef.

Raspberry
Cream.

Potted Cheese.
Cardoons,
stewed.
Lemon Pudding.

Hare.

---

NINE AND SEVEN.

(FIRST COURSE.)

Stewed Carp.

Chickens.
Parsley Butter.
Cod sounds, White.
Currant Jelly.
Stewed Pigeons.

Epergne.

Green Peas Soup.

Cheek of Bacon.
Batter.
Rabbits and Onions.
Gravy.
Cutlets Maintenon.

(*Remove—Haunch Venison.*)

*Vegetables on side table.*

(SECOND COURSE.)

Sweetbreads.

Mushrooms
stewed.

Sauce Robart.

Trifle.

Blancmange in
small forms.

Currant Tart
with Custard.

Bread Sauce.

Roasted Partridges.

Stewed
Cucumbers.

---

NINE AND ELEVEN, AND A REMOVE.

(FIRST COURSE.)

Turbot.

(*Remove—Chickens.*)

Palates.
French Pie.
Veal.
Olives.

Liver and Lemon Sauce.
Carrot Soup.

Butter.

Lamb's Fry.
Tongue in Turnips.
Rabbit Brown in
Fricassee.

Aitchbone of Beef.

(*Vegetables on side table.*)

(SECOND COURSE.)

Wild Fowl.

| Stewed Pippins. | French Beans. | Lobster in Fricassee Sauce. |
|---|---|---|
| Scalloped Oysters. | Solid Syllabub in a glass dish. | Stewed Mushrooms. |
| Cray-fish in Jelly. | Peas. | Apricot Tart, open cover. |
| | Goose. | |

---

NINE DISHES, TWO REMOVES, AND ELEVEN.

Fish.

(*Remove—Stewed Beef.*)

| Oxford Dumplings. | | Fricandeau. |
|---|---|---|
| Small Ham. | White Soup. | Turkey, boiled. |
| Lamb Steaks | | Oyster Sauce. |
| round Potatoes. | | Lobster Patties. |

Fish.

(*Remove — Saddle of Mutton.*)

(SECOND COURSE.)

Sweetbreads, larded.

| French Beans, in White Sauce. | Orange Jelly. | Prawns. |
|---|---|---|
| Open Tart. | Raspberry Cream. | Sago Pudding. |
| Lobster. | Form. | Stewed Mushrooms. |
| | Green Goose. | |

---

(FIRST COURSE.)

Fish.

(*Remove—Hashed Calf's Head.*)

| Rabbit and Onions. | Sauce. | Lamb's Fry. |
|---|---|---|
| Macaroni Pudding. | Transparent Soup. | Beef Steak Pie. |
| Veal Cutlets. | Butter. | Stewed Pigeons with Cabbage. |

Fish.

(*Remove—Sirloin of Beef.*)

(SECOND COURSE.)

Chickens.

| Cheesecakes. | | Stewed Lobster. |
|---|---|---|
| | Raspberry Cream. | |
| Peas. | Trifle. | Asparagus. |
| | Lemon Cream. | |
| Macaroni. | | Apricot open Tart. |
| | Ducklings. | |

ELEVEN AND NINE.
(FIRST COURSE.)
Fish.
(*Remove—Ham Glazed.*)

Pigeons, stewed.

Tongue.

Bole Mutton.

Sauce.
Gravy Soup.

Butter.

Fillet of Veal.

Sweetbread, grilled.

Beef-Steak Pie.

Boiled Chickens.

(SECOND COURSE.)
Pheasant.

Raspberry Tartlets.
Collared Eel.
Stewed
Celery.

Bread Sauce.
Plateau.
Gravy and Jelly
for Hare.
Hare.

Artichokes.
Collared Beef.
Stewed
Pears.

---

ELEVEN AND ELEVEN.
(FIRST COURSE.)
Stewed Beef.

Oxford Puddings.
Ham,
braised.
Lamb Steaks.
Potatoes.

White Soup.

Fish.
Saddle of Mutton.

Veal Fricandeau.
Turkey.
Oyster Sauce.
Lobster
Patties.

(SECOND COURSE.)
Sweetbreads.

French Beans.
White Sauce.
Open Tartlet.
Anchovy Toasts.

Orange Jelly.

Whipped Cream.
Wine Roll.
Green Goose.

Prawns.

Muffin Pudding.
Stewed Mushrooms.

---

ELEVEN AND ELEVEN AND TWO REMOVES.
(FIRST COURSE.)
Salmon.
(*Remove—Brisket of Beef stewed, and high Sauce.*)
Cauliflower.

Fry.
Stewed
Cucumbers.

Cutlets
Maintenon.

Shrimp Sauce.

Giblet Soup.

Potatoes.

Anchovy Sauce.

Pigeon Pie.
Stewed Peas
and Lettuce.

Veal Olives
raised.

Soles, fried.
(*Remove— Quarter Lamb, roasted.*)

P

(SECOND COURSE.)

Young Peas.

Coffee Cream.

Ramakins.

Lobster.

Raspberry Tart.

Trifle.

Orange Tourte.

Grated Beef.

Omelet.

Roughed Jelly.

Ducks.

---

LONG TABLE ONCE COVERED.

Fish.

Fruit Tart.  One Turkey or Two Poults.  Blancmange.

Mock Turtle.

Harico.  Sweetbreads, larded.

Mashed Turnips.  Jerusalem Artichokes,  Stewed

Carrots thick round.  fricasseed.  Spinach.

Cray Fish.  Savoy Cake.  Dried Salmon in

Macaroni Pudding.  papers.

Ham, braised.  Trifle.  Chickens.

French Pie.

Casserole of Rice  Picked Crab.

with Giblets.

Sea Kale.  Stewed Celery.  Young Sprouts.

Apple Pie and Custard.

Fricandeau.  Ox Rumps and

Spanish Onions.

Rich White Soup.

Jelly Form.  Cheesecakes.

Fish.

(*Remove—Venison, or Loin of Veal.*)

---

GENERAL REMARKS ON DINNERS.

**Things used at First Courses.**—Various Soups. Fish, dressed many ways. Turtle. Mock Turtle. Boiled Meats and Stewed. Tongue. Ham. Bacon. Chawls of Bacon. Turkey and Fowls, chiefly boiled. Rump, Sirloin, and Ribs of Beef roasted. Leg, Saddle, and other Roast Mutton. Roast Fillet, Loin, Neck, Breast, and Shoulder of Veal. Leg of Lamb, Loin, Fore-Quarter. Chine. Lamb's-head and Mince. Mutton stuffed and roasted. Steaks, variously prepared. Ragouts and Fricassees. Meat Pies raised, and in Dishes. Patties of Meat, Fish, and Fowl. Stewed Pigeons. Venison. Leg of Pork, Chine, Loin, Sparerib. Rabbits. Hare. Puddings, boiled and baked. Vegetables, boiled and stewed. Calf's Head different ways. Pig's Feet and Ears different ways. In large dinners two Soups and two dishes of Fish.

Things for Second Course.—Birds: and Game of all sorts. Shell Fish, cold and potted. Collared and Potted Fish. Pickled ditto. Potted Birds. Ribs of Lamb roasted. Brawn. Vegetables, stewed or in sauce. French Beans. Peas. Asparagus. Cauliflower. Fricassee. Pickled Oysters. Spinach, and Artichoke bottoms. Stewed Celery. Sea Kale. Fruit Tarts. Preserved-Fruit Tourtes. Pippins stewed. Cheese-cakes, various sorts. All the list of Sweet Dishes, of which abundance are given from page 139 to 164, with directions for preparing them, such as Creams, Jellies, and all the finer sorts of Puddings, Mince Pies, &c. Omelet. Macaroni. Oysters in Scallops, stewed or pickled.

Having thus named the sort of things used for the two courses, the reader will think of many others. For removes of Soup and Fish one or two joints of Meat or Fowl are served; and for one small course, the articles suited to the second must make a part. Where Vegetables and Fowls, &c., are twice dressed, they add to the appearance of the table the first time; three sweet things may form the second appearance without greater expense.

The Bills of Fare which have been given from page 218 to 219, may be modified at discretion.

In some houses, one dish at a time is sent up with the vegetables or sauces proper to it, and this in succession hot and hot. In others, a course of Soups and Fish; then Meats and boiled Fowls, Turkey, &c. Made Dishes and Game follow; and, lastly, Sweet Dishes; but these are not the common modes.

It is worthy observation here, that common cooks do not think of sending up such articles as are in the house, unless ordered; though by so doing, the addition of a collared or pickled thing, some Fritters, fried Patties, or quick-made Dumplings, would be useful when there happened to be accidental visitors; and at all times it is right to better the appearance of the table rather than let things spoil below, by which the expense of a family is more increased than can be easily imagined. Vegetables are put on the side-table at large dinners, as likewise sauces, and servants bring them round: but some inconveniences attend this plan; and when there are not many to wait, delay is occasioned; besides that, by awkardness, the clothes of the company may be spoiled. If the table is of a due size, the articles alluded to will not fill it too much.

## SUPPERS.

Hot suppers are not much in use where people dine very late. When required, the top and bottom, or either, may be Game. Fowls. Rabbit. Boiled Fish, such as Soles, Mackerel. Oysters, stewed or scalloped. French Beans. Cauliflower, or Jerusalem Artichokes, in white Sauce. Brocoli with Eggs. Stewed Spinach and ditto. Sweetbreads. Small Birds. Mushrooms. Potatoes. Scallop, &c. Cutlets. Roast Onions. Salmagundy. Buttered Eggs, on Toast. Cold Neat's Tongue. Ham. Collared things. Hunter's Beef sliced. Rusks buttered with Anchovies on. Grated Hung beef with Butter, with or without Rusks. Grated Cheese

P 2

round, and Butter, dressed in the middle of a plate. Radishes ditto. Custards in glasses with Sippets. Oysters, cold or pickled. Potted Meats. Fish. Birds. Cheese, &c. Good plain Cake, sliced. Pies of Birds or Fruit. Crabs. Lobsters. Prawns, Cray-fish. Any of the list of sweet things. Fruits. A Sandwich set with any of the above articles, placed a little distance from each other on the table, looks well without the tray, if preferred.

The lighter the things, the better they appear, and glass intermixed has the best effect. Jellies, different coloured things, and flowers, add to the beauty of the table. An elegant supper may be served at a small expense by those who know how to make trifles that are in the house form the greatest part of the meal.

*Note.*—Any of the following things may be served as a relish, with the Cheese, after dinner. Baked or pickled Fish, done high. Dutch pickled Herring. Sardines, which eat like Anchovy, but are larger. Anchovies. Potted Char. Ditto Lampreys. Potted Birds made high. Caviare and Sippets of Toast. Salad. Radishes. French Pie. Cold Butter. Potted Cheese. Anchovy Toast, &c. Before serving a Dutch Herring, it is usual to cut to the bones without dividing, at the distance of two inches from head to tail.

# INDEX.

Accounts, necessity of keeping, 6
Acids, stains caused by, 211
Aitch-bone of beef, directions for carving, 14
Ale, various receipts for brewing, 179, 180; refining of, 180
Almond cheesecakes, 127, 128
Almond custards, 126
Almond cream, 144
Almond puddings, different receipts for, 109
Amber pudding, receipt for, 110
American flour, 176
Anchovies, directions for choosing, 100; essence of, ib.; how to keep when the liquor dries, ib.
Anchovy toast, 153
Apple and rice, soufflé of, 139
Apple dumplings, 117
Apple fool, 143
Apple jelly, to preserve at table, 147: for preserving apricots, &c., 160
Apple marmalade, 159
Apple pies, directions for making, 121
Apple pudding, baked, receipt for, 110
Apple puffs, 124
Apple sauce, for goose, &c., 96
Apple trifle, 142
Apple water, for the sick, 204
Apples, red, in jelly, 160; dried, ib.
Apricot cheese, 156
Apricot pudding, receipt for, 115
Apricots, various ways of preparing and preserving, 155, 156
April, list of articles in season during the month of, 218
Arrow-root jelly, for the sick, 199
Artichoke bottoms, dressing of, 130; preservation of, 135
Artichokes, dressing of, 130; Jerusalem, ib.
Articles for domestic use, 9, 10; inventories to be kept, 10
Asses' milk, for the sick, 202; artificial preparations of, 203
Au-Choux, or royal paste, 128
August, list of articles in season during the month of, 218, 219

Bacon, directions for choosing, 35; preparation of, 64; manner of curing Wiltshire bacon, ib.
Barberries, preparations of, for tartlets, 154; in bunches, ib.
Barberry drops, 163
Barley gruel, for the sick, 203
Barley water, for the sick, 204
Batter puddings, receipts for, 112

Bean pudding, green, receipt for, 116
Beans, dressing of, 131
Bechamel, or white sauce, directions for making, 92
Beef, directions for carving the different joints of, 14, 15; directions for choosing, 34; roasting of, 37; keeping and salting of, 40, 41; Dutch way of salting, 40; palates of, 45; cakes for a side-dish, ib.; potting of, ib.; dressing a cold sirloin of, ib.; fricassee of, ib.; dressing cold beef underdone, 45, 46; mincing and basting of, 46; à-la-vingrette, ib.; round of, ib.; rolled that equals ham, ib.; how to make a pasty of, to resemble venison, 125; broth of, for the sick, 198
Beef à-la-mode, 41; fricandeau of, 42; stewing a rump of, ib.; en miroton, 43; stewing brisket of, ib.; how to press, ib.; to make hunter's beef, ib.; an excellent mode of dressing, ib.; collaring of, 44; steaks of, ib.; collop, ib.
Beef-heart, preparations of, 49
Beef-olives, dressing of, 45
Beef-steak pie, receipt for, 104
Beef-steak puddings, receipt for, 114
Beef-steaks, preparation of, 44; with oyster sauce, ib.; Staffordshire, ib.; Italian, ib.
Beef-tea, for the sick, 199
Beet-roots, dressing of, 134; preservation of, 135
Beer, various receipts for brewing, 179, 180; refining of, 180
Benton sauce, for roast beef, 95
Benton tea-cakes, different kinds of, 174
Bills of fare for the different months, 218 et seq.
Birds, small, cooking of, 80; potting of, ib.
Biscuit-cake, making of, 174
Biscuits, hard, 178; plain and crisp ones, 179
Black puddings, directions for making, 61, 62
Black-caps, preparation of, 148
Blacking for shoes, receipt for, 217
Blade-bone of pork, cooking of the, 57
Blanc-mange, receipt for, 142
Blankets, preservation of, 11
Blue, dying the colour of, 212
Boards, how to give a beautiful appearance to, 215; extracting oil from, 216
Boekings, receipt for, 119
Boerhaave's sweet butter-milk for the sick 204
Brandy cream, 143
Brandy pudding, receipt for, 116

Brawn, directions for choosing, 35
Brawn, mock, directions for dressing, 61; souse for, ib.
Bread, for domestic use, 11; on the making and baking of, 176; various kinds of, 177; how to discover adulteration in, ib.
Bread-and-butter pudding, receipt for, 109
Bread cake, a common one, 172
Bread puddings, receipts for, 110, 111
Bread sauce, receipt for, 95
Breast of veal, directions for carving, 15
Brentford rolls, 178
Brewing of ale and wines, and various receipts for, 179 et seq.
Brisket of beef, stewing of, 43
Brocoli, dressing of, 131
Broths, different kinds of, for the sick, 197—9
Brown-bread ice, 149
Browning, to colour and flavour made dishes, 102
Bubble and squeak, dressing of, 49
Buns, plain ones, 175; rice ones, ib.
Burnt cream, 143
Butter, clarifying of, for potted things, 80; to serve as a little dish, 152; observations respecting, 190; making of, ib. preserving of, 191; keeping of, 192; how to choose at market, ib.
Buttermilk, valuable uses of, 192; for the sick, 204
Buttermilk pudding, receipt for, 116
Buttock of beef, directions for carving, 15

CABBAGE, red, different ways of stewing, 132; pickling of, 138
Cakes, colourings for staining, 149; on the making and baking of, 169; various receipts for, 170 et seq.; icing for, 170
Cakes, Yorkshire, 178
Calf's feet jelly, 146, 147
Calf's head, directions for carving, 15; boiling of, 53, 54; hashing, fricasseeing, or collaring of, 54
Calf's-head pie, receipt for, 104
Calf's liver, different preparations of, 56
Calico furniture, directions for cleaning, 213
Calves' feet, broth of, for the sick, 198
Camp vinegar, receipt for, 98
Candles for domestic use, 10
Caper sauce, excellent substitute for, 97
Capers, nasturtiums for, 99; keeping of, 139
Carmel cover for sweetmeats, 146
Carp, directions for choosing, 21; boiled, stewed, and baked, preparation of, 27; sauce for, 94
Carpets, dusting of, 215; cleaning of old ones, ib.
Carrier sauce for mutton, 96
Carrole of rice, 151
Carrot pudding, receipt for, 115
Carrot soup, directions for making, 87
Carrots, boiling and stewing of, 133; preservation of, 135
Carving, utility of, 5; directions for, 13—20

Casserol, edging for a currie, 102
Cast iron, how to clean, 217
Caudle, different preparations of, for the sick and lying-in, 201, 207
Cauliflowers, boiling of, 131; in white sauce, ib.; with parmesan, ib.
Cecils, dressing of, 46
Celery, stewing of, 131
Chalot sauce, receipt for, 95
Chantilly cake, 142
Chapped hands and lips, pastes for, 209
Chardoons, dressing of, 131
Charity, recommended, 8
Charlotte pudding, 117
Cheese, potted, roasted, and melted, 152; toasted, 153; damson and muscle plum, 162; observations respecting, 187; making of, 188—190; preserving of, 190
Cheese puffs, 124
Cheese-cakes, light paste for, 123; directions for making, 126; the various kinds of lemon, orange, potato, almond, &c., 127, 128
Cherries, how to dry them with sugar, 158; without sugar, 159; the best way of drying, ib.; in brandy, ib.; how to keep, 165
Cherry jam, 159
Chicken broth, for the sick, 198
Chicken currie, preparation of, 75, 76
Chicken panada, for the sick, 200
Chicken pie, receipt for, 106; fricassee of, 75; how to pull, ib.; braising of, 76; fattening of, 194
Chimney-pieces, stone, how to blacken the fronts of, 216
China, broken, how to cement, 210
China Chilo, receipt for, 68
China orange juice, 167
Chocolate, &c., preparation of, 12, 202
Chocolate cream, 145
Cider, refining of, 180
Clary wine, making of, 183
Cleaning of furniture, plate, gilding, wainscoting, &c., 213, 214; hearths, stones, &c., 217
Clouted cream, 145
Coals, &c., use of, 12
Cockle ketchup, preparation of, 139
Cocoa, patent, 202
Cod, choosing of, 21; stuffing for, 29; preparing and cooking of, 25, 26; preparation of crimp cod, 26; currie of, ib.; salted, ib.; pie, receipt for, 103
Cod sound ragout, preparation of, 26
Cod sounds, boiled, 26; to look like chickens, ib.
Cod's head, directions for carving, 14
Cod's head and shoulders, 25
Codlin cream, 145
Codlin tart, 122
Codlins, how to scald, 148; how to keep, 165
Coffee, &c., preparation of, 12; making of, 201, 202
Coffee cream, 144
Coffee milk, preparation of, 202

Collared beef, preparation of, 44
College puddings, 111
Colourings to stain jellies, &c., 149
Cook, general hints to the, 12, 13
Cookery, for the sick, 197 *et seq.*; for the poor, 205 *et seq.* (See *Sick.*)
Copper utensils, use of, 12
Cough, fine draught for a, 204
Courses, succession of, at family dinners, 220-6; general remarks on, 226-8
Cow-heels, various modes of dressing, 48; jelly of, 84
Cows, management of, 186, 187
Cowslip mead, making of, 184
Cowslip wine, making of, 182
Crabs, choosing of, 22; directions for dressing, 33
Cracknels, making of, 174
Crack-nuts, making of, 174
Cranberries, different ways of dressing, 167
Cranberry jelly, 147
Crawfish soup, directions for making, 90
Cray-fish, in jelly, 33
Creaking of doors, how to prevent, 217
Cream, a froth to set on, 146; how to manage for whey butter, 191; how to scald, as in the West of England, *ib.*; keeping of, 192; syrup of, *ib.*
Cream cheese, making of, 189, 190
Creams, different preparations of, 143—6
Crickets, how to destroy, 213
Crimp skate, preparations of, 27
Crusts, for custards or fruits, 120; excellent short ones, *ib.*; for orange cheesecakes or sweetmeats, *ib.*
Cucumber vinegar, receipt for, 98
Cucumbers, stewing of, 130; pickling young ones, 137
Cucumbers and onions sliced, pickling of, 137
Cullis, or brown gravy, directions for making, 92
Curd puddings, receipt for, 116
Curd star, preparation of, 141
Curds, preparations of, 141
Curds and whey, Gallino, preparation of, 192
Currant dumplings, 117
Currant jam, 159
Currant jelly, 159
Currant pies, making of, 121, 122
Currant sauce for venison, 96
Currant shrub, making of, 186
Currant water ice, 149
Currant wine, making of, 181; very fine black currant, 182
Currants, how to keep, 165
Currie of cod, preparation of, 26; of lobsters or prawns, 33
Custard, a froth to set on, 146
Custard pudding, receipt for, 115
Custards, raised crusts for, 120; the various kinds of, 126
Cyder. (See *Cider.*)

Dairy, directions for managing, 186 *et seq.*
Damson cheese, 162

Damson dumplings, 117
Damsons, how to keep, 165; for winter pies, 166, 167
Dartford fowls, 192, 193
Daughters, education and duties of, 4
December, list of articles in season during the month of, 219
Deeds, old, making a liquor to wash, 213
Dinners, preparation of, 5; bills of fare for, with the different courses, 220 *et seq.*; general remarks on, 226-8
Dish, a very nice one, 70
Domestic acquirements, observations on, 4 *et seq.*
Dough nuts, receipt for, 128
Draught, a pleasant one for the sick, 200
Dressing fish, observations on, 22, 23
Drinks, refreshing, for the sick, 203
Drops, different kinds of, 163, 164
Duck pie, receipt for, 106
Ducks, directions for choosing, 71; directions for roasting, boiling, stewing, and basting, 76; sauce for, 94; management of, in the poultry yard, 195
Duke of Cumberland's pudding, 112
Dumplings, various receipts for, 117
Dun-birds, cooking of, 81
Dutch puddings, receipts for, 110
Dutch sauce for meat or fish, 95
Dyeing, the linings of furniture, &c., 213

Eel-broth, for the sick, 198
Eel-pie, receipt for, 103
Eel-soup, directions for making, 90
Eels, choosing of, 22; fried and boiled, 30 spitchcock, *ib.*; broth of, 31; collared *ib.*; stewing of, *ib.*
Egg mince pies, 122
Egg-sauce, directions for making, 95
Egg-wine, preparation of, for the sick, 205
Eggs, whites of, 12; how to poach, 153; buttered, *ib.*; Scotch, *ib.*; hatching of, 193; choosing and preserving of, 194; preparation of, for the sick, 200
Elder-wine, making of, 183
English bamboo, pressing and preserving of, 136
Eve's puddings, receipt for, 111

Families, miscellaneous observations addressed to, 3 *et seq.*
Family dinners, bills of fare for, with the different courses, 220-6; general remarks on, 226-8
Fare, bills of, for the different months, 218
Feathers of poultry, 195
February, list of articles in season during the month of, 218
Females, domestic acquirements of, 5, 6
Fillet of veal, directions for carving, 15
Firmity, Somersetshire, 141
Fish, directions for choosing the various kinds of, 21, 22; observations on dressing, 22, 23; frying or boiling, 23, 24; different kinds in season, during each month of the year, 218, 219
Fish-gravy, directions for making, 93

Fish-pie, sauce for, 96; receipt for, 103
Fish-sauce, various receipts for, 96, 97
Fish-soups, stock for brown or white, 90;
    forcemeat for, 101
Flannels, how to make them keep their
    colour, and not shrink, 212
Flat cakes for keeping, 171
Floating island, preparation of, 140
Floor-cloths, choice and preservation of,
    215; cleaning of, ib.
Floors, dusting of, 215
Flounders, choosing of, 22; stewing of, 31
Flour, American, 176
Flour-caudle, for the sick, 201
Flummery, preparations of, 140, 141
Forcemeat, for forcing fowls or meat, 100;
    ingredients of, 101; for cold savoury
    pies, 101; for hares, pikes, soles, &c.,
    ib.; for fish soups, &c., ib.; as for
    turtle, ib.
Fore-hand of pork, directions for cooking, 57
Fowls, directions for carving, 18; direc-
    tions for choosing, 70; boiling of, 72;
    trussing of, for roasting, 73; boiling
    with rice, 74; roasting and boiling of, ib.;
    a nice way to dress one for a small dish,
    ib.; forcing, 75; braising of, ib.; blanch-
    ing of, 83; gravy for, when there is no
    meat to make it of, 92; sauce for, 93,
    94; management of, in the poultry-
    yard, 192 et seq.
French beans, dressing of, 131
French bread, 177
French pie, receipt for, 107
French rolls, 178
French salad, dressing of, 133
Fricassee of cold roast beef, 45
Fricassee of chickens, 75
Fricassee of fowls, &c., white sauce for,
    93
Fricasseed lambstones and sweetbread,
    preparation of, 70
Fritters, the different kinds of, 118, 119
Fruit, scalding of, 12; preparation of, for
    children, 149; biscuit of, 162; how to
    preserve, for tarts, 167; stains, caused
    by, 211; different kinds in season
    during each month of the year, 218, 219;
    how to green them for preserving or
    pickling, 154; how to candy them, ib.
Furniture, &c., dyeing the linings of, 212;
    dyeing gloves, ib.
Furs, how to preserve from moths, 212

GAME, directions in the choice of, 70; di-
    rections for dressing, 71, 72; different
    kinds in season during each month of
    the year, 218, 219
Geese, management of, 195; directions for
    choosing, 71
George pudding, receipt for, 113
German puddings, receipt for, 110
Giblet-pie, receipt for, 106
Giblet-soup, directions for making, 85
Giblets, directions for stewing, 75
Gilding, how to preserve and clean, 214
Ginger drops, a good stomachic, 164

Ginger-wine, making of, 182
Gingerbread, various receipts for making,
    175
Gloucester jelly, for the sick, 199
Gloves, dyeing of, 212
Golden-pippins, stewed, 148
Goose, directions for carving, 17; roasting
    of, 76; apple-sauce for, 96
Gooseberries, how to keep, 165, 166
Gooseberry-fool, receipt for, 142
Gooseberry-hops, 161
Gooseberry-jam, 160, 161
Gooseberry-pudding, 115
Gooseberry-trifle, 142
Gooseberry-vinegar, 98
Grate, cleaning the back of the, 217
Gravies, general directions for making, 83;
    colouring for, 84; a clear brown stock
    for, ib.; different kinds of, 91—93
Gravy, dressing and cleaning of, 91; with-
    out meat, 92; a rich one, ib.; for a fowl,
    ib.; to make mutton eat like venison,
    ib.; strong fish gravy, 93
Gravy soup, directions for making, 87
Green-goose pie, receipt for, 106
Green-peas, how to keep them, 129, 130;
    boiling and stewing of, 130
Green sauce, for green geese, 96
Greengages, how to preserve, 161
Ground-rice milk, for the sick, 202
Ground-rice pudding, 117
Grouse, directions for cooking, 91
Gruel, preparations of, for the sick, 206
Gudgeons, choosing of, 22
Guinea-fowl, dressing of, 81
Guinea hens, management of, 196

HADDOCK, preparation of, 29; stuffing
    for, ib.
Haggett's economical bread, 177
Hair, receipt for preventing its falling off,
    210
Ham, directions for carving, 17; boiling
    of, 37
Ham-sauce, receipt for, 96
Hams, directions for choosing, 35; dif-
    ferent ways of curing, 62, 63; how to
    dress them, 64
Hare, directions for carving, 18
Hare pie, receipt for, 107
Hare soup, directions for making, 88
Hares, directions for choosing, 71; keep-
    ing and paunching of, 81; roasting
    of, 82; jugging, broiling, hashing, and
    potting of, ib.
Hartshorn jelly, 147
Hatching of chickens, 193, 194
Haunch of mutton, directions for carving,
    17
Hay, green, how to preserve it from firing,
    213
Hearth, cleaning the, 217; how to blacken
    the, 217
Hen-house, should be commodious,
    193
Hen-turkey, directions for choosing,
    70

Hens, setting and management of, 193,194; fattening of, 194; to make them lay, ib.
Herb-pie, receipt for, 107
Herbs for domestic use, 11; frying of, 134
Herrings, choosing of, 21; smoking of, 31; frying, broiling, and potting, ib.; dressing red herrings, ib.; baking of, 32; potting of, ib.
Hessian soup and ragout, directions for making, 88
Hog-flesh, various modes of cooking, 54, 57
Hog's cheeks, drying of, 60
Hog's ears, forcing of, 60
Hog's head, how to make excellent meat of, 58
Hog's lard, preparation of, 62
Hog's puddings, white, directions for making, 62
Honey water, preparation of, 210
Hotch-potch, how to prepare an excellent one, 88
Hungary water, receipt for, 209
Hunter's beef, making of, 43
Hunter's pudding, receipt for, 114

Ice, preparation of, for icing, 149
Ice creams, 149
Ice waters, 149
Ices, different kinds of, 149; colourings for staining, ib.
Icing for tarts, 122; for cakes, 170
Imperials, making of, 184
Indian pickle, the different ways of preparing and preserving it, 135, 136
Ink, receipt for making, 210; how to take it out of mahogany, 215
Insects, how to preserve a granary from, 213
Inventory of domestic articles to be kept, 10
Ironmoulds, directions for taking them out of linen, 211
Irons, how to preserve them from rust, 216

Jams, different kinds of, 159; gooseberry, 160, 161; raspberry, ib.
January, list of articles in season during the month of, 218
Jaune-mange, receipt for, 142
Jellies, different preparations of, 146, 147; colourings for staining, 149; different kinds of, for the sick, 199
Jelly, for putting over cod pies, 93; to cover cod fish, ib.; currant, 159; apple, 160; red apple, ib.
Jerusalem artichokes, dressing of, 130.
July, list of articles in season during the month of, 218, 219
June, list of articles in season during the month of, 218

Ketchup, the different kinds of, 138, 139
Kidney pudding, receipt for, 114
Kidneys, dressing of, 56, 68

Lamb, directions for carving the fore quarter, 16; directions for choosing, 35; boiling of, 37; different modes of cooking, 68, 69; fore quarter, breast, and shoulder, 69; steaks and cutlets of, ib.; head and hinge, ib.; a very nice dish from the neck, 70
Lamb pie, receipt for, 105
Lamb's fry, preparation of, 69
Lamb's sweetbreads, 69
Lamb-stones, fricassee of, 70
Lamprey, stewing of, 31
Larks, cooking of, 80
Lavender water, preparation of, 210
Laver, dressing of, 134
Leek pie, receipt for, 108
Leg of mutton, directions for carving, 16
Lemon cheese-cakes, 127
Lemon cream, different preparations of, 144
Lemon custards, 136
Lemon drops, 163
Lemon honeycomb, 150
Lemon juice, how to keep, 167
Lemon marmalade, 156
Lemon mince pies, 122
Lemon peel, preservation of, 135
Lemon pickles, preservation of, 135
Lemon pudding, receipt for, 109
Lemon puffs, 124
Lemon sauce, receipt for, 96
Lemon water, for the sick, 204
Lemon whey, for the sick, 204
Lemon white sauce for boiled fowls, 94
Lemonade, receipt for making different kinds of, 168; preparation of, for the sick, 205
Lemons, use of, 12; pickled, 137; preserving in jelly, 158; for puddings, ib.
Lent potatoes, preparation of, 140
Light puffs, 124
Linen, various receipts for taking stains out of, 211
Liquors, cooling of, 12
Liver, different preparations of, 56
Liver sauce, receipt for, 95
Lobster patties, 124
Lobster pie, receipt for, 103
Lobster salads, dressing of, 133
Lobster sauce, receipts for, 97, 98
Lobster soup, directions for making, 90
Lobsters, choosing of, 22; potting of, 32; stewing, buttering, and roasting of, ib.; currie of, 33
Looking-glasses, directions for cleaning, 204

Macaroni, dressed sweet, 140; various preparations of, 151
Macaroni pudding, receipt for, 115
Macaroni soup, making of, 86
Macaroons, making of, 174
Mackerel, choosing of, 21; different preparations of, 28; pickled, ib.; potting of, 32
Made dishes, browning to colour and flavour, 102

Mahogany, how to give a fine colour to, 214; how to take ink out of, 215

Maids, preparation of, 27

Malt, extract of, for coughs, 180

Marble, how to take stains out of, 216

March, list of articles in season during the month of, 218

March's "Family Book-keeper," utility of, 7

Marmalade, different kinds of, 136; transparent, *ib.*; apple, 159; quince, 162

Married life, duties of, 4

Marrow bones, dressing of, 48

May, list of articles in season during the month of, 218

Meals, articles in preparation for, 10

Meat, directions for choosing the various kinds of, 34, 35; purchasing, keeping, and dressing of, 35—38; boiling and roasting of, 37; how to keep it hot, 38; the different kinds in season during each month of the year, 218, 219

Meat pies, raised crust for, 108

Melon mangoes, preparing and preserving of, 136

Melted butter, directions for making, 98

Mildew, directions for removing, 212

Milk, different preparations for the sick, 202

Milk porridge, preparation of, for the sick, 202; French, *ib.*

Milk punch, making of, 185

Millet pudding, receipt for, 115

Mince pies, directions for making, 121, 122

Mistress of a family, directions for her use, 3 *et seq.*

Mock brawn, directions for dressing, 61

Mock turtle, various preparations of, 55

Moor game, potting of, 80

Morels, preparation of, 84; preservation of, 135

Mortar, preparation of, for outside plastering, 211

Muffins, making of, 178

Mulled wine, for the sick, 201

Mullet, red, preparation of, 28

Mullets, choosing of, 23

Muscle-plum cheese, 162

Mushroom ketchup, different preparations of, 138, 139

Mushroom sauce, for fowls or rabbits, 94

Mushrooms, drying of, 99; powder of, *ib.*; directions for choosing, 132; stewing of, *ib.*; pickling of, 138

Mustard, directions for making, 99

Mutton, directions for carving the different joints, 15, 16, 17; directions for choosing, 35; observations on keeping and dressing, 64, 65; leg, neck, and shoulder, 65; haunch of, *ib.*; roasting saddle of, *ib.*; fillet of braised, 66; harrico of, *ib.*; how to hash, *ib.*; boiling a shoulder of, with oysters, 66; breast and loin of, *ib.*; kebobbed, 68; gravy to make it eat like venison, 92; currie sauce for, 96; how to make a pasty of, to resemble venison, 125; broth of, for the sick, 198

Mutton broth, Scotch, 84

Mutton collops, directions for cooking, 67

Mutton cutlets, cooked in the Portuguese way, 67

Mutton ham, directions for cooking, 67

Mutton pie, receipt for, 105

Mutton puddings, receipts for, 114

Mutton rumps and kidneys, dressing of, 68

Mutton sausages, preparation of, 67

Mutton steaks, different ways of cooking, 67

Nasturtiums, for capers, 99

Nelson puddings, receipts for, 111

Norfolk punch, making of, 186

November, list of articles in season during the month of, 219

Oatmeal pudding, receipt for, 110

October, list of articles in season during the month of, 219

Olives, pickled, 137

Omelets, making of, 151, 152

Onion sauce, receipt for, 95

Onion soup, directions for making, 88

Onions, stewing of, 130; roasting of, 131; preservation of in store, 135; pickled, 137

Orange biscuits, 157

Orange butter, 148

Orange cheesecakes, 127

Orange chips, 157

Orange cream, 145

Orange-flower cakes, 157

Orange fool, 143

Orange jelly, 147

Orange marmalade, 156

Orange puddings, receipt for, 100

Orange tart, 122, 123

Orange wine, making of, 182

Orangeade, for the sick, 205

Oranges, different preparations of, 156—8; cutting of, 156, 157; preserving in jelly, 158; for puddings, *ib.*

Orgeat, receipts for, 168; preparations of, for the sick, 205

Ortolans, roasting of, 81

Ox-cheek, stewing of, 48; dressing of, *ib.*

Ox-feet, various modes of dressing, 48

Ox-rump soup, directions for making, 88

Oxford dumplings, receipt for, 117

Oyster patties, 34, 123

Oyster sauce, receipt for, 97

Oyster soup, directions for making, 91

Oysters, choosing of, 22; how to feed, 33; how to stew, boil, scallop, or fry, *ib.*; oyster loaves, *ib.*; how to pickle, *ib.*

Paint, directions for cleaning, 214

Paste for paper, directions for making, 217

Panada, different kinds prepared for the sick, 199, 200

Pancakes, the different kinds of, 118

Paper, for domestic use, 11

Paper hangings, directions for cleaning, 214

Parsley pie, receipt for, 107

Parsley sauce, how to make, when o
    parsley leaves are to be had, 95
Parsnips, mashing of, 133; fricassee of, ib.;
    preservation of, 135
Partridge pie, receipt for, 107
Partridge soup, directions for making, 85
Partridges, directions for carving, 19; direc-
    tions for choosing, 71; directions for
    cooking, 80; potting of, ib.; sauce for, 94
Paste, different kinds of, for pastry, 119,
    120, 122; for tarts and cheesecakes, 122;
    royal, 128; for chapped hands, 209
Pastry, 102; general directions for making,
    and various receipts for, 119 et seq.;
    observations on, 121; on using pre-
    served fruits in, ib.; how to prepare
    venison for, 125; the different kinds of,
    125, 126
Patterns, preparation of black paper for
    drawing, 210
Patties, the various kinds of—fried, oyster,
    lobster, beef, veal, turkey, sweet ones,
    &c., 123, 124; resembling mince pies,
    124
Pea-fowls, dressing of, 81; management
    of, 196
Pears for domestic use, 11; stewed or
    baked, 148; jargonel, how to preserve,
    160
Peas, green, preserving and dressing of,
    129, 130
Peas, old, stewing of, 130
Peas soup, old and green, directions for
    making, 86
Pepper, kitchen, preparation of, 99
Pepper-pot, receipts for, 86, 153
Peppermint drops, 164
Perch, choosing of, 22; preparation of, 28
Pettitoes, directions for dressing, 59
Pheasant, directions for carving, 19; di-
    rections for cooking, 80
Pickles, that will keep for years, receipt
    for, 63; rules for preparing and preserv-
    ing the different kinds of, 135—138
Pies, cold savoury, forcemeat for, 101
Pies, apple, directions for making, 121
Pies, savoury, general directions for mak-
    ing, and various receipts for, 102—108
Pig, sucking, directions for carving, 17;
    scalding and roasting of, 58, 59
Pig's cheek, how to prepare for boiling,
    59
Pig's feet and ears, different ways of
    dressing, 60; fricasseed, ib.; jelly of, 61
Pig's harslet, directions for dressing, 61
Pig's head, collaring of, 60
Pigeon pie, receipt for, 107
Pigeons, directions for carving, 20; direc-
    tions for choosing, 71; directions for
    dressing, 78; stewing, broiling, roast-
    ing, and pickling, ib.; in jelly, 79; pot-
    ting of, ib.; management of, in the
    poultry yard, 196
Pike, choosing of, 21; baking of, 29; stuf-
    fing for, ib.
Pilchard pie, receipt for, 103
Pink, dyeing the colour of, 212

Pipers, how to dress, 29
Pippin pudding, receipt for, 116
Pippin tarts, receipt for, 122
Pistachio cream, 145
Plaice, dressing of, 30
Plate, directions for cleaning, 213
Plovers, directions for choosing, 71; dress-
    ing of, 81; eggs of, ib.
Plum-cakes, directions for making, 171,
    172
Plum-pudding, receipt for, 115
Plums, magnum bonum, 163
Poached eggs, 153
Pomade divine, receipt for, 208
Pomatum, receipt for, 208
Poor, cookery for the, 197, 205 et seq.
Pork, directions for choosing, 35; boiling
    of, 37; salting of, 40; various ways of
    cooking, 56, 57; leg, loin, shoulder,
    neck, &c., 57; how to dress as lamb, ib.;
    pickling of, 58; apple-sauce for, 96
Pork-griskin, preparation of, 57
Pork-jelly, for the sick, 199
Pork-pies, receipt for making, 105
Pork-steaks, directions for cooking, 58
Porker's-head, how to roast, 59
Porridge, milk, preparation of, 202
Portable soup, directions for, 89
Pot-pourri, receipt for, 208
Potato cheese-cakes, 127
Potato paste, receipt for, 120
Potato fritters, 118
Potato paste, 126
Potato pie, receipt for, 107
Potato puddings, receipts for, 113
Potato rolls, 178
Potatoes, boiling, broiling, roasting, fry-
    ing, and mashing of, 133
Pots, patent pewter, cleaning of, 217
Potting of lobsters, shrimps, mackerel,
    herrings, and trout, 32; of beef, 45; of
    veal, 51; of game, 80; of hares, 82;
    rabbits, 83
Poultry, directions in the choice of, 70;
    directions for cooking, 71, 72; boil-
    ing, 72; roasting, ib.; different kinds,
    in season during each month of the
    year, 218, 219
Poultry-yard, 186; directions for manag-
    ing the, 192 et seq.
Pound-cake, directions for making, 172
Prawn-soup, directions for making, 90
Prawns, choosing of, 22; currie of, 33; in
    jelly, ib.; how to butter, ib.
Preserved fruits, use of, in pastry, 121
Preserves, 139; preparation of, and vari-
    ous receipts, 154 et seq.
Prices of articles, acquaintance with, 7
Prune-tarts, 122
Pudding, a quick-made one, 117
Puddings, 108; general directions for mak-
    ing, and various receipts for, 108 et seq.;
    in haste, 111
Puff-paste, a rich one, 119
Puffs, the various kinds of apple, lemon,
    cheese, &c., 124
Puits d'amour, preparation of, 140

Punch, an excellent method of making, 185; different receipts for, 185, 186

Quails, cooking of, 81
Quaking-pudding, receipt for, 112
Queen-cakes, making of, 173
Quince-marmalade, 162
Quinces, how to preserve them, 163

Rabbit-pie, receipt for, 106
Rabbits, directions for carving, 18; directions for choosing, 71; the different ways of cooking, 82, 83; to make a rabbit taste like a hare, 83; potting of, ib.; blanching of, ib.; management of, 197
Ragout, directions for making, 88, 89
Raised crusts for meat-pies, &c., 108; for custards, 120
Raisin-wine, making of, 183; with and without cider, 183, 184
Ramakins, preparation of, 153
Raspberry brandy, making of, 185
Raspberry cakes, 164
Raspberry cream, 145
Raspberry jam, 161
Raspberry pies, 122
Raspberry tart, with cream, 123
Raspberry vinegar, receipt for, 168
Raspberry vinegar water, for the sick, 204
Raspberry-water ice, 149
Raspberry wine, making of, 181
Ratafia, making of, 184
Ratafia-cream, 143, 144, 149
Ratcliff's restorative pork jelly, 199
Ready money, payment of, 7
Receipts, a variety of, with directions for servants, 208
Reeves, cooking of, 81
Rennet, preparation of, for turning milk, 188
Restoratives, different kinds of, for the sick, 200
Rhubarb-tart, 123
Rice, different preparations of, 150, 151
Rice-bread, 177
Rice-cake, making of, 173
Rice-caudle, for the sick, 201
Rice-jelly, 147
Rice milk, preparation of, 150
Rice puddings, various receipts for, 112, 113
Rolls, receipts for various kinds of, 178
Roman cement, for outside plastering, 211
Rot in sheep, prevention of, 213
Rout drop-cakes, 171
Ruffs, cooking of, 81
Rush-cream cheese, making of, 190
Rusks, directions for making, 175
Russian-seed pudding, 117
Rust, how to preserve irons from, 216; how to take it out of steel, 217

Sack cream, 143
Sack mead, making of, 184
Saddle of mutton, directions for carving, 17
Sage cheese, making of, 189
Sago, for the sick, 207
Sago milk, preparation of, 150

Sago and sago-milk, preparation of, for the sick, 202
Sago-pudding, receipt for, 109
Salmagundy, preparation of, 151
Salmon, choosing of, 21; directions for boiling, broiling, potting, and drying, 24; excellent dish of dried salmon, 25; pickling and collaring of, ib.
Saloop, preparation of, 203
Salting of beef or pork, 40, 41
Sanders, dressing of, 46
Sauce Robart, for rumps or steaks, 95
Sauces, different kinds of, 93 et seq.; sauce to hide the bad colour of fowls, 93; for fricassee of fowls, rabbits, &c., ib.; for wild fowl, carp, turkey, fowls, &c., 94; à-la-maître d'hôtel, ib.; for green geese, 95; for meat or fish, ib.; for rumps or steaks, ib.; for hot and cold roast beef, ib.; for fish pies, 96; for hot or cold meat, ib.; for goose and roast pork, ib.; for venison, ib.; for mutton, ib.; ham sauce, ib.; fish sauce, 96, 97; caper, oyster, and lobster sauces, 97; shrimp and anchovy, 98
Sausages, cooking of, 58; Spadbury's Oxford sausages, ib.
Sausages, mutton, preparation of, 67
Savoury pies. (See Pies, and Puddings.)
Scotch leek soup, directions for making, 86
Sea-kale, boiling of, 134
Seed-cake, a cheap one, 172
September, list of articles in season during the month of, 218, 219
Servants, characters of, 9; various useful receipts for, and general directions to, 208—213 et seq.
Shalot vinegar, receipt for, 98
Shank jelly, for the sick, 199
Shelford pudding, receipt for, 116
Shoulder of mutton, directions for carving, 15
Shrewsbury cakes, making of, 173
Shrimp pie, receipt for, 106
Shrimp sauce, receipt for, 98
Shrimps, choosing of, 22; how to butter, 33; how to pot, ib.
Shrub, white currant, 186
Sick, cookery for the, 197 et seq.; broths, 197, 198; jellies, 199; panadas, 199, 200; sippets, eggs, and restoratives, 200; different kinds of restoratives for the, ib.; caudles, 201, 207; mulled wine, 201; coffee milk, 202; chocolate, saloop, and various preparations of milk, 202, 203; gruel and refreshing drinks, 203; water wheys and buttermilk, 204; orangeade and egg wine, 205; sago, 207
Sippets, preparation of, for the sick, 200
Sirloin of beef, directions for carving, 14; dressing of, 45
Skate, choosing of, 21; preparation of, 27; crimped, ib.
Skate soup, directions for making, 90
Smelts, choosing of, 22; frying of, 30
Snipes, cooking of, 81
Snow-balls, preparation of, 140

Snow cream, 144
Soap, use of, 11
Soda, use of, 11
Sole pie, receipt for, 105
Soles, choosing of, 21; different modes of cooking, 29; in the Portuguese way, 30; Portuguese stuffing for, ib.
Sorrel, stewing of, 132
Souchy, water, preparation of, 31
Souffle of rice and apple, 139
Soup, baked, for the poor, 206
Soup, an excellent kind for the weakly, 207
Soup-à-la sap, directions for making, 89
Soup maigre, directions for making, 89, 90
Soups, general directions for making, 83; various kinds of, 84 et seq.; colouring for, 84; a clear brown stock for, ib.; some excellent ones, 84, 85
Spare-rib of pork, directions for cooking, 57
Spinach, dressing of, 131
Spinach cream, 145
Spinach soup, directions for making, 88
Sponge-cake, 173, 174
Sprats, choosing of, 22; smoking of, 31; baking of, 32; dressing of, ib.; how to make them taste like anchovies, 100
Squab pie, receipt for, 105
Staffordshire dish of fried herbs and liver, 153
Stains, various receipts for taking them out of linen, 211; caused by acids, fruits, &c., ib.; how to take them out of marble, 216
Steak pudding, receipt for, 114
Steaks, lamb, cooking of, 69
Steaks, mutton, different ways of cooking, 67
Steel, how to take rust out of, 217
Stock for brown or white fish soups, 90
Stone, how to extract oil from, 216
Stone stairs and halls, how to clean, 216
Stoves, cleaning the fronts of, 217; how to take the black off the bright bars of, ib.; mixture, for cleaning, ib.
Straw, for domestic use, 11
Strawberries, how to preserve them whole, 158; in wine, ib.
Stucco, an excellent kind which will adhere to wood, 210; Mason's washer for, ib.; yellow, 211
Stuffing for pike, haddock, and small cod, 29
Sturgeon, how to dress, 26; how to roast, 27; excellent imitation of pickled sturgeon, ib.
Sucking pig, how to scald, 58; directions for roasting, 59
Suet, preserving of, 154.
Suet dumplings, 117
Suet puddings, receipts for, 114
Sugar, how to clarify for sweetmeats, 154
Sugar vinegar, receipt for, 98
Sugars, directions for the choice of, 10
Supper dish, a very pretty one, 150
Suppers, bills of fare for, 227

Sweet dishes, preparation of, and various receipts for, 189 et seq.
Sweetbreads, different preparations of, 56; fricassee of, 70
Sweetmeats, 139; a carmel cover for, 146; preservation of, and various receipts for, 154 et seq.; for tarts, 163; observations on, 164
Sweet-pot, receipt for, 209
Sweets, rice paste for, 119
Syllabubs, London, Staffordshire, Somersetshire, Devonshire, and everlasting, 150

TABLE beer, 180
Tansey, preparation of, 140
Tapioca jelly for the sick, 199
Tarts, light paste for, 122; icing for, 122; the various kinds of, 122, 123
Tea cakes, making of, 174
Teal, cooking of, 81
Tench, choosing of, 21; preparation of, 26
Tench broth, for the sick, 199
Thornback, preparation of, 27
Time, on the economy of, 8
Tin covers, how to clean, 217
Tippling cake, receipt for, 128
Toast and water, for the sick, 204
Tomato sauce, receipt for, 96
Tongue, boiling of, 37
Tongues, directions for roasting, 46, 47; pickling and stewing of, 47; an excellent way of doing them to eat cold, ib.
Transparent pudding, receipt for, 112
Trifle, receipt for, 142; apple and cake, ib.; a froth to set on, 143
Tripe, the various modes of dressing, 48; soused, ib.
Trout, how to fry, 28; à-la-Genevoise, ib.; potting of, 32
Truffles, preparation of, 84; preservation of, 135
Trussing, for roasting and boiling (with engravings), 73, 75
Tunbridge cakes, making of, 173
Turbot, directions for choosing, 21; for keeping, 24; for boiling, ib.
Turkey, boiling and roasting of, 72; pulled turkey, ib.; sauce for, 94
Turkey-cock, directions for choosing, 70
Turkey-patties, 124
Turkeys, management of, 195
Turnip pie, receipt for, 107
Turnip soup, directions for making, 86
Turtle, forcemeat for, 101; little eggs for, 102

UDDER, directions for roasting, 46

VEAL, fillet and breast of, directions for carving, 15; directions for choosing, 34; Scotch collops of, 53; keeping and dressing of, 49; leg, knuckle, shoulder, and neck, and the various ways of dressing them, ib.; neck of, à-la-braise, 50; breast of, and the different ways of dressing it, *ib.*; chump of, *à-la-daube*, *ib.*; rolls of, 51; harrico of, *ib.*; a dunelm of, *ib.*; mincing and potting of, *ib.*; cutlets of, 51, 52; callops, scallops, and fricandeau of, 52, 53; olives, cake, and sausages of, 153

Veal broth, directions for making, 84; for the sick, 193

Veal gravy, directions for making, 92

Veal patties, 124

Veal pies, various receipts for, 104

Vegetable marrow, boiling or stewing of, 129

Vegetable pies, receipt for, 107

Vegetable soup, directions for making, 87

Vegetables, to be kept, 11; their tendency to corrode metals, 12; directions for dressing, and various receipts for, 129 *et seq.*; how to boil them green, 129; preservation of, for eating in winter, 134; different kinds in season during each month of the year, 218, 219

Vendor, making of, 185

Venison, haunch of, directions for carving, 16; directions for choosing, 34; keeping and dressing of, 38; roasting, stewing, and hashing of, 40; old currant sauce for, 96: how to prepare it for a pasty, 125

Venison pasty, 40; crust for, 119; different preparations of, 125

Vessels, use of, 12

Vinegar, its tendency to corrode metals, 12; the various kinds of, 98, 99

Vinegar whey, for the sick, 204

Vingaret, for cold fowl or meat, 98

WAFERS, making of, 174

Walnscot oak, how to give a fine gloss to, 214

Walnut ketchup, preparation of, 139

Walnuts, pickling of, 138

Wash-balls, receipt for making, 209

Waters, different preparations of, for the sick, 204

Water cakes, making of, 173

Water-gruel, for the sick, 203

Waters, receipt for different kinds of, 209, 210

Weasels, how to preserve a granary from, 213

Welsh pudding, receipt for, 117

Welsh rabbit, making of a, 153

Wheat bread, 177

Whey butter, how to manage cream for, 191

Wheys, different kinds of, for the sick, 204

Whitings, choosing of, 21; preparation of, *ib.*

Widgeon, cooking of, 81

Wild ducks, cooking of, 81

Wild fowl, roasting of, 81; sauce for, 94

Windsor beans, dressing of, 131

Wine, refining of, 180; mulling of, 201; stains caused by, 211

Wine rolls, 148

Wine vinegar, receipt for, 98

Wine whey, for the sick, 204

Wines, 179; receipts for making different kinds of, 181 *et seq.*; remarks on, 181

Woodcocks, cooking of, 81

Woollen, how to preserve from moths, 213

YEAST, directions for making, 170; preserving of, 180

Yeast dumplings, 117

Yorkshire pudding, receipt for, 117

THE END.

Savill and Edwards, Printers, 4, Chandos-street, Covent-garden.

# CONTENTS.

| | PAGE |
|---|---|
| OBSERVATIONS FOR THE USE OF THE MISTRESS OF A FAMILY | 3 |
| DIRECTIONS FOR CARVING | 13 |
| CHOOSING AND DRESSING OF FISH | 21 |
| CHOOSING OF MEATS, AND DIFFERENT MODES OF COOKING | 34 |
| CHOOSING OF POULTRY, GAME, ETC., AND DIFFERENT WAYS OF COOKING | 70 |
| SOUPS AND GRAVIES | 83 |
| SAUCES, ETC. | 93 |
| PIES, PUDDINGS, AND PASTRY | 102 |
| DRESSING OF VEGETABLES | 129 |
| SWEET DISHES, PRESERVES, SWEETMEATS, ETC. | 139 |
| MAKING AND BAKING OF CAKES, BREAD, ETC. | 169 |
| HOME BREWERY, WINES, ETC. | 179 |
| DAIRY AND POULTRY YARD | 186 |
| COOKERY FOR THE SICK AND FOR THE POOR | 197 |
| VARIOUS USEFUL RECEIPTS, AND DIRECTIONS FOR SERVANTS | 208 |
| BILLS OF FARE, FAMILY DINNERS, ETC. | 218 |
| REMARKS ON DINNERS | 226 |
| GENERAL INDEX | 229 |

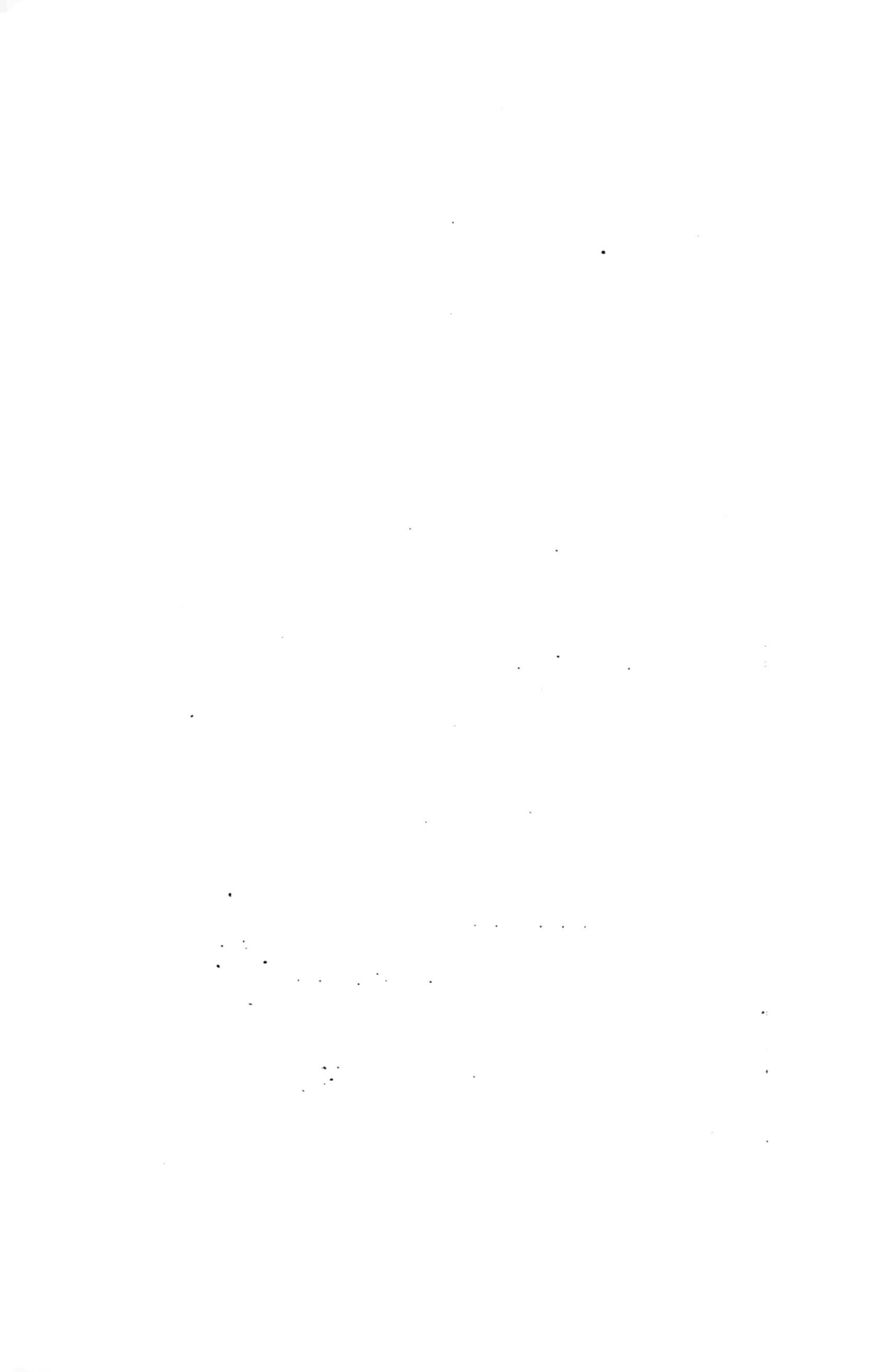

Breinigsville, PA USA
25 November 2009
228199BV00003B/48/P